Permanent Court of Arbitration

Summaries of Awards 1999–2009

This book is dedicated to the memory of

Sir Arthur Desmond Watts KCMG, QC

(November 14, 1931 – November 16, 2007)

Member of the Eritrea-Ethiopia Boundary Commission

Arbitrator in the Malaysia/Singapore, Barbados/Republic of Trinidad and Tobago, and Ireland *v.* United Kingdom (MOX Plant) arbitrations

Chairman of the Tribunal in Saluka Investments B.V. *v.* Czech Republic

Member and friend of the Permanent Court of Arbitration

where he served and inspired others with infinite wit, wisdom, and warmth.

Permanent Court of Arbitration

Summaries of Awards 1999–2009

Edited by

Belinda Macmahon and Fedelma Claire Smith

T·M·C·Asser press

Published by T·M·C·ASSER PRESS
P.O. Box 16163, 2500 BD The Hague, The Netherlands
<www.asserpress.nl>

ISBN 978-90-6704-319-9

The Permanent Court of Arbitration (PCA) is an intergovernmental organization, founded at the first Hague Peace Conference in 1899, and based in the Peace Palace in The Hague. It provides a wide range of dispute resolution mechanisms – including arbitration, conciliation and fact finding – in disputes involving various combinations of states, private parties and intergovernmental organizations. The PCA is committed to meeting the rapidly evolving dispute resolution needs of its member states and the international community.

International Bureau
Permanent Court of Arbitration
Peace Palace
Carnegieplein 2
2517 KJ The Hague
The Netherlands
Telephone: +31 70 302 4165
Facsimile: +31 70 302 4167
Email: bureau@pca-cpa.org
Website: www.pca-cpa.org

FOREWORD

It gives me great pleasure to present this publication, a collection of summaries of the thirty-one public awards and decisions rendered by fifteen arbitral tribunals and commissions for which the Permanent Court of Arbitration (PCA) in The Hague provided registry and administrative services over the decade December 1999 to August 2009, which saw the organization's remarkable revival. When the PCA was created at the First Hague Peace Conference in 1899, it was originally conceived as an intergovernmental mechanism exclusively for the settlement of disputes between States. However, the evolving flexibility of the PCA has allowed it to identify and respond to the changing dispute resolution needs of the international community in a world order that is dramatically different from that of the late nineteenth century, and that continues today.

The present volume provides an overview of the PCA's recent history and follows on from the PCA's 1999 publication *The Permanent Court of Arbitration: International Arbitration and Dispute Resolution: Summaries of Awards, Settlement Agreements and Reports* (Kluwer Law International), which contained summaries of all publicly available awards, decisions and reports rendered with the PCA's assistance over the one hundred years since its establishment. The period of time covered by the previous volume ended with the conclusion of the first phase of the land and maritime boundary proceedings between Eritrea and Yemen; the first summary in the present volume relates to the second phase of those proceedings.

Over the last decade, the broad and diverse range of arbitrations that the PCA has been called upon to administer includes, amongst others, four arbitrations brought under Annex VII of the 1982 United Nations Convention of the Law of the Sea and the recently concluded arbitration between the Government of Sudan and the Sudan People's Liberation Movement/Army. The two commissions established by the peace agreement signed by Eritrea and Ethiopia that brought an end to the war between them that lasted from May 1998 to June 2000 – the Eritrea-Ethiopia Boundary Commission and the Eritrea-Ethiopia Claims Commission – are also featured. The latter only recently completed its mandate with the release of its Final Awards on Damages. The case load of the PCA over the past ten years has thus addressed matters such as State sovereignty, the laws of armed conflict (*jus in bello* and *jus ad bellum*), the delimitation of land and maritime boundaries, and the interpretation of treaties, as well as vital and rapidly-developing fields such as international humanitarian law, the law of the sea, environmental law, and the protection of foreign investors. All of the awards and decisions featured herein are available in full on the PCA's website at www.pca-cpa.org, along with other pertinent information concerning each particular case.

I am greatly indebted to Professor J.G. Merrills, Professor of International Law of the University of Sheffield, United Kingdom, who has – once again – contributed a thorough and in-depth critical analysis on the contribution of these arbitrations to the development of international law and international dispute resolution.

I wish to express gratitude to my predecessor, Tjaco T. van den Hout, Secretary-General of the PCA from 1999 to 2008, whose vision and resolve made this project possible. Thanks are also due for the diligence and skill of former PCA staff members Fedelma Claire Smith, who drafted and co-edited the summaries, and to Belinda Macmahon, who edited and oversaw the composition of the book and project-managed its publication. I am also grateful to the many tribunal chairpersons and presidents who graciously participated in the rigorous review procedure for each summary.

I am certain that this volume will prove to be a valuable research tool for academics and practitioners of public international law and related disciplines, and for anyone wishing to gain an insight into the PCA's work and field of activity in recent years. I am sure that it will also be useful to foreign ministries and other government departments, intergovernmental organizations, and of course any other body which may in future seek to make use of the Permanent Court of Arbitration.

Christiaan KRÖNER

Secretary-General
Permanent Court of Arbitration
The Hague, December 2009

TABLE OF CONTENTS

APPENDICES

ABBREVIATIONS

AFDI	Annuaire français de droit international
Am. J. Int'l L.	American Journal of International Law
ASIL	American Society of International Law
Aust. J. Int'l L.	Australian Journal of International Law
Br. Y.B. Int'l L.	British Yearbook of International Law
Chinese J. Int'l L.	Chinese Journal of International Law
Dublin U. L.J.	Dublin University Law Journal
Eur. Ct. H.R.	European Court of Human Rights
Eur. Env'l L. Rev.	European Environmental Law Review
Geo. Wash. Int'l L. Rev.	George Washington International Law Review
Germ. Y.B. Int'l L.	German Yearbook of International Law
The Global Cmty. Y.B.	The Global Community Yearbook of International Law and Jurisprudence
Griffin's View on Int'l & Comp. L.	Griffin's View on International & Comparative Law
Hague Y.B. Int'l L.	Hague Yearbook of International Law
I.C.J. Rep.	International Court of Justice – Reports of Judgments, Advisory Opinions and Orders
ICSID Rep.	International Centre for Settlement of Investment Disputes (ICSID) Reports
I.L.M.	International Legal Materials
I.L.R.	International Law Reports
Int'l & Comp. L.Q.	International and Comparative Law Quarterly
Int'l J. Marine & Coastal L.	International Journal of Marine & Coastal Law
Int'l L. & Juris.	International Law and Jurisprudence
J. Conflict & Sec. L.	Journal of Conflict & Security Law
JDI	Journal du droit international
J. Env'l L.	Journal of Environmental Law
J. Int'l Arb.	Journal of International Arbitration
J. Int'l Dispute Settlement	Journal of International Dispute Settlement
J. World Inv. & Trade	Journal of World Investment & Trade
Leiden J. Int'l L.	Leiden Journal of International Law
Marine Pol'y	Marine Policy
Neth. Int'l L. Rev.	Netherlands International Law Review
Nordic J. Int'l L.	Nordic Journal of International Law
N.Z. Y.B. Int'l L.	New Zealand Yearbook of International Law
Ocean Dev. & Int'l L.	Ocean Development & International Law

RBDI	Revue Belge de droit international
RGDIP	Revue Générale de Droit International Public
R.I.A.A.	Reports of International Arbitral Awards
RQDI	Revue québécoise de droit international
S.C.R.	Supreme Court of Canada Reports
Sing. L. Rev.	Singapore Law Review
Tilburg Foreign L. Rev.	Tilburg Foreign Law Review
Wis. Int'l L.J.	Wisconsin International Law Journal
World Trade & Arb. Materials	World Trade & Arbitration Materials
Y.B. Int'l Human. L.	Yearbook of International Humanitarian Law

OVERVIEW AND ANALYSIS

THE CONTRIBUTION OF THE PERMANENT COURT OF ARBITRATION TO INTERNATIONAL LAW

1999-2009

by

J.G. Merrills*

When the Permanent Court of Arbitration ("PCA") celebrated its centenary in 1999 it marked the occasion by publishing a volume containing a summary of the cases in which the PCA had been involved since its inception.[1] In an introduction to the work the present writer analysed that jurisprudence in order to demonstrate the manifold ways in which the PCA's activity has contributed to the development of the rules and principles of international law.[2] In 2007 another landmark was reached with the centenary of the Second Hague Peace Conference. The PCA has decided to mark it with this volume, summarising cases in which the PCA has been involved over the past ten years. As before, it was thought helpful to open the work with an essay putting the individual cases in their broader context and identifying elements in the jurisprudence with a wider legal significance. There have, of course, been fewer cases decided in this latest period than in the previous century, but if the number of decisions is relatively small, this is more than compensated for by the complexity of the arguments presented and the range of issues that had to be dealt with. Although it is not possible within the limitations of a general survey to examine any of these recent cases in detail, what follows will, it is hoped, serve to highlight their more important features.

---

* Professor of International Law (Emeritus), University of Sheffield, United Kingdom.

[1] THE PERMANENT COURT OF ARBITRATION: INTERNATIONAL ARBITRATION AND DISPUTE RESOLUTION pp. 3-27 (Phyllis Hamilton *et al.* eds., 1999) [hereinafter THE PCA: INTERNATIONAL ARBITRATION]. *See also* Gilbert Guillaume, *The Contribution of the Permanent Court of Arbitration and its International Bureau to Arbitration between States*, Remarks on the Occasion of a Celebration of the Centenary of the PCA, The Hague, Oct. 18, 2007, *available at* the PCA website, www.pca-cpa.org.

[2] J.G. Merrills, *The Contribution of the Permanent Court of Arbitration to International Law and to the Settlement of Disputes by Peaceful Means*, *in* THE PCA: INTERNATIONAL ARBITRATION, *supra* note 1, at p. 3.

I. TERRITORIAL SOVEREIGNTY

Historically, territorial sovereignty has been one of the fundamental concerns of international law. As international law developed to govern the relations of States, which are territorial entities, so rules and principles to regulate the acquisition of territory, its transfer and the delineation of boundaries were an early requirement and still constitute a key component of the system. In view of the importance attached to territory and the uncertainty of many historic titles, it is not surprising that several of the PCA's early cases, included the well-known *Island of Palmas* case,[3] involved territorial issues. In the period we are concerned with two further cases have been added to the list – the 2002 Decision of the Commission in the *Eritrea-Ethiopia Boundary* case, which was followed by efforts by the same Commission to demarcate the boundary, and the 2009 Award of the Tribunal in the *Abyei* arbitration.

As with the other cases in this survey, it is unnecessary to describe the decision of the Boundary Commission exhaustively, or to review aspects of the case which have already been covered in the literature. However, with territory and boundaries, as with other topics, whilst the general legal framework may now be reasonably clear, only the application of the law to specific situations can clarify its contents in detail. In addition, as well as their substantive contribution, all arbitral decisions have a procedural dimension which may shed light on methods of dispute settlement from the institutional aspect. As we shall see, in both respects the *Eritrea-Ethiopia Boundary* case[4] contains a number of points of interest.

The disputed boundary consisted of three sectors: a central sector and western and eastern sectors, defined by three treaties concluded respectively in 1900, 1902 and 1908, when Ethiopia was an independent State, but Eritrea was an Italian colony. The Boundary Commission's mandate was "to delimit and demarcate the colonial treaty border," based on these treaties, "and applicable international law." Accordingly, at the delimitation stage the Commission's task was mainly one of treaty interpretation. However, guided by the ruling of the International Court of Justice ("ICJ") in the *Kasikili/Sedudu Island* case,[5] the Commission held that the reference to "applicable international law" entitled it to go beyond the law relating to treaty interpretation and to take into account rules of customary international law, even if they might have the effect of altering the position as laid down in the treaty.[6] In the

[3] Island of Palmas (U.S./Neth.), 2 R.I.A.A. p. 829 (1928), *also available at* www.pca-cpa.org; *see also* THE PCA: INTERNATIONAL ARBITRATION, *supra* note 1, pp. 3-6 and 118-128.

[4] *See* p. 144 of this volume.

[5] Kasikili/Sedudu Island (Bots./Namib.), Judgment, I.C.J. REP. p. 1045 (1999).

[6] *See* Eritrea-Ethiopia Boundary Commission, Decision Regarding Delimitation of the Border between the State of Eritrea and the Federal Democratic Government of Ethiopia, Apr. 13, 2002, paras. 3.14 and 3.15, *available at* www.pca-cpa.org.

context of territorial acquisition and boundaries this is plainly an important facility as it enables an arbitrator to take into account, amongst other factors, arguments relating to prescription, acquiescence, or other legally significant conduct, which either or both of the parties may wish to have considered.

The way in which subsequent conduct can vary the parties' treaty rights is particularly evident in the Boundary Commission's decision on the location of the boundary in the central sector. In one area it adjusted the boundary by taking account of an admission made in the course of the proceedings by Ethiopia; in another it found Eritrean activity sufficient to justify treating the region as part of that State; while in two further places it found the conduct of both parties supported the conclusion that they belonged to Ethiopia. In this sector map evidence was also significant. The evidence of maps is, of course, something which can vary greatly in value, as international courts and tribunals have often explained.[7] Here, however, the description of the boundary in the 1900 Treaty was somewhat vague, but a map which was more explicit had been annexed to it. The Commission therefore concluded that this map could be relied on and should be interpreted as part of the treaty.

In the western sector the Boundary Commission faced a problem of a type that is all too common in boundary disputes. The 1902 Treaty defined part of the boundary by referring to a named river, but the parties were in disagreement as to which of two possible rivers was meant. To resolve this issue the Commission employed the full range of material relevant to treaty interpretation, taking into account the meaning of the key words in the light of the object and purpose of the treaty, its context and negotiating history and the subsequent conduct of the parties in its application. The Commission finally came down in favor of Eritrea's interpretation, an important factor being the finding that the object and purpose of the treaty explicitly included the assignment of a named tribe to Eritrea. Having identified the relevant river, the Commission then had to identify a further part of the boundary which had not been delimited in the 1902 Treaty. This it did by using maps produced later by the parties which it found amounted to subsequent conduct or practice of the parties evidencing their acceptance of the line claimed by Eritrea. Here therefore, as in the central sector, maps were again significant, though in a rather different way.

In the eastern sector the boundary was defined by the 1908 Treaty as a line "parallel to and at a distance of 60 kilometres from the coast." The question here was essentially one of implementation and the Commission decided that the best method was to take a satellite image of the relevant coastline and project it inland so as to produce the necessary boundary line. This decision, which is a good example of how modern technology can assist boundary-making, generated a provisional boundary line, which the Commission then reviewed in the light of the parties' subsequent

---

[7] *See* J.G. Merrills, *The International Court of Justice and the Adjudication of Territorial and Boundary Disputes*, 13 Leiden J. Int'l L. p. 873, at pp. 887-888 (2000).

conduct, finding that in one place a small adjustment was needed to reflect their common agreement.

When the delimitation decision (which was unanimous) was rendered in 2002, both parties immediately accepted it. The Commission then began its further task of demarcating the boundary, but soon encountered obstacles. Although demarcation started successfully in the eastern sector, in the central and western sectors the work was obstructed. Having failed to secure the parties' agreement to its activity on the ground, the Commission eventually decided to identify the location of points for the emplacement of boundary pillars by using image processing and terrain modelling techniques. By this means it was able in due course to provide the two governments with a complete list of boundary points. Since the Commission could not remain in existence indefinitely, it decided at the end of 2006 that if within twelve months it had been unable to resume its activity, that list should be regarded as fulfilling its mandate. No further co-operation from the parties was forthcoming, and so in November 2007 the Commission decided to terminate its activity.[8]

The Boundary Commission evidently did its best in very difficult circumstances. Although it is possible that the delimitation stage would have benefited from more time, the Commission had to operate within the time scale laid down by the parties and produced a careful and well-reasoned decision. With the benefit of hindsight it may be questioned whether it was wise to give the Commission the additional task of demarcating the boundary, or whether, as is more commonly the case, that work should have been entrusted to others.[9] But if the case highlights some of the problems of combining the two functions, there is no doubt that when it encountered obstacles the Commission took practical steps to overcome them. The *Eritrea-Ethiopia Boundary* case, though less than ideal in its outcome, therefore contains much of interest to boundary-makers.

The *Abyei* arbitration[10] involved boundary questions of a rather different kind. Sudan achieved independence at the beginning of 1956, but soon afterwards civil war broke out between the north and the south. In 1972 that war was ended by an agreement providing for a referendum to allow certain areas to remain in Northern Sudan or to join a new autonomous Southern Sudan. However, subsequent disputes over self-determination and other issues led in 1983 to a second civil war. The Abyei Area in the middle of the country was the geographical centre of the conflict which in the next two decades claimed over two million lives. In 2002 the Sudanese Govern-

[8] On the problems encountered by the Commission in demarcating the boundary *see* Malcolm N. Shaw, *Title, Control and Closure? The Experience of the Eritrea-Ethiopia Boundary Commission*, 56 INT'L COMP. L.Q. p. 755, at pp. 786-793 (2007).

[9] On this point *see id.* p. 794.

[10] The Government of Sudan/The Sudan People's Liberation Movement/Army ("Abyei Arbitration"), Final Award, July 22, 2009, *available at* www.pca-cpa.org. Further details of this case can be found at p. 296 of this volume.

ment and the Sudan People's Liberation Movement ("SPLM"), representing the south, concluded an agreement providing for an eventual referendum on secession and various interim arrangements.

In 2005 the Government of Sudan and the SPLM signed a Comprehensive Peace Agreement, confirming that the Abyei Area was to have a special administrative status and also providing that the Abyei Boundaries Commission ("ABC") should define and demarcate the Area. The Commission's functions were to be performed by five experts "knowledgeable in history, geography and any other relevant expertise." The ABC Experts did their work and presented their Report in July 2005, but the Government of Sudan rejected it, claiming that the Experts had exceeded their mandate. In July 2008 the Government and the SPLM agreed to submit the dispute to arbitration, utilizing the PCA Optional Rules for Arbitrating Disputes between Two Parties of Which Only One is a State. A five member Tribunal was appointed to hear the parties' arguments and handed down its decision in July 2009.

The main issue for the Tribunal was whether the ABC Experts had exceeded their mandate when establishing the boundaries of the Abyei Area. The Government's case was that they had relied on three distinct lines of argument. First, the Government maintained that the Experts had made various procedural errors; second, it claimed that their Report contained substantive deficiencies; and third, it alleged that in carrying out their task the Experts had violated a number of mandatory criteria, including a failure to support their conclusions with adequate reasons. In the event of the Tribunal's finding that the Experts had exceeded their mandate, the Arbitration Agreement provided that the Tribunal itself should delimit the Abyei Area.

In a lengthy and detailed Award the Tribunal rejected most of the Government's arguments. It held that violations of procedural rights could not here amount to an "excess of mandate" and further that, given the limited scope of the Tribunal's authority, the applicable standard of review was the reasonableness of the Experts' treatment of their mandate, a test which the Tribunal found had been satisfied. Most of the supposed "mandatory criteria" were likewise dismissed, but crucially one, the requirement to provide adequate reasons, was found to have been transgressed in relation to the Experts' treatment of three of the four boundaries of the Abyei Area. Here therefore the Tribunal, having considered the evidence, redrew the relevant boundaries. This revision reduced the overall size of the Abyei Area and most significantly excluded from it two important oil fields.

The focus of argument in this case was on the scope for subsequent review when a decision is challenged, not by way of appeal on the merits, but on the more limited ground of an "excess of mandate." The Award therefore contains a wealth of material on this issue, including a discussion of the subtle relationship between the mission in a given case and the general principles of judicial review. In this regard the Tribunal's treatment of the need to provide reasons together with how this should be interpreted in practice are particularly useful. In contrast, the part of the Award concerned with actually delimiting the Abyei Area is largely taken up with an analysis of the particular facts and so contains less material with wider legal relevance. The Award does, however, make a point of confirming the Experts' decision that the traditional grazing rights of the local population should be preserved on both sides of the northern boundary. In the Tribunal's view this was not only required by the Comprehensive Peace Agreement, but also supported by the general principle that, unless the contrary is indicated, boundary delimitations do not extinguish traditional rights.

Before leaving this topic it is worth adding that in 1998 another Award relating to territory was made by an arbitral tribunal established to resolve a number of issues of territorial sovereignty and maritime delimitation between Eritrea and Yemen.[11] Although falling outside the time frame of the present survey, that Award is relevant here for several reasons. Like the Decision of the Boundary Commission in 2002, the earlier decision was based on a bilateral agreement with Eritrea providing for arbitration. Similarly, like the Boundary Commission's Decision, the treatment of substantive issues by the arbitrators is notable for a meticulous analysis of the historical evidence and for its endorsement and application of the principles of international law relating to territory and boundaries.[12] It also included a ruling that whilst sovereignty over certain islands lay with Yemen, the traditional fishing regime in the region should continue. This ruling, which is discussed further below, bears some similarity to a reference by the Boundary Commission to the customary rights of the population to have access to local rivers, pending demarcation of the boundary.[13] Finally, and most importantly, the Arbitration Agreement between Eritrea and Yemen envisaged resolution of the matters in dispute in two stages. At the first stage, which was concluded by the 1998 Award, the Tribunal's main task was to determine title to certain islands in the Red Sea ("*Eritrea/Yemen I*"). Having resolved that issue, it would then, at a second stage, address the question of maritime delimitation. In accordance with this scheme the Tribunal duly rendered its second Award in 1999 ("*Eritrea/Yemen II*"). Falling, as it does, within our time frame, this further phase of the case is considered in the next section.

---

[11] Eritrea-Yemen Arbitration, Award of the Arbitral Tribunal in the First Stage of the Proceedings (Territorial Sovereignty and Scope of the Dispute), Oct. 9, 1998, 40 I.L.M. p. 900 (2001); THE ERITREA-YEMEN ARBITRATION AWARDS 1998 & 1999 p. 19 (PCA Award Series 2005); *also available at* www.pca-cpa.org [hereinafter *Eritrea/Yemen I*]. *See also* THE PCA: INTERNATIONAL ARBITRATION, *supra* note 1, pp. 196-201.

[12] *See* Nuno Sergio Marques Antunes, *The Eritrea-Yemen Arbitration: First Stage – The Law of Title to Territory Re-Averred*, 48 INT'L COMP. L.Q. p. 362 (1999).

[13] *See Eritrea/Yemen I*, Award, *supra* note 11, paras 7.1-7.3.

II. MARITIME BOUNDARIES

Like territory and the issue of land boundaries, maritime boundaries have long been a matter of concern to States. Accordingly, they too have frequently given rise to disputes which the parties have sometimes been able to resolve by utilising international courts and tribunals. Until relatively recently, international law restricted States' maritime jurisdiction to the belt of coastal waters known as the territorial sea; as a result when boundary disputes occurred they concerned this relatively narrow area, along with associated matters such as fishing rights. However, with the extension of States' maritime jurisdiction to 200 nautical miles or more, through the emergence in the second half of the last century of the concepts of the continental shelf and the exclusive economic zone ("EEZ"), disputes over maritime boundaries have acquired a new dimension. Accordingly, while the tribunals in two early PCA cases that addressed such boundaries both involved coastal waters,[14] the three cases decided more recently all range farther afield.

In the *Eritrea/Yemen II* case,[15] the Tribunal had to decide the location of a maritime boundary in a rather complex situation. Eritrea and Yemen lie on opposite sides of the Red Sea with several groups of islands in between. At the first stage of the case in 1998 the Tribunal had resolved the issue of sovereignty over the islands, assigning some to Eritrea and some to Yemen. At the second stage it now had to determine the maritime boundary, which meant specifically deciding what effect, if any, the various islands should have on a median line based on the mainland coasts. The Tribunal's task was somewhat simplified by the fact that as a result of its ruling at the first stage, every island had been allocated to the State with the nearer mainland coast. Even so, numerous questions remained to be resolved, the significance of several islands located near the median line being a particular matter of interest.

In the northern section of the boundary the most significant feature of the decision was the contrasting treatment given to the Dahlak archipelago, which was held to be an integral part of Eritrea's coastline, and two Yemeni islands which, being barren and further out to sea, were allowed no effect on the median line. This section also called for a number of decisions about the appropriateness of employing straight base-lines when a coast is fringed with islands. In the central section the parties' respective islands were situated very close together and the Tribunal decided that a median line giving each State a territorial sea of about two and a half miles was appropriate. In the southern section, on the other hand, there were no islands and so the boundary was a simple median line dividing the coasts.

---

[14] *See The Grisbadarna* case (Nor./Swed.), 11 R.I.A.A. p. 147 (1909), *and* North Atlantic Coast Fisheries (Gr. Brit./U.S.), 11 R.I.A.A. p. 167 (1910), both *also available at* www.pca-cpa.org. *See also* THE PCA: INTERNATIONAL ARBITRATION, *supra* note 1, at pp. 51-56 and 57-68 respectively.

[15] Eritrea-Yemen Arbitration, Award of the Arbitral Tribunal in the Second Stage of the Proceedings (Maritime Delimitation), Dec. 17, 1999 [hereinafter *Eritrea/Yemen II*]. *See* p. 39 of this volume.

Although this was not the first boundary case to involve islands, the number and variety of islands here meant that the Tribunal was presented with a unique situation and the knowledge that its ruling would be scrutinised, not just by the parties, but also by numerous other States with unresolved maritime boundaries. In the absence of detailed rules in treaties or custom, judicial decisions have come to play a key role in establishing the framework for maritime delimitations. It has been observed that the delimitation in the *Eritrea/Yemen* case was "consistent with current developments in the law."[16] Consequently the Tribunal's decision, which was unanimous, has added usefully to the jurisprudence.[17] The handling of the base-lines issue, though obviously a subsidiary element, is also worth noting as this aspect of the law of the sea, which is closely bound up with the question of delimitation, had hitherto received relatively little judicial attention.

Finally, an unusual feature of this case was that a large part of the Tribunal's judgment at the second phase was taken up by explaining what it had meant by ruling in the first phase that in exercising sovereignty over certain islands "Yemen shall ensure that the traditional fishing regime of free access and enjoyment for the fishermen of both Eritrea and Yemen shall be preserved … ." Since the parties' interpretations of this obligation were very different, the Tribunal in its second judgment had to explain itself in more detail, by, in effect, constructing a special regime and spelling out its implications. This can be regarded either as a laudable example of judicial creativity, or alternatively as a salutary warning against giving hostages to fortune.[18] Either way it is a reminder that maritime boundaries, like their counterparts on land, have social as well as political consequences.

Fishing was an even more important element in the *Barbados/Trinidad and Tobago* case[19] which was decided in 2006. Barbados and Trinidad and Tobago are island States which lie opposite each other in the southern Caribbean. Following unsuccessful attempts to negotiate a maritime boundary, the issue was referred to arbitration by Barbados under the provisions of the 1982 United Nations Law of the Sea Convention ("the Convention," "UNCLOS"), which provides for compulsory adjudication of certain disputes involving the Convention, utilising what is called "Annex VII arbitration." The *Barbados/Trinidad and Tobago* case was not the first

---

[16] W. Michael Reisman, *Note*, 94 AM. J. INT'L L. p. 721, at p. 727 (2000).

[17] *See* Barbara Kwiatkowska, *The Eritrea-Yemen Arbitration: Landmark Progress in the Acquisition of Territorial Sovereignty and Equitable Maritime Boundary Delimitation*, 32 OCEAN DEV. & INT'L L. p. 1 (2001). But for a more cautious approach *see* Malcolm D. Evans, *The Maritime Delimitation between Eritrea and Yemen*, 14 LEIDEN J. INT'L L. p. 141 (2001).

[18] For discussion of this aspect of the case *see* Reisman, *supra* note 16, at pp. 722-723 and 729-731; *see also* Nuno Sergio Marques Antunes, *The 1999 Eritrea-Yemen Maritime Delimitation Award and the Development of International Law*, 50 INT'L COMP. L.Q. p. 299, at pp. 301-316 (2001).

[19] *See* p. 97 of this volume.

to involve this procedure,[20] but it was the first such case to result in a decision on the merits.

Both States accepted that part of the boundary should be a median line, but otherwise held very different views as to its location. In the western sector, Barbados sought a boundary to protect its fishing interests that extended its waters well beyond the median line and restricted Trinidad and Tobago to a partial enclave. In the eastern sector, on the other hand, Trinidad and Tobago sought a matching large adjustment as a way of increasing its access to the Atlantic. Faced with these conflicting claims, the Tribunal began by reviewing the law, finding that as embodied in previous decisions, an approach was required that combined predictability and stability with flexibility and the exercise of judicial discretion in order to achieve an equitable outcome. Having drawn a provisional equidistance boundary, following normal practice, the Tribunal then considered whether it needed adjustment. Its conclusion was that in general it did not. Consequently, the maritime boundary was held to be an equidistance line with only one minor modification in the south.

The Tribunal rejected Barbados's argument that to take account of its fishing interests in the western sector it must either adjust the equidistance boundary, or, as in the *Eritrea/Yemen* case, create a special fishing regime within Trinidad and Tobago's waters. Instead, finding that it lacked jurisdiction to rule on the fisheries regime that should apply within the latter's EEZ, it ruled that the parties were under an obligation to agree upon measures to co-ordinate and ensure the conservation and development of flying fish stocks and to negotiate in good faith and conclude an agreement that would provide Barbados with access to the fishery.[21]

In reaching its conclusion on the boundary, which was unanimous, the Tribunal also rejected arguments based on the parties' oil practice, as failing to meet the test laid down by the ICJ in the *Cameroon/Nigeria* case.[22] It also rejected the boundary proposed by Trinidad and Tobago on the ground that this was not an adjustment to equidistance, but a substitution for it, employing what the Tribunal called "a wholly artificial construction."[23] However, in order to take account of the broad coastal frontages of the islands of Trinidad and Tobago and "the resulting disparity in coastal lengths between the Parties," the Tribunal did introduce a relatively minor adjustment to the boundary in favour of Trinidad and Tobago in the south.[24]

---

[20] For previous cases *see* J.G. MERRILLS, INTERNATIONAL DISPUTE SETTLEMENT pp. 193-195 (4th ed. 2005).

[21] The jurisdictional limitation stemmed from Article 297(3) of the 1982 UNCLOS, and the conservation obligation from Article 63.

[22] Land and Maritime Boundary between Cameroon and Nigeria (Cameroon v. Nig., Eq. Guinea intervening), Merits, Judgment, I.C.J. REP. p. 303 (2002).

[23] Barbados/Republic of Trinidad & Tobago, Award, Apr. 11, 2006, para. 360, *available at* www.pca-cpa.org.

[24] *Id.* paras. 372-379.

Prior to examining the substantive issues, the Tribunal addressed a number of jurisdictional points which, like its ruling on the boundary, may be highly relevant in future Annex VII arbitrations. These included the scope of Article 281 of the Convention, which the Tribunal found to be relatively narrow, and of Article 283, which calls for an "exchange of views" as to the means of settlement to be adopted and which the Tribunal ruled must not be interpreted formalistically. The Tribunal also decided that the scope of the dispute submitted to arbitration gave it jurisdiction over delimitation of the continental shelf beyond 200 nautical miles, although in the event the boundary line it adopted meant that no such delimitation was needed.

The award in the *Barbados/Trinidad and Tobago* case has been described as "strengthening compulsory jurisdiction under Part XV of the [Law of the Sea] Convention" and "reinforcing and enriching the doctrine of maritime boundary delimitation."[25] Both assessments seem well justified, the former because the various jurisdictional issues presented were dealt with in a balanced and sensible way; the latter because the decision on the boundary accurately reflected the current emphasis on equidistance, while at the same time acknowledging the need for a careful review of the range of factors which may be relevant when parties urge that this line should be modified.

The third and most recent case involving maritime delimitation was also the simplest. Guyana and Suriname are adjacent States with coastlines on the Atlantic Ocean. They therefore required a maritime boundary to separate their respective areas of territorial sea and exclusive economic zone but, despite several rounds of negotiations, were unable to agree on its location. Since both States are parties to the 1982 Law of the Sea Convention, when a dispute arose involving the activities of holders of oil concessions granted by Guyana, the latter referred the dispute to arbitration in accordance with Articles 286 and 287 of the Convention. Like the *Barbados/Trinidad and Tobago* case, the *Guyana/Suriname* case[26] was therefore an arbitration under Annex VII of the 1982 Convention.

Dealing first with delimitation in the territorial sea, the Tribunal had to decide whether there were any "special circumstances" to justify departing from the median line approach which is laid down as the normal basis for such boundaries in Article 15 of the Convention. It decided that there were, on the ground that the United Kingdom and the Netherlands, as the parties' predecessors, had chosen a different solution, "the 10° Line," to facilitate access to the coast of Suriname which Guyana had subsequently recognised, at least as far as the three mile limit. Both

---

[25] Barbara Kwiatkowska, *Note*, 101 AM. J. INT'L L. p. 149, at p. 156 (2007). *See also* the same writer's more detailed appraisal, *The 2006 UNCLOS Annex VII Barbados/Trinidad and Tobago Award: Landmark Progress in Compulsory Jurisdiction and Maritime Boundary Delimitation*, 19 HAGUE Y.B. INT'L L. p. 33 (2006).

[26] *See* p. 117 of this volume. *See also* Stephen Fietta, *Note*, 102 AM. J. INT'L L. p. 119 (2008).

parties having now extended their territorial seas to twelve miles without addressing the effect on the maritime boundary, the Tribunal had to decide how it should be extended, a question on which the Tribunal was surprised to find little guidance in precedents. Having again considered the navigational rationale for the 10° Line, its conclusion on this point was that a simple straight line boundary, joining the end of that Line to the beginning of the parties' continental shelf and exclusive economic zone boundary, would meet the requirements of the Convention.

When determining the continental shelf and EEZ boundary the Tribunal began by emphasising that in accordance with the approach adopted in *Barbados/Trinidad and Tobago* and other cases, delimitation should begin by identifying a provisional equidistance line which could then be adjusted, if necessary, to achieve an equitable solution. This approach, which now seems to have become standard in delimitation cases, has the merit of creating a presumption in favor of an equidistance boundary, thereby putting the onus on a State which disagrees to show why a different solution is required. In the present case, Guyana and Suriname both argued for another boundary, relying for this purpose on local geographical circumstances, but the Tribunal found their arguments unconvincing, ruling that there were no features in the configuration of the relevant coastlines to warrant a departure from equidistance. In this connection, a further point on which the Tribunal followed established doctrine was its unwillingness to attach any significance to the parties' oil practice in the absence of evidence that the location of such concessions reflected an agreement between them.[27]

Whilst the issue of boundary delimitation in *Guyana/Suriname* was relatively straightforward, the judgment, which was again unanimous, contains several further points of interest. Each party claimed that the other had breached its obligations under Articles 74(3) and 83(3) of the 1982 Convention which create an obligation "to enter into provisional arrangements of a practical nature," pending agreement on delimitation.[28] The Tribunal's finding that both States had violated this obligation is helpful both in clarifying its scope and in reminding governments that, vague as these provisions are, they are not a dead letter. The case also involved a claim for damages by Guyana arising out of an alleged unlawful threat of force by Suriname, and a procedural wrangle over the disclosure of documents. These issues are discussed below.

Finally, it is intriguing to observe that in October 2007, less than a month after the decision in *Guyana/Suriname*, the ICJ in the *Nicaragua/Honduras* case delimited a maritime boundary between adjacent States using "angle bisector methodol-

[27] This was the approach taken in the *Barbados/Trinidad and Tobago* case and earlier in the *Cameroon/Nigeria* case, note 22 *supra*.

[28] For discussion of these provisions *see* NATALIE KLEIN, DISPUTE SETTLEMENT IN THE UN CONVENTION ON THE LAW OF THE SEA pp. 248–249 (2005).

ogy," which the Arbitral Tribunal had rejected.[29] This does not, of course, cast doubt on the correctness of either decision, or the competence of their respective judges. It does, however, show that circumstances alter cases and underlines a point which was emphasised in *Barbados/Trinidad and Tobago*: that adjudicating maritime boundaries always requires the exercise of discretion.

In addition to the three cases mentioned, the location of a maritime boundary was an issue in one other case in the period with which we are concerned. This was the *Land Reclamation* case between Malaysia and Singapore where the main question, as we shall see shortly, was the possible impact of a reclamation project on the marine environment, but as part of its claim Malaysia also sought a delimitation of the two States' territorial waters. In the event, however, no decision on this point was necessary. For, as explained in the next section, the whole dispute was settled on agreed terms in 2005 in an arrangement under which the parties agreed that "the issue pertaining to the maritime boundaries be resolved through amicable negotiations without prejudice to the existing rights of the Parties under international law to resort to other means of pacific settlement."

III. ENVIRONMENTAL ISSUES

At the beginning of the twentieth century, international law had little to say about the environment or the obligations of States with regard to its protection. As a result, only a handful of cases brought before international courts and tribunals dealt with these matters. The PCA, for example, had only one case of this type in its early years – the *North Atlantic Coast Fisheries* arbitration[30] – concerned in part with the "reasonable and equitable" regulation of fishing rights, along with other law of the sea issues. However, since the celebrated Stockholm Declaration of 1972, international environmental law and policy have become much more important and, as the substantive law has grown, so there has been an increase in litigation concerned with its application.[31] In the period under review, for example, PCA tribunals have been required to address disputes involving environmental issues on no less than five occasions. As we shall see, the outcome of these cases has varied a good deal, but the general lesson is clear. Broadening the scope of international law to include novel environmental obligations has had a significant impact on the work of the PCA.

---

[29] *See* Philippe Sands, *The Permanent Court of Arbitration: Remarks on the Occasion of a Celebration of the Centenary of the PCA* (The Hague, Oct. 18, 2007), p. 6, *available at* www.pca-cpa.org.

[30] *See* note 14 *supra*.

[31] For analysis of these developments *see* PATRICIA BIRNIE & ALAN BOYLE, INTERNATIONAL LAW AND THE ENVIRONMENT (2d ed. 2002) *and* PHILIPPE SANDS, PRINCIPLES OF INTERNATIONAL ENVIRONMENTAL LAW (2d ed. 2003).

In the *Rhine Chlorides* case between the Netherlands and France,[32] the question submitted to arbitration concerned the scope of the parties' financial obligations under the 1991 Additional Protocol to the 1976 Convention on the Protection of the Rhine against Pollution by Chlorides ("Additional Protocol"), which requires measures to be taken to reduce chloride discharges into the Rhine River and lays down a scheme allocating the costs among the contracting parties. The issue in the case was therefore essentially one of treaty interpretation and the main interest of the case, beyond its immediate outcome, is to be found in the Tribunal's exposition of the principles of interpretation and their application to the particular facts. As regards the general approach to be adopted, the decision confirmed the common understanding that Articles 31 and 32 of the 1969 Vienna Convention on the Law of Treaties ("Vienna Convention") must be regarded as reflecting the position under customary law. It also emphasised that the various elements of Article 31 of the Convention should be viewed as an integral whole and that the supplementary means in Article 32 may be used to confirm the meaning derived from Article 31, as well as when the application of the latter leaves the meaning ambiguous or obscure, or leads to a result which is manifestly absurd or unreasonable.

The application of these principles to the facts demanded a close analysis of the text of the Additional Protocol, its context, and object and purpose. The Tribunal also considered what might qualify as subsequent practice, together with relevant rules of international law, as prescribed in Article 31(3)(c) of the Vienna Convention. Here it made the significant point that the "polluter pays" principle, relied on by the Netherlands, could not be regarded as part of general international law.[33] Having applied Article 31, the Tribunal then considered the preparatory work of the Protocol in accordance with Article 32 and found that this confirmed its interpretation. With the meaning of the Protocol established, it only remained for the Tribunal to calculate the sum due from France, which it did in the final part of its judgment.

The dispute which gave rise to the *Rhine Chlorides* case arose because, as Judge Guillaume explained in his declaration, forecasts were made in 1989 about the coefficient of flow of the Rhine that turned out to be completely wrong. The situation thus bore some resemblance to that in an earlier environmental dispute, the *Gabcikovo-Nagymaros Project* case,[34] where the ICJ likewise had to examine the impact of changing circumstances on a treaty. In the present case Judge Guillaume indicated that he regarded the situation as one falling under Article 62(1) of the

---

[32] *See* p. 73 of this volume.

[33] *See* Case *Concerning the Auditing of Accounts between the Kingdom of the Netherlands and the French Republic Pursuant to the Additional Protocol of 25 September 1991 to the Convention on the Protection of the Rhine Against Pollution by Chlorides of 3 December 1976*, Arbitral Award of Mar. 12, 2004 (unofficial English translation), para. 103, *available at* www.pca-cpa.org.

[34] Gabcikovo-Nagymaros Project (Hung./Slovk.), Judgment, I.C.J. REP. p. 7 (1997).

Vienna Convention. In his view, then, the 1991 Additional Protocol had been terminated by reason of a change of circumstances and the issue of payments should now be resolved by good faith negotiations between the parties. Although this approach did not commend itself to his colleagues, it has certain advantages over relying on Articles 31 and 32, not least that in a new and unexpected situation it enables governments to start afresh, rather than saddling them, through interpretation of their original treaty, with unwelcome and unanticipated burdens.[35]

New circumstances of another kind lay at the heart of the *Iron Rhine* arbitration,[36] where again the interpretation of treaty obligations was the central issue. The case arose when Belgium wished to reactivate a railway line connecting Antwerp with the Rhine basin in Germany and which ran across the Netherlands' territory. The railway, which was in use from 1879 to 1991, had been authorised by treaties concluded between Belgium and the Netherlands in 1839 and 1873, but the proposed reactivation led to a dispute about how this was to be paid for and the parties' respective rights to regulate the conditions under which it could be used. In 2003 these matters were referred to arbitration and in May 2005 the Tribunal handed down its Award, followed by a minor correction and a further decision interpreting the Award in September 2005.

The questions set out in the Arbitration Agreement were of some complexity, relating as they did to the respective powers of regulation of the Dutch and Belgian authorities and the allocation of the costs and financial risks of the reactivation between the parties. While it is unnecessary to describe the Tribunal's answers in detail, several features of its reasoning are worth noting.

As in the *Rhine Chlorides* case, the Tribunal prefaced its review of the particular treaty provisions with an outline of its general approach to interpretation. Again, like its predecessor tribunal, it held that interpretation was governed by the 1969 Vienna Convention, which it found to reflect the position in customary law. In important rulings it held that Article 31(3)(c) enabled it to take account of developments in European law and international environmental law when determining the obligations of the Netherlands[37] and observed that, following the *Gabcikovo-Nagymaros* case, an "evolutive" interpretation, taking into account today's standards, was here more appropriate than an interpretation limited by the parties' original intentions.[38] However, qualifying these remarks with a cautionary note, the Tribu-

---

[35] On the available approaches to cases of this kind *see* J.G. Merrills, *The Mutability of Treaty Obligations*, *in* MATTHEW CRAVEN & MALGOSIA FITZMAURICE, INTERROGATING THE TREATY p. 89 (2005).

[36] *See* p. 81 of this volume.

[37] *See* In the Arbitration Regarding the Iron Rhine ("IJzeren Rijn") Railway between the Kingdom of Belgium and the Kingdom of the Netherlands, Award, May 24, 2005, paras. 58 and 79, *available at* www.pca-cpa.org [hereinafter *Iron Rhine* Award].

[38] *Id.* para. 80.

nal added that application of the principle of effectiveness in interpretation does not "entitle a Tribunal to revise a treaty."[39]

Although the Tribunal answered all the questions in the Arbitration Agreement, it stated that it was not its task "to investigate questions of considerable scientific complexity as to which measures will be sufficient to achieve compliance with the required levels of environmental protection,"[40] or to assess the costs of reactivation of the railway, or of its possible benefits to the Netherlands. In a move we shall also find adopted in the next case, it therefore recommended that the parties set up a group of independent experts for this purpose. Another feature of the case we shall encounter again was that before addressing the merits, the Tribunal had to consider the role of European law in the arbitration in order to avoid trespassing on the prerogatives of the European Court of Justice under certain articles of the EC Treaty. This aspect of the case is discussed below, together with the subsequent decision on interpretation in which the Tribunal clarified several aspects of the Award.

The *Land Reclamation* case[41] involved proceedings brought by Malaysia against Singapore in 2003 in response to reclamation activities being undertaken by the latter in the Straits of Johor, which are shared with Malaysia. The Malaysian Government took the view that the reclamation projects were damaging the marine environment and likely to cause coastal erosion. Malaysia claimed that as the disputed activities had been carried out without notification of, or consultation with, Malaysia, Singapore had breached its obligations under the 1982 Law of the Sea Convention to which both States are parties. Malaysia therefore sought a suspension of the reclamation work until a full assessment of it had been undertaken, involving Malaysia, and also requested a delimitation of the two States' territorial waters.

As noted earlier, the 1982 Convention, as well as laying down rights and duties for States, also includes elaborate arrangements for resolving disputes about its interpretation and application. These include arrangements for compulsory arbitration using an Annex VII tribunal of the type employed in two of the delimitation cases described above,[42] and Malaysia's ultimate objective was to have the dispute over Singapore's reclamation activities heard by such a tribunal. However, the Convention also provides that while an Annex VII tribunal is being set up, a State may request the International Tribunal for the Law of the Sea ("ITLOS") to order provisional measures of protection. Malaysia accordingly asked the ITLOS for an order suspending land reclamation activities by Singapore, requiring the latter to provide

---

[39] *Id.* para. 49. *See also* CHESTER BROWN, A COMMON LAW OF INTERNATIONAL ADJUDICATION pp. 46, 47, 51 & 52 (2007); Duncan French, *Environmental Dispute Settlement: The First (Hesitant) Signs of Spring?*, 19 HAGUE Y.B. INT'L L. p. 3, at pp. 7 & 8 (2006).

[40] *See Iron Rhine* Award, *supra* note 37, para. 235.

[41] *See* p. 93 of this volume.

[42] *See* the *Barbados/Trinidad and Tobago* case and the *Guyana/Suriname* case and the text accompanying notes 19 and 26, *supra*.

information about the projects and to give Malaysia an opportunity to comment, together with an undertaking to negotiate with Malaysia on outstanding unresolved issues, pending the establishment of the Annex VII tribunal.

To deal with Malaysia's request, the ITLOS had to address two rather different issues. As a preliminary matter it had to decide whether it was competent to deal with the case at all. This involved examining the scope of the provisions for compulsory dispute settlement in the Convention, a matter which was also relevant to the jurisdiction of the Annex VII tribunal. Having decided this point in favor of Malaysia, the ITLOS then had to address the main question and decide whether provisional measures were needed. Here it was assisted by the fact that during the hearings the two States had reached agreement on the main issues raised by Malaysia's request. Therefore although the Tribunal rejected Malaysia's request for a suspension of the reclamation work, it made an Order putting on record the parties' undertakings with regard to the sharing of information and co-operation, and in particular requiring them to set up a group of independent experts to investigate the dispute and make recommendations.[43] In addition, the ITLOS required them to report on their progress in fulfilling these undertakings early in 2004. Thus, in this case, the ITLOS made an Order requiring certain provisional measures, but in terms different from those requested.

In accordance with the terms of the Order, Malaysia and Singapore undertook consultations and informed the ITLOS of the results, which included the establishment of the expert group as required by the provisional measures. In the meantime the Annex VII Tribunal had been appointed, although the ITLOS Order for provisional measures remained in force. The expert group submitted an interim report in September 2004 and a final report in November which was then considered at a conference in January 2005. At the conference the parties informed the Annex VII Tribunal they were in the process of settling the dispute on the basis of the experts' recommendations. The Settlement Agreement was concluded in April 2005 and notified to the arbitrators in May. Under the Agreement, the dispute with regard to land reclamation was settled on agreed terms, which the Annex VII Tribunal was requested to adopt in the form of a final and binding award. This the arbitrators did in an Award of September 1, 2005, which terminated the proceedings.[44]

The text of the final Settlement Agreement is set out in an annex to the arbitral Award. It is unnecessary to describe its provisions, but it is interesting to note that as well as dealing with technical issues relating to the reclamation work and various other matters, the Agreement also set up joint mechanisms involving Malaysia and

---

[43] Case *Concerning Land Reclamation by Singapore in and around the Straits of Johor (Malay. v. Sing.)*, Request for Provisional Measures, Order of Oct. 8, 2003, 126 I.L.R. p. 487 (2005).

[44] Case *Concerning Land Reclamation by Singapore in and around the Straits of Johor (Malaysia v. Singapore)*, Award on Agreed Terms, Sept. 1, 2005, *available at* www.pca-cpa.org.

Singapore and designed to promote their future co-operation. As mentioned earlier, the issue of maritime boundaries was left to later negotiation. As regards the main dispute, it is clear that Annex VII arbitration was used here to endorse a solution which had already been reached by negotiation. This is, of course, a rather different use of arbitration from that normally encountered, though one which was perfectly legitimate in the circumstances of the case. Thus, as well as highlighting the value of provisional measures in moving the parties towards accommodation and the role of the ITLOS, the *Land Reclamation* case demonstrates that when negotiations take place against the background of compulsory arbitration, States have an added incentive to agree, so rendering third party resolution of their differences unnecessary.[45]

The *OSPAR* case[46] was one of two arbitrations prompted by the British decision to build a mixed oxide ("MOX") plant at Sellafield in Cumbria on the Irish Sea coast. Both cases were brought by Ireland, which opposed the new plant on environmental and security grounds, the basis of claim here being the 1992 Convention for the Protection of the Marine Environment of the North-East Atlantic ("OSPAR Convention"), to which Ireland and the United Kingdom are both parties and which contains an arbitration clause. More specifically, Ireland's claim relied on Article 9 of the Convention, which is entitled "Access to Information" and which, according to Ireland, the UK had violated by not providing various information relating to the MOX plant which Ireland had requested. In response, the UK argued that the Tribunal lacked jurisdiction and the claim was inadmissible and that in any case, when correctly interpreted, Article 9 did not cover Ireland's request.

In a lengthy and closely reasoned Award, the Tribunal addressed three principal issues. The first was how widely it should cast its net in seeking to elucidate the OSPAR Convention. The Tribunal accepted that "current international law and practice"[47] were relevant to interpretation by reason of Article 31(3)(c) of the 1969 Vienna Convention and that it was necessary to avoid "anachronistic results that are inconsistent with current international law."[48] However, it was not prepared to admit as part of this process principles that had yet to acquire full normative status, or treaties that had not yet been accepted by the parties. This ruling was important because Ireland sought to support its case with extensive reference to such material and, more generally, because international environmental law, as an evolving subject, is at present replete with matter of this kind.

---

[45] For a more detailed appraisal of this case *see* J.G. Merrills, *New Horizons for International Adjudication*, 6 THE GLOBAL COMTY. Y.B. INT'L L. & JURIS. p. 47, at pp. 48-57 (2006).

[46] *See* p. 52 of this volume.

[47] Dispute Concerning Access to Information under Article 9 of the OSPAR Convention, Ireland v. United Kingdom, Final Award, July 2, 2003, para. 101, *available at* www.pca-cpa.org [hereinafter *OSPAR* Award].

[48] *Id.* para. 103.

The second issue was whether, as Ireland maintained, Article 9(1) of the OSPAR Convention created a direct right for Ireland to receive information, or whether, as the UK argued, it was concerned only with the obligation to establish "a domestic regulatory framework" for the disclosure of information. The Tribunal decided this point in favor of Ireland, basing itself on a careful evaluation of the text of the provision in the context of the rest of the agreement and supporting its reading with references to both European law and the international law of State responsibility. Ireland's submission – that its argument that Article 9(1) created an "obligation of result" was supported by the ICJ's decision in the *LaGrand* case[49] – found favor with one member of the Tribunal, but the majority held that their position on textual interpretation made it unnecessary to invoke such material.

The third and ultimately decisive issue was whether the information sought by Ireland fell within Article 9(2) of the OSPAR Convention, which covers information "on the state of the maritime area, on activities or measures adversely affecting or likely to affect it and on activities or measures introduced in accordance with the Convention." Ireland had requested fourteen categories of information concerned with the economics of the MOX plant and related matters, which it maintained could be brought within a broad interpretation of Article 9(2). The UK, emphasising that the OSPAR Convention is not a freedom of information treaty, disagreed and argued that its disclosure obligations were limited to environmental information not covered by Ireland's request. The Tribunal agreed with the UK and, in a decision underlining the significance of its earlier ruling on evolving law and practice, rejected the Irish claim.

In this case, unlike most of those we are considering, the Tribunal's decision was not unanimous, as one of its three members dissented on the interpretation of Article 9(1) of the OSPAR Convention and another on the issue of Article 9(2). From the dissenting opinion on the latter point, it is clear that behind the technical questions of treaty interpretation in cases like this lie significant issues of judicial policy,[50] notably the weight to be assigned to developments outside the particular treaty and to the wider legal context. As noted earlier, similar issues were considered by the Tribunals in both the *Rhine Chlorides* case and the *Iron Rhine* case, and can almost be guaranteed to arise in environmental disputes.

The final environmental case, the *MOX Plant* case,[51] stemmed from the same situation as the *OSPAR* case. When the Irish Government learned of the British intention to open the new facility at Sellafield, at the same time as the *OSPAR* proceedings, it initiated arbitration under the 1982 Law of the Sea Convention, claim-

---

[49] LaGrand (Germ. v. U.S.), Judgment, I.C.J. REP. p. 466 (2001).

[50] *See* the dissenting opinion of Gavan Griffith QC, and for a view supporting the majority's approach, T.L. McDorman, *Note*, 98 AM. J. INT'L L. p. 330 (2004).

[51] *See* p. 136 of this volume.

ing that operation of the new plant would contribute to the pollution of the Irish Sea and that transporting material to the plant by sea would pose further risks. In view of these dangers, Ireland claimed that the United Kingdom had breached its duties under the Convention, to which both States are parties, and which contains a number of provisions dealing with marine pollution.

As in the *Land Reclamation* case, although the claimant's objective was to have the dispute heard by an Annex VII arbitral tribunal, it began by seeking provisional measures of protection through an application to the ITLOS. In its request, Ireland asked for an order with the aim of delaying the opening of the MOX plant and suspending the movement of vessels associated with it, pending the establishment of the Annex VII tribunal. After deciding that it was competent to deal with the request, the ITLOS rejected Ireland's specific request and instead made an Order requiring Ireland and the UK to enter into consultations and exchange information about the possible risks posed by the MOX plant.[52] Thus, like the *Land Reclamation* case, the ITLOS Order required certain provisional measures, but in terms different from those that had been requested.

In accordance with the terms of the Order, the two States undertook consultations and informed the ITLOS of the results. In 2002 an Annex VII tribunal was appointed to hear the case and in 2003 the Tribunal considered a request from Ireland for further provisional measures. This request was rejected on the ground that additional measures were not needed, but the measures ordered by the ITLOS were affirmed.[53] Whilst these rulings are a useful addition to the extensive case law on provisional measures, the main interest in the case is to be found in the way the Annex VII Tribunal dealt with various jurisdictional issues in relation to both provisional measures and its ability to rule on the merits. In particular, the relation of the current proceedings to those before two other courts needed to be considered: namely the *OSPAR* Tribunal, which was already functioning, and the European Court of Justice ("ECJ"), which might be involved in the future.

As regards the former, the UK argued that the Annex VII Tribunal lacked even *prima facie* jurisdiction to deal with the case on the grounds, *inter alia*, that the parties had agreed to resolve it through another binding procedure, as demonstrated by the *OSPAR* proceedings. This argument, which relied on Article 282 of the UNCLOS, had been rejected by the ITLOS when Ireland made its initial application for provisional measures, and was also rejected by the Annex VII Tribunal. It acknowledged that the OSPAR Convention was "relevant to at least some of the ques-

---

[52] *MOX Plant* Case (Ir. v. U.K.), Request for Provisional Measures, Order of Dec. 3, 2001, 126 I.L.R. p. 259 (2005).

[53] *MOX Plant* case, Order No. 3, Suspension of Proceedings on Jurisdiction and Merits, and Request for Further Provisional Measures, June 24, 2003, 26 I.L.R. p. 259, at p. 310 (2005) [hereinafter MOX, Order No. 3]; *also available at* www.pca-cpa.org.

tions in issue between the Parties,"[54] but considered that this did not alter the character of the dispute as one essentially involving the interpretation and application of the UNCLOS, adding that it was "not persuaded that the OSPAR Convention substantially covers the field of the present dispute so as to trigger the application of Articles 281 or 282 of the Convention."[55]

The possibility that some of the issues might fall within the exclusive jurisdiction of the ECJ was likewise raised, but similarly held to be no bar to a finding of *prima facie* jurisdiction for the purpose of considering provisional measures. However, the Annex VII Tribunal also held that "before proceeding to any final decision on the merits, the Tribunal must satisfy itself that it has jurisdiction in a definitive sense."[56] But if the ECJ were to hold that the interpretation of the Law of the Sea Convention in its entirety fell within the Court's exclusive competence as between Members of the Union, then the Tribunal's jurisdiction would be precluded by virtue of Article 282 of the Convention. Noting that the scope and effects of European Community law were essentially for the ECJ to determine, the Tribunal therefore concluded that "bearing in mind considerations of mutual respect and comity which should prevail between judicial institutions,"[57] it would be inappropriate for it to proceed further with a hearing on the merits. It therefore decided to suspend the proceedings.

The last stage of the *MOX Plant* litigation took place before the Grand Chamber of the ECJ in 2006. The proceedings were brought against Ireland by the Commission of the European Communities which sought a declaration that by instituting proceedings against the United Kingdom under the Law of the Sea Convention, Ireland had failed to fulfil its obligations under a number of provisions of European law. An awareness that these proceedings were in contemplation was the reason the Annex VII Tribunal had suspended its proceedings. In the event, the case initiated by the Commission resulted in a decision by the ECJ that Ireland's claims under the Convention did fall within its exclusive jurisdiction.[58] Accordingly, in instituting the Annex VII arbitration, Ireland had failed to fulfil its obligations under European law. Naturally the same question could be asked about the *OSPAR* arbitration, which, as noted above, had concluded with a decision on the merits in 2003. However, the ECJ indicated that the terms of the Commission's application meant that this point did not have to be decided.

---

[54] *Id.* para. 18.

[55] *Id.* This perhaps suggests that in some cases at least disputes under two conventions may be so similar in their subject matter as to preclude multiple litigation. If so, the ITLOS appeared to take a different view. *See* J.G. Merrills, *The Mosaic of Dispute Settlement Procedures: Complementary or Contradictory?*, 54 NETH. INT'L L. REV. p. 361, at pp. 373-374 (2007).

[56] MOX, Order No. 3, *supra* note 53, para. 15.

[57] *Id.* para. 28.

[58] Case C-459/03, Commission v. Ireland. For a summary *see* C.P.R. Romano, *Note*, 101 AM. J. INT'L L. p. 171 (2007).

Whether the ECJ was correct to interpret its competence so broadly will not be considered here, but its decision clearly has major consequences both for members of the regional organization and for the work of international courts and tribunals. When justifying its decision to suspend proceedings, the Annex VII Tribunal observed that "a procedure that might result in two conflicting decisions would not be helpful to the resolution of the dispute between the Parties."[59] While that is certainly so, it is interesting to note that when faced with a similar problem, the Tribunal in the *Iron Rhine* arbitration considered that it was in a "position analogous to that of a domestic court within the EC"[60] and decided that only in certain special circumstances would it be required to yield to the ECJ. This reasoning has been called "imaginative,"[61] but it achieved a result which respected the parties' mutual desire to have their dispute resolved by arbitration. The relationship between different courts and tribunals, as these cases have shown, is therefore something that will continue to be debated.

IV. MIXED ARBITRATIONS

The Permanent Court of Arbitration was originally envisaged as an institution whose *raison d'être* was to encourage the use of arbitration in inter-State disputes. Its early cases all involved such disputes and, as is evident from the cases already considered, it is still used for that purpose. In 1935, however, the PCA took on a broader role when in the *Radio Corporation of America* case[62] it was for the first time employed in an arbitration between a State on one side and a commercial corporation on the other. Since that time, as Professor Crawford has explained,[63] such "mixed arbitrations" have formed a significant part of the PCA's work and steps have been taken to encourage its use for cases of this kind. The four mixed arbitrations described in this section affirm both the value and continuing significance of this work.

In *Larsen/Hawaiian Kingdom* ("*Larsen*"),[64] a resident of the state of Hawaii claimed that the "Hawaiian Kingdom" was liable for failing to protect him from the

---

59 MOX, Order No. 3, *supra* note 53, para. 28.

60 *Iron Rhine* Award, *supra* note 37, para. 103.

61 *See* Paul James Cardwell & Duncan French, *Who Decides? The ECJ's Judgment on Jurisdiction in the* MOX Plant *Dispute*, 19 J. ENV'L L. p. 121, at p. 127 (2007).

62 Radio Corporation of America v. China (1935) 1 R.I.A.A. p. 7, *also available at* www.pca-cpa.org, *and see* THE PCA: INTERNATIONAL ARBITRATION, *supra* note 1, at pp. 145–148.

63 *See* James Crawford, *The Permanent Court of Arbitration and Mixed Arbitration: Remarks on the Occasion of a Celebration of the Centenary of the PCA* (The Hague, Oct. 18, 2007), p. 1, *available at* www.pca-cpa.org.

64 *See* p. 46 of this volume. *See also* David J. Bederman & K.R. Hilbert, *Note*, 95 AM. J. INT'L L. p. 927 (2001).

United States on the ground that the invasion of Hawaii in 1893 and the coup which overthrew its queen was illegal. The PCA was designated as the registry of the arbitration, which the parties agreed should be governed by the Arbitration Rules of the United Nations Commission on International Trade Law ("UNCITRAL Rules"). On a preliminary point, the Tribunal held that the UNCITRAL Rules could be employed for a non-contractual dispute, but then decided that, as there was no real dispute between the parties, the claim should be dismissed. It added that even if there was a dispute, the Tribunal could not address it, because the United States, which was not present, but whose conduct was in issue, was an indispensable third party. In drawing these conclusions the Tribunal sought to apply the pertinent case law of the International Court of Justice.[65] Consequently, whilst the situation in *Larsen* is unlikely ever to be repeated, the Tribunal's rulings on the various issues of justiciability raised by the case have some lasting value.

The *Bank for International Settlements* case,[66] though another mixed arbitration, was different from *Larsen* in almost every respect. The Bank for International Settlements ("BIS") was founded in 1930 to deal with German reparations from the First World War, subsequently widening its functions to become effectively an international financial organization and central bank. When the BIS was set up, it was as a company with shareholders, most of which were States, but which also included a number of private individuals and concerns. This unusual arrangement was seen as increasingly anomalous by the Bank's management and its State shareholders and so in 2001 its Statutes were modified to permit the recall of the shares in private hands in return for compensation. This action led to a dispute with the private shareholders in which the main issue was the level of compensation offered, but a further question, raised by one claimant, was whether the forced redemption was lawful. These matters were referred to arbitration in accordance with the 1930 Settlement Agreement. A tribunal was therefore appointed which, in 2002, issued a Preliminary Award, holding that the share recall was lawful and indicating the applicable standards for valuation of the shares, and then a Final Award in 2003 specifying the sums due.

The decisions made by the Tribunal, though naturally concerned with the particular circumstances, contain a number of points of wider interest. Thus it decided that the BIS possessed international legal personality in view of its functions and widespread recognition, and also that the share recall was lawful on the basis of the Bank's constituent instrument. As regards the latter, however, the Tribunal went on

---

65 The cases cited included, on the dispute point, the *Northern Cameroons* case, I.C.J. REP. p. 15 (1963) *and* the *East Timor* case, I.C.J. REP. p. 90 (1995); and on the indispensable third party point, the *Monetary Gold* case, I.C.J. REP. p. 19 (1954); the *Nicaragua* case, I.C.J. REP. p. 215 (1984); the *Nauru* case, I.C.J. REP. p. 240 (1992); and the *East Timor* case (above).

66 *See* p. 62 of this volume. *See also* David J. Bederman, *The Unique Legal Status of the Bank for International Settlements Comes into Focus*, 16 LEIDEN J. INT'L L. p. 787 (2003).

to consider the possible relevance to the case of the substantive standards of international law which apply when expropriations are carried out by States. On the question of valuation the Tribunal again referred to the law of expropriation, finding that this normally requires "full" rather than "appropriate" compensation. Here, however, compensation was governed by the *lex specialis* of the Bank's constituent instruments. In the Tribunal's view this meant that the Bank's shares should be valued according to the "net asset value" method favoured by the claimants rather than the lower "dividend perpetuity model" proposed by the Bank. In the event, this resulted in the claimants receiving significantly more than the amount for their shares that had originally been offered.

As well as its substantive rulings, the Tribunal dealt with a number of procedural issues which also merit attention. It decided that a counter-claim by the Bank against one of the claimants was not only admissible but also well-founded, on the grounds that the claimant in question had sued the Bank in the United States, contrary to the undertaking to arbitrate. In various preliminary orders the Tribunal addressed such questions as the scope for discovery of documents in relation to attorney-client privilege,[67] and the extent to which non-parties to a case may claim disclosure of information about the parties and their claims.[68] Issues of this type have arisen before and are increasingly common in mixed arbitrations.[69] The manner in which they were handled here is therefore instructive.

Every mixed arbitration has its own distinctive features, but the next case to be considered, *Saluka Investments v. The Czech Republic*,[70] can be thought of as in many respects the most conventional. Following the end of communist rule in 1990, the Czech Government privatised one of the country's principal banks, IPB, by selling the State's shareholding to Nomura, a Japanese group, which then transferred the shares to a subsidiary, Saluka Investments, incorporated under the law of the Netherlands. In 2000 the Czech Government put IPB into forced administration, alleging mismanagement, and sold it to another bank for a symbolic price of one crown. Nomura, which held a 46% stake in IPB, responded by initiating arbitration through Saluka on the basis of a bilateral investment treaty ("BIT") between the Netherlands and the Czech Republic. In its Partial Award in 2006 the Tribunal rejected a challenge to its jurisdiction from the Government and upheld Saluka's claim in part. The question of compensation was reserved. The case was settled and resolved following issuance of the Partial Award.

---

[67] *See* the Tribunal's Procedural Order No. 6 (Order with Respect to the Discovery of Certain Documents for which Attorney-Client Privilege has been Claimed), June 11, 2002, *available at* www.pca-cpa.org.

[68] *See* the Tribunal's Procedural Order, In the matter of Reginald H. Howe, on the Request of Reginald H. Howe for Exceptional Remedies, Aug. 31, 2001.

[69] *See* Crawford, *supra* note 63, at p. 5. *See also* BROWN, *supra* note 39, at pp. 83-119.

[70] *See* p. 126 of this volume.

On the merits there were two main issues for the Tribunal to consider: whether the Government's conduct with regard to IPB had violated Article 3 of the BIT, which guaranteed fair and equitable treatment, or Article 5, which covered deprivation of investment. As regards the latter, it decided that there had been no violation, ruling that the Government's action was "valid and permissible as within its regulatory powers,"[71] notwithstanding its drastic effect on Saluka's investment. However, the claim based on Article 3 was more successful. For here, the Tribunal decided that the Government's failure to treat IPB in the same way as three other banks to which assistance had been given amounted to a failure to accord it fair and equitable treatment. Furthermore, the Tribunal found that the Government had frustrated efforts by IPB and the shareholders to resolve the bank's crisis, and decided that this too constituted a failure to provide fair and equitable treatment.

From a systemic perspective, the significance of this case lies in the way the guarantee of "fair and equitable treatment" was interpreted and applied. There are now more than 2,000 BITs and as nearly all of them provide this guarantee, it has been aptly described as "a cornerstone of the evolving international law on the protection of investors and their investments."[72] The precise contents of the standard are therefore a matter of great importance. A study in 1999 found arbitral jurisprudence on the point to be "almost non-existent,"[73] and whilst that is no longer true, *Saluka* is a cogent addition to the growing case law. It should also be noted that in this case, as in the *Bank for International Settlements* case, the Tribunal had to deal with a counter-claim. Unlike the previous case, however, here it was unsuccessful. Although the Tribunal ruled that counter-claims could be entertained in principle, it decided that the particular counter-claim which was being put forward was not sufficiently connected with the main claim to be considered.

The last mixed arbitration, the *Eurotunnel* case,[74] arose from a dispute between the two companies which built and operate the Channel Tunnel, on one side, and the British and French Governments, on the other. In 1986 the two governments concluded the Treaty of Canterbury under which they agreed that a tunnel linking England and France would be constructed and financed by private investment. The companies selected – one British and one French – then concluded a Concession Agreement with the two governments, setting out the agreed terms for building and operating the Tunnel. The Tunnel was built and opened in 1994, but then problems emerged which led to this arbitration. One problem was that migrants wishing to

[71] *See* Saluka Investments B.V. v. The Czech Republic, Partial Award, Mar. 17, 2006, para. 276, *available at* www.pca-cpa.org.

[72] Peter Muchlinski, '*Caveat Investor'? The Relevance of the Conduct of the Investor under the Fair and Equitable Treatment Standard*, 55 Int'l & Comp. L.Q. p. 527 (2006).

[73] Stephen Vasciannie, *The Fair and Equitable Treatment Standard in International Investment Law and Practice*, 70 Br. Y.B. Int'l L. p. 99, at p. 130 (1999).

[74] *See* p. 106 of this volume.

enter the UK illegally began to gather in large numbers near the entrance to the Tunnel at Calais, seriously disrupting the service and causing the operators to incur significant costs. The companies claimed that the governments had not done enough to stop this illegal activity and that by failing to protect the Tunnel they were in breach of their obligations under the Concession Agreement. A second problem was that the French Government was alleged to be subsidising a cross channel ferry service, run by another French company. The Tunnel operators claimed that this constituted unfair competition and was a further violation of the Concession Agreement.

The main issue for the Tribunal was thus the scope of the obligations owed by the governments under the Concession Agreement and whether, on the facts, those obligations had been broken. Interpretation of the Agreement was a complex matter, since the document itself was long and detailed, there were differences between the English and the French texts (which were equally authoritative), and the extent to which the Treaty of Canterbury and related material could be taken into account was a matter of disagreement. There were also different views on the factual aspects of the case, including the scale and circumstances of the illegal incursions and the nature of the alleged French subsidy. After hearing argument on all these points the Tribunal upheld the first of the applicants' claims, holding that the governments were under a duty to provide adequate security arrangements and that this duty had been broken, but dismissed the second claim, ruling that there were no obligations under the Concession Agreement with regard to the subsidising of competitors. The Partial Award, which was made in 2007, resolved the issue of liability. As in the *Bank for International Settlements* arbitration and the *Saluka* case, the quantum of compensation was reserved for a subsequent phase of the proceedings.

The Award, running to nearly 400 paragraphs and accompanied by a dissenting opinion from one of the arbitrators,[75] covers a huge amount of ground, embracing not only interpretation, but jurisdiction and the issue of applicable law, joint and several liability (where the Tribunal referred to the International Law Commission Articles on State Responsibility), and the role of national and European law in the arbitration, as well as a number of incidental issues. On the subsidy point it is interesting to note that the Tribunal's conclusion that an obligation here could not be inferred, but required express words, was identical to the decision in the *Radio Corporation of America* case on a similar point some seventy years earlier.[76] More generally, it has been observed that the *Eurotunnel* case "shows the use of internationalized contracts in developed economies as a means of securing long-term infrastructure investments,"[77] as well, of course, as confirming the particular value of mixed arbitration when disputes over the meaning of such contracts arise.

---

[75] Lord Millett, who dissented on the scope of the responsibility of the United Kingdom.

[76] *See* Crawford, *supra* note 63, at p. 2.

[77] *Id.* p. 4.

V. THE USE OF FORCE

Disputes concerning the lawfulness of the use of force in international affairs, whether the *jus ad bellum* or the *jus in bello*, tend to be of a highly political nature. Since consent has always been fundamental to the exercise of jurisdiction by international courts and tribunals, historically such disputes have generally been dealt with by other means. The PCA, for example, had only one case raising issues of this kind in its early years: the *Venezuelan Preferential Claims* case[78] in 1904, where the point was raised indirectly. In recent years, however, resort to courts and tribunals to resolve such questions has become rather more frequent. It is therefore not altogether unexpected that in the latest period use of force issues have been addressed by PCA tribunals on two occasions.

In the *Guyana/Suriname* arbitration the point in issue related to the *jus ad bellum*. A dispute arose when an oil rig and drill ship operated by the holder of a concession from Guyana were ordered by Suriname to leave an area which both States claimed, and were then escorted from the scene. As noted earlier, Guyana referred the question of maritime delimitation to arbitration and also made a claim for damages arising from both the initial incident and the subsequent warning off of two other concession holders. In its Award the Tribunal, having rejected various jurisdictional objections from Suriname, along with its attempt to invoke the "clean hands" doctrine, decided that there had been a threat of force and that in the light of ICJ case law, this threat was unlawful. In reaching this conclusion the Tribunal rejected Suriname's argument that its action constituted reasonable and proportionate law enforcement measures, or alternatively could be justified as countermeasures. As regards remedies, however, the Tribunal rejected Guyana's claim for compensation on the ground that no damage had been proved, and also held that an order prohibiting further threats of force was unnecessary as this issue was sufficiently addressed by the Tribunal's ruling on delimitation.

The Eritrea-Ethiopia Claims Commission, which was set up in 2000 to hear claims concerning violations of international law relating to the recent war between Eritrea and Ethiopia, rendered a number of notable Awards.[79] For the most part, these concerned the *jus in bello*, but in one, the *Jus Ad Bellum* Award, the rules regulating resort to the use of force had to be considered. Ethiopia claimed that Eritrea had invaded its territory in May and June 1998 and that this action violated Article 2(4) of the United Nations Charter. In its Award the Commission upheld the claim, rejecting Eritrea's argument that border skirmishes had amounted to an "armed at-

---

[78] Preferential Treatment of Claims of Blockading Powers against Venezuela (Gr. Brit., Germ. and Italy/Venez.), 9 R.I.A.A. p. 99 (1904), *and see* THE PCA: INTERNATIONAL ARBITRATION, *supra* note 1, p. 17 and pp. 35-37.

[79] *See* pp. 155-295 of this volume.

tack," entitling it to act in self-defence. This Commission likewise rejected Eritrea's claim that it was merely recovering unlawfully occupied territory, pointing out that force is not a legitimate means of resolving border disputes. Whilst these are not unexpected rulings, they are a further demonstration of the justiciability of at least some use of force disputes.

Most of the issues dealt with by the Eritrea-Ethiopia Claims Commission concerned the *jus in bello*. There is no need to describe the various claims individually, but some examples may be useful to give an idea of their range and juridical significance. Claims brought by both sides relating to the treatment of prisoners of war ("POWs") required the Commission to consider allegations of killing and abuse of prisoners immediately after capture and the conditions in which they were subsequently detained. Among the specific matters ruled on by the Commission here were the provision of medical care for POWs, conditions of labor during detention, permissible and prohibited methods of interrogation, and the obligation on the parties to provide the International Committee of the Red Cross with access to POWs, which the Commission held to be an obligation under customary international law.

The treatment of civilians and their property also featured prominently in the Commission's decisions. A number of claims concerned the conduct of warfare, including the selection of targets for aerial bombardment, the use of anti-personnel landmines, and the destruction of cultural property. Others related specifically to mistreatment of the civilian population, and included allegations of murder, rape, beatings, abductions, and looting. In evaluating these claims, the Commission had to consider both the state of the law, notably the relation between the 1949 Geneva Conventions, together with other treaties, and customary law, but also, since most of the allegations were contested, the relevant evidential standards on which the Commission made a number of significant pronouncements.

Amongst the legal issues presented was precisely when territory should be regarded as "occupied" by a belligerent for the purposes of international law. On this point the Commission ruled that when combat in an area is still in progress, it does not so qualify, but as soon as control is established, even if for only a few days, the rules of belligerent occupation must be applied. When examining this concept the Commission also addressed a novel argument put forward by Eritrea to the effect that in territory which was later awarded to it by the decision of the Eritrea-Ethiopia Boundary Commission, the law of belligerent occupation was not applicable. Understandably the Claims Commission rejected this argument, ruling that the relevant legal instruments contained no suggestion that the concept of belligerent occupation applied only to territory whose title is clear and uncontested.

Civilian claims considered by the Commission also included claims concerning deprivation of nationality, expulsion, detention, deprivation of property, and separation of families. Like the claims already mentioned, these raised many issues relating to the applicable law and the assessment of evidence. It was, for example, necessary for the Commission to review the law on dual nationality in relation to certain individuals, to determine when deprivation of nationality may be permissible, and what constitutes an "arbitrary" deprivation. Expulsion raised, amongst other issues, the question of what may be regarded as a "constructive" expulsion, and property and detention claims brought up matters such as the scope of a State's powers under international humanitarian law and human rights law with regard to enemy nationals. In relation to claims that were upheld, the Commission had to give a further ruling on remedies, deciding that this should normally take the form of monetary compensation.

Some claims required the Commission to go beyond international humanitarian law and consider the impact of war in a wider legal context. Thus both sides made claims for loss, damage and injury to their diplomatic missions, consular posts and personnel, while Ethiopia claimed (successfully) that Eritrean officials had interfered with its diplomatic bag. The Commission's treatment of these issues usefully clarifies the scope of diplomatic law and more particularly, how it applies in the unusual situation where States elect to maintain diplomatic relations during wartime. Similarly, claims for economic loss by Ethiopia called for the Commission to examine the effect of war on bilateral treaties. Another claim involved the scope of a belligerent's right to control trade and restrict access to its ports and its obligations with regard to stranded property and the delivery of humanitarian aid. And an unusual claim relating to the payment of pensions called for discussion of the doctrines of State succession and unjust enrichment.

As already indicated, in discharging its mandate the Eritrea-Ethiopia Claims Commission dealt with complex evidential issues, made many important pronouncements on the law, then conscientiously applied that law to the facts. The Commission's approach has been described as "pragmatic yet principled,"[80] no doubt the best course when States which have just fought a war elect to submit the delicate matter of its conduct and aftermath to international arbitration.

VI. THE ADMINISTRATION OF INTERNATIONAL JUSTICE

The awards of arbitral tribunals have had a major part to play in developing the rules and principles of international law concerned with the conduct of litigation, including those relating to a range of procedural matters, to evidence, to the review of awards, and to judicial remedies. Thus the early cases administered by the PCA included a high proportion of those decided when the framework for modern arbitration was being established, and so contain numerous rulings on these matters

[80] J. Romesh Weeramantry, *Note*, 99 AM. J. IN'TL L. p. 465, at p. 471 (2005). *See also* the same author's later Notes *in* 100 AM. J. IN'TL L. p. 201 (2006) *and* 101 AM. J. IN'TL L. p. 616 (2007).

which have subsequently been influential.[81] In the latest period this trend has continued, with recent tribunals being required to address a variety of issues relating to the administration of justice; some already the subject of a good deal of international practice, others of a more novel character.

An unusual point that had to be decided in the *Eurotunnel* case concerned a provision in the Treaty of Canterbury which forbade the arbitrators appointed by the Concessionaires from participating "in that part of any decision relating to the interpretation or application of the Treaty." Since the Concession Agreement might need to be interpreted in the light of the Treaty and the scope of the intended prohibition was by no means clear, the application of this provision presented obvious difficulties. However, the Tribunal resolved the problem by ruling that it was for the full Tribunal to consider the significance of the Treaty in any given case by virtue of its "competence competence,"[82] so giving the provision a relatively narrow interpretation. It therefore concluded that, should the need arise, it was for the full Tribunal to hear argument and discuss the issue, the sole effect of the exclusion being to prevent the arbitrators appointed by the claimants from voting on the point.

In *Larsen/Hawaiian Kingdom*, the Tribunal gave a striking demonstration of the principle that tribunals are masters of their own procedure by refusing to give effect to a revised *compromis* in which the parties asked it to verify "the continued existence of Hawaiian Statehood" in an interlocutory award. By way of explanation, the Tribunal held that it was not open to the parties to redefine essential issues as interlocutory, pointing out that in accordance with the UNCITRAL Rules "and with the general principles of arbitral procedure, it is for the Tribunal to determine which issues need to be dealt with and in what order."[83] Further examples of the exercise of this power may be seen in the resolution by the Tribunal in the *OSPAR* arbitration of a disagreement between the parties as to the sequencing of argument and examination of witnesses,[84] and in the ruling by the Tribunal in the *MOX Plant* arbitration that it was competent to order provisional measures *ultra petita*.[85]

In the *Eritrea/Yemen* arbitration, the Tribunal had to apply a choice of law clause providing for the application of the Law of the Sea Convention and "any other

---

[81] *See* THE PCA: INTERNATIONAL ARBITRATION, *supra* note 1, pp. 17-21.

[82] In the Matter of an Arbitration before a Tribunal Constituted in Accordance with Article 19 of the Treaty between the French Republic and the United Kingdom of Great Britain and Northern Ireland Concerning the Construction and Operation by Private Concesssionaires of a Channel Fixed Link Signed at Canterbury on 12 February 1986, between 1. The Channel Tunnel Group Ltd. 2. France-Manche S.A. and The Secretary of State for Transport of the Government of the United Kingdom of Great Britain and Northern Ireland 2. Le Ministre de l'equipement, des transports, de l'amenagement du territoire, du tourisme et de la mer du Gouvernement de la Republique Francaise, Partial Award, Jan. 30, 2007, para. 90 [hereinafter *Eurotunnel* Award], *available at* www.pca-cpa.org.

[83] *Larsen*, Arbitral Award, Feb. 5, 2001, para. 6.5, citing the Tribunal's Procedural Order No. 4 of Sept. 5, 2000. *See also* on this point BROWN, *supra* note 39, p. 65.

[84] *OSPAR* Award, *supra* note 47, paras. 60 and 65.

[85] MOX, Order No. 3, *supra* note 53, para. 43.

pertinent factor." Having interpreted this, very sensibly, as referring to the various factors "that are generally recognised as being relevant to the process of delimitation,"[86] the Tribunal went on, more controversially, to justify its treatment of the "artisanal fishing regime" by reference to Islamic law, an explanation that has been criticised as both unwise and unnecessary.[87] Choice of law was also an important issue in the *Eurotunnel* case, where the Tribunal emphasised the crucial distinction between jurisdiction and choice of law, or, as the Tribunal put it, "the scope of the rights and obligations which an international tribunal has jurisdiction to enforce and the law which it will have to apply in doing so."[88] As the Tribunal explained, this distinction was also emphasised in the *MOX Plant*[89] and *OSPAR* arbitrations.[90]

Evidential issues were prominent in the work of the Eritrea-Ethiopia Claims Commission where, in relation to many of the claims considered, the sworn declarations by each side were completely contradictory. The Commission decided that in view of the gravity of some of the claims, including the mistreatment of POWs and civilians, a "clear and convincing" standard of proof should be adopted.[91] Not surprisingly, therefore, many claims were dismissed for lack of proof. In the *Eritrea-Ethiopia Boundary* case, in contrast, much of the disputed evidence consisted of maps, leading the Commission in that case to observe that

> [t]he effect of a map that is not part of a treaty will vary according to its provenance, its scale and cartographic quality, its consistency with other maps, the use of it made by the parties, the degree of publicity accorded to it and the extent to which, it at all, it was adopted or acquiesced in by the parties adversely affected by it, or the extent to which it is contrary to the interests of the party that produced it.[92]

In several of the cases with which we are concerned, tribunals were assisted in their work by experts of various kinds. As already mentioned, in the *Iron Rhine* case the Tribunal recommended the appointment of a committee of independent experts to establish the costs of reactivating the railway and certain related matters, whilst in the *Land Reclamation* case the Award on agreed terms which the Tribunal endorsed was based largely on the work of an expert group prescribed earlier by the

---

[86] *Eritrea/Yemen II* Award, *supra* note 15, para. 130.

[87] *See* Reisman, *supra* note 16, at p. 729.

[88] *Eurotunnel* Award, *supra* note 82, para. 152.

[89] MOX, Order No. 3, *supra* note 53, para. 19.

[90] *OSPAR* Award, *supra* note 47, para. 85.

[91] *See, e.g.*, Prisoners of War, Eritrea's Claim 17 between the State of Eritrea and the Federal Democratic Republic of Ethiopia, Partial Award, July 1, 2003, para. 46; Prisoners of War, Ethiopia's Claim 4 between the Federal Democratic Republic of Ethiopia and the State of Eritrea, Partial Award, July 1, 2003, para. 37, both *available at* www.pca-cpa.org.

[92] *Eritrea-Ethiopia Boundary Commission* Decision, *supra* note 6, para. 3.21. *See also* Shaw, *supra* note 8, at pp. 777-779.

ITLOS. In each of three maritime delimitation cases the tribunal itself appointed an expert in hydrography or geodesy to assist it, as is now standard practice in such cases, and in one, the *Guyana/Suriname* case, the person appointed conducted a site visit to the area.[93] In that case, too, when a dispute arose between the parties over the disclosure of documents held in the Netherlands' National Archives, the Tribunal appointed another independent expert to help them resolve the matter.[94]

The scope and availability of judicial remedies is a further issue on which the cases under review contain a rich and varied jurisprudence. In the *MOX Plant* case, it will be recalled, the Tribunal decided to suspend proceedings, pending the resolution of certain jurisdictional issues by the ECJ, and its ruling has already been followed by an ICSID tribunal in what it saw as an analogous situation.[95] In contrast, in the *Eritrea/Yemen* case, the Tribunal seemed to envisage its continuation indefinitely in case Eritrea wished to raise the question of its fishermen's rights for further consideration.[96] This could not only present practical difficulties, but also offers a rather surprising possibility, given that it went beyond what Eritrea was asking for.

Damages, one of the key issues in many past arbitral awards, have been awarded and assessed only by the Eritrea-Ethiopia Claims Commission and in the *Bank for International Settlements* case. The final award in this case contains a valuable discussion of both the standard of compensation required and the different methods of valuing shares, both of which issues will no doubt arise in future cases. The Eritrea-Ethiopia Claims Commission, having resolved the question of liability in a series of Partial Awards, then addressed the issue of compensation in two wide-ranging Final Awards dealing with the parties' respective claims. These contain a detailed treatment of compensation for loss of property, personal injury (including rape), deprivation of nationality, wrongful expulsion and a number of other injuries and, as well as the Commission's assessment of the facts, feature rulings on legal issues such as evidential standards and causation. Notable rulings also include the Commission's rejection of claims for both "consequential" and "moral" damages and its handling of the difficult question of compensation for violations of the *jus ad bellum.* Before leaving this topic it should, of course, be added that in the *Eurotunnel* arbitration there has been a partial award upholding some or all of the claims on the merits. In due course, therefore, a final award assessing the damages due in this case may be expected.

---

[93] *Guyana v. Suriname* Award, Sept. 17, 2007, paras. 121, 122, *available at* www.pca-cpa.org.

[94] *Id.* paras. 62-102.

[95] *See SGS v. Philippines*, ICSID Case No. ARB/02/6, Decision on Jurisdiction of Jan. 29, 2004, para. 175. *See also* Yuval Shany, *Contract Claims vs. Treaty Claims: Mapping Conflicts between ICSID Decisions on Multisourced Investment Claims*, 99 AM. J. INT'L L. p. 835, at pp. 841-842 (2005); *and* BROWN, *supra* note 39, pp. 251-252.

[96] *Eritrea/Yemen II* Award, *supra* note 15, at para. 101. *And see* Reisman, *supra* note 16, at p. 731.

The possibility of awarding remedies other than monetary compensation was recognised by the Eritrea-Ethiopia Claims Commission which, in an early Decision, ruled that non-monetary remedies could be granted where such remedies were "in accordance with international practice" and "would be reasonable and appropriate in the circumstances."[97] This acknowledges that remedies such as satisfaction in the form of a declaration of wrongfulness may well be fitting for certain types of claims. In a situation of a rather different kind, it is worth noting that the Tribunal in the *Guyana/Suriname* case was asked by Guyana for an order precluding Suriname from resorting to further threats of force, but decided that, in accordance with the ICJ's decision in the *Cameroon/Nigeria* case, this point was sufficiently addressed by its ruling on delimitation.

Finally, three of the cases under review raised a rather specialized aspect of the administration of international justice, namely the powers of a tribunal to interpret or correct an award. Shortly after rendering its Decision, the Eritrea-Ethiopia Boundary Commission rejected a "Request for Interpretation, Correction and Consultation" from Ethiopia, on the ground that what was being sought went beyond the Commission's powers of interpretation or revision, and as such was inadmissible.[98] The Eritrea-Ethiopia Claims Commission, likewise, rejected a request for an interpretation of one of its partial awards on similar grounds. On the other hand, the Tribunal in the *Iron Rhine* case, having made a minor correction to its Award at the request of Belgium,[99] also issued an Interpretation of the Award answering a number of questions from the same State relating to its scope and implications.[100] Dr. Brown has pointed out that "judicial and arbitral practice on the exercise of the power of interpretation is somewhat limited,"[101] and so all these decisions, though reflecting the very different nature of the three arbitrations, are a useful addition to the case law.

VII. CONCLUSION

Writing in 1970, a leading member of the International Court observed that "[s]ince specific legislative action with direct binding effect is not at present possible in the international field, judicial pronouncements of one kind or another constitute the principal method by which the law can find some concrete measure of clarification

---

[97] *See* the Commission's Decision No. 3, Remedies, July 24, 2001, *available at* www.pca-cpa.org; *see also* J. Romesh Weeramantry, *Note*, 100 AM. J. INT'L L. p. 201 at pp 205-207 (2006).

[98] Eritrea-Ethiopia Boundary Commission, Decision on Interpretation, June 24, 2002, *available at* www.pca-cpa.org.

[99] *Iron Rhine*, Correction of Award, Sept. 20, 2005, *available at* www.pca-cpa.org.

[100] *Iron Rhine*, Interpretation of Award, Sept. 20, 2005, *available at* www.pca-cpa.org.

[101] BROWN, *supra* note 39, at p. 173.

or development."[102] Forty years on, many today would perhaps be more inclined to agree with another distinguished international judge who in 1995 cautioned against attaching too much significance to the words of judges and suggested that international law may now be "getting beyond the stage when one hoped for more cases before the Court simply to get the law authoritatively stated and developed."[103] But if there is now a great deal more international law than there used to be, there is, as a consequence, also more for international courts to interpret and apply and a greater demand for their services, owing to a renewed interest in adjudication. In this situation, as should be evident from our survey of the recent awards of the PCA, "judicial pronouncements of one kind or another" have certainly not lost their value. It is, of course, necessary to remember that the awards described here are only a fraction of the now burgeoning international case law, that some of them will inevitably be more influential than others, and that in any event, as already indicated, judicial decisions are not the main means by which the law develops today, if indeed they ever were. All that having been said, however, it is clear that without this recent jurisprudence, not only might a number of troubling disputes have remained unresolved, but international law as a whole would be much poorer.

---

[102] Judge Sir Gerald Fitzmaurice, separate opinion in the *Barcelona Traction* case, I.C.J. REP. p. 3, at p. 65 (1970).

[103] Robert Y. Jennings, *The International Court of Justice after Fifty Years*, 89 AM. J. IN'TL L. p. 493, at p. 498 (1995). Judge Sir Robert Y. Jennings was a Member of the International Court of Justice from 1982 to 1995, serving as its President from 1991 to 1994. He was also President of the Tribunal in the *Eritrea/Yemen* case.

ARBITRAL TRIBUNALS

Eritrea/Yemen – Maritime Delimitation

Parties: Eritrea/Yemen

Date of Arbitration Agreement: October 3, 1996

Arbitrators: Prof. Sir Robert Jennings (President), Judge Stephen M. Schwebel, Dr. Ahmed Sadek El-Kosheri, Mr. Keith Highet, Judge Roslyn Higgins

Date of Award: December 17, 1999

Summary

Delimitation of maritime boundary between Eritrea and Yemen – fisheries practices of Parties held not to affect the delimitation line – interpretation of traditional fishing regime referred to in First Award of the Tribunal – delimitation effected by single line in accordance with Arbitration Agreement and United Nations Convention on the Law of the Sea.

Legal Subject Matters

Oceans:
- Law of the sea
  - Maritime delimitation
    - Fisheries practice
    - Proportionality
    - Third States

Sources of international norms:
- Customary international law
- Islamic law
- Regional legal traditions

Bibliography

Award published in:
- The Eritrea-Yemen Arbitration Awards 1998 and 1999 (Permanent Court of Arbitration Award Series, TMC Asser Press 2005);
- XXII R.I.A.A. p. 335 (1999).

Commentary:
- Jean-Pierre Queneudec, *The Eritrea-Yemen Arbitration: Its Contribution to International Law, in* The Eritrea-Yemen Arbitration Awards 1998 and 1999 (Permanent Court of Arbitration Award Series 2005);

- Nuno Sérgio Marques Antunes, THE 1999 ERITEA-YEMEN MARITIME DELIMITATION AWARD AND THE DEVELOPMENT OF INTERNATIONAL LAW (Almedina 2004);
- Barbara Kwiatkowska, *The Eritrea/Yemen Arbitration: Landmark Progress in the Acquisition of Territorial Sovereignty and Equitable Maritime Boundary Delimitation*, 32 OCEAN DEV. & INT'L L. p. 1 (2001);
- Nuno Sérgio Marques Antunes, *The 1999 Eritrea-Yemen Maritime Delimitation Award and the Development of International Law*, 50 INT'L & COMP. L. Q. p. 299 (2001);
- Malcolm D. Evans, *The Maritime Delimitation between Eritrea and Yemen*, 14 LEIDEN J. INT'L L. p. 141 (2001);
- *In the Second Stage of the Proceedings in the Matter of the Arbitration Between Eritrea and Yemen (Maritime Delimitation)*, 6 Y.B. ISLAMIC & MIDDLE EASTERN LAW p. 465 (2001);
- Yoshifumi Tanaka, *Reflections on the Eritrea/Yemen Arbitration of 17 December 1999 (Second Stage: Maritime Delimitation)*, 48 NETH. INT'L. L. REV. p. 197 (2001);
- Barbara Kwiatkowska, *The Eritrea/Yemen Arbitration: Landmark Progress in the Acquisition of Territorial Sovereignty and Equitable Maritime Boundary Delimitation*, I.B.R.U. BOUNDARY & SECURITY BULL. p. 66 (2000);
- Giovanni Distefano, *La sentence arbitrale du 17 décembre 1999 sur la délimitation des frontières maritimes entre l'Érythrée et le Yemen : quelques observations complémentaires*, 46 AFDI p. 255 (2000);
- W. Michael Reisman, *Eritrea-Yemen Arbitration (Award, Phase II: Maritime Delimitation)*, 94 AM. J. INT'L L. p. 721 (2000);
- Constance Johnson, *Eritrea-Yemen Arbitration*, 13(2) LEIDEN J. INT'L L. p. 426 (2000);
- Jean-François Dobelle & Jean-Michel Faure, *Le différend entre l'Érythrée et le Yemen : la sentence arbitrale du 17 décembre 1999 sur la délimitation des frontières maritimes*, 45 AFDI p. 554 (1999) ;
- W. Michael Reisman, *International Decisions*, 93 AM. J. INT'L L. p. 668 (1999).

Facts

The State of Eritrea ("Eritrea") and the Republic of Yemen ("Yemen") both claimed sovereignty over a group of islands in the Red Sea and disagreed as to the location of their common maritime boundary. This Award in the Second Stage of the Arbitration ("Award in the Second Stage") was rendered pursuant to the Arbitration Agreement dated October 3, 1996 ("Arbitration Agreement") between the Government of the State of Eritrea and the Government of the Republic of Yemen (the "Parties"). The Arbitration Agreement was preceded by an "Agreement on Principles" between the Parties, done at Paris on May 21, 1996. Pursuant to the Arbitration Agreement, on October 9, 1998, the Tribunal rendered an Award in the First Stage ("First Award"), in which it made its determinations concerning sovereignty over the disputed islands. In the First Award, the Tribunal found that Eritrea had sovereignty over the Mohabbakhs, the Haycocks, and the South West Rocks, and it found that Yemen had sovereignty over the Zubayr group and the Zuqar-Hanish group.[1]

On May 25, 1999, Mr. Tjaco van den Hout, Secretary-General of the Permanent Court of Arbitration ("PCA"), succeeded as Registrar on the retirement of Mr. Hans Jonkman. Pursuant to Article 7(2) of the Arbitration Agreement, the First Secretary of the PCA served as Secretary to the Tribunal. On July 8, 1999, pursuant to Article 7(4) of the Arbitration Agree-

---

[1] For a summary of the First Award, *see* Eritrea/Yemen – Sovereignty of Various Red Sea Islands, *in* THE PERMANENT COURT OF ARBITRATION: INTERNATIONAL ARBITRATION AND DISPUTE RESOLUTION: SUMMARIES OF AWARDS, SETTLEMENT AGREEMENTS AND REPORTS pp. 196–201 (Kluwer Law International 1999).

ment, the Tribunal designated Ms. Ieltje Anna Elema, Head of the Geodesy and Tides Department of the Hydrographic Service of the Royal Netherlands Navy, as its expert in geodesy. The Oral Proceedings in the second stage of the Arbitration were held from July 5 to 16, 1999, in the Peace Palace in The Hague. On August 13, 1999, the Parties submitted written responses to questions put to them by the Tribunal on July 13 and 16. The Tribunal issued its unanimous Award in the Second Stage on December 17, 1999.

Summary of Matters Submitted to Arbitration

Article 2(3) of the Arbitration Agreement provided:

> The second stage shall result in an award delimiting maritime boundaries. The Tribunal shall decide taking into account the opinion that it will have formed on questions of territorial sovereignty, the United Nations Convention on the Law of the Sea, and any other pertinent factor.

Award

Arguments of the Parties

In its summary of the main arguments of the Parties as to the location of their common maritime boundary,[2] the Tribunal addressed the question of the location of the northern and southern ends of that boundary. It noted that, in those areas, the delimitation could potentially prejudice other boundary disputes with neighboring countries. With respect to the northern end of the boundary, the Kingdom of Saudi Arabia, by letter to the Registrar of the Tribunal dated August 31, 1997, had pointed out that its boundaries with Yemen were disputed, had reserved its position, and had suggested that the Tribunal restrict its decisions to areas "that do not extend north of the latitude of the most northern point on Jabal al-Tayr island."[3] The Tribunal took this statement, and the responses of the Parties, into consideration.[4]

With respect to the southern end of the boundary line, the third States concerned had not made any representations to the Tribunal. The Tribunal noted that the question of the possible effect upon the course of the boundary line of the Island of Perim might clearly involve the views of Djibouti. The Tribunal concluded that the boundary line determined by it should stop short of the place where any influence upon it of Perim Island would begin to take effect.[5]

The General Question of Fishing in the Red Sea

The Tribunal considered, next, the arguments of the Parties based on their respective fisheries practices.[6] It found that neither Party had demonstrated that the line of delimitation

---

[2] Award of the Arbitral Tribunal in the Second Stage – Maritime Delimitation [hereinafter "Award"], paras. 10–46.

[3] Award, para. 44.

[4] Award, para. 46.

[5] Award, para. 46.

[6] Award, paras. 48–71.

proposed by the other would produce catastrophic or inequitable effects on the fishing activity of its nationals, or detrimental effects on fishing communities or economic dislocation of its nationals.[7] Thus, the Tribunal could neither accept nor reject the line of delimitation proposed by either Party on fisheries grounds. These general fishing issues did not affect the legal reasons supporting the Tribunal's own selection of a delimitation line.[8]

Petroleum Agreements and Median Lines

The Tribunal then considered the pertinence and probative force, with respect to the delimitation of the maritime boundary, of petroleum contracts and concessions entered into by Yemen and by Eritrea or Ethiopia. It ruled that concession lines that had been drawn without regard to uninhabited islands, when the sovereignty of those islands was indeterminate, could not be taken as governing once that sovereignty had been determined.[9]

The Traditional Fishing Regime

Eritrea argued that, in paragraphs 526 and 527(vi) of the First Award, the Tribunal had established "resource zones" that the Tribunal was to delimit in its Award in the Second Stage.[10] Yemen, in contrast, asserted that, according to paragraph 526 of the First Award, it was for Yemen, in the exercise of its sovereignty, to ensure the preservation of the traditional fishing regime. Yemen further asserted that the Tribunal had not made any finding that there should be joint or common resource zones.[11]

The Tribunal recalled the respect for regional legal traditions on which it had based the disputed aspect of its First Award. In particular, the Tribunal recalled that the Islamic concept that all humans are "stewards of God" on earth,[12] applied equally to States in their mutual relations.[13] The Tribunal held that the sovereignty it had awarded to Yemen over the islands of Jabal al-Tayr, the Zubayr group, and the Zuqar-Hanish group was subject to the Islamic legal concepts of the region.[14]

The Tribunal held that the traditional fishing regime was not "an entitlement in common to resources."[15] Rather, it entitled both Eritrean and Yemeni fishermen to engage in artisanal fishing around the islands that the Tribunal had attributed to Yemen in its First Award.[16] The Tribunal specified that the term "artisanal fishing," which it used in contrast to "industrial fishing," did not exclude improvements in fishing techniques. However, this term did not extend to large-scale commercial or industrial fishing, nor to any fishing by nationals of third States in the Red Sea.[17] The traditional fishing regime, which the Parties were free to

[7] Award, para. 72.
[8] Award, paras. 73–74.
[9] Award, para. 83.
[10] Award, paras. 87–89.
[11] Award, para. 90.
[12] Award, para. 92.
[13] Award, para. 93.
[14] Award, para. 94.
[15] Award, para. 103.
[16] *Id.*
[17] Award, para. 106.

regulate by mutual agreement,[18] was not limited to the territorial waters of specified islands[19] and was not qualified by the maritime zones specified under 1982 United Nations Convention on the Law of the Sea ("Convention").[20] The traditional fishing regime operated throughout those waters that lie beyond the territorial waters of each of the Parties, as well as in their territorial waters and ports, as specified in paragraph 107 of the First Award.[21]

Accordingly, in the Tribunal's view, the traditional fishing regime did not depend, either for its existence or for its protection, upon the drawing of an international boundary by the Tribunal, or on any further agreement between the Parties. Nor was the drawing of the maritime boundary conditioned by the finding, in the First Award, that such a regime existed.[22]

The Delimitation of the International Boundary

Eritrea was not a party to the Convention. In the Tribunal's view, in the Arbitration Agreement, Eritrea had accepted the application of those provisions of the Convention that the Tribunal found to be relevant to the present stage of the proceedings.[23] There was no reference in the Arbitration Agreement to the customary law of the sea, but the Tribunal held that many of the relevant elements of customary law were incorporated in the provisions of the Convention.[24]

The Tribunal ruled that the international maritime boundary between the Parties "shall be a single all-purpose boundary ... that ... should, as far as practicable, be a median line between the opposite mainland coastlines."[25] This solution was not only in accord with practice and precedent in like situations but was also familiar to both Parties, as reflected by the offshore petroleum agreements entered into by Yemen, Eritrea, and Ethiopia.[26] In making this determination, the Tribunal relied on the definition of the median line found in Article 15 of the Convention as a line "every point of which is equidistant from the nearest points on the baselines from which the breadth of the territorial seas of the two States is measured,"[27] as well as on the definition of the "normal" baseline of the territorial sea set out in Article 5 of the Convention.[28]

The Tribunal had neither competence nor authority to delimit any of the boundaries between either of the Parties and neighboring States, at the northern and southern extremities of the international boundary line.[29] It was therefore necessary for the Tribunal, first, to determine the location of base points controlling the median line so as to produce a boundary line, and, second, to decide how to terminate the ends of that boundary line in such a way as to avoid trespassing on an area where other claims might fall to be considered.[30]

---

18 Award, para. 108.
19 Award, para. 109.
20 *Id.*
21 *Id.*
22 Award, paras. 110–111.
23 Award, para. 130.
24 *Id.*
25 Award, para. 132.
26 *Id.*
27 Award, para. 133.
28 *Id.*
29 Award, para. 136.
30 *Id.*

In the northernmost stretch of the boundary line, the Tribunal had to decide how to accommodate three groups of islands: (i) the Dahlaks on the Eritrean side; (ii) the lone mid-sea island of Jabal al-Tayr and the mid-sea island group of Jabal al-Zubayr; and (iii) the cluster of islands and rocks off the northern coast of Yemen.

As regards the Dahlaks, the Parties differed as to the effect of the "Negileh Rock," which was a reef that was never above water at any state of the tide. Recalling Articles 6 and 7(4) of the Convention, the Tribunal held that the Eritrean claim to the existence of a straight baseline system foreclosed any right to employ a reef that was not proud of the water at low-tide as a baseline of the territorial sea.[31] Further, the Tribunal decided that the single island of al-Tayr and the island group of Jabal al-Zubayr should have no effect on the median line international boundary due to their barren and inhospitable nature and their position well out to sea.[32] As to the base points to be used for the northern part of the coast of Yemen, where there was a considerable scattering of islands, the Tribunal ruled that one significant controlling base point was on the westernmost extremity of the large, inhabited island of Kamaran.[33] The Tribunal found that the islands of Tiqfash, Kutama, and Uqban were a "fringe system" of the kind contemplated by Article 7 of the Convention, even though Yemen had not claimed it as such. It therefore decided also to use Uqban and Kutama as median line base points.[34] These decisions enabled the Tribunal to compute and plot the northern stretch of the boundary line, the entire length of which, the Tribunal held, was a mainland-coastal median, or equidistance, line.[35]

The Tribunal turned, next, to the boundary in the narrow seas between the south-west extremity of the Hanish group, on the one hand, and the Eritrean islands of the Mohabbakahs, High Island, the Haycocks, and the South West Rocks, on the other. These islands generated overlapping territorial seas of the Parties.[36] The Tribunal rejected the Yemen claim line, which left the Haycocks and South West Rocks isolated and outside the territorial sea proper. Given that an island, however small, could generate a territorial sea of up to 12 nautical miles ("nm") according to Article 121(1) of the Convention, it followed that a chain of islands that were less than 24 nm apart could generate a continuous band of territorial sea. The Tribunal applied this rule to the Eritrean islands out to, and including, the South West Rocks.[37]

The Tribunal held that, under Article 3 of the Convention, each island created a further low-water baseline, from which the coastal territorial sea was to be measured.[38] With respect to the area of Eritrean mainland coast territorial sea, potentially extending beyond the South West Rocks and the Haycock group of islands, on the one hand, and overlapping the territorial sea generated by the Yemen islands of the Hanish group, on the other, the Tribunal

---

[31] Award, para. 145.
[32] Award, paras. 147–148.
[33] Award, para. 150.
[34] Award, para. 151.
[35] Award, para. 152.
[36] Award, para. 154.
[37] Award, para. 155.
[38] Award, para. 156.

held that no variance to the median line was required by Article 15 of the Convention.[39] This line was also "entirely equitable," in the Tribunal's opinion.[40]

The Tribunal then described that part of the boundary line connecting the "mainland coastal median line" and the line delimiting the overlapping territorial seas.[41] The boundary line was diverted to the west round the Zuqar-Hanish group of islands, in order to respect the territorial seas which, in the opinion of the Tribunal, these islands generated. The Tribunal used straight geodetic lines in this part of the boundary line.[42] From the southernmost turning point on the overlapping territorial seas median line, where the boundary turned generally south-eastwards to rejoin the mainland-coastal median line, the Tribunal used a geodetic line connecting this point to the intersection of the extended overlapping territorial seas median line and the coastal median line.[43] In the Tribunal's view, the terminal points of the boundary line were well short of where the boundary line might be disputed by any third State.[44]

The Tribunal then applied the principle of proportionality to this delimitation. The Parties disagreed about the respective lengths of their coasts for this purpose.[45] The Tribunal ruled that the relevant portion of the Eritrean coast ceased where the general direction of that coast met a line drawn from the northern terminus of the Yemen land frontier at right angles with the general direction of the Yemen coast. The Tribunal determined the southern end point to be considered for the computation of the length of the Yemen coast in the same way.[46] The Tribunal calculated the ratio of the coastal lengths thus determined, and ruled that the line of delimitation it had decided upon resulted in no disproportion.[47]

The Tribunal set out the geographical coordinates of the international maritime boundary in the *Dispositif* of the Award.[48] Appended to the Award were the following Annexes: (1) the Parties' Arbitration Agreement of October 3, 1996; (2) "Yemen's Answer to Judge Schwebel's Question Put to Yemen on Tuesday, 13 July 1999" and "Eritrea's Answer to Judge Schwebel's Question"; and (3) English and Arabic versions of the "Memorandum of Understanding between the State of Eritrea and the Republic of Yemen For Cooperation in the Areas of Maritime Fishing, Trade, Investment and Transportation," dated November 15, 1994, and the "Treaty Establishing the Joint Yemeni-Eritrean Committee for Bilateral Cooperation Between the Government of the Republic of Yemen and the Government of the State of Eritrea," dated October 16, 1998.

---

[39] Award, para. 158.
[40] Award, para. 159.
[41] *See* text accompanying note 36 *supra*.
[42] Award, paras. 160–161.
[43] Award, para. 163.
[44] Award, para. 164.
[45] Award, para. 166.
[46] Award, para. 167.
[47] Award, para. 168.
[48] Award, para. 169.

Larsen v. Hawaiian Kingdom

Parties:	Lance Paul Larsen/the Hawaiian Kingdom by its Council of Regency
Date of Arbitration Agreement:	October 30, 1999
Arbitrators:	Prof. James Crawford SC, Dr. Gavan Griffith QC, Prof. Christopher Greenwood QC
Date of Award:	February 5, 2001

Summary

Agreement to arbitrate between private individual and "the Hawaiian Kingdom" under the UNCITRAL Arbitration Rules – status of "the Hawaiian Kingdom" – applicability of the UNCITRAL Arbitration Rules – requirement that a tribunal decline to exercise jurisdiction over a dispute if the rights of a third party will necessarily be affected – requirement of a justiciable dispute between the parties – question submitted to arbitration necessarily concerned actions of the United States of America – no dispute between parties on any matter that could be defined without reference to the actions of the United States of America – arbitral proceedings not maintainable.

Legal Subject Matters

Settlement of disputes:
- Arbitration
  - Applicable law
  - Jurisdiction of the arbitral tribunal
    - Justiciability
    - *Monetary Gold* principle
  - Rules of procedure
    - Permanent Court of Arbitration Optional Rules for Arbitrating Disputes Between Two Parties of Which Only One is a State
    - UNCITRAL Arbitration Rules

State:
- Sovereignty
- Statehood
- Territory
  - Annexation

Bibliography

Award published in:
- 119 I.L.R. p. 566 (2001)

Commentary:
- Patrick Dumberry, *The* Hawaiian Kingdom Arbitration Case *and the Unsettled Question of the Hawaiian Kingdom's Claim to Continuity as an Independent State under International Law*, 1 CHINESE J. INT'L L. p. 655 (2002);
- David J. Bederman & Kurt R. Hilbert, *Lance Paul Larsen v. The Hawaiian Kingdom*, 95 AM. J. INT'L L. p. 927 (2001).

Facts

In the nineteenth century, the Hawaiian Kingdom was recognized as an independent State by, *inter alia*, the United States of America ("United States") and the United Kingdom, through, among other things, exchanges of diplomatic or consular representatives and the conclusion of treaties. On July 6, 1898, the United States House of Representatives and Senate passed Joint Resolution No. 55, providing for the annexation of the Hawaiian Islands to the United States. This followed an uncompleted process of annexation attempted during the administration of President Grover Cleveland in 1893.

On October 30, 1999, the Claimant, Lance Paul Larsen, a resident of Hawaii, and the Hawaiian Kingdom by its Council of Regency ("Respondent") (together, the "Parties") concluded an Agreement ("Arbitration Agreement"), pursuant to which the Claimant commenced arbitral proceedings by a Notice of Arbitration dated November 8, 1999. The Claimant described the Notice of Arbitration as "a demand pursuant to Article 3, Section 1 of the Permanent Court of Arbitration Optional Rules For Arbitrating Disputes Between Two Parties Of Which Only One Is a State" ("PCA Optional Rules"). By a "First Amendment to Notice of Arbitration," dated December 3, 1999, the Claimant and the Respondent amended the Notice of Arbitration and the Arbitration Agreement by substituting the "UNCITRAL [United Nations Commission on International Trade Law] Arbitration Rules as at Present in Force" ("UNCITRAL Rules") for the PCA Optional Rules as the governing rules for the arbitration.

Clause 6 of the Notice of Arbitration stated that the arbitral tribunal should consist of one arbitrator, to be chosen by Keoni Agard, Esq., a Hawaiian national resident in Hawaii ("Appointing Authority"). By a "Special Agreement" of January 25, 2000, the Parties agreed on several procedural matters for the arbitration, including, under Article IV, confirmation that the UNCITRAL Rules applied. By an "Amendment to the Special Agreement," dated February 28, 2000, the Parties agreed that the arbitral tribunal should comprise three arbitrators, one to be chosen by each party through the Appointing Authority, with the two arbitrators so appointed choosing the presiding arbitrator. In April 2000, the Appointing Authority appointed Dr. Gavan Griffith QC and Professor Christopher J. Greenwood QC as arbitrators. These two arbitrators jointly appointed Professor James Crawford SC as the President of the Tribunal. Pursuant to clause 6 of the Arbitration Agreement, and the Amendment to the Special Agreement, the Permanent Court of Arbitration was appointed to provide secretariat services and facilities for the arbitration.

By Procedural Order No. 3 of July 17, 2000, the Tribunal raised three preliminary issues that the Parties had not addressed in their pleadings. Oral hearings were held on December 7, 8, 11, and 12, 2000, at the Peace Palace in The Hague.

Questions Submitted to Arbitration

In the Arbitration Agreement dated October 30, 1999, the Parties agreed to submit the following questions to arbitration:

(a) The Claimant's allegation that the Respondent was "in continual violation of its 1849 Treaty of Friendship, Commerce and Navigation with the United States of America, and in violation of the principles of international law laid down in the Vienna Convention on the Law of Treaties, 1969, by allowing the unlawful imposition of American municipal laws over claimant's person within the territorial jurisdiction of the Hawaiian Kingdom";[1]
(b) The Claimant's allegation that the Respondent was also in continual violation of the principles of international comity "by allowing the unlawful imposition of American municipal laws over the claimant's person within the territorial jurisdiction of the Hawaiian Kingdom";[2] and
(c) Whether, if the rights of the Claimant under international law as a Hawaiian subject were being violated, the Claimant had any redress against the Respondent.[3]

Award of the Tribunal

The Award of the Tribunal addressed the preliminary issues raised in Procedural Order No. 3 of July 17, 2000, namely:

a. The applicability of the UNICTRAL Rules to the arbitration;
b. Whether there was a justiciable dispute between the Parties; and
c. Whether the United States was a necessary party to such dispute, with the consequence that the Tribunal lacked jurisdiction over the dispute in its absence.[4]

Status of the Hawaiian Kingdom as Represented by its Council of Regency

In order to consider the merits of the dispute, the Tribunal determined that it would have to address, *inter alia*, the question whether the Respondent constituted "the Hawaiian Kingdom represented by its Council of Regency."[5] The Parties had sought to avoid this difficulty by stipulating as between them that the Hawaiian Kingdom continued to exist as a sovereign State. According to the Tribunal, it was required to examine this agreed position carefully in the context of the merits, having regard, *inter alia*, to the lapse of time since the annexation

---

[1] Arbitration Agreement, Art. I(1)(a).
[2] *Id.*, Art. I(1)(b).
[3] Special Agreement, Art. II.
[4] Award, para. 9.5.
[5] Award, para. 9.1.

of the Hawaiian Islands to the United States, subsequent political, constitutional, and international developments, as well as relevant changes in international law since the 1890s.[6] The Parties agreed that such examination should be postponed, and that the Tribunal should first consider the three preliminary issues identified in Procedural Order No. 3.[7]

Application of the UNCITRAL Arbitration Rules

Concerning the applicability of the UNCITRAL Rules, the Tribunal held that, having regard to the non-prescriptive and non-coercive nature of the UNCITRAL Rules, there was no reason why those rules could not be adapted to apply to a non-contractual dispute.[8] It found that the parties effectively had agreed to apply the UNCITRAL Rules with such necessary adaptations as arise from the terms of the Arbitration Agreement and the nature of the issues referred to in the arbitration.[9]

Justiciable Dispute and Necessary Parties

The Tribunal then turned to the questions whether the pleadings and oral submissions disclosed a "justiciable dispute" between the parties to the proceedings, and whether the United States was a "necessary party" to any such dispute. Both Parties had argued that "these principles" were "inapplicable in the present proceedings" and were "binding, if at all, only on the International Court of Justice and other tribunals exercising jurisdiction in State to State matters."[10]

Requirement of a Justiciable Dispute Between the Parties

The Tribunal held that there were several aspects to the requirement of the existence of a justiciable dispute between the Parties, including that the dispute must be one actually existing between the parties at the time of the proceedings and not one that had become moot so that any decision given would be devoid of purpose.[11] It was not the function of an international arbitral tribunal to decide purely historical issues or controversies that bore no relation to the legal rights and obligations of the parties at the time of the decision, whatever symbolic significance or effect may be attributed to those historical issues.[12] The Tribunal noted that the requirement of a dispute between the parties was explicit in the UNCITRAL Rules and Article 1(1) of the PCA Optional Rules.[13] According to the Tribunal, the nature of the arbitral function required it to scrutinize carefully the arguments of the Parties, in order to determine whether those arguments did in fact disclose a dispute, and to decline to exercise jurisdiction if it was not satisfied on that score.[14]

---

[6] Award, para. 9.2.
[7] Award, para. 9.3.
[8] Award, para. 10.7.
[9] Award, para. 10.10.
[10] Award, para. 11.2.
[11] Award, para. 11.3.
[12] *Id.*
[13] Award, para. 11.6.
[14] Award, para. 11.7.

Necessary Parties – the Monetary Gold *Principle*

The Tribunal then turned to the question whether the United States was a necessary party to the proceedings. In this connection, it examined the principle, established in the jurisprudence of the International Court of Justice ("ICJ") in the *Monetary Gold* case,[15] that an international tribunal may not decide a dispute between the parties before it if the very subject matter of the decision would be the rights or obligations of a State which is not a party to the proceedings ("*Monetary Gold* principle"). The Tribunal also recalled the subsequent jurisprudence of the ICJ confirming the *Monetary Gold* principle.[16] Each Party contended that the *Monetary Gold* principle was confined to proceedings before the ICJ and did not extend to arbitral proceedings of a mixed character. The Tribunal disagreed. It held that an international arbitral tribunal operates within the general confines of public international law and, like the ICJ, cannot exercise jurisdiction over a State which is not a party to its proceedings. The *Monetary Gold* principle was thus applicable in the present proceedings.[17] Accordingly, the Tribunal could not rule on the lawfulness of the conduct of the Respondent in the present case if the decision would entail or require, as the necessary foundation for the decision between the Parties, an evaluation of the lawfulness of the conduct of the United States, or of any other State which was not a party to the proceedings before the Tribunal.[18]

The Tribunal noted that there may be exceptions to the *Monetary Gold* principle, for example, where the finding involving an absent third party is merely a finding of fact. In the present case, however, the Parties had not sought to rely on any exceptions to the *Monetary Gold* principle, and they accepted that the Tribunal was called upon to decide more than purely factual issues.[19]

Application of the Monetary Gold *Principle – No Justiciable Dispute Between the Parties*

The Tribunal observed that the Parties could, by agreement, determine the extent of the Tribunal's jurisdiction as between themselves. However, it held that the Parties could not thereby entitle, let alone compel, the Tribunal to ignore the fundamental requirements of international law that there must be a real dispute between the Parties and that the Tribunal must not make a decision which evaluates the legality of the conduct of a State not party to the proceedings.[20] The Tribunal found that, in the present case, there was no dispute between the Parties on which it could adjudicate without falling foul of the *Monetary Gold* principle.[21] If the dispute was defined without reference to the actions of the United States in

---

[15] Monetary Gold Removed from Rome in 1943 (Italy v. Fr., U.K. and U.S.), 1954 I.C.J. REP. p. 19 (June 15).

[16] Award, paras. 11.11–11.15, citing, *inter alia*, Certain Phosphate Lands in Nauru (Nauru v. Austl.), 1992 I.C.J. REP. p. 240, at pp. 258–262 (June 26); and East Timor (Port. v. Austl.), 1995 I.C.J. REP. p. 90, at paras. 28–35 (June 30).

[17] Award, para. 11.17.

[18] Award, para. 11.23.

[19] Award, para. 11.24.

[20] Award, para. 12.6.

[21] Award, para. 12.10.

Hawaii, it had to be reduced to an abstract question about whether the Respondent had a duty to protect the Claimant, on which question there was no dispute between the Parties.[22]

An identified dispute only emerged in respect of whether the Respondent had discharged its duty of protection towards the Claimant.[23] This question could not be addressed unless the Tribunal determined that there was something against which the Respondent should have acted to protect the Claimant. Consideration of this question "inevitably and inexorably" forced the Tribunal "back to allegations regarding the acts of the United States of America."[24] Moreover, the Tribunal held, the United States' actions of which the Claimant claimed to be the victim would not give rise to a duty of protection in international law unless they were themselves unlawful in international law.[25] The Tribunal thus could not determine whether the Respondent had failed to discharge its obligations towards the Claimant without ruling on the legality of the acts of the United States.[26]

Fact-Finding Enquiry

The Tribunal noted that, at one stage of the proceedings, the question was raised whether some of the issues which the parties had presented might be dealt with "by way of a fact-finding process."[27] It emerged during the course of argument, however, that there was no essential question of fact as to the situation of the Parties or of the Hawaiian islands that was in dispute. The Parties accordingly did not press the issue of a possible fact-finding commission.[28]

Dispositif

The Tribunal determined, as a matter of international law, (a) that there was no dispute between the Parties capable of submission to arbitration, and (b) that, in any event, the Tribunal was precluded from the consideration of the issues raised by the Parties, because the United States was not a party to the proceedings and had not consented to them. Accordingly, the Tribunal found that that the arbitral proceedings were not maintainable.

---

[22] Award, para. 12.11.
[23] Award, para. 12.14.
[24] *Id.*
[25] *Id.*
[26] Award, para. 12.15.
[27] Award, para. 13.1.
[28] Award, para. 13.3.

3

Dispute Concerning Access to Information under Article 9 of the OSPAR Convention

Parties:	Ireland/United Kingdom of Great Britain and Northern Ireland
Arbitration Agreement:	Article 32 of the 1992 Convention for the Protection of the Marine Environment of the North-East Atlantic ("OSPAR" Convention)
Arbitrators:	Professor W. Michael Reisman (Chairman), Dr. Gavan Griffith QC, The Rt. Hon. Lord Mustill
Date of Award:	July 2, 2003

Summary

Commissioning of a mixed oxide ("MOX") plant by United Kingdom Government – preparation of reports by private consultancy firm as part of approval process – reports subsequently published with commercially sensitive information redacted – request by Ireland based on Article 9 of the 1992 OSPAR Convention for access to information redacted from reports – Article 9(1) of OSPAR held to give rise to an obligation to provide information – information requested by Ireland held not to fall within categories of information which United Kingdom obliged to disclose under Article 9(2) of OSPAR – consideration of permissible exceptions under Article 9(3) of OSPAR therefore not necessary.

Legal Subject Matters

Sources of international norms:
- Customary international law
- European Communities
- International environmental law
- Treaties
  - Good faith
  - Interpretation
  - Object and purpose
  - Status
  - Terms

Bibliography

Award published in:

- THE OSPAR ARBITRATION (IRELAND–UNITED KINGDOM) AWARD OF 2003 (Permanent Court of Arbitration Award Series, TMC Asser Press 2009);

- XXIII R.I.A.A. p. 59 (2003);
- 42 I.L.M. p. 1118 (2003).

Commentary:
- Daniel Bodansky, *The OSPAR Arbitration of The MOX Plant Dispute, in* THE OSPAR ARBITRATION (IRELAND–UNITED KINGDOM) AWARD OF 2003 (PCA Award Series, 2009);
- Freya Baetens, *Muddling the Waters of Treaty Interpretation? Relevant Rules of International Law in the MOX Plant OSPAR Arbitration and EC Biotech Case*, 77(3) NORDIC J. INT'L L. p. 197 (2008);
- Robin Churchill & Joanne Scott, *The MOX Plant Litigation: The First Half-Life*, 53 INT'L & COMP. L.Q. p. 643 (2004);
- Yuval Shany, *The First MOX Plant Award: The Need to Harmonize Competing Environmental Regimes and Dispute Settlement Procedures*, 17 LEIDEN J. INT'L L. p. 815 (2004);
- Ted L. McDorman, *Access to Information under Article 9 of the OSPAR Convention (Ireland v. United Kingdom)*, 98 AM. J. INT'L L. p. 330 (2004);
- Malgosia Fitzmaurice, *Dispute Concerning Access to Information under Article 9 of the OSPAR Convention*, 18 INT'L J. MARINE & COASTAL L. p. 541 (2003).

Facts

A dispute arose between the Government of the Republic of Ireland ("Ireland") and the Government of the United Kingdom of Great Britain and Northern Ireland ("United Kingdom") (the "Parties"). This dispute concerned access to information that had been redacted from reports published as part of the approval process for the commissioning of a mixed oxide fuel ("MOX") plant in the United Kingdom ("MOX Plant").

The MOX Plant was constructed in 1996, by a corporation owned by the United Kingdom, for the reprocessing of spent nuclear fuel. Pursuant to the law of the United Kingdom, the United Kingdom Environment Agency ("Agency"), which was responsible for approving the MOX Plant, was required to ensure that whatever environmental detriments the MOX Plant might cause be economically justified. Accordingly, between 1997 and 2001, the Agency held five rounds of public consultations. As part of this process, at the Agency's request, two confidential reports ("Reports") on the economic justifications of the MOX Plant were prepared by private consulting firms for governmental consideration. The Reports were released to the public in redacted form, omitting information that was deemed by the Agency to be commercially sensitive. The first of the Reports, by the PA Consulting Group, London ("PA Report"), was published in December 1997, and the second, by the consulting firm Arthur D. Little ("ADL Report"), was published in March 2001.

Ireland objected to the commissioning of the MOX Plant. Beginning in July 1999, Ireland made repeated requests that the United Kingdom provide it with the information redacted from the Reports. From October 2000, Ireland based its requests for the redacted information on Article 9 of the 1992 Convention for the Protection of the Marine Environment of the North-East Atlantic, also known as the OSPAR Convention ("OSPAR"),[1] which provides:

[1] Convention for the Protection of the Marine Environment of the North-East Atlantic, Sept. 22, 1992, 32 I.L.M. p. 1069.

ACCESS TO INFORMATION

1. The Contracting Parties shall ensure that their competent authorities are required to make available the information described in paragraph 2 of this Article to any natural or legal person, in response to any reasonable request, without that person's having to prove an interest, without unreasonable charges, as soon as possible and at the latest within two months.
2. The information referred to in paragraph 1 of this Article is any available information in written, visual, aural or data-base form on the state of the maritime area, on activities or measures adversely affecting or likely to affect it and on activities or measures introduced in accordance with the Convention.
3. The provisions of this Article shall not affect the right of Contracting Parties, in accordance with their national legal systems and applicable international regulations, to provide for a request for such information to be refused where it affects:
   a. the confidentiality of the proceedings of public authorities, international relations and national defence;
   b. public security;
   c. matters which are, or have been, *sub judice*, or under enquiry (including disciplinary enquiries), or which are the subject of preliminary investigation proceedings;
   d. commercial and industrial confidentiality, including intellectual property;
   e. the confidentiality of personal data and/or files
   f. material supplied by a third party without that party being under a legal obligation to do so;
   g. material, the disclosure of which would make it more likely that the environment to which such material related would be damaged.
4. The reasons for a refusal to provide the information requested must be given.

On June 15, 2001, Ireland initiated arbitral proceedings against the United Kingdom pursuant to Article 32 of OSPAR, which provides, in relevant part:

SETTLEMENT OF DISPUTES

1. Any disputes between Contracting Parties relating to the interpretation or application of the Convention, which cannot be settled otherwise by the Contracting Parties concerned, for instance by means of inquiry or conciliation within the Commission, shall at the request of any of those Contracting Parties, be submitted to arbitration under the conditions laid down in this Article.

Ireland appointed Dr. Gavan Griffith QC as an arbitrator, and the United Kingdom appointed Lord Mustill as an arbitrator. On October 30, 2001, the party-appointed arbitrators designated Professor W. Michael Reisman as chairman. The Parties agreed that the Permanent Court of Arbitration ("PCA") would act as the Registry and designated The Hague as the seat of the arbitration. The Tribunal adopted its Rules of Procedure by its Decision No. 1 of February 21, 2002.

By its Decisions No. 2 and 3 of October 12 and 18, 2002, the Tribunal acknowledged the agreement of the United Kingdom to make available the unredacted Reports to the Tribunal and to independent counsel for Ireland, and set forth the procedures for access to the unredacted Reports. Hearings were held at the Peace Palace from October 21 to 25, 2002.

Questions Submitted to Arbitration

1. Does Article 9(1) of OSPAR require a contracting party to disclose, or to set up a procedure to disclose, "information" within the meaning of Article 9(2)?

2. If so, does the material, the disclosure of which Ireland has requested, constitute "information" for the purposes of Article 9 of OSPAR?
3. If so, has the United Kingdom redacted and withheld any and what information requested by Ireland, in contravention to Article 9(3)(d) of OSPAR?

Award of the Tribunal

Applicable Law[2]

As to the applicable principles of interpretation, despite Ireland not being a party to the Vienna Convention on the Law of Treaties ("Vienna Convention"), the Parties agreed that the interpretation provisions of the Vienna Convention governed the construction of OSPAR.[3]

Neither Article 9(1) nor Article 9(2) of OSPAR referred specifically to any bodies of substantive conventional law to which the Tribunal should have recourse.[4] The Parties disagreed as to the relevance of Article 9(3)(d) of OSPAR, which states that contracting parties have the right to refuse a request for information under Article 9(2) "in accordance with their national legal systems and applicable international regulations" where the information affects "commercial and industrial confidentiality, including intellectual property … ." Ireland contended that "applicable international regulations" included "international law and practice." Ireland relied, *inter alia*, on the 1998 Aarhus Convention on Access to Information, Public Participation in Decision-making and Access to Justice in Environmental Matters ("Aarhus Convention"), which entered into force on October 30, 2001. Neither the United Kingdom nor Ireland had ratified the Aarhus Convention at the time of the arbitration.[5] Ireland contended that the applicable instruments had to be interpreted in light of "the evolving international law and practice on access to environmental information."[6] The United Kingdom asserted that there were no "applicable international regulations" under Article 9(3)(d) of OSPAR, other than EC Directive 90/313/EEC of June 7, 1990, on the Freedom of Access to Information on the Environment ("Directive 90/313"),[7] which had been implemented in United Kingdom law.[8]

The Tribunal, noting that the issue was one of interpretation in good faith, "as required by Article 31(1) of the Vienna Convention, if not by an essential ingredient of law itself," stated that "[a] treaty is a solemn undertaking and States Parties are entitled to have applied to them and to their peoples that to which they have agreed and not things to which they have not agreed."[9] It further noted that, in order to avoid an anachronistic result, a tribunal must engage in "*actualization* or contemporization"[10] when construing an international instru-

[2] This part of the Tribunal's decision was supported by a majority comprising Professor Reisman and Lord Mustill.

[3] Final Award [hereinafter "Award"], para. 81.

[4] Award, para. 92.

[5] Award, para. 97.

[6] Award, para. 98.

[7] Council Directive 90/313/EEC, 1990 O.J. (L 158) 56.

[8] Award, para. 96.

[9] Award, para. 102.

[10] Award, para. 103, citing Legal Consequences for States of the Continued Presence of South Africa in Namibia (South West Africa) notwithstanding Security Council Resolution 276 (1970), Advisory Opinion, 1971 I.C.J. Rep. p. 3 (June 21). Emphasis in the original.

ment concluded in an earlier period. However, this principle applied only to developments in the law and did not include material that had not yet become law. The Tribunal therefore rejected Ireland's proposal that the Aarhus Convention or "draft proposals for a new EC Directive" be applied.[11]

Findings with respect to Article 9(1) of OSPAR

Ireland claimed that, pursuant to Article 9(1) of OSPAR, the United Kingdom was required to disclose "information" within Article 9(2) of OSPAR. The United Kingdom argued that Ireland's Article 9(1) claim fell outside the Tribunal's jurisdiction and was inadmissible. The Tribunal, however, unanimously held that the question posed by Ireland with respect to Article 9(1) was one of substance, namely, the purport of Article 9(1) under the facts of the present case.[12] Thus, Ireland's Article 9(1) claim was admissible and fell within the Tribunal's jurisdiction.

The Tribunal[13] first examined the meaning of the obligation under Article 9(1) in the context of the OSPAR regime, taking into account the objects and purposes of OSPAR, and also the dispute settlement clause found in Article 32.[14] In the Tribunal's view, the entire text of the Convention disclosed a carefully crafted hierarchy of obligations to achieve the disparate objectives of OSPAR.[15] The obligation in Article 9(1), by the requirement that a contracting party "shall ensure" the stipulated result, reflected a deliberate choice of vocabulary.[16] The Tribunal sought to interpret Article 9 in conformity with the rest of OSPAR, and held, as a result, that the obligation in Article 9(1) was mandatory.[17]

The Tribunal found support for its textual interpretation in the relevant rules of international and European Union law.[18] The Parties agreed that Article 9(1) of OSPAR was derived from Article 4 of Directive 90/313.[19] The United Kingdom referred to the definition of a directive, in Article 249 of the European Community ("EC") Treaty, as a measure which "shall be binding as to the result to be achieved, upon each Member State to which it is addressed, but shall leave to the national authorities the choice of form and words." It argued that, by adopting the language of Directive 90/313, the contracting parties to the OSPAR Convention evinced an intention to adopt the approach provided in Article 249 of the EC Treaty, so that a Member State's only obligation would be to take such legislative or administrative measures as may be appropriate to achieve the stated objective.[20] The Tribunal held that, while the language of the sources used by the drafters of a treaty may be instrumental in tracing and understanding the origins of specific treaty terms, "their normative value should

[11] Award, para. 104.

[12] Award, para. 118.

[13] This part of the Tribunal's reasoning was supported by a majority comprising Dr. Griffith and Lord Mustill.

[14] Award, para. 126.

[15] Award, para. 130.

[16] Award, para. 133.

[17] Award, para. 134.

[18] Award, para. 139.

[19] *See* text accompanying note 7, *supra*.

[20] Award, paras. 140–142.

not be attributed to similarly worded legal obligations imposed by that treaty."[21] It held that the primary purpose of employing similar language in both was to create uniform and consistent legal standards in the field of the protection of the marine environment, and not to create precedence of one set of legal remedies over the other.[22]

The Tribunal considered that its reading of the OSPAR Convention was consistent with contemporary principles of State responsibility. According to those principles, a State covenanting with other States to put in place a domestic framework and review mechanisms remains responsible to those other States for the adequacy of this framework and the conduct of its competent authorities.[23] This was confirmed by Articles 4 and 5 of the International Law Commission's Draft Articles on State Responsibility.[24] The Tribunal therefore determined that, on its proper construction, Article 9(1) of OSPAR requires an outcome of result, namely, that information falling within the meaning of Article 9(2) "is in fact disclosed" in accordance with Article 9.[25]

Findings with Respect to Article 9(2) of OSPAR

Ireland argued that Article 9(2) of OSPAR did not require a contracting party claiming information under Article 9(1) to demonstrate that the information sought related directly to activities that adversely affect the maritime area.[26] Ireland contended that the information omitted, at the Agency's request, from the redacted PA and ADL Reports "relates closely to various important aspects of [MOX production] and contributed to the determination whether that activity should be permitted."[27] It further contended that "[i]t would be unduly restrictive to read Article 9(2) as referring only to environmental information about such an activity."[28] Ireland relied on the broad definition of "environmental information" in Article 2(3) of the Aarhus Convention, which included "cost-benefit and other economic analyses and assumptions used in environmental decision-making." Ireland contended that this definition should be applied to OSPAR according to Article 31(3)(c) of the Vienna Convention.[29]

The United Kingdom argued that the relevant question was not whether MOX production would affect the maritime area, because "all such information has been in the public domain for many years."[30] According to the United Kingdom, rather, the information contemplated in Article 9(2) of OSPAR was information on activities or measures "adversely affecting or likely to affect the maritime area."[31] This narrower reading prevented the OSPAR Convention from being used to conduct "fishing expeditions."[32]

The United Kingdom had argued that Ireland's claim under Article 9(2) of OSPAR fell outside the Tribunal's jurisdiction and was inadmissible. The Tribunal unanimously held

---

[21] Award, para. 141.
[22] Award, para. 143.
[23] Award, para. 144.
[24] Award, para. 145.
[25] Award, para. 148.
[26] Award, para. 149.
[27] *Id.*
[28] *Id.*
[29] Award, para. 150.
[30] Award, para. 153.
[31] *Id.*
[32] *Id.*

that Ireland's claim under Article 9(2) was one of substance, because it concerned "the purport of Article 9(2) under the facts of this case."[33]

The Tribunal[34] held that the issue for determination was the application of Article 9(2) of OSPAR to a specific controversy over 14 categories of information redacted from the "PA and ADL Reports," namely:

1. Estimated annual production capacity of the MOX facility;
2. Time taken to reach this capacity;
3. Sales volumes;
4. Probability of achieving higher sales volumes;
5. Probability of being able to win contracts for recycling fuel in "significant quantities";
6. Estimated sales demand;
7. Percentage of plutonium already on site;
8. Maximum throughput figures;
9. Life span of the MOX facility;
10. Number of employees;
11. Price of MOX fuel;
12. Whether, and to what extent, there are firm contracts to purchase MOX from Sellafield;
13. Arrangements for transport of plutonium to, and MOX from, Sellafield;
14. Likely number of such transports.[35]

It was manifest to the Tribunal that none of these items could plausibly be characterized as "information … on the state of the maritime area."[36] Ireland argued that the information fell within the scope of Article 9(2) because, without the Reports, "there would be no discharges from the MOX Plant into the Irish Sea."[37] The Tribunal called this argument an interpretative theory of "inclusive causality," according to which theory anything, no matter how remote, which facilitated the performance of an activity, was to be deemed part of that activity.[38]

In the Tribunal's view, the three categories of "information … on the state of the maritime area" under Article 9(2) of OSPAR were:

1. "any available information" on "the state of the maritime area";
2. "any available information" on "activities or measures adversely affecting or likely to affect … the maritime area"; and
3. "any available information" on "activities or measures introduced in accordance with the Convention."

---

[33] Award, para. 159.

[34] This part of the Tribunal's reasoning was supported by a majority comprising Professor Reisman and Lord Mustill.

[35] Award, para. 161.

[36] Award, para. 163.

[37] Award, para. 164.

[38] *Id.*

The Tribunal focused on the second category referred to in Article 9(2).[39] It considered, first, the meaning of the phrase "the maritime area," which was defined by Article 1(a) and (b) of OSPAR,[40] and of the phrase "activities or measures."[41] The Tribunal noted that each of the three categories in Article 9(2) was cast in the broad terms that were consistent with the "any information" formula, and that, as such, they might warrant an interpretation of "inclusive causality."[42] However, the second category contained an "additional threshold of inclusion/exclusion that is manifestly designed by the drafters to be more restrictive than the first and third categories," because it qualified the obligation to provide "any available information" on activities or measures "adversely affecting or likely to affect" the maritime area.[43] The Tribunal held that:

> Ireland has failed to demonstrate that the 14 categories of redacted items in the PA and ADL Reports, insofar as they may be taken to be activities or measures with respect to the commissioning and operation of a MOX Plant at Sellafield, are "information ... on the state of the maritime area" or, even if they were, are likely adversely to affect the maritime area.[44]

Although it was arguable that Ireland's claim might have succeeded under some of the draft treaties relied on by Ireland, the Tribunal was "not empowered to apply legally unperfected instruments."[45]

The Tribunal therefore concluded that Ireland had not established that the class of redacted information it was seeking fell within the scope of Article 9(2) of OSPAR.[46] As a consequence, it held that Ireland's claim that the United Kingdom had breached its obligations under Article 9 of OSPAR by refusing, on the basis of Article 9(3)(d),[47] to make available information, did not arise.[48] The Tribunal ordered that the costs of the arbitration be divided equally between the Parties, and that there be no other order for costs.[49]

Declaration of Professor W. Michael Reisman

In Professor Reisman's view, Ireland's proposed interpretation of Article 9(1) of OSPAR should have been rejected. Article 9(1) was "not expressed in terms to establish an obligation on the international plane to provide information, with the performance of that obligation in specific cases to be subject to the jurisdiction of a Tribunal established under Article 32."[50] It would be "anomalous and duplicative" for Article 9(1) to require contracting parties to ensure that their national competent authorities should do something and to prescribe

[39] Award, para. 169.
[40] Award, para. 170.
[41] Award, paras. 171–172.
[42] *See* text accompanying note 38, *supra*.
[43] Award, para. 174.
[44] Award, para. 179.
[45] Award, para. 180.
[46] Award, para. 182.
[47] *See* text accompanying note 1 *supra*.
[48] Award, para. 185.
[49] Award, para. 184.
[50] Award, Declaration of Professor W. Michael Reisman, para. 6.

how it should be done, yet then to assign the application role in specific cases to an international tribunal. The more plausible reading of Article 9(1) was that the implementation of the obligations and exceptions to those obligations for providing access to information was to be effected by the competent authorities of the contracting parties.[51]

According to Professor Reisman, Article 9 was the only provision in OSPAR that referred to a dispute resolution mechanism other than Article 32. To Professor Reisman, this suggested that the contracting parties did not intend to subject those aspects of Article 9 that were assigned to a municipal remedy to the international provisions of Article 32.[52] This result was consistent with a common treaty practice in which States are obliged to make adjustments in domestic law and, to the extent that they do so appropriately, they have fulfilled their treaty obligations.[53] Where, as here, international law assigned a competence to national law, the assumption was that claims were to be pursued through the review mechanisms of that national system.[54]

Dissenting Opinion of Dr. Gavan Griffith QC

Applicable Law

Dr. Griffith dissented as to the law applicable to the interpretation of OSPAR. According to Dr. Griffith, the Aarhus Convention, which both Parties had signed, did have a relevant normative and evidentiary value, even though neither Party had yet ratified it.[55] He noted that the United Kingdom had maintained its intention to be bound by, and to implement, the obligations set down by the Aarhus Convention.[56] Further, in Dr. Griffith's view, since the European Union ("EU") was a party to OSPAR, the subsequent practice of the EU, including legislative proposals of the European Community, should have been taken into account in the interpretation of OSPAR under Article 32(2)(b) of the Vienna Convention.[57]

Findings with Respect to Article 9(2) of OSPAR

According to Dr. Griffith, the second and third categories of information under Article 9(2) of OSPAR were not confined to information "on the state of the maritime area."[58] The exceptions from disclosure were to be determined under Article 9(3); there was thus no scope for an intervening limitation within Article 9(2).[59]

In Dr. Griffith's view, given that neither Party had contended that the PA and ADL Reports were in themselves activities or measures with respect to the commissioning and operation of the MOX Plant, the primary point of dispute was whether those Reports contained

---

[51] *Id.* para. 7.
[52] *Id.* para. 9.
[53] *Id.* para. 12.
[54] *Id.* para. 16.
[55] Award, Dissenting Opinion of Dr Gavan Griffith QC, paras. 10–16.
[56] *Id.* para. 17.
[57] *Id.* paras. 22–24.
[58] *Id.* paras. 36–38.
[59] *Id.* paras. 51–52.

information on activities or measures within the scope of Article 9(2) of OSPAR.[60] The context of the justification exercise engaged in by the United Kingdom was that "the negative effect arising from the commissioning of the MOX Plant was a given" and that the Plant "should not be approved unless the proven economic effect outweighed the detriment."[61] Thus, "it was not open to the majority to find no adverse effect as a determinative finding of fact."[62]

Burden of Proof

According to Dr. Griffith, the majority erred in assuming the burden of proof to fall on Ireland. The precautionary principle, an established customary principle of international law that was embraced by Article 2(2)(a) of OSPAR, shifted the burden to the United Kingdom to prove no adverse effect within the meaning of Article 9(2).[63] The finding by the majority that Ireland had "failed to demonstrate" adverse effect thus "ignores Article 2(2)(a)" of OSPAR.[64]

---

[60] *Id.* para. 68.
[61] *Id.* para. 69.
[62] *Id.* para. 71.
[63] *Id.* para. 72.
[64] *Id.* para. 75.

Bank for International Settlements

Parties:	1. Dr. Horst Reineccius, 2. First Eagle SoGen Funds, Inc., 3. Mr. Pierre Mathieu/Bank for International Settlements
Arbitration Agreement:	1930 Agreement Regarding the Complete and Final Settlement of the Question of Reparations
Arbitrators:	Prof. W. Michael Reisman, Prof. Dr. Jochen A. Frowein, Prof. Dr. Matthias Krafft, Prof. Dr. Paul Lagarde, Prof. Dr. Albert Jan van den Berg
Date of Awards:	Partial Award, November 22, 2002; Final Award, September 19, 2003

Summary

Bank for International Settlements ("Bank") – international organization created in 1930 to promote cooperation of national central banks and to provide additional facilities for international financial operations – Bank established as a company limited by shares – some shares in Bank held by private shareholders – compulsory recall of privately held shares by Bank – dispute between Bank and three former private shareholders as to lawfulness of compulsory recall and whether amount of compensation adequate – compulsory recall held to be lawful – appropriate method of compensation held to be based on per-share net asset value of Bank.

Legal Subject Matters

Arbitration:
- Arbitration agreement
  - Breach
  - Costs
    - Access to justice
  - Damages
- Jurisdiction of the arbitral tribunal

Conflict of laws

Expropriation:
- Discrimination
- Public interest
- Standard of compensation

International organizations:
- Constituent instruments

- Immunities
- Powers

Law of treaties:
- Interpretation

Bibliography

Partial Award published in:
- XXIII R.I.A.A. p. 153 (2002);
- 15(2) World Trade & Arb. Materials p. 73 (2003).

Final Award published in:
- 43 I.L.M. p. 893 (2004);
- XXIII R.I.A.A. p. 252 (2003).

Both Awards published in:
- The Bank for International Settlements Arbitration Awards of 2002 and 2003 (Permanent Court of Arbitration Award Series, TMC Asser Press 2007).

Commentary:
- V. V. Veeder, *The Bank for International Settlements Arbitration: Its Contribution to International Law*, *in* The Bank for International Settlements Arbitration Awards of 2002 and 2003 (Permanent Court of Arbitration Award Series, 2007);
- Scott Armstrong Spence, *Organizing an Arbitration Involving an International Organization and Multiple Private Parties: The Example of the Bank for International Settlements Arbitration*, 21 J. Int'l Arb. p. 309 (2004);
- David J. Bederman, *The Unique Legal Status of the Bank for International Settlements Comes into Focus*, 16 Leiden J. Int'l L. p. 787 (2003).

Facts

The Bank for International Settlements ("Bank") was established by the Governments of Germany, Belgium, Great Britain, Italy, Japan, and Switzerland through the Convention Respecting the Bank for International Settlements ("Convention"), dated January 20, 1930. The Convention included the Constituent Charter and the Statutes of the Bank (hereinafter, the Convention, the Constituent Charter and the Statutes of the Bank will be referred to collectively as the "Constituent Instruments"). The Bank was organized by Article 1 of the Statutes as "a Company limited by shares," and its objects, according to Article 3, were "to promote the cooperation of central banks and to provide additional facilities for international financial operations; and to act as trustee or agent in regard to international financial settlements entrusted to it under agreements with the parties concerned."

Article 16 of the Statutes of the Bank ("Statutes") stated that "[a]ny subscribing institution or banking group may issue, or cause to be issued to the public, the shares which it has subscribed." In accordance with this option, as of 2000, 13.73% of the Bank's shares were held by private shareholders. The shares did not convey any rights in the governance of the Bank. According to Article 13 of the Statutes:

> [t]he shares shall carry equal rights to participate in the profits of the Bank and in any distribution of assets under Articles 51, 52 and 53 of the Statutes.

On January 8, 2001, the Board of Directors held an Extraordinary General Meeting, at which it amended the Statutes by introducing Article 18A, which provided for the compulsory recall of all privately held shares. The Bank paid compensation of CHF 16,000 for each share thus recalled. The level of compensation was based on a recommendation by J.P. Morgan, which had prepared a report ("J.P. Morgan Report") for the Bank dated September 7, 2000.

Three former private shareholders of the Bank, Dr. Horst Reineccius ("Dr. Reineccius"), First Eagle SoGen Funds, Inc. ("First Eagle"), and Mr. Pierre Mathieu on behalf of himself and of the Société Hippique de la Châtre (collectively, "Mr. Mathieu") (hereinafter, collectively, "Claimants"), disputed the amount of compensation they had been paid following the compulsory recall under Article 18A of the Statutes. Dr. Reineccius submitted a Notice of Arbitration and Statement of Claim on March 7, 2001. First Eagle filed a Notice of Arbitration on August 31, 2001. Mr. Mathieu submitted a Notice of Arbitration on October 10, 2001. The Claimants invoked the jurisdiction of the Arbitration Tribunal established pursuant to Article XV of the Agreement regarding the Complete and Final Settlement of the Question of Reparations, signed at The Hague on January 20, 1930 ("1930 Hague Agreement"). The Bank filed its Statement of Defense and Counterclaim on January 14, 2002. In its Counterclaim, the Bank claimed damages in respect of legal proceedings that First Eagle had initiated against the Bank in the domestic courts of the United States.[1]

The Tribunal Concerning the Bank for International Settlements ("Tribunal") was constituted pursuant to Article XV of the 1930 Hague Agreement. The members of the Tribunal, appointed by the Governments of Belgium, France, Germany, Italy, and the United Kingdom for a term of five years, were: Prof. W. Michael Reisman, Chairman, Prof. Jochen A. Frowein, Prof. Dr. Matthias Krafft, Prof. Dr. Paul Lagarde, and Prof. Dr. Albert Jan van den Berg. The procedures of the Tribunal are set out in Annex XII of the 1930 Hague Agreement, which incorporates Chapter III of the Hague Convention of 1907 for the Pacific Settlement of International Disputes ("1907 Hague Convention"), except as modified by the 1930 Hague Agreement.

On January 17, 2001, the Tribunal designated Mrs. Phyllis Hamilton of the PCA as its Secretary, and the International Bureau of the PCA as Registry, for the proceedings. On March 23, 2001, the Tribunal adopted the "Rules for Arbitration between the Bank and Private Parties" ("Rules for Arbitration"). Public hearings pursuant to Article XV of the 1930 Hague Agreement and Article 20 of the Rules for Arbitration were held in The Hague from August 26 to 28, 2002. At the request of the Parties, their separate claims were heard in parallel. In accordance with the 1930 Hague Agreement, simultaneous translations in English, French, and German were provided at the hearings.[2]

---

[1] First Eagle SoGen Funds, Inc. v. Bank for International Settlements, No. 01 Civ. 0087(RO), 2001 WL 1150323 (S.D.N.Y., Sept. 28, 2001); 252 F.3d 604 (2nd Cir. 2001).

[2] Partial Award on the Lawfulness of the Recall of the Privately Held Shares on 8 January 2001 and the Applicable Standards for Valuation of those Shares [hereinafter "Partial Award"], para. 51.

Summary of Matters Submitted to Arbitration

(i) Whether the compulsory recall of shares by the Bank on January 8, 2001, was lawful;
(ii) The identification of the applicable standards for the valuation of the compulsorily recalled shares;
(iii) The application of the standards in (ii) above to the shares which were compulsorily recalled; and
(iv) Whether First Eagle had breached Article 54 of the Statutes of the Bank by initiating court proceedings against the Bank in the United States.

Awards
Partial Award

Legal Nature and Status of the Bank

First Eagle disputed that the Bank was an international organization, on the basis that the Bank had private shareholders, and that it performed some commercial activities common to private sector banks.[3] Dr. Reineccius and Mr. Mathieu accepted the identity of the Bank as an international organization.[4] The Tribunal noted that the Bank was established under international law and was not subordinated to Swiss law, despite the applicability of Swiss law to the Bank in some situations.[5] It held that the functions of the Bank were quintessentially public international in character[6] and concluded that the Bank was "a *sui generis* creation which is an international organization."[7]

Lawfulness of Compulsory Recall of Privately Held Shares

The Claimants contested the legality of the compulsory share recall principally under the Statutes and, secondarily, under principles of international law regarding expropriation. The Bank had adopted Article 18A of the Statutes for the compulsory recall of the privately held shares, based on the procedure for amendment of unreserved articles of the Statutes provided for in Article 57 of the Statutes.[8] Article 18A of the Statutes provides, in part:

> In accordance with the resolutions of the Extraordinary General Meeting held on 8 January 2001 and in order to implement Article 15 of the Statutes as amended, the Bank will, on a compulsory basis, repurchase each share which, as of that date, is registered in the name of a shareholder other than a central bank (a "private shareholder"), against payment of compensation of CHF 16,000 for each share … .

[3] Partial Award, paras. 116–117.
[4] Partial Award, para. 116.
[5] Partial Award, paras. 106–108.
[6] Partial Award, para. 113.
[7] Partial Award, para. 118.
[8] Partial Award, para. 131.

The Tribunal examined the question whether the modification of the Statutes, assuming conformity with principles of international law, was carried out in accordance with Articles 57 and 58 of the Statutes.[9] Article 57 provides:

> Amendments of any Articles of these Statutes other than those enumerated in Article 58 may be proposed by a two-thirds majority of the Board to the General Meeting and if adopted by a majority of the General Meeting shall come into force, provided that such amendments are not inconsistent with the provisions of the Articles enumerated in Article 58.

Article 58 provides:

> Articles 2, 3, 8, 14, 19, 24, 27, 44, 51, 54, 57 and 58 cannot be amended except subject to the following conditions: the amendment must be adopted by a two-thirds majority of the Board, approved by a majority of the General Meeting and sanctioned by a law supplementing the Charter of the Bank.

The Tribunal noted that Article 57 of the Statutes introduced no substantive limitation on the amendment competence of the General Meeting other than the requirement that those amendments not be inconsistent with the articles enumerated in Article 58 of the Statutes. There was no indication in Article 57 that the mode of formulation of an amendment, whether as an addition to an existing article or as an entirely new article designated by a new number, had any legal significance. The Tribunal thus held that "an interpretation of the Statutes in good faith in accordance with the ordinary meaning to be given to the terms of the Treaty, must find the amendment under discussion as valid and *intra vires* the Statutes."[10]

The Tribunal took account of the subsequent conduct of the Bank, pursuant to Article 31(3)(b) of the Vienna Convention on the Law of Treaties and the decision of the International Court of Justice ("ICJ") in *Reparations for Injuries Suffered in the Service of the United Nations.*[11] It noted that the Bank had, on a number of occasions, amended its Statutes by the introduction of a new article.[12] In the Tribunal's view, Article 18A of the Statutes could not be plausibly construed as engaging any of the reserved articles in Article 58 of the Statutes "or any of the concerns that animated that provision."[13] The Tribunal therefore found that "the Bank had the authority to add Article 18A to its Statutes and that the compulsory recall of the shares, including the procedures by which it was accomplished, was *intra vires* the Statutes and was, accordingly, a valid exercise of the Bank's powers."[14]

The Tribunal then turned to the question whether the recall by the Bank and the valuation that the Bank set upon the shares held by private parties were unlawful under general international law.[15] Mr. Mathieu contended that the Bank's actions violated two of international

[9] Partial Award, para. 142.

[10] Partial Award, para. 144.

[11] Reparations for Injuries Suffered in the Service of the United Nations, Advisory Opinion, 1949 I.C.J. REP. p. 174, at p. 180 (Apr. 11).

[12] Partial Award, para. 145.

[13] Partial Award, para. 147.

[14] Partial Award, para. 148.

[15] *Id.*

law's cardinal requirements for a lawful expropriation: that the taking be in the public interest and that it be non-discriminatory.[16]

The Tribunal held that, when applied to an actor which is an international entity, but not a State, the "public interest" must be understood, *mutatis mutandis*, as an action rationally, proportionately, and necessarily related to the performance of one of the legitimate international public purposes of the actor undertaking it.[17] The Bank had submitted evidence that the presence of private shareholders increased certain costs for the Bank and impeded the performance of some of its international public functions.[18] Thus, *prima facie*, the Bank was able to show that, were the international law of expropriation to be applied, it could meet, *mutatis mutandis*, the public interest requirement.[19]

The Tribunal held, further, that the Bank's actions with regard to the shareholders would not be characterized as discriminatory under the international law of expropriation.[20] The very nature of the Bank as an international organization imported a different treatment, for some purposes, of central banks and private shareholders. This difference was most apparent in governance rights, none of which could be acquired by private shareholders.[21]

The Tribunal concluded that the decision to recall the privately held shares by the Extraordinary General Meeting of January 8, 2001, was *intra vires* the Statutes and a lawful exercise of the Bank's powers. Nor did this exercise of the Bank's power violate any principles of international law that might apply.[22]

Adequacy of Compensation

The Bank submitted that the share redemption price satisfied international human rights law. It argued that the applicable standard of compensation was that of "appropriate, reasonable, fair or equitable" compensation, in accordance with, *inter alia*, Article 21(2) of the American Convention on Human Rights, which provides for "just" as opposed to "full" compensation.[23] According to the Tribunal, the "mainstream of general international law" in cases of expropriation of the shares of foreign investors required "full compensation,"[24] namely, "prompt, adequate and effective" compensation.[25] The Tribunal rejected the Bank's "unpersuasive" analogy of itself to a State taking the property of its own nationals.[26] The Tribunal also noted that the Bank had actually paid the shareholders almost double the market exchange value of the recalled shares, even though it had only argued for the application of the stock market price in the arbitration.[27]

---

[16] Partial Award, para. 149.

[17] Partial Award, para. 150.

[18] Partial Award, para. 151.

[19] *Id.*

[20] Partial Award, para. 152.

[21] Partial Award, para. 154.

[22] Partial Award, para. 158.

[23] Partial Award, para. 91.

[24] Partial Award, para. 168.

[25] Partial Award, para. 169, *citing* Biloune and Marine Drive Complex Ltd v. Ghana Investments Centre and the Government of Ghana, 95 I.L.R. p. 183 (1993).

[26] Partial Award, para. 168.

[27] Partial Award, para. 171.

The Parties agreed that the issue of the required level of compensation had to be resolved primarily by reference to the Bank's Constituent Instruments, and by international law only if the Constituent Instruments should fail to provide an answer. The Tribunal held that "the *lex specialis* of this case," namely, the 1930 Hague Agreement and the Constituent Instruments, was conceived as self-contained, and did not incorporate general international law, except insofar as the *lex specialis* failed to provide an answer to a question that might arise or violated a fundamental principle of international law.[28] Applying the *lex specialis*, the Tribunal determined that "the specific provisions of the Statutes establishing the equal rights of the shares"[29] prescribed a higher amount of compensation than general international law.[30] The Tribunal held, further, that there was "no ground for [it] to depart from the *lex specialis* applicable to the Parties and to use the international law standard which would apply market value for the shares."[31]

Valuation

All three Claimants submitted that the appropriate method for valuation should be based on a per share proportionate part of the undiscounted net asset value ("NAV") of the Bank.[32] The Bank disagreed, on the basis that the shares lacked fundamental characteristics of equity ownership, because (i) sale of shares was subject to approval of both the Bank and the central bank to whose national issue the shares belonged; and (ii) shares did not carry any governance rights.[33] The Tribunal examined how the Bank itself had understood the appropriate valuation prior to the recall of the privately held shares.[34] It found that, from 1936 onwards, the Bank, in its internal deliberations, seemed to have assumed that all shares were entitled to an equal proportionate share of the assets of the Bank; to have priced new shares on that basis; and to have taken for granted that, if it were compulsorily to repurchase its private shares, the Statutes would require it to price the shares by using a method of valuation of shares based on some form of the net assets of the Bank.[35]

The Question and Scope of a Possible Discount

The Tribunal ruled that the per share proportionate NAV should be discounted by 30%. It relied on an internal document of the Bank, which had been prepared in 1969 in order to calculate a share premium ("1969 Report").[36] The 1969 Report had calculated the NAV of the Bank on the basis of a hypothetical liquidation of the Bank, taking into account "the impacts which would have occasioned a liquidation," and had suggested a discount of 30%.[37]

---

[28] Partial Award, para. 174.

[29] Statutes, Article 13.

[30] Partial Award, paras. 174–175.

[31] Partial Award, para. 175.

[32] Partial Award, para. 183.

[33] Partial Award, para. 187.

[34] Partial Award, para. 193.

[35] Partial Award, para. 194.

[36] "Agenda for the Three Hundred and Eighteenth Meeting of the Board of Directors of the Bank for International Settlements," Nov. 17, 1969.

[37] Partial Award, para. 197.

The Tribunal also found that the Bank had consistently used a discount of 30% in pricing shares issued to new central banks. [38]

Conclusions of Partial Award

The Tribunal concluded that the appropriate compensation for the recalled shares, as required by the Statutes, was a proportionate share of the NAV of the Bank, discounted by 30%, subject to the additional NAV assessment for real estate. As the Bank had paid less than this amount, it was obliged to pay the difference to each private shareholder.[39] The Tribunal reserved, for the next and final phase of the arbitration, the determination of the Bank's NAV as discounted,[40] the calculation of the precise sum due plus interest,[41] the expert determination of the value of the Bank's real estate,[42] the Bank's counterclaim against First Eagle,[43] and the question of costs. [44]

Final Award

Determination of the Exact Amount Owed by the Bank for International Settlements per Share

The Tribunal held that the amount which was owed in Swiss francs to the private shareholders for the compulsory purchase of their shares was the per share value of the Bank's NAV, as calculated in the J.P. Morgan Report, discounted by 30%, plus the per share value of the Bank's real estate, discounted by 30%. The Tribunal used the figure of CHF 33, 936 for the value per share, which it discounted by 30% to produce a remainder of CHF 23,755. As the Bank had paid each private shareholder CHF 16,000, the Bank owed each of the Claimants a supplementary payment of CHF 7,755.20 per share.[45] To this sum had to be added the discounted per share value of the Bank's real estate. The expert appointed in accordance with the Partial Award[46] valued the real estate of the Bank, as of September 7, 2000, at CHF 168, 094,000.[47] The per share value of the Bank's real estate, when discounted by 30%, thus resulted in an additional payment to the Claimants of CHF 222.36 per share.[48]

Interest

The Claimants proposed different rates of interest, varying from 3.25% to 7%, based upon different theories of public international law, international commercial law, and Swiss

---

[38] Partial Award, para. 201.

[39] Partial Award, para. 202.

[40] Partial Award, para. 203.

[41] Partial Award, para. 204.

[42] Partial Award, para. 205.

[43] Partial Award, paras. 206–207.

[44] Partial Award, para. 208.

[45] Final Award on the Claims for Compensation for the Shares Formerly Held by the Claimants, Interest Due Thereon and Costs of the Arbitration and on the Counterclaim of the Bank against First Eagle SoGen Funds, Inc. [hereinafter "Final Award"], para. 78.

[46] *See* text accompanying note 42, *supra*.

[47] Final Award, para. 100.

[48] Final Award, para. 102.

practice.[49] Neither the 1930 Hague Agreement, nor the 1907 Hague Convention, nor the Statutes of the Bank prescribed a rate of interest for any purpose.[50] In determining the proper rate of interest, the Tribunal noted the frequent practice, in situations where the laws of several different legal systems could potentially be applied, of selecting the law of the legal system with which the question to be decided has, in the specific case, the closest contacts.[51] Article 2 of the Statutes designated Basle, Switzerland, as the place where the registered office of the Bank should be situated, and Switzerland had "consistently been the *siège* and operational center of the activities of the Bank."[52] The Tribunal determined that the Swiss legal system was the one having the closest contacts with this question, and therefore referred to Swiss law, which applies a 5% simple rate for moratory interest.[53]

The Tribunal ruled that, for all the Claimants, there was a debt owing from the Bank for the supplementary payment resulting from the difference between what the Bank paid on January 8, 2001, and "the application of the formula of NAV minus 30%."[54] Accordingly, the Tribunal calculated 5% simple interest for all Claimants from January 8, 2001, until the date of the Final Award with respect to that supplementary payment,[55] including the per share value of the Bank's real estate.[56]

Counterclaim

The Bank claimed that First Eagle's suit in the United States breached Article 54 of the Statutes.[57] Article 54(1) of the Statutes provides:

> If any dispute shall arise between the Bank, on the one side, and any central bank, financial institution, or other bank referred to in the present Statutes, on the other side, with regard to the interpretation or application of the Statutes of the Bank, the same shall be referred for final decision to the Tribunal provided for by the Hague Agreement of January, 1930.

The Bank argued that its status as an international organization required that disputes to which it was a party be determined on a uniform and consistent basis.[58] It argued, further, that the *lex specialis* of the Bank's Statutes provided for interim measures of protection, and First Eagle was therefore not free to seek interim measures from a municipal court.[59] First Eagle defended its recourse to domestic litigation in the United States as action that did not breach Article 54(1) of the Statutes because "courts are entitled to review the existence and validity of the arbitration agreement on which the arbitrators' jurisdiction is based."[60]

---

[49] Final Award, para. 89.
[50] Final Award, para. 90.
[51] Final Award, para. 91.
[52] *Id.*
[53] Final Award, para. 92.
[54] Final Award, para. 97.
[55] *Id.*
[56] Final Award, para. 103.
[57] Final Award, para. 104.
[58] Final Award, para. 107.
[59] Final Award, para. 108.
[60] Final Award, para. 112.

According to the Tribunal, a private shareholder of the Bank, by purchasing shares, accepted the dispute resolution regime provided for by Article 54 of the Statutes, including the immunity of the Bank from national courts and the competence of a Tribunal formed under the 1930 Hague Agreement and the Statutes to decide its own jurisdiction and to issue provisional measures.[61] A power or option provided by domestic law could not be used to justify violation of a commitment that operated on the level of international law.[62] The Tribunal concluded that First Eagle had unlawfully required the Bank to expend a considerable amount in defending its rights under the Statutes, giving the Bank a right to reparation, and that First Eagle had to reimburse the Bank for the Bank's expenses in the U.S. litigation.[63]

Declaratory Relief

As part of its Counterclaim, the Bank had requested that the Tribunal render an award "declaring that the Tribunal has exclusive jurisdiction over any claims against the Bank arising out of or in connection with the validity, procedures and amount of compensation provided in the 8 January 2001 redemption of the Bank's privately held shares."[64] The Tribunal noted that Dr. Reineccius had requested that it "expressly forbid the Bank from making upcoming payments dependent on signing a waiver" by the Claimants of rights to resort to ordinary courts to obtain a more favorable judgment,[65] and that First Eagle had opposed the Bank's request for the declaratory Award.[66] It therefore found that the Bank had demonstrated "a specific interest that the Tribunal must address."[67] The Tribunal declared that, as between the Parties to this Arbitration, its decision was final and binding, and no other remedy was available to the Parties *inter se* with respect to the issues determined in it.[68]

Expenses of the Parties and Costs of the Arbitration

Annex XII of the 1930 Hague Agreement provides:

> In particular Article 85 of the Hague Convention shall apply to these proceedings, and each Party shall pay its own expenses and an equal share of the expenses of the Tribunal.

The Tribunal interpreted this provision in light of the principle of effective access to justice.[69] It relied on the holding of the European Court of Human Rights, in *Waite & Kennedy v. Germany*,[70] that a correlative of the immunity of international organizations is an obligation to provide for fair access to justice.[71] Dr. Reineccius and Mr. Mathieu were individual

---

[61] Final Award, para. 115.
[62] Final Award, para. 116.
[63] Final Award, para. 119.
[64] Final Award, para. 120.
[65] Final Award, para. 121.
[66] Final Award, para. 122.
[67] Final Award, para. 123.
[68] Final Award, para. 124.
[69] Final Award, para. 125.
[70] Waite & Kennedy v. Germany, 30 Eur. Ct. H.R. p. 261 (1999).
[71] Final Award, para. 126.

claimants with limited financial resources. Because Dr. Reineccius was not represented by counsel, the Tribunal found that it was only necessary for the Bank to pay the expenses incurred by Mr. Mathieu.[72] In the Tribunal's view, effective access to justice was not at issue for First Eagle in defending its claims, and First Eagle should therefore pay its own expenses.[73]

The Tribunal determined, further, that Article 54(1) of the Statutes had to be interpreted in such a way as to make access to justice for every shareholder, not only theoretically possible, but, in reality, feasible.[74] Considering all the circumstances, the Tribunal held that the Bank would bear the full costs of the Arbitration.[75]

[72] *Id.*
[73] Final Award, paras. 127–128.
[74] Final Award, para. 133.
[75] Final Award, para. 135.

The Rhine Chlorides Arbitration concerning the Auditing of Accounts

Parties:	Netherlands/France
Arbitration Agreement:	1976 Convention on the Protection of the Rhine against Pollution by Chlorides, Article 13, and the 1991 Additional Protocol, Article 7
Arbitrators:	Judge Krzysztof Skubiszewski (President), Judge Gilbert Guillaume, Judge Pieter H. Kooijmans
Date of Award:	March 12, 2004[1]

Summary

Additional Protocol of 1991 to the 1976 Convention on the Protection of the Rhine against Pollution by Chlorides – Protocol providing for France to reduce discharges of waste chlorides into the Rhine from Alsace Potassium Mines during period 1991-1998 – France to store the chlorides on land – contracting parties to make annual payments to France in respect of costs – France to reimburse payments at end of period – Protocol setting out method of calculation to be used for reimbursement of surplus payments – amounts of chlorides to be stored in fact much lower than predicted – costs of storage per ton accordingly much higher – disagreement between Parties as to basis of calculation of sums to be reimbursed – interpretation of Protocol in accordance with law of treaties – determination of the method of calculation to be used according to that interpretation of Protocol – determination of amounts to be reimbursed according to that calculation.

Legal Subject Matters

Sources of international norms:
- Customary international law
- General principles of international law
- Treaties
  - Application
  - Effectiveness
  - Good faith
  - Interpretation
  - Object and purpose
  - Terms

---

[1] The Award was rendered in French. This summary is based on the unofficial English translation *available at* www.pca-cpa.org.

Bibliography

Award published in:

- THE RHINE CHLORIDES ARBITRATION CONCERNING THE AUDITING OF ACCOUNTS (NETHERLANDS–FRANCE) AWARD OF 2004 / *L'ARBITRAGE « PROTECTION DU RHIN CONTRE LES CHLORURES »* (Permanent Court of Arbitration Award Series, TMC Asser Press 2008);
- XXV R.I.A.A. p. 267 (2004).

Commentary:

- Laurence Boisson de Chazournes, *L'arbitrage « Protection du Rhin contre les chlorures » concernant l'apurement des comptes (Pays-Bas–France) : sa contribution au droit international / The "Rhine Chlorides" Arbitration Concerning the Auditing of Accounts (Netherlands-France: Its Contribution to International Law, in* THE RHINE CHLORIDES ARBITRATION CONCERNING THE AUDITING OF ACCOUNTS (NETHERLANDS–FRANCE) AWARD OF 2004 (PCA Award Series, 2008);
- Anne Rainaud, *Les aléas du débit de l'eau face à la rigueur financière du Protocole Additionnel à la Convention relative à la protection du Rhin contre les chlorures: Arbitrage sur la liquidation des comptes opposant les Pays-Bas et la France*, 17 RGDIP p. 1 (2004).

Facts

The Convention on the Protection of the Rhine against Pollution by Chlorides (the "Convention"), signed by France, Germany, Luxembourg, the Netherlands, and Switzerland, provides for the reduction by France of discharges of waste chlorides from the Alsace Potassium Mines into the Rhine. In the Additional Protocol to the Convention signed on September 25, 1991 ("Protocol"), the contracting parties agreed on further measures to be taken. In French territory, France was to reduce chloride discharges and temporarily store the chlorides on land when the chloride concentration in the Rhine at the German-Netherlands border exceeded 200 milligrams per liter ("mg/l"). In Netherlands territory, the Netherlands was to limit chloride concentrations in the waters of the IJsselmeer by discharging the briny waters from the Wieringermeer polder into the Waddenzee, rather than into the IJsselmeer.

The Protocol provided in Article 4 for the contracting parties to bear the costs of these measures in the following shares: France 30%, Germany 30%, the Netherlands 34%, and Switzerland 6%. The contracting parties agreed on maximum expenditures of 400 million French francs for the period 1991-1998 for the measures to be taken in France. These expenditures were to include the costs of investment, which were themselves limited to 40 million French francs, and running costs for storage and removal from storage of the chlorides. The amount thus agreed constituted a spending limit beyond which France was released from its storage obligations.

A dispute arose between the Netherlands and France (the "Parties") concerning the interpretation and implementation of the Protocol, which the Parties were unable to settle by negotiation. By a *note verbale* dated October 21, 1999, the Netherlands requested that the dispute be submitted to arbitration in accordance with Article 13 of the Convention and Article 7 of the Protocol. On December 17, 1999, the Netherlands appointed as an arbitrator Mr. Pieter H. Kooijmans, and France appointed as an arbitrator Judge Gilbert Guillaume. The two party-appointed arbitrators chose as the third arbitrator Judge Krzysztof Skubiszewski, who, on February 1, 2000, agreed to serve as President of the Netherlands-France Arbitral Tribunal (the "Tribunal"). On June 21, 2000, the Tribunal held a meeting in

The Hague, at which it adopted its Rules of Procedure, and following which it was agreed that the International Bureau of the Permanent Court of Arbitration would serve as Registry of the Tribunal. In accordance with the Rules of Procedure, a hearing was held in closed session on October 3, 2002, at the International Conference Centre in Paris. Further documents and written submissions were exchanged following the hearing up to January 9, 2004. The Tribunal issued its Award on March 12, 2004.

Question Submitted to Arbitration

The Netherlands and France agreed to submit the following question to the Tribunal:

> Taking into account all relevant provisions of the Additional Protocol to the Convention of 3 December 1976 on the Protection of the Rhine against Pollution by Chlorides and its Annexes, interpreted in accordance with international law, what is the sum that must be transferred between the Parties to the dispute in order that the accounts be audited pursuant to point 4.2.1 of Annex III to the said Protocol?

Award of the Tribunal

The Applicable Law

The question submitted to the Tribunal referred to "the relevant provisions of the Additional Protocol ... interpreted in accordance with international law." The Tribunal accordingly began by recalling the law applicable to treaty interpretation, as expressed in Articles 31 and 32 of the Vienna Convention on the Law of Treaties of May 23, 1969 ("Vienna Convention").[2] Given that France was not a party to the Vienna Convention, the Tribunal made particular reference to international judicial dicta affirming that Articles 31 and 32 of the Vienna Convention are a codification of customary law.[3] It noted that international jurisprudence has adhered to the general rule of interpretation codified in Article 31 of the Vienna Convention. The Tribunal considered that this rule should be viewed as an integral whole, the constituent elements of which cannot be separated.[4]

The Parties' divergent positions as to the applicable law concerned mostly the importance to be attached to each of the various elements of the general rule of interpretation. For the Netherlands, the determining element was the ordinary meaning of the terms used. For France, those terms were only the point of departure, and other factors must also be taken into account, such as good faith, context, and the object and purpose of the treaty.[5] In the Tribunal's view, "factors other than the ordinary meaning of the words cannot be cast aside; in the same way, neither can that meaning be ignored."[6] It emphasized that the ordinary meaning of the terms does not always have to be adopted; in fact, according to Article 31(4) of the Vienna Convention, "a special meaning shall be given to a term if it is established that

---

[2] Award, paras. 54–55.
[3] Award, paras. 59–61.
[4] Award, para. 62.
[5] Award, para. 64.
[6] *Id.*

the parties so intended."[7] The Tribunal also examined the relationship between Articles 31 and 32 of the Vienna Convention. It held that Article 32 does not restrict the use of supplementary means of interpretation to cases in which the result of the application of the provisions of Article 31 would be ambiguous, obscure, or manifestly absurd or unreasonable, but that recourse may be had to Article 32 in order to confirm the meaning resulting from the application of Article 31. The Tribunal considered that its approach was in line with international jurisprudence.[8]

The Tribunal gave examples of the wealth of long-standing and consistent arbitral jurisprudence from which Article 32 of the Vienna Convention originated.[9] France contended that customary law, where it is the only law binding on the two Parties, should not be applied with the same kind of minute and analytical rigor as would be the case if the treaty codifying that custom were itself binding on the two Parties. The Tribunal observed that France had not identified any specific respect in which the customary rules might differ from Articles 31 and 32 of the Vienna Convention, and that Articles 31 and 32 were "not as rigid in nature as France appears to claim." The Tribunal concluded that those articles must be taken as a faithful reflection of the current state of customary law and were therefore applicable in the present case.[10]

Resolution of the Dispute

The dispute between the Parties related to the interpretation of point 4.2.1 of Annex III of the Protocol ("Annex III"), which provides:

> For expenditure in French territory, payments made in advance [for each year in the period 1991–1998] are not payments in full discharge, and the accounts shall be audited by 31 December 1998 at the very latest by comparing the actual expenditure, calculated according to the conditions specified in points 1.2.3, 1.2.4 and 1.2.6 above, with the spending limits [for the respective years in the period 1991–1998] set out in point 2 above increased by any amount [of the spending limit of a preceding year not spent in that year plus interest] carried over pursuant to point 3.2.3[11] above. In the event that actual expenditure by France is less than the amount referred to in point 1.2 [i.e. 400 million French francs], France undertakes to return the surplus received plus 11/12 of the yearly interest on this amount at the annual long-term interest rate on national loans. In this connection, the rate of price rises shall also be taken into account.

Point 1.2.6 of Annex III reads:

> Each year, France shall be released from its storage obligations once the expenditure ["*dépenses effectuées*"] in that year has reached the spending limit [for the year concerned] as determined by point 2 and point 3.2.3. For this purpose, the running costs ["*dépenses engagées*"] for France shall be calculated at a rate of 61.5 French francs (1988 French francs adjusted for inflation) per ton stored. For the first year, investment costs shall be added on (40 million 1988 French francs adjusted for inflation).

---

[7] Award, para. 67.
[8] Award, paras 70–72.
[9] Award, paras 73–76.
[10] Award, para. 77.
[11] *See infra* for the text of point 3.2.3.

This mechanism of calculation, which the Tribunal set out in detail, was put in place under Article 4 of the Protocol and Annex III, because it was impossible to predict the quantities of chlorides that would have to be stored each year.[12]

Throughout the relevant period, the quantities of chlorides actually stored by France remained well below the upper limits set out by the contracting parties; as a result, France was obliged to repay to the other contracting parties the surplus amounts it had been paid. The subject of the dispute between the Parties was the manner in which the surplus to be reimbursed should be calculated under Annex III. For the Netherlands, the "*dépenses engagées*" ["expenditures incurred"] by France were the costs of investment, plus the amount of 61.5 French francs multiplied by the number of tons of chloride stored and removed from storage. For France, the only purpose of the 61.5 French francs per ton stipulated in point 1.2.6 of Annex III was to calculate the spending limits during the 1991-1998 period; and at the time of the final auditing, the actual costs of storage and removal from storage were to be used. In France's submission, these actual costs were much higher than 61.5 French francs per ton because of the small amounts of chlorides that were in practice stored and removed from storage.[13]

The Tribunal acknowledged the fundamental nature of the principle that "[a] treaty shall be interpreted in good faith," but held that there was no reason to doubt the good faith of the interpretations of the Protocol put forward respectively by the Netherlands and France.[14] It therefore proceeded to examine the terms of point 4.2.1 of Annex III, the meaning of which was in issue between the Parties, and which had to be interpreted in good faith.[15] Recalling the terms of point 4.2.1, the Tribunal observed that the main issue between the Parties was how the phrase "actual expenditure, calculated according to the conditions specified in points 1.2.3, 1.2.4 and 1.2.6" should be interpreted.

France argued that the provisions of point 1.2.6 of Annex III referred to the running costs only for the purpose of calculating the spending limits. The Tribunal held that the reference in point 4.2.1, for the purposes of auditing, to the calculation methods in point 1.2.6, gave these methods a new purpose in addition to that laid down in point 1.2.6.[16] It then considered the use in point 4.2.1 of the term "*comparaison*" and the disagreement between the Parties on the consequences of this use. The Tribunal was of the view that the immediate context supported the interpretation of this term as synonymous with "mathematical difference." It concluded that France had not shown that the contracting parties intended to invest the term "*comparaison*" with a particular meaning that referred back to a method based on actual costs.[17] The Tribunal found that the expressions "*engagées*" and "*effectuées*" had been used synonymously, and, moreover, that they had been used interchangeably in the German, French, and Dutch texts. It held, further, that the presumption of effectiveness militated against an interpretation that would draw a distinction between these terms.[18]

In accordance with Article 31(2) and (3) of the Vienna Convention, the Tribunal then examined the context of point 4.2.1 of Annex III. In this regard, France attached special

[12] Award, paras. 80–83.
[13] Award, para. 84.
[14] Award, para. 86.
[15] Award, paras. 87–92.
[16] Award, para. 89.
[17] Award, para. 91.
[18] Award, para. 92.

importance to the apportionment formula in Article 4 of the Protocol. However, the Tribunal noted that that provision referred back to Annex III for the calculation of the amounts due. Article 4 of the Protocol was thus not decisive with respect to the issue of the basis of this calculation.[19] The Tribunal was unable to find other instruments that could be helpful in the interpretation of the Protocol and its Annexes.[20] The Tribunal found the object and purpose of the Protocol not to be decisive. The interpretations of both Parties were compatible with the object of organizing the fight against chloride pollution of the Rhine by guaranteeing that the measures taken by France and the Netherlands would be jointly financed.[21]

The Tribunal found the subsequent practice of the Parties, as reflected in the method used in the texts relied on by the Netherlands – namely, the annual reports and the provisional balance sheet prepared by France as at the end of 1996 – did not reflect agreement by the Parties as to the interpretation to be given to point 4.2.1 of Annex III.[22] The Tribunal also took into account relevant rules of international law applicable in the relations between the Parties under Article 31(3)(c) of the Vienna Convention. It did not view the "polluter pays" principle, to which the Netherlands had referred in support of its claim, as forming part of general international law,[23] nor did it accord any particular status to the Netherlands by virtue of its geographical position.[24] Having regard to this analysis, the Tribunal was of the opinion that the calculation for the purpose of the final auditing must be based on the amount of 61.5 (1988) French francs per ton.[25]

The Tribunal went on to examine, in accordance with Article 32 of the Vienna Convention, the various documents submitted by the Parties as "preparatory documents" for the Protocol.[26] Based on its analysis of these documents, the Tribunal found that the figure of 37.5 French francs per ton for removal from storage had been maintained substantially unchanged since 1988, while the quantities to be removed from storage fell from 16.3 million to 5.1 million and finally to 4.4 million tons in October 1990.[27] The Tribunal determined that the Parties had adopted the figure of 37.5 French francs per ton in the knowledge that it comprised both fixed and variable costs. The Parties had taken the view that, given the forecasts they had made for the coefficient of flow of the Rhine, there was no need, when deciding on the cost per ton, to take account of the variations that might occur in the quantities to be stored. Using these forecasts, the Tribunal concluded that the Parties had adopted the figure of 61.5 French francs per ton as a lump sum figure, irrespective of those quantities.[28] This finding was supported, in particular, by the preparatory document closest in time to the date of signature of the Protocol, namely, the record of the decisions of the 56th Plenary Meeting of the International Commission for the Protection of the Rhine held on July 2, 1991 ("document PLEN 30/91").[29]

---

[19] Award, para. 94.
[20] Award, para. 95.
[21] Award, para. 98.
[22] Award, para. 101.
[23] Award, para. 103.
[24] Award, para. 104.
[25] Award, para. 105.
[26] Award, paras. 106–127.
[27] Award, para. 125.
[28] Award, para. 127.
[29] *Id.*

The Tribunal found that the Parties had not foreseen that the coefficient of flow of the Rhine would increase, thereby reducing the resulting quantities to be stored so as to throw their costs forecasts into disarray.[30] In the Tribunal's view, the preparatory documents in its possession did not lead it to a different conclusion from that reached by applying the general rule of interpretation in accordance with Article 31 of the Vienna Convention.[31]

Calculation of the Amount to be Reimbursed

The Parties' calculations yielded different results with respect to the amount to be reimbursed. Exclusive of interest, the Netherlands, applying its favored method of calculation, claimed reimbursement of the sum of 102.33 million French francs, while France, based on its method, concluded that it should reimburse the Netherlands the sum of 55,793,779 French francs.[32] In the Tribunal's view, the method proposed by the Netherlands was incomplete since: (1) this method took no account of the fact that the expenditures, both for operation and investment, were to be calculated in 1988 French francs adjusted for inflation, while the payments in advance were made in francs at current value, and (2) the Netherlands claimed interest without indicating how that interest should be calculated.[33]

The Tribunal performed the auditing calculation in two stages: in the first stage, by calculating the amount of excess paid by the Netherlands to France (the "Annual Surplus") and, in the second stage, by calculating the interest due by France on that amount.[34]

The Tribunal calculated the Annual Surplus as follows: first, using the calculation method provided for in point 1.2.6 of Annex III, it determined the total amount actually expended by France and then it calculated 34% of that total expenditure, to arrive at the agreed contribution of the Netherlands under Article 4 of the Protocol (the "Agreed Contribution"). Next, the Tribunal calculated the difference between the Agreed Contribution and the sum of the annual payments actually made by the Netherlands to arrive at the Annual Surplus.[35]

The Tribunal determined that the interest due by France on the Annual Surplus up to December 31, 1998, was to be calculated pursuant to, and in accordance with, point 3.2.3 of Annex III. Point 3.2.3 provides:

> In the event that actual storage costs calculated in this way are below the limit initially set for the year concerned (point 2.1.1), the difference (plus 11/12 of the yearly interest on this amount at the annual long-term interest rate on national loans) shall be carried over to the following year, thereby raising the spending limit for the following year accordingly.

The Tribunal noted that, after January 1998, the Netherlands must have known that the annual payments it was making to France would not be used in the depollution of the Rhine pursuant to the Protocol. In those circumstances, the Tribunal held that the payments made by the Netherlands after January 1998 should not bear interest.[36] With respect to the pay-

[30] Award, para. 129.
[31] Award, para. 131.
[32] Award, paras. 84, 134.
[33] Award, para. 135.
[34] Award, para. 136.
[35] Award, para. 137.
[36] Award, para. 139.

ments made before January 1998, the Tribunal used the rate of interest provided for in point 3.2.3 of Annex III, namely, the rate of the *Crédit National*. For 1997 and 1998, when the *Crédit National* rate was no longer in existence, the Tribunal used a rate of interest agreed by the Parties in the arbitral proceedings, namely, the interest rates on French 10-year State bonds.[37]

After setting out the amounts of the interest and balance carried over as at December 31, 1998, the Tribunal calculated the interest due after December 31, 1998, as required by point 4.2.1 of Annex III, making a distinction between expenditures for storage and those for removal from storage.[38]

According to the Tribunal's calculations, the surplus that France was obliged to reimburse to the Netherlands was 128,855,162 French francs. This was the total amount carried forward as at December 31, 1998, representing the sum of the amount of 117,136,937 French francs and interest in the amount of 11,718,225 French francs.[39] Pursuant to the provisions of Chapter III of Annex 4 of document PLEN 30/91,[40] the Tribunal found that the cost overruns on removal from storage resulting from the rise in prices after 1998 fell to be deducted from that amount. The Tribunal held that it was up to the Parties to determine the amount of these cost overruns as soon as the removals from storage were completed, and that the amount of 10 million French francs should be set aside for the purpose.[41] The Tribunal found that France was under an obligation, after the determination of the cost overruns by the Parties, to deduct these from the amount set aside and transfer the remaining balance to the Netherlands, with no interest payable.[42]

Declaration of Judge Guillaume

Judge Guillaume made a Declaration in which he set out the circumstances of the adoption of the Treaty. He observed that the "fundamental difficulty" of the case was that "the forecasts made in 1989 about the coefficient of flow of the Rhine turned out to be completely wrong." Judge Guillaume examined the conditions laid down in Article 62(1) of the Vienna Convention concerning "fundamental change of circumstances," and took the view that those conditions had been fulfilled in this case. After examining comparable provisions of domestic law in several jurisdictions, Judge Guillaume stated his regret that the Tribunal had been led to adopt an unreasonable solution that should have been reviewed, in the light of the fundamentally changed circumstances, by good faith negotiations between the Parties.

---

[37] *Id.*
[38] Award, para. 140.
[39] Award, para. 141.
[40] *See* text accompanying note 28, *supra.*
[41] Award, para. 142.
[42] Award, para. 143.

The Iron Rhine ("IJzeren Rijn") Arbitration

Parties:	Belgium/Netherlands
Date of Arbitration Agreement:	July 22 and 23, 2003
Arbitrators:	Judge Roslyn Higgins (President), Prof. Guy Schrans, Judge Bruno Simma, Prof. Alfred H.A. Soons, Judge Peter Tomka
Date of Award:	May 24, 2005
Interpretation of the Award:	September 20, 2005

Summary

1839 Treaty of Separation between Belgium and the Netherlands provided for Belgian right of transit over Netherlands territory – Iron Rhine Treaty subsequently provided for right of transit to be exercised by building of a railway – route of Belgian right of transit agreed in Treaty of Separation as amended by Iron Rhine Treaty – Iron Rhine railway built pursuant to said Treaties and used occasionally from 1879 until 1991 – the Netherlands designated parts of agreed route as nature reserves during ensuing period of disuse – Belgium initiated discussions on reactivation of the Iron Rhine railway in 1998 – reactivation more expensive due to Netherlands environmental protection measures – determination of nature and scope of Belgium's right of transit – determination of allocation of costs for reactivation – determination of above issues in light of Parties' obligations under EC law – interpretation of the Award.

Legal Subject Matters

General principles of international law:
- International environmental law
- Sustainable development

Settlement of disputes:
- Arbitration
- Jurisdiction of the arbitral tribunal
  - European Community law

Sources of international norms:
- Treaties
  - Interpretation
    - Effectiveness
    - Intertemporality
    - Object and purpose
    - Terms

Bibliography

Award published in:

- The Iron Rhine Arbitration ("*IJzeren Rijn*") (Belgium–Netherlands) Award of 2005 (Permanent Court of Arbitration Award Series, TMC Asser Press 2007);
- XXVII R.I.A.A. p. 35 (2007).

Commentary:

- Colin Warbrick, *The Iron Rhine ("IJzeren Rijn") Arbitration (Belgium-Netherlands): Its Contribution to International Law*, *in* The Iron Rhine Arbitration (Belgium–Netherlands) Award of 2005 (PCA Award Series, 2007);
- Pierre d'Argent, *De la fragmentation à la cohésion systémique : la sentence arbitrale du 24 mai 2005 relative au « Rhin de Fer » (IJzeren Rijn)*, *in* *Droit du pouvoir, pouvoir du droit : Mélanges offerts à Jean Salmon* (Bruylant 2007);
- Ineke van Bladel, *The Iron Rhine Case and the Art of Treaty Interpretation: The Application of Nineteenth Century Obligations in the Twenty-first Century*, *in* The Netherlands in Court: Essays in Honour of Johan G. Lammers p. 1 (Nijhoff 2006);
- Virginie Barral, *La sentence du Rhin de Fer, une nouvelle étape dans la prise en compte du droit de l'environnement par la justice internationale*, 3 RGDIP p. 647 (2006);
- Ineke van Bladel, *The Iron Rhine Arbitration Case: On the Right Legal Track? An Analysis of the Award and of Its Relation to the Law of the European Community*, 18 Hague Y.B. Int'l L. p. 3 (2006);
- Nikolas Lavranos, *The MOX Plant and IJzeren Rijn Disputes: Which Court is the Supreme Arbiter?*, 19(1) Leiden J. Int'l L. p. 223 (2006);
- J. Harrison, *Case Comment: Iron Rhine Railway Arbitration*, J. Env. L. p. 505 (2006)
- Philippe Weckel, *Sentence du 24 Mai 2005, Chemin de fer du Rhin (Belgique/Pays-Bas)*, 3 RGDIP p. 715 (2005);
- Frans Tonnaer, *De Reactivering van de IJzeren Rijn : Discussie op een dwaalspoor?*, *in* Grensoverschrijdend recht p. 1 (2006);
- Pieter Van Nuffel, *Uitspraak van het Arbitragetribunaal van 24 mei 2005 in het geschil tussen Belgie en Nederland betreffende de Ijzeren Rijn-spoorlijn*, *in* 30 Tijdschrift voor Europees en economisch recht (SEW) p. 129 (2006);
- Ernst M.H. Hirsch Ballin, *De IJzeren Rijn*, *in* Ars Aequi p. 1058 (Dec. 2005);
- *Arbitrage inzake de IJzeren Rijn*, *in* 9 Nederlands Juristenblad (NJB) pp. 536–537 (Mar. 3, 2006).

Facts

Article XII of the 1839 "Treaty between Belgium and the Netherlands relative to the Separation of their Respective Territories" ("Treaty of Separation") provided for a right of transit by Belgium over a specified route through Netherlands territory. In 1868, the Netherlands agreed that Belgium could build a railway line under Article XII ("Iron Rhine railway"). In 1873, the Netherlands and Belgium entered into the "Iron Rhine Treaty,"[1] Article IV, paragraph 4, of which modified the route specified in the Treaty of Separation.

The revised route linked the port of Antwerp in Belgium to the Rhine basin in Germany. The Iron Rhine railway came into use on this route from 1879. Apart from brief interruptions

[1] Convention between Belgium and the Netherlands relative to the Payment of the Belgian Debt, the Abolition of the Surtax on Netherlands Spirits, and the Passing of a Railway Line from Antwerp to Germany across Limburg of 1873.

in the two World Wars, the line was used from 1879 to 1991. From 1991 to the date of the arbitration, the Iron Rhine railway had not been used for through traffic between Belgium and Germany, although internal traffic was continued on certain sections of the track within the Netherlands. During the 1990s, the Government of the Netherlands enacted several measures aimed at environmental protection. These included the designation as nature reserves of certain areas lying across the route of the Iron Rhine railway.

In 1987 and during the 1990s, there were a number of communications between government officials of Belgium and the Netherlands (the "Parties") concerning possible reactivation of the Iron Rhine railway. Formal discussions on this issue were initiated by the Prime Minister of Belgium on June 12, 1998. These led to the adoption of a Memorandum of Understanding on March 28, 2000 ("MoU"), between the Parties. The MoU provided, amongst other things, for (i) completion of an international study jointly with Germany on the consequences of reactivation and possible alternative routes, and (ii) completion of an Environmental Impact Assessment ("EIA") procedure by the Netherlands for that part of the Iron Rhine railway located on Dutch territory. Both studies, completed in May 2001, concluded that the preferred option would be the historic route.

Further implementation of the MoU having failed due to disagreements between the Parties concerning the conditions of use and allocation of costs, particularly with respect to plans for so-called "temporary use" of the Iron Rhine railway, discussions led to the conclusion of the Arbitration Agreement between the Parties in July 2003.

The Parties subsequently agreed on Rules of Procedure for the arbitration, which were based on the PCA Optional Rules for Arbitrating Disputes between Two States. In accordance with Article 5(1) of the Rules of Procedure, Belgium appointed as arbitrators Professor G. Schrans and Judge B. Simma, and the Netherlands appointed Professor A.H.A. Soons and Judge P. Tomka. On September 22, 2003, the four arbitrators appointed Judge R. Higgins as President of the Arbitral Tribunal ("Tribunal"). Article 1(3) of the Rules of Procedure designated the PCA as Registry of the Tribunal. The Parties filed their written pleadings in accordance with the timetable set forth in the Rules of Procedure. No request for an oral hearing was made by either Party or sought by the Tribunal.

Questions Submitted to Arbitration

The Arbitration Agreement posed the following questions:

> 1. To what extent is Dutch legislation and the decision-making power based thereon in respect of the use, restoration, adaptation and modernisation of railway lines on Dutch territory applicable, in the same way, to the use, restoration, adaptation and modernisation of the historical route of the Iron Rhine on Dutch territory?
>
> 2. To what extent does Belgium have the right to perform or commission work with a view to the use, restoration, adaptation and modernisation of the historical route of the Iron Rhine on Dutch territory, and to establish plans, specifications, and procedures related to it according to Belgian law and the decision-making power based thereon? Should a distinction be drawn between the requirements, standards, plans, specifications, and procedures related to, on the one hand, the functionality of the rail infrastructure in itself and, on the other hand, the land use planning and the integration of the rail infrastructure, and, if so, what are the implications of this? Can the Netherlands unilaterally impose the building of underground and above-ground tunnels, diversions, and the like, as well as the proposed associated construction and safety standards?

3. In the light of the answers to the previous questions, to what extent should the cost items and financial risks associated with the use, restoration, adaptation and modernisation of the historical route of the Iron Rhine on Dutch territory be borne by Belgium or by the Netherlands? Is Belgium obliged to fund investments over and above those that are necessary for the functionality of the historical route of the railway line?

The Arbitration Agreement requested the Tribunal "to render its decision on the basis of international law, including European law if necessary, while taking into account the Parties' obligations under Article 292 of the EC Treaty."

Award of the Tribunal

Legal Basis and Scope of Belgium's Transit Right

The Tribunal began by considering the applicable rules and principles relevant to the basis and scope of Belgium's right of transit. These included the relevant provisions of the Treaty of Separation,[2] the Iron Rhine Treaty,[3] and the arrangements concerning ownership of the railway lines on Belgian and Netherlands territory. The Treaty of Separation was concluded in Dutch and French.[4] The Tribunal noted the particular importance of Article XII of the Treaty of Separation, of which the Tribunal set out its own translation:

> In the case that in Belgium a new road would have been built or a new canal dug, which would lead to the Maas facing the Dutch canton of Sittard, then Belgium would be at liberty to ask Holland, which in that hypothesis would not refuse it, that the said road, or the said canal be extended in accordance with the same plan, entirely at the cost and expense of Belgium, through the canton of Sittard, up to the borders of Germany. This road or canal, which could be used only for commercial communication, would be constructed, at the choice of Holland, either by engineers and workers whom Belgium would obtain authorization to employ for this purpose in the canton of Sittard, or by engineers and workers whom Holland would supply, and who would execute the agreed works at the expense of Belgium, all without any burden to Holland, and without prejudice to the exclusive rights of sovereignty over the territory which would be crossed by the road or canal in question.
>
> The two Parties would set, by common agreement, the amount and the method of collection of the duties and tolls which would be levied on the said road or canal.

Concerning the applicable principles of interpretation, the Tribunal highlighted the importance of "the problem of intertemporality" in the interpretation of certain phrases contained in Article XII of the 1839 Treaty of Separation.[5] It also paid particular attention to principles of international environmental law, noting that "both international and EC law require the integration of appropriate environmental measures in the design and implementation of economic development activities."[6] Having regard to Principle 4 of the Rio Dec-

[2] Award, paras. 30–36.
[3] Award, paras. 37–39.
[4] Award, para. 32.
[5] Award, para. 57.
[6] Award, paras. 57, 59.

laration on Environment and Development, the Tribunal held that "[e]nvironmental law and the law on development stand not as alternatives but as mutually reinforcing, integral concepts, which require that where development may cause significant harm to the environment there is a duty to prevent, or at least mitigate, such harm."[7] The Tribunal applied these principles in its interpretation of the disputed elements of Article XII of the Treaty of Separation.

The Treaty of Separation did not deal expressly with the question of modernization and adaptation of the line. The Parties disagreed as to whether the Belgian request was a request for a new road or canal or railway line to be extended across the Netherlands within the meaning of Article XII, or whether it was a request for the adaptation of a transit right already in existence under Article XII. The Netherlands contended that the work needed for the Belgian reactivation was so substantial that it amounted to a request for the extension of a new railway on Belgian territory on to Netherlands territory. For the Netherlands, therefore, the Article XII provisions on the costs applied. Belgium assimilated its request to the maintenance of an existing line, for which the costs were to be borne by the Netherlands under Article XI of the Treaty of Separation.[8] By applying the rule of intertemporal law and the principle of effectiveness, the Tribunal held that Article XII continued to apply to upgrading and improvements. It concluded that a request for reactivation of a line long dormant, with a considerably increased freight capacity, was not a mere matter of maintenance of the existing railway line, nor was it to be regarded as a request for a new line.[9]

The Tribunal interpreted the phrase "[w]ithout prejudice to the exclusive rights of sovereignty over the territory which would be crossed by the road or canal in question"[10] in accordance with the object and purpose of the Treaty of Separation. It held that the Netherlands had forfeited no more sovereignty than that which was necessary for the track to be built and to operate to allow a commercial connection from Belgium to Germany across Limburg.[11] The Tribunal held that designation of any territory over which the historic route ran as a nature reserve did not in theory constitute a limitation of the right of transit. There was therefore no legal obligation for the Netherlands to have consulted Belgium prior to such designation.[12]

The Role of European Law in the Arbitration

The Tribunal held that the combined effect of Articles 292, 227, and 239 of the EC Treaty was to establish the exclusive competence of the European Court of Justice ("ECJ") "to ensure that in the interpretation and application of [the EC Treaty] the law is observed."[13] It noted that, if Member States submit to a "non-EC" tribunal a legal dispute that requires that tribunal to interpret or apply provisions of EC law, proceedings may be instituted against them by the European Commission for violation of Article 292 of the EC Treaty.[14]

---

[7] Award, para. 59.
[8] Award, paras. 74–75.
[9] Award, paras. 75–84.
[10] Award, paras. 85–96.
[11] Award, para. 87.
[12] Award, para. 95.
[13] Award, para. 101, *citing* Art. 220 of the EC Treaty.
[14] Award, para. 101.

The Tribunal then considered Article 234 of the EC Treaty, pursuant to which a national court faced with the interpretation of EC law may, and in certain cases shall, request the ECJ to give a preliminary ruling. It noted ECJ jurisprudence on the discretion of the national court in deciding whether to request a preliminary ruling and the circumstances in which such a request may be rejected by the ECJ.[15] The Tribunal considered itself to be "in a position analogous to that of a domestic court within the EC"[16] and that "not all mention of EC law brings with it the duty to refer."[17] It took guidance from ECJ and domestic jurisprudence, according to which national courts are under an obligation to refer a question to the ECJ if the interpretation of EC law is necessary to enable them to decide the case under consideration.[18]

On this basis, the Tribunal considered whether the interpretation of EC law was necessary in order for the Tribunal to decide the dispute in relation to the issues of EC law in dispute between the Parties, which were: (i) the system of Trans-European Networks ("TEN"); and (ii) European environmental legislation.[19]

Concerning the TEN system, the Tribunal noted that the Iron Rhine railway had been earmarked as a priority project within the system of Trans-European Networks provided for in Articles 154 to 156 of the EC Treaty.[20] The Tribunal held that the TEN system did not give any rights to Belgium going beyond the right of transit claimed by it under Article XII of the Treaty of Separation.[21] It therefore concluded that the inclusion of the Iron Rhine railway as a priority project in the TEN system did not engage the exclusive competence of the ECJ, because the points of law put forward by the Parties were not conclusive for the task of the Tribunal.[22]

The second disputed EC law aspect of the case turned on the fact that the Netherlands had designated the Meinweg area, through which the historic route of the Iron Rhine railway ran, as a special area of conservation under Council Directive No. 92/43/EEC of May 21, 1992, on the conservation of natural habitats and of wild fauna and flora ("Habitats Directive").[23] The Netherlands had also identified the Meinweg as a national park and as a "Silent Area" under its domestic legislation, making it necessary in its view to build a tunnel in that area should the Iron Rhine railway be reactivated.[24] The Tribunal considered whether it had to engage in the interpretation of the Habitats Directive in order to decide the issue of the reactivation of the Iron Rhine railway and the costs involved.[25] It did so by examining whether

[15] Award, para. 102, *citing* Case C-373/95, Maso, Gazzetta *et al.* v. Istituto Nazionale della Previdenza Sociale (INPS), 1997 E.C.R. I-4051, para. 26; Case C-186/90, Durighello v. Istituto Nazionale della Previdenza Sociale (INPS), 1991 E.C.R. I-5773, para. 9.

[16] Award, para. 103.

[17] Award, para. 104, *citing* Case 283/81, Srl CILFIT and Lanificio di Gavardo SpA v. Ministero della Sanità, 1982 E.C.R. 3415.

[18] Award, para. 105, *citing* H.P. Bulmer Ltd. v. J. Bollinger SA, Court of Appeal (Civil Division), [1974] 2 C.M.L.R. 91, [1974] 2 All E.R. 1226.

[19] Award, paras. 105–106.

[20] Award, paras. 107–120.

[21] Award, para. 117.

[22] Award, para. 119.

[23] Award, para. 128.

[24] Award, para. 128.

[25] Award, para. 121.

it would arrive at different conclusions on the application of Article XII of the Treaty of Separation to the Meinweg tunnel project if the Habitats Directive did not exist. It found that its decision would be the same under both Article XII and Netherlands environmental legislation alone.[26] Thus, the questions of EC environmental law in the case did not "trigger any obligations under Article 292 of the EC Treaty."[27]

The Belgian Request for Reactivation and the Memorandum of Understanding

In reviewing the circumstances preceding the signature of the MoU,[28] the Tribunal found that the position of the Netherlands with respect to Belgium's interest in the future use of the Iron Rhine railway had consistently been based on two principles: (i) the Netherlands did not contest Belgium's right of transit with respect to the Iron Rhine railway; and (ii) any reactivation of the Iron Rhine railway must comply with Netherlands legislation, particularly legislation concerning the protection of the environment.[29]

After setting out the content of the MoU, the Tribunal determined its legal significance.[30] The Tribunal noted that, while the Parties agreed that the MoU was not a binding instrument as a matter of international law, they did not treat it as legally irrelevant.[31] The Tribunal held, therefore, that the principles and procedures laid down in the MoU remained to be interpreted and implemented in good faith, and provided useful guidelines to the Parties' interpretation of both Article XII of the Treaty of Separation and the Iron Rhine Treaty.[32]

The Measures Envisaged by the Netherlands in light of Article XII of the Treaty of Separation

The Tribunal reviewed the applicable legislation and decision-making procedures in the Netherlands, notably, the *Wet Geluidhinder* ("Noise Abatement Act") and legislation on the protection of the natural environment.[33] The exact measures to be prescribed for the reactivation of the Iron Rhine railway on Netherlands territory were still uncertain. The Tribunal therefore examined the measures that had been the specific focus of the arguments of both Parties, which measures were set out in a preparatory document ("Draft Order") that had been prepared by the Netherlands' infrastructure manager in July 2003.[34]

The Draft Order described the route of the Iron Rhine railway over Netherlands territory in four track segments, labeled A to D from west to east; for each segment, it also described in detail all the measures to be taken for the long-term reactivation of the Iron Rhine railway.[35] The Tribunal found that the Parties had agreed, in principle, to reroute the track in

---

[26] Award, para. 137.
[27] Award, para. 137.
[28] Award, paras. 143–153.
[29] Award, para. 151.
[30] Award, paras. 154–158.
[31] Award, paras. 156–157.
[32] Award, para. 157.
[33] Award, paras. 167–182.
[34] Award, paras. 183–201.
[35] Award, paras. 184–185, *and see* text accompanying notes 61–66, *infra*.

segment C to avoid the centre of the town of Roermond, through which the historic route ran.[36]

The main sources of disagreement between the Parties were the proposed measures for nature protection in segments A and D, and those for noise abatement along the entire length of the track. The Netherlands had designated the Meinweg area in segment D and the Weerter-en Budelerbergen in segment A as specially protected natural areas.[37] As a result, more costly measures of protection were envisaged for those sections of the historic track, including the building of a tunnel in the Meinweg area.[38] Belgium did not contest the Netherlands' right to make these designations but disagreed as to the financial consequences for the Parties.[39] It submitted that the Netherlands' application of its noise abatement legislation amounted to an unnecessary interference with Belgium's right of transit.[40]

The Tribunal held that Article XII of the Treaty of Separation did not require the Netherlands to apply its national legislation more favorably to the Iron Rhine railway than to other railways in the Netherlands, unless such non-discriminatory application would amount to a denial of Belgium's transit right or rendered the exercise of that right unreasonably difficult.[41] It concluded that the measures envisaged by the Netherlands could not be regarded as a denial of Belgium's transit right, nor did they render the exercise of that right unreasonably difficult.[42] It was not disputed that the measures envisaged by the Netherlands flowed exclusively from the application of the Netherlands' national legislation. The Tribunal therefore did not find it necessary to address any issue of EC law.[43]

Allocation of Costs

The Tribunal observed that the 1839 Treaty of Separation did not refer to "financial risks" – the term that the Parties used, without explaining its meaning, in their third question. The Tribunal took the view that the Party that bore the costs would also have to bear the financial risks.[44]

Belgium contended that its obligation to bear expenses under Article XII of the Treaty of Separation related to the *construction* of a railway on Netherlands territory as a prolongation of a new railway on Belgian territory, but not to the exercise of Belgium's right of transit.[45] It argued that the exercise of the right of transit was subject only to moderate toll fees.[46] According to Belgium its present request for reactivation did not amount to a request for a "new road" within the meaning of Article XII of the 1839 Treaty of Separation. Belgium also argued that the Netherlands had rendered impossible the use of the railway by dismantling parts of its infrastructure, by failing to provide for maintenance, and by interrupting works

---

36 Award, paras. 198–201.
37 Award, paras. 189, 194.
38 Award, paras. 191, 195, *and see* text accompanying notes 23–27, *supra*.
39 Award, paras. 193, 197.
40 Award, para. 187.
41 Award, para. 204.
42 Award, para. 205.
43 Award, para. 206.
44 Award, para. 209.
45 Award, para. 212. Emphasis in the original.
46 *Id.*

aimed at restoring the railway to a standard necessary for temporary use, and had thus violated Belgium's right of transit. Belgium concluded that the costs of restoring the historic route, which would not have arisen but for the Netherlands' violation of its obligations, should be borne by the Netherlands.[47]

The Netherlands submitted that Belgium's request for reactivation amounted to a request under Article XII of the Treaty of Separation for the extension of a new railway originating in Belgium into and over Netherlands territory, because reactivation required "a very considerable adaptation and modernization."[48] The Netherlands thus interpreted Article XII of the Treaty of Separation as requiring Belgium to bear the full costs incurred in connection with its request for adaptation and modernization of the existing infrastructure.[49]

The Tribunal observed that "although Article XII was directed towards the construction of, and regime for, the Iron Rhine, the right of transit there provided for also covered the reactivation of the track and its use through time."[50] A major adaptation and modernization of an existing railway must today include necessary environmental protection measures as an integral component of such a project.[51] Rules of international law on the protection of the environment were applicable law between the Parties in the interpretation of the conventional regime for the Iron Rhine railway.[52]

The Tribunal, however, held that "the financial burdens associated with the reactivation must not fall in such a way as effectively to prevent or render unreasonably difficult the exercise of Belgium's right of transit under Article XII of the 1839 Treaty of Separation."[53] These elements, taken together, suggested that the costs were not to be borne solely by Belgium as if the railway were "a new road"; but neither were they to be borne solely by the Netherlands. The financial obligations of the Parties therefore had to be subjected to careful balancing.[54]

The Tribunal noted that today, in international environmental law, a growing emphasis is being placed on the duty of prevention.[55] It observed, further, that much of international environmental law has been formulated by reference to the impact that economic activities of one State may have on the territory of another, whereas in the present case it was faced with the possible impact of the exercise of a treaty-guaranteed right of one State in the territory of another State. The Tribunal held that, in such circumstances, "by analogy, where a state exercises a right under international law, considerations of environmental protection also apply."[56] It concluded that the reactivation of the Iron Rhine railway could not be viewed in isolation from the environmental protection measures necessitated by the intended use of the railway line, which were to be fully integrated into the project and its costs.[57]

---

[47] Award, paras. 213, 214.
[48] Award, para. 217.
[49] *Id.*
[50] Award, paras. 219, 82–84.
[51] Award, para. 220.
[52] Award, paras. 220, 58–59.
[53] Award, para. 220.
[54] *Id.*
[55] Award, para. 223.
[56] *Id.*
[57] *Id.*

Rather than specifying the allocation of costs in monetary terms, the Tribunal indicated the relevant criteria and principles that the Parties should apply in making such allocation.[58] It held that Belgium had an obligation to fund the environmental element of the overall costs of the reactivation, which obligation was integral to the exercise of its right of transit. A reasonable interpretation of Article XII of the Treaty of Separation also required that, on those parts of the line where both Iron Rhine trains and Netherlands trains would pass, the Netherlands contribute to the total cost to the extent that those measures represented particular quantifiable benefits to the Netherlands.[59] In this sense, the Tribunal took into account the development of the Netherlands railway transport system ("autonomous development").[60] The Tribunal went on to apply these principles to each segment of the proposed line.[61]

With respect to the first part of segment A, namely, the line between the Belgian-Netherlands border and the junction with the railway line Eindhoven-Weert, the Tribunal concluded that the costs of reactivation were to be borne by Belgium.[62] With respect to the second part of segment A ("A2"), east of the junction with the railway line Eindhoven-Weert up to the municipality of Nederweert, the Tribunal held that, while the overall financial obligation was that of Belgium, certain costs caused by the anticipated development of the Netherlands railway transport envisaged for 2020 ("autonomous development") and quantifiable benefits to the Netherlands were to be taken into account in the apportioning of costs between the Parties.[63]

With regard to segment B, the line between the municipalities of Nederweert and Haelen, the Tribunal found that the current and planned use of the railway line was similar to that in segment A2; thus, it took the view that the costs of the reactivation of the railway line should also be apportioned between the Parties according to the same principles.[64] Segment C covered the municipalities of Swalmen and Roermond. The Tribunal found that, if a loop around Roermond deviating from the historic route was agreed, Belgium would be obliged to fund the amount that would have been required for the reactivation of the historic route in its current location, while the Netherlands would be obliged to bear costs incurred above that amount due to the rerouting of the line.[65]

The line in segment D, between the Asenrayerweg and the German-Netherlands border, had been out of use since 1991 and in the future was only to be used for the connection between Belgium and Germany. Belgium would therefore have to bear the cost of the reactivation of the track, specifically with respect to noise barriers to be built near dwellings and compensatory conservation measures. The major cost factor in this segment was the envisaged tunnel in the Meinweg, which was required due to the designation of the Meinweg as a nature reserve by the Netherlands. The Tribunal found that the construction of the tunnel was also required because of the intensive use envisaged by Belgium, of which Belgium had not informed the Netherlands in a timely fashion. It concluded that the costs of the tunnel in

---

[58] Award, para. 224.
[59] Award, para. 226.
[60] Award, para. 229.
[61] Award, para. 227, *and see* text accompanying note 35, *supra*.
[62] Award, para. 228.
[63] Award, para. 230.
[64] Award, para. 231.
[65] Award, para. 232.

the Meinweg should be apportioned equally between the Parties, as both Parties had contributed to the occurrence of a situation which now required much more costly measures.[66]

The Tribunal recommended that the Parties set up, within four months of the date of the Award, a committee of independent experts, which would be tasked to determine, within six months of its establishment:

1. the costs of the reactivation of the Iron Rhine railway;
2. the costs of the autonomous development; and
3. the particular, quantifiable financial benefits to the Netherlands of the reactivation.

The Tribunal instructed the Parties to use the findings of this committee to determine their respective shares of the costs associated with the upgrading of the Iron Rhine railway in segments A2 and B.

In the final chapter of its Award, the Tribunal set out the above findings in the form of "Replies of the Tribunal to the Questions put by the Parties."[67]

Interpretation of the Award of the Arbitral Tribunal

On July 25, 2005, Belgium submitted three Requests for Interpretation of the Award ("Requests"). The Netherlands submitted its comments on each of the Requests on August 15, 2005. On September 20, 2005, the Tribunal issued its responses to each of the Requests in the "Interpretation of the Award of the Arbitral Tribunal."

The first Request posed the following question:

> Should the Award be interpreted as meaning that the Netherlands is under the obligation to bring at its own expenses the Iron Rhine railway back to a level allowing for a use of the Iron Rhine comparable to the one that prevailed during the regular albeit light use of the line prior to discontinuation of such use in 1991?

The Tribunal responded that the allocation of costs of any agreed reactivation of the Iron Rhine Railway should include "the obligation of the Netherlands to bear that portion of the costs that represents the expenses that would have been incurred for outstanding maintenance of the track, including its safety features, to permit use comparable to the one that existed in 1991."[68] It ruled that the financial obligations of the Netherlands would relate to such safety standards as current Netherlands legislation would require and not as they may have been applicable in 1991.[69]

The second Request posed the following questions:

> Should the Award be interpreted as meaning that Belgium has no right to temporary use of the Iron Rhine line?
> Should the finding that the Netherlands' requirements may not amount to a denial of Belgium's right of transit nor render unreasonably difficult the exercise by Belgium of its right of transit

[66] Award, para. 234.
[67] Award, paras. 238–244.
[68] Award, para. 12.
[69] Award, para. 13.

(§§ 239(c) and 241(e)) be interpreted as applying to the issue of temporary use of the Iron Rhine, together with the Tribunal's findings on the principles and procedures laid down in the March 2000 MoU, contained in paragraphs 157 and 158 of the Award?

The Tribunal responded that the Award was not to be interpreted as meaning that Belgium had no right to temporary use, nor did the Award contain any pronouncement by the Tribunal upon the circumstances in which any such right may be exercised.[70] The Tribunal recalled its findings that the application of Dutch legislation and the decision-making powers based thereon may not amount to a denial of Belgium's right of transit over the historic route, nor render unreasonably difficult the exercise by Belgium of its right of transit.[71] It ruled that those findings were applicable to any use of the Iron Rhine.[72]

The third Request posed the following question:

Should the Tribunal's ruling on the apportionment of costs in segment C if a loop around Roermond is agreed, be interpreted as laying with Belgium the costs of a reactivation of the historic route through Roermond, when such costs result from measures required by the Netherlands after the award had been rendered, over and above those included in the figures presented to the Tribunal, the Dutch legislation of general application remaining unchanged?

The Tribunal responded that its ruling on the apportionment of costs in segment C, if a loop around Roermond was agreed,[73] was "to be interpreted as applicable to the scenario before it and not to any other hypothetical alternative."[74]

---

[70] Award, para. 18.

[71] *See* text accompanying notes 41–43, *supra.*

[72] Award, para. 21.

[73] *See* text accompanying note 65, *supra.*

[74] Award, para. 26.

Case Concerning Land Reclamation by Singapore In and Around the Straits of Johor

Parties: Malaysia/Singapore

Arbitration Agreement: 1982 United Nations Law of the Sea Convention

Arbitrators: Mr. M. Christopher W. Pinto (President), Dr. Kamal Hossain, Prof. Bernard Oxman, Prof. Ivan Shearer, Sir Arthur Watts KCMG QC[†]

Date of Award: September 1, 2005

Summary

Singapore carried out certain land reclamation works in the Straits of Johor – land reclamation works alleged to infringe Malaysia's rights in the area – Order for provisional measures issued by International Tribunal for the Law of the Sea – Parties requested Arbitral Tribunal to render an award on agreed terms – Arbitral Tribunal acceded to Parties' request.

Legal Subject Matters

Arbitration:
- Settlement

Oceans:
- Law of the sea
- International Tribunal for the Law of the Sea
  - Judges Ad Hoc
  - Provisional measures

Bibliography

Award published in:
- XXVII R.I.A.A. p. 133 (2007).

Commentary:
- Nico Schrijver, *Practising International Law at the International Tribunal for the Law of the Sea: The Case Concerning Land Reclamation In and Around the Straits of Johor (Malaysia v. Singapore), Application for Provisional Measures*, 6 Griffin's View on Int'l & Comp. L. p. 35 (2005);
- Jeremy Leong, *Singapore and Malaysia: Recent Bilateral Developments*, 24 Sing. L. Rev. p. 1 (2004).

[†] Deceased November 16, 2007.

Facts

A dispute arose between Malaysia and Singapore ("Parties") concerning certain land reclamation activities, carried out by Singapore in and around the Straits of Johor, that allegedly affected Malaysia's rights under the 1982 United Nations Convention on the Law of the Sea ("UNCLOS"). On July 4, 2003, Malaysia instituted proceedings against Singapore pursuant to Article 287 of UNCLOS and Article 1 of Annex VII to UNCLOS ("Annex VII"). In its Notification of July 4, 2003, Malaysia appointed Dr. Kamal Hossain as an arbitrator. On July 29, 2003, Singapore appointed Professor Bernard H. Oxman as an arbitrator.

On September 5, 2003, Malaysia transmitted to the International Tribunal for the Law of the Sea ("ITLOS") a request for provisional measures under Article 290 of UNCLOS. Because ITLOS did not include upon the bench judges of the nationalities of the Parties, Dr. Hossain, chosen by Malaysia, and Professor Oxman, chosen by Singapore, were admitted to sit as judges *ad hoc* in the case on September 24, 2003. On October 8, 2003, following a hearing held at the facilities of ITLOS in Hamburg, Germany, ITLOS issued an Order ("Order") prescribing certain procedural measures "pending a decision by the Annex VII arbitral tribunal."[1] In the Order, ITLOS directed the Parties to enter into consultations in order to

> (a) establish promptly a group of independent experts with the mandate
> (i) to conduct a study, on terms of reference to be agreed by Malaysia and Singapore, to determine, within a period not exceeding one year from the date of this Order, the effects of Singapore's land reclamation and to propose, as appropriate, measures to deal with any adverse effects of such land reclamation;
> (ii) to prepare, as soon as possible, an interim report on the subject of infilling works in Area D at Pulau Tekong;
> (b) exchange, on a regular basis, information on, and assess risks or effects of, Singapore's land reclamation works;
> (c) implement the commitments noted in this Order and avoid any action incompatible with their effective implementation, and, without prejudice to their positions on any issue before the Annex VII arbitral tribunal, consult with a view to reaching a prompt agreement on such temporary measures with respect to Area D at Pulau Tekong, including suspension or adjustment, as may be found necessary to ensure that the infilling operations pending completion of the study referred to in subparagraph (a)(i) with respect to that area do not prejudice Singapore's ability to implement the commitments referred to in paragraphs 85 to 87.

In the Order, ITLOS also directed Singapore not to conduct its land reclamation in ways that might cause irreparable prejudice to the rights of Malaysia or serious harm to the marine environment, taking especially into account the reports of the group of independent experts.[2]

Following issuance of the ITLOS Order, the Parties established the group of independent experts ("GOE"), and the President of ITLOS, acting pursuant to Article 3(e) of Annex VII, appointed Mr. Christopher Pinto (President), Prof. Ivan Shearer, and Sir Arthur Watts KCMG QC as further members of the Annex VII arbitral tribunal ("Tribunal").

The GOE submitted its report to the Parties on November 5, 2004, and completed its work with a presentation to the Parties on December 22, 2004.

---

[1] Order, *Dispositif*, para. 1.

[2] *Id.*, para. 2.

The Tribunal met with the Parties on January 10, 2005. At that meeting, the Parties informed the Tribunal that they had agreed *ad referendum* on the text of a draft Settlement Agreement. By letter dated May 18, 2005, the Parties notified the Tribunal that the Settlement Agreement had been signed on April 26, 2005. The Settlement Agreement entered into force in accordance with its terms.

Question Submitted to Arbitration

Whether certain land reclamation activities carried out by Singapore in and around the Straits of Johor infringed Malaysia's rights under UNCLOS.

Award on Agreed Terms

With respect to the dispute submitted by Malaysia to the Tribunal on July 4, 2003, the Settlement Agreement provided:

> 13. This Agreement is in full and definitive settlement of the dispute with respect to the land reclamation and all other issues related thereto. The Parties agree that the issue pertaining to the maritime boundaries be resolved through amicable negotiations, without prejudice to the existing rights of the Parties under international law to resort to other pacific means of settlement.
> 14. This Agreement accordingly terminates the *Case Concerning Land Reclamation by Singapore In and Around the Straits of Johor (Malaysia v. Singapore)* upon the agreed terms.
> 15. The Parties shall forthwith jointly request that the Arbitral Tribunal in the *Case Concerning Land Reclamation by Singapore In and Around the Straits of Johor (Malaysia v. Singapore)* adopt the terms of this Agreement in the form of an agreed Award which is final and binding upon the Parties.

The Tribunal acceded to the joint request by the Parties and delivered a final Award binding upon the Parties in the terms set out in the Settlement Agreement.[3] It did so by attaching the text of the Settlement Agreement as an Annex to the Award.

Settlement Agreement

The Parties agreed on the actions to be taken by Singapore relating to the land reclamation works, as recommended in the GOE report, including the compensation of Malaysian fishermen.[4] Singapore reassured Malaysia that the Pulau Tekong reclamation would not adversely affect the safe and smooth passage of ships through Kuala Johor and Calder Harbour.[5] The Parties agreed to expand the terms of reference of the Malaysia-Singapore Joint Committee on the Environment ("MSJCE") to include monitoring activities.[6]

The Settlement Agreement was in full and definitive settlement of the dispute with respect to the land reclamation and all other issues related thereto. The Parties agreed that the

[3] Award on Agreed Terms, *Dispositif*, para. 2.
[4] Annex, paras. 1–7.
[5] Annex, para. 8.
[6] Annex, paras. 9–12.

issue pertaining to the maritime boundaries be resolved through amicable negotiations, without prejudice to the existing rights of the Parties under international law to resort to other pacific means of settlement.[7] The Agreement accordingly terminated the *Case Concerning Land Reclamation In and Around the Straits of Johor (Malaysia v. Singapore)* upon the agreed terms.[8] Annexed to the Settlement Agreement was a map showing the location of the land reclamation activities.

[7] Annex, para. 14.
[8] Annex, para. 15.

Barbados / Republic of Trinidad and Tobago

Parties:	Barbados/Republic of Trinidad and Tobago
Arbitration Agreement:	Article 286 of the 1982 United Nations Convention on the Law of the Sea
Arbitrators:	Judge Stephen M. Schwebel (President), Mr. Ian Brownlie CBE QC, Prof. Vaughan Lowe, Prof. Francisco Orrego Vicuña, Sir Arthur Watts KCMG QC[†]
Date of Award:	April 11, 2006

Summary

Maritime delimitation of continental shelf and exclusive economic zone ("EEZ") of Barbados and the Republic of Trinidad and Tobago – delimitation carried out according to provisional distance line adjusted for relevant circumstances – Barbados claimed an adjustment in the west to allow for traditional fishing in waters off Tobago – claim of Barbados rejected – Parties in agreement as to delimitation in central sector – provisional equidistance line in the east adjusted to take account of the lengths of the coasts of the Parties – Tribunal lacking jurisdiction to make an order concerning fisheries access by Barbados to EEZ of Trinidad and Tobago.

Legal Subject Matters

Oceans:
- Law of the sea
  - Maritime delimitation
  - Access to resources

Settlement of disputes:
- Arbitration
  - Jurisdiction of the arbitral tribunal

Sources of international norms:
- Treaties
  - Interpretation

[†] Deceased November 16, 2007.

Bibliography

Award published in:

- The Barbados/Trinidad and Tobago Arbitration Award of 2006 (Permanent Court of Arbitration Award Series, TMC Asser Press 2009);
- 45 I.L.M. p. 800 (2006);
- XXVII R.I.A.A. p. 147 (2007).

Commentary:

- Bernard H. Oxman, *The Law of Maritime Delimitation: Back to the Future*, *in* The Barbados/Trinidad & Tobago Arbitration Award of 2006 (Permanent Court of Arbitration Award Series, TMC Asser Press 2009);
- Andon Blake & Gary A. Campbell, *Conflict over Flying Fish: The Dispute Between Trinidad & Tobago and Barbados*, 31 Marine Pol'y p. 327 (2007);
- Barbara Kwiatkowska, *The Landmark 2006 UNCLOS Annex VII Barbados/Trinidad and Tobago Maritime Delimitation (Jurisdiction and Merits) Award*, 39(3) Geo. Wash. Int'l L. Rev. p. 573 (2007);
- Barbara Kwiatkowska, *The 2006 Barbados/Trinidad and Tobago Maritime Delimitation (Jurisdiction and Merits) Award*, *in* Law of the Sea, Environmental Law and Settlement of Disputes: Liber Amicorum Judge Thomas A. Mensah (Nijhoff 2007);
- Barbara Kwiatkowska, *The 2006 UNCLOS Annex VII "Barbados/Trinidad and Tobago" Award: Landmark Progress in Compulsory Jurisdiction and Equitable Maritime Boundary Delimitation*, 19 Hague Y.B. Int'l L. p. 33 (2007);
- Barbara Kwiatkowska, *Barbados/Trinidad and Tobago: Award on Jurisdiction and Merits: UN Convention on the Law of the Sea Annex VII Arbitral Tribunal, April 11, 2006*, 101 Am. J. Int'l L. p. 149 (2007);
- Barbara Kwiatkowska, *The 2006 Barbados/Trinidad and Tobago Award: A Landmark in Compulsory Jurisdiction and Equitable Maritime Boundary Delimitation*, 22 Int'l J. Marine & Coastal L. p. 7 (2007);
- Clifford E. Griffin, *Friends versus Interests: Strategic Rationality in the Barbados-Trinidad and Tobago Maritime Dispute*, *in* Intervention, Border & Maritime Issues in CARICOM (2007);
- David A. Colson, *Permanent Court of Arbitration (PCA): In the Matter of an Arbitration Between: Barbados and the Republic of Trinidad and Tobago (April 11, 2006)*, 45 I.L.M. p. 798 (2006);
- Yoshifumi Tanaka, *Arbitral Tribunal Award, Annex VII Law of the Sea Convention: Barbados v. Trinidad and Tobago*, 21(4) Int'l J. Marine & Coastal L. p. 523 (2006);
- Phillippe Weckel & Guillaume Aerou, *Sentence du 11 mai 2006, Délimitation de la ZEE et du plateau continental (Barbade c. Trinité-et-Tobago)*, 3 RGDIP p. 713 (2006).

Facts

Over a period of some three decades up to 2004, Barbados and the Republic of Trinidad and Tobago (the "Parties") held high-level diplomatic meetings and conducted negotiations concerning the use of resources in the maritime spaces they were claiming. In February 1978, Barbados adopted an "Act to provide for the establishment of Marine Boundaries and Jurisdiction" for the purpose of extending its jurisdiction beyond its territorial sea, and in order to claim its EEZ and the rights appertaining thereto. In 1986, Trinidad and Tobago adopted the "Archipelagic Waters and Exclusive Economic Zone Act" in order to define Trinidad and Tobago as an archipelagic state, and to claim its EEZ in accordance with the 1982 United Nations Convention on the Law of the Sea ("UNCLOS"). On several occasions during the period 1988 to 2004, Trinidad and Tobago arrested Barbadians fishing off Tobago and accused them of illegal fishing. Following a series of bilateral negotiations from July 2000 to November 2003, the Parties agreed to hold further negotiations in February 2004. On February 6, 2004, Trinidad and Tobago arrested Barbadian fisherfolk and accused them of illegal fishing.

On February 16, 2004, Barbados filed a Notice of Arbitration and Statement of Claim pursuant to Article 286 of UNCLOS. In its Notice of Arbitration, Barbados appointed Professor Vaughan Lowe as a member of the arbitral tribunal to be constituted under Annex VII of UNCLOS. Trinidad and Tobago subsequently appointed Mr. Ian Brownlie CBE QC. The remaining three members of the Tribunal, duly appointed in accordance with Article 3 of Annex VII, were Judge Stephen M. Schwebel, Professor Francisco Orrego Vicuña, and Sir Arthur Watts KCMG QC. On April 16, 2004, the PCA agreed to serve as Registry for the proceedings.

On August 23, 2004, the Tribunal met with the Parties and heard arguments from them on Trinidad and Tobago's application of August 17, 2004, for disclosure of certain information and documentation from Barbados. On December 23, 2004, Trinidad and Tobago filed a Statement of Preliminary Objections, in which it objected to the jurisdiction and admissibility of Barbados' claim and stated that these objections should be determined in the Tribunal's final Award. Hearings were held at the International Dispute Resolution Centre in London during the period October 17 to 28, 2005. On October 23, 2005, the Tribunal appointed a Hydrographer, Mr. David Gray, as an expert to assist the Tribunal pursuant to Article 11(4) of the Rules of Procedure.

Summary of Matters Submitted to Arbitration

1. The delimitation by a single unified maritime boundary line of the exclusive economic zone and continental shelf between Barbados and the Republic of Trinidad and Tobago, as provided under Articles 74 and 83 of UNCLOS; and
2. Jurisdiction of the Tribunal to carry out the above delimitation, in accordance with Article 283 of UNCLOS.

Award of the Tribunal

Jurisdiction

Trinidad and Tobago contested the jurisdiction of the Tribunal on the grounds that the negotiations between the Parties were ongoing and had been at an early stage when Barbados initiated arbitral proceedings.[1] Trinidad and Tobago argued that, for this reason, neither of the preconditions under Article 283(1) of UNCLOS, namely, (i) the existence of a dispute, and (ii) an exchange of views having taken place regarding settlement by negotiation or other peaceful means, had been met. According to Trinidad and Tobago, should the Tribunal hold that it does have jurisdiction to hear the dispute, then the dispute should also involve the continental shelf boundary beyond 200 nautical miles ("nm").[2]

[1] Award, paras. 73–79.
[2] Award, paras. 83–87.

According to Barbados, five years and nine rounds of unsuccessful negotiations, involving extensive but unproductive exchanges of views, had led it reasonably to conclude that a sufficient period of time had elapsed.[3] Barbados argued that the Tribunal lacked jurisdiction to make any determination with respect to Trinidad and Tobago's continental shelf, because the dispute submitted to the Tribunal did not relate to delimitation of any potential outer continental shelf entitlement beyond 200 nm of either of the Parties.[4]

Both Parties were, at all relevant times, parties to UNCLOS, and neither had made a written declaration choosing one of the particular means of dispute settlement set out in Article 287(1) of UNCLOS. Accordingly, the Tribunal recalled that, under Article 287(3) of UNCLOS, both Parties were deemed to have accepted arbitration in accordance with Annex VII of UNCLOS.[5] Neither Party had made declarations under Article 298 of UNCLOS, which allows States to exclude the operation of the procedures in Section 2 with respect to certain categories of disputes.[6]

The Tribunal took the view that the Parties had negotiated for a reasonable period of time, and that, no agreement having been reached, the Parties were under an obligation to resort to the dispute resolution procedures provided for in Part XV of UNCLOS.[7] The existence of a dispute was not precluded by the fact that the precise scope of the dispute had not been fully articulated, since the record indicated with reasonable clarity the scope of the legal differences between the Parties.[8] Nor was the existence of a dispute precluded by the fact that negotiations could theoretically have continued, since it was well established that the obligation to negotiate does not require the Parties to continue with negotiations that in advance show every sign of being unproductive.[9]

The Tribunal considered that the dispute before it included the extended continental shelf – that is, the continental shelf beyond 200 nm – since (i) it either formed part of, or was sufficiently closely related to, the dispute submitted by Barbados; (ii) the record of the negotiations showed that it was part of the negotiations; and (iii) in any event there was in law only a single "continental shelf" rather than an inner continental shelf and a separate extended or outer continental shelf.[10]

Maritime Delimitation: General Considerations

The Tribunal set out the guiding principles concerning maritime delimitation that the Parties had put forth, starting with the applicable law.[11] It also focused on the evolution of the legal approach to maritime delimitation in the EEZ and continental shelf, particularly the specific applicable criteria.[12] The continental shelf and the EEZ coexisted as separate institutions, and decisions on the determination of a single maritime boundary line had been

[3] Award, para. 69.
[4] Award, paras 80–82.
[5] Award, para. 191.
[6] Award, para. 192.
[7] Award, para. 195.
[8] Award, para. 198.
[9] Award, para. 199.
[10] Award, para. 213.
[11] Award, paras. 220–223.
[12] Award, paras. 228–233.

based on the agreement of the parties. However, State practice, with very few exceptions, had overwhelmingly resorted to the establishment of single maritime boundary lines, and courts and tribunals had endorsed this practice.[13] The Tribunal observed that the determination of the line of delimitation normally follows a two-step approach: first, the positing of a provisional line of equidistance; and second, the examination of this provisional line in the light of relevant circumstances, to determine whether it is necessary to adjust the provisional equidistance line in order to achieve an equitable result.[14] The process of achieving an equitable result being thus constrained by legal principle, the Tribunal concluded that it had both the right and the duty to exercise judicial discretion in order to achieve an equitable result.[15] The Tribunal then proceeded to undertake this process of delimitation in respect of the dispute submitted to it.[16]

Delimitation in the West: The Flyingfish Fishery and Barbados' Claim to Adjust the Equidistance Line

Trinidad and Tobago maintained that the provisional equidistance line in the west should be the line of delimitation.[17] Barbados maintained that the requisite equitable solution was to be achieved by application of the "equidistance/special circumstances" rule. The governing special circumstance was the fact that Barbadian fisherfolk had traditionally fished by artisanal methods off the island of Tobago, principally for "flyingfish, a species of pelagic fish that moves seasonally to the waters off Tobago."[18] Barbados based its claim on three core factual circumstances: (i) there was a centuries-old history of Barbadian artisanal fishing in the waters off Tobago; (ii) Barbadian fisherfolk, and the economy of Barbados, were critically dependent on the maintenance of access to that fishery; and (iii) the fisherfolk of Trinidad and Tobago did not fish in those waters for flyingfish and therefore did not depend on that fishery for their livelihoods.[19]

The Tribunal determined that the three core factual circumstances invoked by Barbados had not been proved, and therefore it was not necessary to decide whether the circumstances pleaded by Barbados were of the requisite character to fall within the "equidistance/special circumstances rule."[20] The Tribunal found confirmation of its conclusions in previous recognition by Barbados that its nationals were fishing in waters of the EEZ of Trinidad and Tobago, and that, insofar as they fished without the licensed permission of Trinidad and Tobago, they were subject to lawful arrest.[21] It also found recognition by Barbados of the EEZ of Trinidad and Tobago in the fishing agreement under negotiation on the eve of the initiation of these arbitral proceedings.[22] In the light of the foregoing analysis, the Tribunal

---

[13] Award, para. 235.
[14] Award, para. 242.
[15] Award, para. 244.
[16] Award, para. 245.
[17] Award, para. 246.
[18] Award, para. 247.
[19] Award, paras. 247–250.
[20] Award, para. 265.
[21] Award, para. 270.
[22] *Id.*

concluded that the equidistance line in the west should be the line of delimitation between Barbados and Trinidad and Tobago.[23]

The Tribunal concluded, further, that it did not have jurisdiction to make an award establishing a right of access for Barbadian fisherfolk to flyingfish within the EEZ of Trinidad and Tobago. Such an award would be outside the Tribunal's jurisdiction by virtue of the limitation set out in Article 297(3)(a) of UNCLOS and would be *ultra petita* in the context of the dispute submitted to the Tribunal.[24] However, both Parties had requested the Tribunal to express a view on the question of Barbadian fishing within the EEZ of Trinidad and Tobago. Trinidad and Tobago had requested the Tribunal "to find that there was no fishing by Barbados in the area claimed prior to the late 1970s."[25] It being common ground that the flyingfish migrate through the waters of both Parties, the Tribunal drew the attention of the Parties to Article 63(1) of UNCLOS. According to this provision, the Parties were under a duty "to agree upon the measures necessary to co-ordinate and ensure the conservation and development" of the flyingfish stocks.[26]

Both Parties had expressly stated before the Tribunal their willingness to find a reasonable solution to the dispute over access to flyingfish stocks. The Tribunal noted that "commitments made by Agents of States before international tribunals bind the State, which is thenceforth under a legal obligation to act in conformity with the commitment so made."[27] It therefore held that Trinidad and Tobago had assumed an obligation, which was consistent with its obligations under UNCLOS, to negotiate in good faith an agreement with Barbados. Such an agreement was to give Barbados access to fisheries within the EEZ of Trinidad and Tobago, subject to the right and duty of Trinidad and Tobago to conserve and manage the living resources within its jurisdiction.[28]

Central Segment of the Line: Equidistance not Disputed

The Parties did not argue for any adjustment of the provisional equidistance line in light of any relevant circumstance in the central segment of the delimitation line. This segment extended for 16 nm from Point D of Barbados' claim to Point A of Trinidad and Tobago's claim.[29] The equidistance line was accordingly agreed to in this short segment.[30]

Delimitation in the East

Barbados requested the Tribunal to determine a single maritime boundary for the EEZ and continental shelf of the Parties. Trinidad and Tobago objected to this request, on the basis that the continental shelf and the EEZ are separate institutions, but accepted that there was no reason for the Tribunal to draw different boundary lines for the EEZ and continental shelf within 200 nm of its own baselines. Accordingly, the Tribunal determined a single

---

[23] Award, para. 271.
[24] Award, para. 283.
[25] *Id.*
[26] Award, para. 285.
[27] Award, para. 291.
[28] Award, paras. 292–293.
[29] *See* Map I, between pages 12 and 13 of the Award, and Map II, between pages 14 and 15.
[30] Award, para. 294.

boundary line for the delimitation of both the continental shelf and the EEZ to the extent of the overlapping claims, without prejudice to the separate legal existence of the EEZ and the continental shelf.[31]

The Parties agreed that delimitation was to be effected by resort to the equidistance/ special circumstances method, whereby the Tribunal should consider whether there were relevant circumstances making departures from a provisional equidistance line necessary to attain an equitable solution.[32] Accordingly, the Tribunal examined in turn the relevant circumstances invoked by Trinidad and Tobago to justify the adjustment of the equidistance line in the east: (i) the projection of the relevant coasts and the avoidance of any cut-off effect or encroachment; (ii) the proportionality of relevant coastal lengths; and (iii) the regional implications of the delimitation.

The Tribunal accepted that coastal frontages were a circumstance relevant to delimitation and that their relative lengths could require an adjustment of the provisional equidistance line. This circumstance did not, however, require the drawing of a delimitation line in a manner mathematically determined by the exact ratio of the lengths of the relevant coastlines.[33] Barbados argued that, except for those basepoints affecting the equidistance line, Trinidad and Tobago's coastline had for the most part a southeasterly orientation facing away from the disputed area, and that this coastline could not be taken into account without refashioning nature.[34] According to the Tribunal, coastal frontages represented a circumstance relevant to delimitation to the extent they abutted as a whole on the disputed area by a radial or directional presence relevant to the delimitation. In this connection, the island of Trinidad had a coastal frontage that clearly abutted upon the disputed area, and this was also true of the coastline off the island of Tobago. Thus, these coastal frontages were a relevant circumstance to be taken into account in the adjustment of the equidistance line.[35]

Trinidad and Tobago asserted that the adjustment it claimed would lead to 49% of the overlapping EEZ entitlements being attributed to Barbados and 51% attributed to Trinidad and Tobago, a result that it considered equitable in the light of the test of proportionality and thus consistent with Article 74 of UNCLOS.[36] The Tribunal held that proportionality was a relevant circumstance to be considered in reviewing the equity of a tentative delimitation, and that the Tribunal's role was "to examine the final outcome of the delimitation effected, as the final test to ensure that equitableness is not contradicted by a disproportionate result."[37]

Trinidad and Tobago also invoked the effect of the delimitation for the region as a whole as a relevant circumstance. Trinidad and Tobago asserted that the delimitation between Trinidad and Tobago and Venezuela in the region south of Barbados, and that between France (Guadeloupe and Martinique) and Dominica in the region north of Barbados, needed to be considered as they represented "a recognition of a departure from the equidistance line in order to avoid a cut-off effect."[38] Trinidad and Tobago referred to the Treaty on the "Delimi-

[31] Award, para. 298.
[32] Award, para. 300.
[33] Award, paras. 327–328.
[34] Award, para. 330.
[35] Award, para. 331.
[36] Award, para. 335.
[37] Award, para. 337.
[38] Award, para. 340.

tation of Marine and Submarine Areas" of April 18, 1990, between Trinidad and Tobago and Venezuela (the "1990 Trinidad-Venezuela Agreement"). It contended that one purpose of the 1990 Trinidad-Venezuela Agreement, which was to allow Venezuela access to the Atlantic, would be impeded by an equidistance line delimitation between Trinidad and Tobago and Barbados in that area. Trinidad and Tobago also invoked the Agreement of September 7, 1987, between France and Dominica (the "1987 France-Dominica Agreement"), where a tentative equidistance line was adjusted to avoid a cut-off effect and to prevent Dominica and Martinique from being deprived of an outlet to the Atlantic.[39] Barbados contested the relevance of both these agreements.[40]

The Tribunal ruled that the 1987 France-Dominica Agreement had no relevance in the current dispute. It held that it was bound to take into account the 1990 Trinidad-Venezuela Agreement, "not as opposed in any way to Barbados or any other third country, but in so far as it determined what the maritime claims of Trinidad and Tobago might be."[41] Similarly, the Barbados/Guyana Joint Cooperation Zone Treaty dated December 2, 2003, which had been invoked by Barbados,[42] was *res inter alios acta* in respect of Trinidad and Tobago and as such could not influence the delimitation in the current dispute, except in so far as it would reflect the limits of Barbados' maritime claim.[43]

After examining the record of the conduct of the Parties in the area claimed by Trinidad and Tobago north of the equidistance line, the Tribunal did not consider that the activities of either Party, or the responses of each Party to the activities of the other, themselves constituted a factor that had to be taken into account in the drawing of an equitable delimitation line.[44]

Trinidad and Tobago's Claim to an Outer Continental Shelf

Trinidad and Tobago principally justified its claim to the adjustment of the equidistance line on the ground of an entitlement to a continental shelf out to the continental margin defined in accordance with Article 76(4)-(6) of UNCLOS. Trinidad and Tobago argued that its continental shelf extended to an area beyond 200 nm from its own baselines that lay within and beyond Barbados' 200 nm EEZ. Trinidad and Tobago asserted that its rights to the continental shelf could not be trumped by Barbados' EEZ.[45] The Tribunal concluded that it had jurisdiction to decide upon the delimitation of a maritime boundary in relation to that part of the continental shelf extending beyond 200 nm. However, the single maritime boundary determined by the Tribunal was such that, as between the Parties, there was no single maritime boundary beyond 200 nm. The Tribunal found that there was no need for it to deal with problems posed by the relationship in that maritime area of continental shelf and EEZ rights, and took no position on the substance of the problem posed by the argument advanced by Trinidad and Tobago.[46]

---

[39] Award, para. 342.
[40] Award, para. 343.
[41] Award, para. 347.
[42] Award, para. 103.
[43] Award, para. 349.
[44] Award, paras. 361–366.
[45] Award, para. 367.
[46] Award, para. 368.

The Adjustment of the Equidistance Line

The Tribunal found that there was one relevant circumstance invoked by Trinidad and Tobago that needed to be considered in order to determine whether it was necessary to adjust the equidistance line and, if so, where and to what extent. That circumstance was the existence of the significant coastal frontage of Trinidad and Tobago abutting directly upon the area to be delimited.[47]

The appropriate point of deflection of the equidistance line was located where the provisional equidistance line met the geodetic line that joined (a) the archipelagic baseline turning point on Little Tobago Island with (b) the point of intersection of Trinidad and Tobago's southern maritime boundary with its 200 nm EEZ limit.[48] This point gave effect to the presence of the coastal frontages of both the islands of Trinidad and Tobago.[49] The Tribunal drew the delimitation line from this point in a straight line in the direction of its terminal point, which was located at the point of intersection of Trinidad and Tobago's southern maritime boundary with its 200 nm EEZ limit. This intersection of the delimitation line with the Trinidad and Tobago-Venezuela agreed maritime boundary established the southernmost limit of the area claimed by Trinidad and Tobago. This terminal point marked the end of the single maritime boundary between Barbados and Trinidad and Tobago and of the overlapping maritime areas between the Parties.[50] In the Tribunal's view, this deflection respected the principle of proportionality in the drawing of the equidistance line,[51] and did not result in giving effect to the relevant coastal frontages in a manner that could itself be considered disproportionate. The bending of the equidistance line thus reflected a reasonable influence of the coastal frontages on the overall area of delimitation, with a view to avoiding reciprocal encroachments which would otherwise result in some form of inequity.[52]

The Tribunal then gave a verbal description of the maritime boundary and a list of the precise governing coordinates, with two illustrative maps.[53] The technical Report of the Tribunal's Hydrographer was appended to the Award.

---

[47] Award, para. 372.
[48] Award, para. 373.
[49] *Id.*
[50] Award, para. 374.
[51] Award, paras. 376–378.
[52] Award, para. 379.
[53] Award, paras. 381–382.

Eurotunnel Arbitration

Parties: 1. The Channel Tunnel Group Limited, 2. France-Manche S.A. v. 1. The Secretary of State for Transport of the Government of the United Kingdom of Great Britain and Northern Ireland, 2. Le Ministre de l'équipement, des transports, de l'aménagement du territoire, du tourisme et de la mer du gouvernement de la République Française

Arbitration Agreement: Article 19 of the Treaty Between the French Republic and the United Kingdom of Great Britain and Northern Ireland Concerning the Construction and Operation by Private Concessionaires of a Channel Fixed Link signed at Canterbury on February 12, 1986

Arbitrators: Prof. James Crawford SC (Chairman), Me Yves Fortier CC QC, H.E. Judge Gilbert Guillaume, The Rt. Hon. Lord Millett, Mr. Jan Paulsson

Date of Partial Award: January 30, 2007

Summary

Claimants constructed and operated a fixed link across the Channel between England and France pursuant to Concession Agreement with French and United Kingdom Governments – opening by France of hostel for refugees near terminal of fixed link – clandestine attempts by hostel inhabitants to reach the United Kingdom via fixed link – Claimants suffered loss and damage due to incursions – failure of French and United Kingdom Governments to prevent incursions – discrimination by Respondents in assistance given to other operators faced with clandestine incursions – United Kingdom Government imposed penalties on Claimants in respect of clandestine migrants gaining entry via Fixed Link – Respondents held liable for failure to prevent incursions – claim concerning discrimination rejected – United Kingdom liable for penalties imposed on Claimants – complaint that France allegedly subsidized ferry company SeaFrance ("SeaFrance claim") – SeaFrance claim rejected – deferral of question of quantification of damages to later stage.

Legal Subject Matters

Arbitration:
- Jurisdiction of the arbitral tribunal
  - Constitution

Law of treaties:
  - Interpretation
  - Interpretation of agreements between States and private entities

Principle of non-discrimination

State responsibility:
- Plurality of responsibility of States

Bibliography

Award published in:
- 132 I.L.R. p. 1.

Commentary:
- Mathias Audit, *Un arbitrage aux confins du droit international public: observations sur la sentence du 30 janvier 2007 opposant le Groupe Eurotunnel au Royaume-Uni et à la République française*, 3 Revue de l'Arbitrage p. 445 (2007);
- Jean-Marc Thouvenin, *L'arbitrage Eurotunnel*, 52 Annuaire français de droit international p. 199 (2006).

Facts

On April 2, 1985, the Government of the French Republic ("France") and the Government of the United Kingdom of Great Britain and Northern Ireland ("United Kingdom") (hereinafter, collectively, "Governments," "Principals," "Respondents") issued an Invitation to Promoters ("Invitation"). The Invitation called for tenders to develop, finance, construct, and operate a fixed link across the Channel between England and France ("Fixed Link"). On January 20, 1986, the Governments announced the selection of the Channel Tunnel Group Limited and France-Manche S.A. (hereinafter, collectively, "Claimants," "Concessionaires") as the Concessionaires of the Fixed Link in accordance with the terms of the Invitation.

On February 12, 1986, the Governments concluded the Treaty concerning the Construction and Operation by Private Concessionaires of a Channel Fixed Link ("Treaty of Canterbury"), which laid down the international legal framework to permit the construction and operation of the Fixed Link by private enterprise. Pursuant to the Treaty of Canterbury, an Intergovernmental Commission ("IGC") was created to supervise, in the name and on behalf of the Governments, all matters concerning the construction and operation of the Fixed Link. On March 14, 1986, the Parties signed the Concession Agreement, which granted the Claimants a concession to develop, finance, construct, and operate the Fixed Link. The Channel Fixed Link was opened in 1994, with terminal areas at Coquelles in the French *Département du Pas de Calais* and at Cheriton in the County of Kent.

In the autumn of 1999, France established a reception and accommodation centre for immigrants at Sangatte ("Sangatte Hostel"), approximately 2.5 kilometres from the Channel Tunnel entrance at Coquelles. From late 1999, increasing numbers of clandestine migrants, who were residents of the Sangatte Hostel, made attempts to reach the United Kingdom by breaking into the perimeter of the terminal site at Coquelles and seeking to smuggle themselves into shuttle trains bound for the United Kingdom. During the period from 1999 to October 2002, incursions by clandestine migrants frequently occurred at Coquelles, at the nearby Fréthun terminal belonging to the Société Nationale des Chemins de Fer Français ("SNCF"), and at the Port de Calais ferry terminal. From September 2000, the Claimants made requests to the French Government for the closure of the Sangatte Hostel. On July 12, 2002, the responsible French and British Ministers agreed in principle to the closing of the Sangatte Hostel. Following discussions between the two Governments and an agreement by the United Kingdom to allow the entry of many of its remaining residents, France closed the Hostel on December 30, 2002.

The United Kingdom introduced a civil penalty regime pursuant to the Immigration and Asylum Act 1999 ("civil penalty regime") in April 2000. Carriers held to be responsible under this regime were liable to a penalty of £2,000 for every clandestine migrant transported to the United Kingdom. From October 1, 2001, the civil penalty regime applied to the Claimants. The United Kingdom also rendered the Claimants liable for the costs of detention and removal in respect of persons brought to the United Kingdom via the Fixed Link who had been refused leave to enter or who were illegal entrants ("removal requirements").

In December 1999, the French cross-Channel sea link, the ferry company SeaFrance, was recapitalized with the approval of France. As part of the recapitalization plan, SeaFrance availed itself of certain benefits including a tax exemption scheme administered by France and a scheme for refunds of employers' social security contributions.

On December 17, 2003, the Claimants commenced arbitration proceedings against the United Kingdom and France pursuant to Clause 40 of the Concession Agreement. Clause 40.1 of the Concession Agreement provides that any dispute between the Parties relating to the application of the Concession Agreement shall be submitted to arbitration in accordance with the provisions of Article 19 of the Treaty of Canterbury. The Claimants sought compensation for alleged breaches by the Governments of the Concession Agreement, the Treaty of Canterbury, and certain related instruments, as well as alleged breaches of relevant rules of international law and of English and French laws.

The Claimants appointed Me Yves Fortier CC QC and Mr. Jan Paulsson as arbitrators. On February 11, 2004, France appointed H.E. Judge Gilbert Guillaume as an arbitrator. On February 16, 2004, the United Kingdom appointed the Rt. Hon. Lord Millett as an arbitrator. The arbitrators appointed by the Governments, with the agreement of the other two Party-appointed arbitrators, appointed Professor James Crawford as the Chairman of the Tribunal. The Parties agreed that the Permanent Court of Arbitration would act as the Registry for the proceedings.

On February 15, 2005, the Respondents filed an "Application to Hive Off Issues of Quantum to a Subsequent Phase of the Proceedings." The Tribunal acceded to the Respondents' request by letter dated April 1, 2005, reserving to a later stage the issue of quantification of compensable damages. Hearings for oral argument and witness examination were held in The Hague from May 8 to 13 and 15 to 18, 2006. The Tribunal rendered its Partial Award on January 30, 2007.

Summary of Matters Submitted to Arbitration

A. The "Sangatte claim," concerning:

(i) The Governments' alleged failure to protect the Fixed Link from multiple incursions and delays, damage, and expenses caused by large numbers of clandestine migrants resident in the Sangatte Hostel;

(ii) The Governments' alleged discrimination against the Fixed Link in favor of other operators faced with the clandestine migrant problem; and

(iii) The United Kingdom's alleged failure to meet its obligations in applying its civil penalty regime and in charging the costs of detention and removal of clandestine migrants arriving in the United Kingdom via the Fixed Link; and

B. The "SeaFrance claim," concerning the Governments' alleged granting, or failure to prevent the granting, of subsidies to SeaFrance, allowing it to compete with the Fixed Link on an unfair basis.

Award

The Tribunal dealt with the following preliminary questions before examining the issues of jurisdiction and merits.

Constitution of Tribunal for the Purpose of Interpreting the Treaty of Canterbury

The Parties disagreed as to whether, according to Article 19(2)(f) of the Treaty of Canterbury, the arbitrators appointed by the Concessionaires should take part in any decision of the Tribunal dealing with the interpretation of that Treaty. Article 19(2)(f) of the Treaty of Canterbury, so far as material, provides:

> The arbitrators appointed by the Concessionaires shall not participate in that part of any decision relating to the interpretation or application of the Treaty.

The Tribunal held that the purpose of Article 19(2)(f) was to prevent the Government-appointed arbitrators from being outvoted on an issue of interpretation of the Treaty of Canterbury,[1] and Article 19(2)(f) should be interpreted no more widely than necessary to give effect to this purpose.[2] The Tribunal held that, in deciding claims submitted to it, it may become necessary for the Tribunal to interpret the Treaty of Canterbury as such, "but it will be for the full Tribunal to decide whether it is necessary to do so in any given case."[3] In order to determine any question before it, including the question whether Article 19(2)(f) of the Treaty of Canterbury applied, the Tribunal had to be able to hear argument on and discuss the issue.[4]

Principles of Interpretation

The Parties agreed that the principles of interpretation laid down in the Vienna Convention on the Law of Treaties ("Vienna Convention") were declaratory of customary international law relating to agreements between States and private parties under international law, as well as that relating to agreements between States.[5] So far as linguistic discrepancies were concerned, the Tribunal was thus called upon to apply Article 33 of the Vienna Con-

---

[1] Partial Award, para. 87.
[2] Partial Award, para. 90.
[3] *Id.*
[4] *Id.*
[5] *Id.*

vention.[6] The Tribunal held that correspondence and other records of the negotiations could be referred to, with due caution, under Article 32 of the Vienna Convention.[7]

Jurisdiction and Applicable Law

In the Tribunal's view, there was no doubt that there was a subsisting dispute between the Claimants and both Respondents concerning the various aspects of the Sangatte claim.[8] However, the Tribunal held that there was no dispute between the Concessionaires and the United Kingdom concerning the SeaFrance claim at the time the arbitration proceedings were commenced; thus, the SeaFrance claim, to the extent directed against the United Kingdom, was outside its jurisdiction.[9]

Joint and Several Responsibility

The Claimants argued that the acts and omissions with respect to the Sangatte claim were attributable to France and the United Kingdom, both individually and collectively.[10] France argued that "if there is to be a responsibility that responsibility … has to be accepted jointly and severally."[11] The United Kingdom argued that the Claimants had to establish the specific responsibility of the United Kingdom for any alleged breach, and concluded that "there is no basis in international law for claims of joint liability or joint and several liability."[12]

The Tribunal addressed the issue in light of Article 47 of the International Law Commission ("ILC") Articles on State Responsibility, which provides:

> Plurality of responsible States
> 1. Where several States are responsible for the same internationally wrongful act, the responsibility of each State may be invoked in relation to that act.
> 2. Paragraph 1:
>   a. does not permit any injured State to recover, by way of compensation, any more than the damage it has suffered;
>   b. is without prejudice to any right of recourse against the other responsible States.

Citing the ILC commentary to Article 47, the Tribunal examined the terms of the Treaty of Canterbury and of the Concession Agreement to establish whether these established or implied "any general principle of solidary responsibility for breaches of obligation."[13] In this regard, whilst Clause 20 of the Concession Agreement provided for the joint and several liability of the Concessionaires to the Principals under the Concession Agreement, there was no equivalent provision concerning the responsibility of the Principals to the Concessionaires.[14] The Tribunal held that, "[t]o the extent that the Claimants' case depended on the

---

[6] Partial Award, para. 93.
[7] Partial Award, para. 94.
[8] Partial Award, para. 138.
[9] Partial Award, para. 143.
[10] Partial Award, para. 163.
[11] Partial Award, para. 170.
[12] Partial Award, para. 171.
[13] Partial Award, paras. 176–186.
[14] Partial Award, para. 176.

thesis of joint and several responsibility, namely, the *per se* responsibility of one State for the acts of the other, it must fail."[15] However, the core commitments towards the Concessionaires to permit the uninterrupted operation of the Fixed Link required the continuing cooperation of both Governments, directly and through the IGC. Whether breaches of the Concession Agreement resulted from the fault of one or the other or both States would depend on the particular obligation violated and on all the circumstances.[16]

The Merits of the Sangatte Claim

After summarizing the positions of the Parties,[17] the Tribunal examined each of the four bases of the Sangatte claim which had "at least an arguable foundation in the Concession Agreement," namely: (i) the failure to protect the Coquelles site against incursions; (ii) discrimination against the Fixed Link; (iii) breaches of French or English law; and (iv) the civil penalty regime and removal requirements.[18]

Failure to Protect the Coquelles Site Against Incursions

The Claimants alleged that the French Government's decision to establish the Sangatte Hostel, and the policy of keeping it open despite repeated requests – including requests from the United Kingdom – for closure, were unilateral measures in contravention of the Concession Agreement and the applicable law.[19] The Claimants also alleged that the Governments failed significantly to increase levels of policing and security so as to combat effectively the activities of clandestine migrants around the Coquelles terminal, despite requests for assistance from the Concessionaires to the French Government, to the United Kingdom Government concerning the United Kingdom control zone at Coquelles, and to the IGC.[20]

According to the Claimants, the Governments had undertaken "to ensure that … the construction and operation of the Fixed Link would not be interfered with in any way that would jeopardize the flow of revenues required" to finance the cost of the private investment.[21] The Claimants relied primarily[22] on Clause 2.1 and Clause 27 of the Concession Agreement. Clause 2.1 provides, in relevant part:

> The Principals shall, in a manner which they will endeavour to coordinate between them, adopt such legislative and regulatory measures, and take such steps, including approaches to international organisations, as are necessary for the development, financing, construction and operation of the Fixed Link in accordance with this Agreement … .

Clause 27 provides, in relevant part:

---

[15] Partial Award, para. 187.
[16] *Id.*
[17] Partial Award, paras. 194–273.
[18] Partial Award, para. 276.
[19] Partial Award, para. 194.
[20] Partial Award, para. 207.
[21] Partial Award, para. 218.
[22] Partial Award, para. 295.

> 27.1 In accordance with Article 10 of the Treaty, the Intergovernmental Commission is established to supervise, in the name and on behalf of the Principals, all matters concerning the construction and operation of the Fixed Link.
>
> ...
>
> 27.7 The Principals shall ensure that in the performance of their functions the Intergovernmental Commission and the Safety Authority shall take the necessary steps to facilitate the implementation of this Agreement. The Principals, the Intergovernmental Commission and the Safety Authority shall give due consideration to the reasonable commercial objectives of the Concessionaires, including the avoidance of unnecessary costs and delays.

The Governments argued that the Claimants had the primary responsibility for security and policing around the Coquelles site,[23] and that the Governments had accepted no positive obligation to act in such a way so as to safeguard the revenue flows of the Fixed Link.[24] They argued that the Claimants had accepted the risk for the security problems at Coquelles, in reliance on Clause 2.1 of the Concession Agreement. The Tribunal disagreed. It held that the Claimants had not assumed the risk of the Governments' failure to comply with their own commitments under the Concession Agreement.[25]

According to the Tribunal, the establishment of the Sangatte Hostel was well within the margin of appreciation of the French authorities.[26] Thus, neither the opening of the Sangatte Hostel, nor its operation in the period prior to September 13, 2000, amounted to a breach of the Concession Agreement.[27] However, in the Tribunal's view, by January 2001 at the latest, it should have been sufficiently clear to the Principals and the IGC that the Sangatte Hostel was being used as a base for criminal activity.[28] The Tribunal held that, under Clauses 2.1 and 27.1 of the Concession Agreement, the IGC should have taken the necessary steps to ensure the orderly operation of the Fixed Link; yet, "at crucial periods, the IGC sought to shift the whole burden of security on to Eurotunnel."[29]

The Tribunal held, further, that, although issues of policing outside the control zone were exclusively a matter for France, the overall responsibility for the security of the Fixed Link was shared and not divided. It was not the case that the United Kingdom was responsible for the security of the Fixed Link on its side of the boundary fixed by Article 3(1) of the Treaty of Canterbury, with France responsible on the continental side. Rather, both States shared that responsibility, and, under Clause 27.7, they had to ensure that the IGC took the necessary steps to facilitate the implementation of that Agreement, including Clause 2.1.[30]

The Tribunal concluded, in the circumstances of the clandestine migrant problem as it existed in the Calais region in the period from September 2000 to December 2002, that it was incumbent on the Principals, acting through the IGC and otherwise, to maintain conditions of normal security and public order in and around the Coquelles terminal; that they failed to take appropriate steps in this regard and thereby breached Clauses 2.1 and 27.7 of

---

[23] Partial Award, paras 227, 231.

[24] Partial Award, paras. 228–229, 232.

[25] Partial Award, para. 281.

[26] Partial Award, para. 306.

[27] Partial Award, para. 308.

[28] Partial Award, para. 309.

[29] *Id.*

[30] Partial Award, para. 317.

the Concession Agreement; and that the Claimants were entitled to recover the losses directly flowing from this breach.[31]

Favoring the SNCF Terminal and Port of Calais to the Detriment of the Fixed Link

The Claimants argued that the Governments, in breach of Clause 15.3 of the Concession Agreement, had treated other cross-Channel operators more favorably when they faced similar, or even lesser, problems.[32] The Tribunal, after examining Clauses 15.3 and 27.5 of the Concession Agreement, held that there was no general obligation on the Principals under the Concession Agreement to observe the principle of non-discrimination between different cross-Channel operators in respect of operational requirements such as security and safety.[33] It concluded that such differential treatment of the Fixed Link, compared with the SNCF terminal and the Port of Calais, as there may have been in the relevant period, was not in breach of the Concession Agreement.[34]

Breach of English or French Law

The Claimants argued that France had breached certain obligations of loyalty and protection owed to them under French law,[35] and that the United Kingdom had breached its obligations in connection with policing over the Fixed Link under a number of provisions of English law.[36] The Claimants relied on the second sentence of Clause 40.4 of the Concession Agreement, which provides:

> The rules of English law or the rules of the French law may, as appropriate, be applied when recourse to those rules is necessary for the implementation of particular obligations under English law or French law.

The Tribunal emphasized that international law, rather the law of either State, was the proper law of the Concession Agreement.[37] In the Tribunal's view, the Sangatte claim did not depend on "the implementation of particular obligations under English law or French law"; it depended on the Concession Agreement itself.[38] It was therefore unnecessary to consider whether the Claimants' interpretations of French and English law were correct.[39]

The United Kingdom's Civil Penalties and the Costs of Detention and Removal

The Claimants argued that, as a result of the extension of the civil penalties scheme, the Concessionaires found themselves paying effectively double for the Governments' failures

---

[31] Partial Award, para. 319.
[32] Partial Award, paras. 241–248.
[33] Partial Award, paras 321–324.
[34] Partial Award, para. 335.
[35] Partial Award, paras. 258–259.
[36] Partial Award, para. 261.
[37] Partial Award, para. 338.
[38] Partial Award, para. 339.
[39] Partial Award, para. 340.

to provide effective policing and security over the Fixed Link.[40] The Claimants also objected to their being made liable by the United Kingdom under the removal requirements.[41] The Claimants argued that to have imposed the removal requirements in respect of persons whose presence in the United Kingdom resulted from the failure of that State to maintain the security of the Fixed Link was unfair and compounded the breach represented by the first ground of the Sangatte claim.

The Tribunal addressed, first, the question whether the application of the civil penalty regime was a breach of the Concession Agreement so far as the Claimants were concerned.[42] The Tribunal noted that no penalties had ever been paid, and that the costs incurred by the Concessionaires in opposing them had been paid by the United Kingdom. Under these circumstances, the dispute over the Concessionaires' liability for civil penalties under the Concession Agreement remained an abstract one.[43]

The Tribunal turned, next, to the Claimants' objection to the removal requirements.[44] The Tribunal treated this claim as a possible head of damages rather than as a distinct basis for responsibility. It therefore deferred, until the quantum stage, the question whether some proportion of the costs of detention and removal should form part of the damages payable for the breaches of the Concession Agreement it had analyzed.[45]

Extent of Responsibility as between the Respondents

The Tribunal deferred until the second phase of the proceedings the quantum of the Claimants' loss, taking into account the conclusions it had reached and the questions whether and on what basis any damages should be apportioned as between the Respondents.[46]

The Merits of the SeaFrance Claim

The Claimants argued that the Respondents had unfairly and improperly sponsored competition with the Fixed Link by giving substantial financial support to the ferry company SeaFrance, in breach of Clause 34.3 of the Concession Agreement, the implied obligation of loyalty and protection *vis-à-vis* the Concessionaires, and relevant principles of international law.[47]

As noted, the Tribunal dismissed for want of jurisdiction the SeaFrance claim to the extent it was directed against the United Kingdom. In examining the merits of the SeaFrance claim against France, the Tribunal addressed the question whether the assistance given to SeaFrance was capable of violating any express provision of the Concession Agreement.[48]

---

[40] Partial Award, para. 264.
[41] Partial Award, para. 269.
[42] Partial Award, paras. 342–344.
[43] Partial Award, para. 344.
[44] Partial Award, paras. 345–350.
[45] Partial Award, para. 350.
[46] Partial Award, para. 351.
[47] Partial Award, para. 353.
[48] Partial Award, para. 368.

The Claimants relied primarily on Clause 34 of the Concession Agreement,[49] which provides, in relevant part:

> 34.1 The Concessionaires recognise that, in due course, the construction of a drive through link may become technically and financially viable. They undertake as a result to present to the Principals between now and the year 2000 a proposal for a drive through link which shall be added to the first link when technical and economic conditions for realisation of such a link shall permit it and the increase of traffic shall justify it without undermining the expected return on the first link.
>
> 34.2 The Principals undertake not to facilitate the construction of another fixed link whose operation would commence before the end of 2020. However, after 2010, and in the absence of agreement with the Concessionaires on the implementation of their proposal for the construction of a drive through link and as to its timetable, the Principals shall be free to issue a general invitation for the construction and operation of such a link. This new link shall not enter into operation before the end of 2020.
>
> ...
>
> 34.3 The Principals agree that throughout the Concession Period no link shall be financed with the support of public funds, either directly or by the provision of government guarantees of a financial or commercial nature.
>
> ...

The Tribunal noted that Clause 34 of the Concession Agreement was concerned with a second fixed link, namely, a drive-through link. It noted, further, that "no link of any kind was to be financed by public funds."[50] The context of Clause 34.3 was thus that of protection for the Concessionaires against a second fixed link.[51] The Tribunal observed that nowhere in the Treaty of Canterbury and the Concession Agreement were ferry services described as a link, and that Clause 34 had no relevance to the financial aid to SeaFrance of which the Claimants complained.[52] The Tribunal concluded that the SeaFrance claim failed in its entirety.[53]

Partially Dissenting Opinion of Lord Millett

Lord Millett dissented from the holding of the majority on the liability of the United Kingdom with respect to the Sangatte Claim.[54] In Lord Millett's opinion, the closure or securing of the Sangatte Hostel, which the Tribunal had held was necessary for the operation of the Fixed Link from September 2000 onwards, was something that only the French Government could do.[55] The United Kingdom had not been obliged to take the action it took in allowing a number of the migrants in the Sangatte Hostel to enter the United Kingdom, and its failure to do so earlier was not a breach of the Concession Agreement.[56]

---

[49] *Id.*

[50] Partial Award, para. 370.

[51] Partial Award, para. 375.

[52] Partial Award, para. 381.

[53] Partial Award, para. 394.

[54] Dissenting Opinion of Lord Millett [hereinafter "Dissenting Opinion"], para. 1.

[55] Dissenting Opinion, para. 5.

[56] Dissenting Opinion, para. 7.

As regards the failure to protect the Coquelles Terminal against mass incursions, Lord Millett agreed with the view of the majority[57] that the overall responsibility for the maintenance of public order and the security of the Fixed Link was shared by both Respondents, but held that each Respondent was separately and solely responsible for public order within its own territory – the United Kingdom in Kent and France in the Pas de Calais.[58] Lord Millett was of the opinion, further, that the IGC, not being a party to the Concession Agreement, owed no contractual obligations of its own to the Claimants and had no operational responsibilities.[59] Clause 27.7 and Clause 2.1 of the Concession Agreement each imposed obligations on both Respondents to take action, in the one case directly and in the other through the medium of the IGC, and here the breach of both Clause 27.7 and Clause 2.1 consisted of the failure of France to take the necessary action.[60]

In Lord Millett's view, France alone was capable of closing or securing the Sangatte Hostel and maintaining public order in the Pas de Calais.[61] The incidence of liability should therefore have been dealt with as part of the hearing on liability.[62] Similarly, in Lord Millett's opinion, the imposition by the United Kingdom of removal requirements was a breach for which the United Kingdom was solely responsible and which did not engage the liability of France.[63]

---

[57] *See* text accompanying note 31, *supra*.
[58] Dissenting Opinion, para. 10.
[59] Dissenting Opinion, para. 12.
[60] Dissenting Opinion, para. 18.
[61] Dissenting Opinion, para. 21.
[62] Dissenting Opinion, para. 28.
[63] Dissenting Opinion, para. 30.

Guyana / Suriname

Parties: Guyana/Suriname

Arbitration Agreement: 1982 United Nations Convention on the Law of the Sea

Arbitrators: H.E. Judge L. Dolliver M. Nelson (President), Prof. Thomas Franck, Dr. Kamal Hossain, Prof. Ivan Shearer, Prof. Hans Smit

Date of Award: September 17, 2007

Summary

Maritime delimitation between States with adjacent coasts – delimitation of territorial sea – special circumstances – delimitation by a single maritime boundary of continental shelf and exclusive economic zone according to an unadjusted equidistance line – exploratory oil drilling by Guyanese concession holder in area under dispute – concession holder ordered to leave disputed area by Surinamese navy – Surinamese naval action an illegal threat of use of force – request for compensation denied – obligations under Articles 74(3) and 83(3) of the United Nations Convention on the Law of the Sea pending delimitation to make provisional arrangements of a practical nature – both States in breach – declaratory relief granted – determination by expert in document production dispute – site visit by Tribunal expert.

Legal Subject Matters

Force:
- Threat of use of force

Oceans:
- Law of the sea
  - Maritime delimitation
  - Obligations pending final delimitation

Remedies:
- Declaratory relief
  - Just satisfaction
- State responsibility

Settlement of disputes:
- Arbitration
  - Jurisdiction of the arbitral tribunal

Sources of international norms:
- Treaties
  - Contemporaneity doctrine
  - Estoppel and acquiescence
  - Interpretation
  - Modification by conduct

Bibliography

Award published in:
- 47 I.L.M. p. 166 (2008).

Commentary:
- Gao Jianjun, *Comments on Guyana v. Suriname*, 8(2) CHINESE J. IN'TL L. p. 191 (2009);
- Alex G. Oude Elferink, *De zeegrenzen van Suriname in het licht van de arbitrage tussen Suriname en Guyana onder het Zeerechtverdrag van de Verenigde Naties* (Ministerie van Buitenlande Zaken van de Republiek Suriname 2008);
- Patricia Jimenez Kwast, *Maritime Law Enforcement and the Use of Force: Reflections on the Categorisation of Forcible Action at Sea in the Light of the Guyana/Suriname Award*, 13 J. CONFLICT & SEC. L. p. 49 (2008);
- Dominic Roughton, *Rights (and Wrongs) of Capture: International Law and the Implications of the Guyana/Suriname Arbitration*, 26 J. ENERGY & NAT. RESOURCES L. p. 374 (2008);
- Stephen Fietta, *Award: UN Convention on the Law of the Sea Annex VII Arbitral Tribunal, September 17, 2007*, 102(1) AM. J. INT'L L. p. 119 (2008).

Facts

Attempts to delimit the maritime boundary between Guyana and Suriname (the "Parties") date back to colonial times. In 1799, the border between Suriname and Berbice, a colony then situated in the eastern part of modern Guyana, was agreed by colonial authorities to run along the west bank of the Corentyne River. In 1936, a Mixed Boundary Commission established by the United Kingdom and the Netherlands, colonial predecessors of Guyana and Suriname, respectively, recommended that the northern end of the land boundary be fixed at a specific point on the west bank of the Corentyne River ("Point 61," the "1936 Point"); it concluded, further, that the maritime boundary in the territorial sea should be fixed at an azimuth of N10°E from Point 61 (the "10° Line") to the limit of the territorial sea, which was then three nautical miles ("nm"). Subsequent efforts to conclude a treaty on the maritime delimitation on this basis having failed, in 1966, shortly after Guyana achieved independence, the United Kingdom hosted direct negotiations between Guyana and Suriname referred to as the "Marlborough House talks." Those negotiations failed due to the Parties' inability to reach agreement on the location of the land boundary. In 1991, following further negotiations, the Parties provisionally agreed on the granting of oil concessions in the boundary area, and on joint exploration activities; this agreement, however, was never implemented. Guyana and Suriname ratified the 1982 United Nations Convention on the Law of the Sea ("UNCLOS," the "Convention") on November 16, 1993, and July 9, 1998, respectively.

A dispute arose in May 2000 regarding the activities of CGX Resources Inc. ("CGX"), the holder of an oil concession granted by Guyana, in the area subject to the Parties' overlapping maritime boundary claims. An oil rig and drill ship, the *C.E. Thornton*, belonging to

CGX, were ordered to leave and were escorted from the area by the Surinamese navy on June 3, 2000 (the "CGX incident").[1] In September 2000, two other holders of Guyanese oil concessions ceased operating in the area: one was ordered to leave by Suriname and the other chose to leave in light of Suriname's actions vis-à-vis the other concession holders.[2] In view of what it deemed a lack of progress in further attempts to settle the Parties' differences through negotiations,[3] Guyana initiated arbitral proceedings on February 24, 2004, pursuant to Articles 286 and 287 of the Convention.

In accordance with Article 3 of Annex VII to the Convention ("Annex VII"), Guyana appointed Professor Thomas Franck as an arbitrator, and Suriname appointed Professor Hans Smit as an arbitrator. The remaining three members appointed in accordance with Annex VII were: H.E. Judge L. Dolliver M. Nelson (President); Dr. Allan Phillip; and Dr. Kamal Hossain. On June 16, 2004, the PCA accepted the joint request of the Parties that it serve as Registry for the proceedings. At a procedural meeting held on July 30, 2004, the Tribunal adopted, with the Parties' consent, its Rules of Procedure and Terms of Appointment. On September 3, 2004, Dr. Phillip tendered his resignation; he died later that month. At the request of the Parties, the Tribunal selected Professor Ivan Shearer as substitute arbitrator in accordance with Article 6(1)(b) of its Rules of Procedure.

Following procedural meetings with the Parties held in The Hague on July 7 and 8, 2005, on July 18, 2005, the Tribunal decided that Suriname's preliminary objections[4] to the Tribunal's jurisdiction would be ruled on in the Tribunal's final award.[5] The disclosure of documents by Suriname became a contentious issue when Suriname asked the Netherlands not to release to Guyana certain documents held in the Netherlands' National Archives.[6] The Tribunal appointed an independent expert, Professor Hans van Houtte, who, pursuant to the terms of his appointment, provided assistance in dealing with requests for disclosure and the production of documents.[7] On November 27, 2006, after consultation with the Parties, the Tribunal appointed Mr. David Gray ("Hydrographer") as an expert to assist the Tribunal, "should it determine that it has jurisdiction to do so, in the drawing and explanation of the maritime boundary line or lines in a technically precise manner."[8]

Hearings were held in Washington, D.C., at the headquarters of the Organization of American States ("OAS"), from December 7 to 20, 2006. On May 31, 2007, pursuant to the Tribunal's Order No. 8 of May 21, 2007, the Hydrographer conducted a site visit in Guyana, accompanied by the Registrar and the representatives of the Parties. The Tribunal issued its unanimous Award on September 17, 2007.

Summary of Matters Submitted to Arbitration

1. The delimitation of the maritime boundary between the Parties, in respect of which Guyana submitted that "[f]rom the point known as Point 61 (5° 59' 53.8" north and longitude 57°

[1] Award, para. 151.

[2] Award, para. 152.

[3] Award, paras. 154–156.

[4] Filed on May 20, 2005.

[5] *See* Order No. 2 of July 18, 2005, entitled "Preliminary Objections," and Award, para. 48.

[6] Award, paras. 16–21, 24–28, 30–34, 36, 44.

[7] Award, paras. 62 *et seq.*, and Order No. 1 of July 18, 2005, entitled "Access to Documents"; Order No. 3 of Oct. 12, 2005; Order No. 4 of Oct. 12, 2005; Order No. 5 of Feb. 16, 2006.

[8] Award, para. 108, and Order No. 6 of Nov. 27, 2006, at para. 3.1.

08' 51.5" west), the single maritime boundary which divides the territorial seas and maritime jurisdictions of Guyana and Suriname follows a line of 34° east and true north for a distance of 200 nautical miles"; and Suriname requested the Tribunal "[t]o determine that the single maritime boundary between Suriname and Guyana extends from the 1936 Point as a line of 10° east of true north to its intersection with the 200-nautical mile limit measured from the baseline from which the breadth of Suriname's territorial sea is measured";

2. Guyana's claim for damages resulting from Suriname's allegedly unlawful activities, first, with respect to the June 3, 2000, incident concerning the *C.E. Thornton* drilling rig and, subsequently, with respect to the departure of two additional Guyanese concession holders;[9] and
3. Whether either Party breached its obligations under Articles 74(3) and 83(3) of UNCLOS to "make every effort to enter into provisional arrangements of a practical nature" and to make every effort "not to jeopardize or hamper the reaching of the final agreement."

Award of the Tribunal

Jurisdiction of the Tribunal

Following a short summary of the procedural history, the geographic and historical background, and the arguments of the Parties, the Tribunal turned its attention to Suriname's preliminary objections, in accordance with its Order No. 2 of July 18, 2005. Suriname, which had objected to the jurisdiction of the Tribunal, contended that, if there was no agreement between the Parties on the maritime boundary in the territorial sea, then there had also been no agreement between the Parties or their colonial predecessors as to the location of the land boundary terminus; thus, the Tribunal lacked jurisdiction to resolve the maritime delimitation issue submitted by Guyana.[10] The Tribunal found no need to consider Suriname's jurisdictional objection to Guyana's maritime delimitation claim in light of its finding that there was an agreed boundary in the territorial sea and Suriname's acceptance that, if there were such an agreed boundary, "then the terminus of the maritime boundary provides a perfectly adequate starting point, and every issue that this Tribunal would have to decide would be governed by the provisions of the Law of the Sea Convention."[11]

Delimitation in the Territorial Sea

Suriname supported its claim that the 10° Line was an agreed boundary for the territorial sea in reliance on historical evidence of acceptance of that line by the United Kingdom and the Netherlands from 1936 by reason of navigational and administrative considerations, namely, the need to safeguard the navigational control by the Netherlands over the approaches to the Corentyne River. This acceptance had not been altered by the extension of the breadth of the territorial sea to twelve miles, in application of the inter-temporal law, according to which a treaty should be interpreted in accordance with the circumstances prevailing at the

[9] *See* text accompanying notes 1 & 2, *supra.*
[10] Award, paras. 176–181.
[11] Award, para. 280.

time.[12] Guyana maintained that the delimitation of the territorial sea should follow what it termed the "historical equidistance line" along an azimuth of N34°E for a distance of 12 nm to a point at the outer limit of the territorial sea (the "N34°E Line").[13] Guyana submitted that the N34°E Line had been treated as an equidistance line by the Parties, and therefore should be given effect as such. Moreover, the adoption of the 10° Line, as a "special circumstance" under Article 15 of UNCLOS, had been provisional in nature and reflected a navigational need which no longer existed.[14]

In its delimitation of the territorial sea, the Tribunal recalled the terms of Article 15 of UNCLOS, which places primacy on the median line as the delimitation line between the territorial sea of opposite or adjacent States. Since there was no evidence before the Tribunal to suggest that some form of historic title to the territorial waters in dispute had inured to either Party, nor were there any geographical features such as low-tide elevations or islands that it would have to consider in delimiting the territorial sea,[15] the Tribunal examined the question whether there were any special circumstances that might justify a departure from the median line approach prescribed by Article 15 of UNCLOS. With regard to the meaning of "special circumstances,"[16] the Tribunal noted that navigational interests had previously been found to constitute such special circumstances.[17] It concluded that "special circumstances of navigation may justify deviation from the median line," and that

> the record amply supports the conclusion that the predecessors of the Parties agreed upon an N10°E delimitation line for the reason that all of the Corentyne River was to be Suriname's territory and that the 10° Line provided appropriate access through Suriname's territorial sea to the western channel of the Corentyne River.[18]

Relying on Guyana's own admission that there had previously been recognition of the 10° Line up to 3 nm,[19] the Tribunal therefore held that the 10° Line was established between the Parties from the starting point to the 3 nm limit.

Both Parties had extended the breadth of their territorial seas from 3 to 12 nm after gaining independence, without addressing directly the question of the continuation of the 10° Line from 3 nm. The question therefore arose how, in the absence of an agreement to do so, a delimitation should be extended from the previous limit of territorial seas to a newly established limit. The Tribunal noted that this issue appeared not to have engaged the attention of States, courts, or commentators.[20] The Tribunal recognized that, in order to prevent Guyana's territorial sea from cutting across the approaches to the Corentyne River at the 3 nm limit, thereby defeating the navigational purpose of this line, a line needed to be drawn from the point at which the 10° Line ended at 3 nm. The Tribunal considered that need in

---

[12] Award, paras. 281–287.

[13] Award, para. 288.

[14] Award, paras. 289–294.

[15] Award, para. 297.

[16] Award, paras. 300–304.

[17] Award, para. 304, *citing* Beagle Channel Arbitration (Arg. v. Chile), 17 I.L.M. p. 634, at p. 673, para. 110 (1978).

[18] Award, para. 306.

[19] *Id.*

[20] Award, para. 311.

itself to be a special circumstance under Article 15 of UNCLOS.[21] Bearing this need in mind, the Tribunal arrived at a line continuing from the seaward terminus of the 10° Line at 3 nm and drawn diagonally by the shortest distance to meet the line adopted to delimit the Parties' continental shelf and exclusive economic zone. The Tribunal held this approach to be in conformity with UNCLOS. It avoided a sudden crossing of the area of access to the Corentyne River, and interposed a gradual transition from the 3 nm to the 12 nm point. It also ensured that the line was convenient for navigational purposes.[22]

Delimitation of the Continental Shelf and Exclusive Economic Zones

The Tribunal recalled the terms of Articles 74 and 83 of UNCLOS, which provide that the delimitation of the exclusive economic zone and continental shelf between States with opposite or adjacent coasts "shall be effected by agreement on the basis of international law, as referred to in Article 38 of the Statute of the [International Court of Justice] ICJ, in order to achieve an equitable solution."[23] The Tribunal noted that its mandate to determine a single maritime boundary delimiting both the continental shelf and the exclusive economic zone involved a concept originating in State practice and the law as developed by international courts and tribunals.[24] The Tribunal found that the case-law of the ICJ and arbitral jurisprudence gave clear guidance that the delimitation process should, in appropriate cases, begin by positing a provisional equidistance line which may be adjusted in the light of relevant circumstances in order to achieve an equitable solution.[25]

Having first established the coasts of the Parties "from which will be determined the location of the baselines and the pertinent basepoints which enable the equidistance line to be measured,"[26] and noting the role of coastal geography in making that determination,[27] the Tribunal considered the arguments of the Parties with respect to the provisional equidistance line.[28] Observing that, due to the geographical circumstances of the area to be delimited, neither Guyana nor Suriname considered the provisional equidistance line to represent an equitable delimitation as required by international law,[29] the Tribunal stated that international courts and tribunals dealing with maritime delimitation had to be mindful of not remaking or wholly refashioning nature.[30] It found that there were no features in the geographical configuration of the relevant coastlines that would justify an adjustment of the equidistance line.[31] As regards the conduct of the Parties, with particular reference to oil

---

[21] Award, para. 323.

[22] Award, paras. 322–325.

[23] Award, paras. 330–331.

[24] Award, paras. 334–341, *citing*, in particular, In the Matter of an Arbitration Between Barbados and the Republic of Trinidad and Tobago (Barb. v. Trin. & Tobago), 45 I.L.M. p. 798 (2006); Maritime Delimitation and Territorial Questions between Qatar and Bahrain (Qatar v. Bahr.), 2001 I.C.J. REP. p. 40 (Mar. 16); Land and Maritime Boundary between Cameroon and Nigeria (Cameroon v. Nig.), 2002 I.C.J. REP. p. 303 (Oct. 10).

[25] Award, para. 342.

[26] Award, paras. 343–352.

[27] Award, paras. 353–357.

[28] Award, paras. 358–368.

[29] Award, para. 373.

[30] Award, para. 374.

[31] Award, para. 377.

concessions, the Tribunal found in the jurisprudence of international courts and tribunals a marked reluctance to accord significance to the oil practice of the parties in the determination of the delimitation line unless such practice was based on the parties' express or tacit agreement.[32] Having found no evidence of any agreement between the Parties, the Tribunal ruled that the oil practice of the Parties could not be taken into account.[33] The Tribunal also ruled that boundary negotiations conducted between Suriname and France with respect to French Guiana were not relevant to the present case.[34] The Tribunal concluded that there were no relevant circumstances in the continental shelf or exclusive economic zone that would require an adjustment to the provisional equidistance line.[35] The Tribunal accepted the baselines provided by the Parties for their respective low-water lines that were relevant to the drawing of the equidistance line beyond the territorial sea.[36] Having recomputed some of the turning points submitted by the Parties, the Tribunal set out the precise coordinates governing the line thus determined.[37]

The Use of Force

Guyana in its third submission sought recovery for damages suffered as a result of Suriname's allegedly unlawful actions in the *C.E. Thornton* incident, as well as actions subsequently taken by Suriname with respect to the additional Guyanese concession holder.[38] The Tribunal rejected Suriname's jurisdictional objections to this claim, namely: that the Tribunal had no jurisdiction to adjudicate alleged violations of the United Nations Charter and general international law;[39] that Guyana had failed to comply with the obligation to exchange views;[40] and that the claim fell outside the Tribunal's jurisdiction pursuant to Part XV, section 3, of UNCLOS.[41] The Tribunal held that the obligation to exchange views did not apply in the particular circumstances. It rejected, further, Suriname's objection that Guyana's conduct was such as to warrant the application of the clean hands doctrine, "to the extent that such a doctrine may exist in international law."[42]

On a review of the evidence and witness statements relating to the CGX incident, particularly the order given by the Surinamese naval officer to the crew of the rig and drill ship to leave the area within twelve hours or "the consequences would be theirs,"[43] the Tribunal took the view that this order constituted a threat that force might be used if the order was not

---

[32] Award, paras. 380–390, *citing*, in particular, Continental Shelf (Tunis./Libya), 1982 I.C.J. REP. p. 18, at para. 118 (Feb. 24); Delimitation of the Maritime Boundary in the Gulf of Maine Area (Canada/U. S.), 1984 I.C.J. REP. p. 246, at para. 150 (Oct. 12); Continental Shelf (Libya/Malta), 1985 I.C.J. REP. p. 13, at para. 25 (June 3); *Cameroon v. Nig.*, note 24 *supra*, at para. 304 and *Barb. v. Trin. & Tobago*, note 24 *supra*, at para. 364.

[33] Award, para. 390.

[34] Award, para.391.

[35] Award, para. 392.

[36] Award, paras. 393–396.

[37] Award, paras 397–400.

[38] Award, para. 401.

[39] Award, paras. 402–406.

[40] Award, paras. 407–410.

[41] Award, paras. 411–416.

[42] Award, paras. 417–422.

[43] Award, paras. 432–439.

complied with.[44] It then turned to the question whether this threat breached the terms of UNCLOS, the UN Charter, and general international law, in light of the ICJ's practice concerning the threat of use of force.[45] The Tribunal rejected on the facts Suriname's argument that the measures it undertook on June 3, 2000, were of the nature of reasonable and proportionate law enforcement measures to preclude unauthorized drilling in a disputed area of the continental shelf.[46] In rejecting Suriname's alternative argument that the measures were lawful countermeasures taken in response to an internationally wrongful act by Guyana, the Tribunal pointed to the well-established principle of international law that countermeasures may not involve the use of force.[47]

Regarding the issue of State responsibility, the Tribunal concluded, with particular reference to the Judgment of the ICJ in the *Case Concerning the Land and Maritime Boundary between Cameroon and Nigeria*,[48] that Guyana's request for an order precluding Suriname from resorting to further threats of force was sufficiently addressed by the Tribunal's maritime delimitation.[49] Being of the view, further, that damages had not been proven to the satisfaction of the Tribunal, it rejected Guyana's claim for compensation.[50]

The Parties' Obligations under Articles 74(3) and 83(3) of UNCLOS

Each Party claimed that the other had breached its obligations, under Articles 74(3) and 83(3) of UNCLOS, to make every effort to enter into provisional arrangements of a practical nature pending agreement on the delimitation of the continental shelf and exclusive economic zone and to make every effort not to jeopardize or hamper the reaching of a final agreement. Guyana also made a claim for reparation, which it withdrew during the proceedings.

In light of the objectives of UNCLOS, the Tribunal found that the obligation to make every effort to enter into provisional arrangements of a practical nature pending a final delimitation imposes a duty to negotiate in good faith. The Tribunal also observed that joint exploration of resources that straddle maritime boundaries has been particularly encouraged by international courts and tribunals.[51] Further, the Tribunal noted that the obligation to make every effort not to jeopardize or hamper the reaching of a final agreement was not intended to preclude all unilateral activities in a disputed maritime area "so long as those activities would not have the effect of prejudicing the final agreement." It held that such an effect would follow from activities causing a permanent physical change to the marine environment, such as exploratory oil drilling, the unilateral undertaking of which was therefore not permissible.[52]

---

[44] Award, para. 439.

[45] Award, paras. 439–440, *citing* Legality of the Threat or Use of Nuclear Weapons, Advisory Opinion, 1996 I.C.J. REP. p. 226, at para. 47 (July 8); and Military and Paramilitary Activities (Nicar. v. U.S.), 1986 I.C.J. REP. p. 14, at para. 190 (June 27).

[46] Award, paras. 441–445.

[47] Award, para. 446.

[48] *Cameroon v. Nig.*, note 24 *supra*.

[49] Award, paras. 448–451, citing, in particular, *Cameroon v. Nig.*, note 24 *supra*, at para. 319.

[50] Award, paras. 451–452.

[51] Award, paras. 460– 464.

[52] Award, paras. 465–467.

Having reviewed the activities of the Parties in light of these obligations, the Tribunal found that at all times Suriname had been under an obligation to make every effort to reach a provisional arrangement. This obligation "became particularly pressing and relevant" when Suriname became aware of CGX's planned exploratory drilling in disputed waters.[53] However, instead of accepting the option then available to it of dialogue with Guyana, Suriname resorted to self-help through its threat of use of force and thus failed, in the build-up to the CGX incident, in its duties under Articles 74(3) and 83(3) of UNCLOS.[54] Guyana, which had been planning to carry out exploratory drilling for some time, also violated its obligation to make every effort to enter into provisional arrangements, by failing to inform Suriname directly of such plans or to attempt to engage Suriname in discussions at an earlier stage.[55] The Tribunal found that both Parties had violated their obligations to make every effort not to jeopardize or hamper the reaching of a final agreement by failing to have recourse to the options for peaceful settlement envisaged by Part XV and Annex VII of UNCLOS.[56] In respect of the violations thus established, the Tribunal granted declaratory relief.[57]

The International Maritime Boundary Between Guyana and Suriname

In setting out its findings in the *dispositif*, the Tribunal described the International Maritime Boundary between Guyana and Suriname in full by reference to "a series of geodetic lines joining the points in the order listed as set forth in paragraphs 328 and 400 of this Award."[58] The Technical Report of the Hydrographer was appended to the Award.

---

[53] Award, para. 476.
[54] *Id.*
[55] Award, para. 477.
[56] Award, paras. 482–484.
[57] Award, paras. 485–486.
[58] Award, para. 488, subpara. 1.

Saluka Investments B.V. v. The Czech Republic

Parties: Saluka Investments B.V./The Czech Republic

Arbitration Agreement: 1991 Agreement on Encouragement and Reciprocal Protection of Investments Between the Kingdom of The Netherlands and the Czech and Slovak Federal Republic

Arbitrators: Sir Arthur Watts KCMG QC (Chairman),† Me Yves Fortier, CC, QC, Prof. Dr. Peter Behrens

Date of Award: March 17, 2006

Summary

Claimant a private investor incorporated in the Netherlands – investment made during privatization of Czech banking sector in post-Communist era – sale of IPB bank to Claimant – IPB one of "Big Four" former State-owned banks – bad debt problem arising in Czech banking sector resulting from post-Communist economic policies – provision of State aid by Czech Government to "Big Four" banks to overcome bad debt problem – exclusion of IPB bank from State aid due to private ownership – exclusion from State aid resulting in bankruptcy of IPB bank – bankruptcy of IPB resulting in loss of investment – whether breach of obligations of Czech Government under Czech-Netherlands Bilateral Investment Treaty – breach of duty to provide fair and equitable treatment – breach of duty of non-impairment – claim for unlawful expropriation rejected – claim for failure to provide full protection and security rejected – question of quantum of damages deferred to second phase.

Legal Subject Matters

Protection of foreign investors:
- Bilateral investment treaty
  - Compensation for breach
  - Quantum
  - Interpretation
- Obligations of the host State
  - Expropriation
  - Fair and equitable treatment
  - Full protection and security
  - Non-impairment

† Deceased November 16, 2007.

Settlement of disputes:
- Arbitration
  - Jurisdiction of the arbitral tribunal
  - Jurisdiction under bilateral investment treaty
    - Definition of qualified investment
    - Definition of qualified investor
    - Jurisdiction over counterclaims

Bibliography

Commentary:
- George Stephanov Georgiev, *The Award in* Saluka Investments v. Czech Republic, *in* THE REASONS REQUIREMENT IN INTERNATIONAL INVESTMENT ARBITRATION: CRITICAL CASE STUDIES p. 149 (Nijhoff 2008);
- Rudolf Dolzer & André von Walter, *Fair and Equitable Treatment – Lines of Jurisprudence on Customary Law, in* INVESTMENT TREATY LAW: CURRENT ISSUES II p. 99 (British Institute of International and Comparative Law 2007);
- Vladimír Balaš, *Saluka Investments B.V. (the Netherlands) v. The Czech Republic: Comments on the Partial Arbitral Award of 17 March 2006*, 7 J. WORLD INV. & TRADE p. 371 (2006);
- Peter Muchlinski, '*Caveat Investor'? The Relevance of the Conduct of the Investor under the Fair and Equitable Treatment Standard*, 55 INT'L & COMP. L.Q. p. 527 (2006).

Facts

A dispute arose following certain transactions between the Government of the Czech Republic ("Czech Republic") and the Nomura Group, a Japanese merchant banking group. The Nomura Group comprised (i) the overall Nomura enterprise ("Nomura"); (ii) an English-incorporated Nomura subsidiary, Nomura Europe plc ("Nomura Europe"); and (iii) the Dutch-incorporated Nomura subsidiary, Saluka Investments B.V. ("Saluka").

Following the end of the Communist period in 1990, the Czech Republic privatized and reorganized the Czech banking sector. By about 1994, the formerly centralized Czech banking system had separated into four large State-owned commercial banks, namely, Ceská sporitelna a.s. ("CS"); Komercní banka a.s. ("KB"); Ceskoslovenská obchodní banka a.s. ("CSOB"); and Investicní a Poštovní banka a.s. (later known as IP banka a.s., or "IPB") (hereinafter, collectively, the "Big Four banks"). The Czech banking sector was administered and regulated by the Czech National Bank ("CNB"). The Czech Government, through a State agency called the National Property Fund ("NPF"), retained a significant minority stake in and control over the Big Four banks until the period 1998–2001.

In mid-1996, Nomura began negotiations for the purchase of the Czech Government's shares in IPB. At that time, Nomura Europe already held approximately 10% of IPB's shares. In about February 1998, Nomura agreed with certain significant counterparties to an option ("Put Option") whereby Nomura Europe could put any shares it held in IPB towards the purchase of other assets, including shares in the Czech brewery that produces Pilsner Urquell beer ("Pilsner Urquell"). On March 8, 1998, Nomura Europe signed a Share Purchase Agreement with the NPF for the purchase of NPF's shares in IPB, whereby Nomura Europe acquired a further 36% of IPB's shares, bringing its total shareholdings in IPB to some 46%. By June 1999, Nomura had acquired 84% of the shares in Pilsner Urquell by successfully operating the Put Option. Nomura later disposed of the Pilsner Urquell shares at a profit.

Nomura Europe was nevertheless able to transfer its IPB shares to Saluka in October 1998 and February 2000. At the time the arbitration was initiated, Saluka continued to be the registered holder of the IPB shares.

By 1998, due to problems in the Czech banking system caused by a combination of liberal credit policies and inadequate creditors' rights, the Big Four banks had a large non-performing loan problem ("bad debt problem"), estimated at 34% for KB, 23.3% for CS, 16.6% for CSOB, and 21.75% for IPB. From early 1998 onwards, the Czech Government took a number of steps to assist one or other of the Big Four banks to overcome the difficulties with which they were faced as a result of the bad debt problem. State assistance was given to KB, CS, and CSOB on the basis that they were banks in which the State had a major shareholding interest, while IPB was not given such assistance as, after March 1998, it was regarded as a private institution the fate of which was a matter for its private shareholders.

From August 30 until November 5, 1999, the CNB carried out a regulatory inspection of IPB, which uncovered serious financial difficulties. As a result of this inspection, the CNB concluded that IPB was not performing prudently, and that IPB needed to create at least 40 billion Czech Republic Koruny (CZK) in provisions. Discussions subsequently took place between representatives of the CNB and the Czech Ministry of Finance and representatives of IPB and Nomura, during which IPB and Nomura presented various proposals to resolve IPB's financial crisis to the Government and to the CNB, which were rejected. Whilst these discussions were underway, media speculation concerning the possible forced administration of IPB caused a run on that bank in the week of February 28, 2000, and another on June 12 to 14, 2000. On June 16, 2000, the CNB put IPB into forced administration and appointed an administrator to exercise the forced administration of IPB, and on June 19, 2000, the CNB transferred IPB to CSOB in a transaction that included various guarantees and indemnities provided by the Czech Government.

The sale of IPB to CSOB was effected despite questions having been raised as to the lawfulness of the transfer under Czech law relating to aspects of the forced administration and to the granting of State aid in connection with the transaction. On June 16, 2002, the forced administration of IPB ended and Nomura resumed control over IPB. On December 4, 2002, the Czech Republic and the NPF inititated the "NPF arbitration" against Saluka and Nomura, seeking the transfer of Saluka's IPB shares to CSOB, and later that month an arbitral tribunal ordered Nomura to transfer Saluka's IPB shares to CSOB. IPB was declared bankrupt on February 5, 2004. On February 16, 2004, CSOB was registered as the new owner of Saluka's IPB shares.

Saluka initiated arbitration proceedings against the Czech Republic by Notice of Arbitration dated July 18, 2001, under Article 8 of the Agreement on Encouragement and Reciprocal Protection of Investments Between the Kingdom of The Netherlands and the Czech and Slovak Federal Republic, signed on April 29, 1991 ("Treaty"). In accordance with Article 8(5) of the Treaty, the arbitral tribunal ("Tribunal"), in determining its own procedure, was to apply the arbitration rules of the United Nations Commission for International Trade Law ("UNCITRAL Rules").

Within the time limits provided in Article 8 of the Treaty, Saluka appointed Mr. Daniel Price as an arbitrator, the Czech Republic appointed Dr. Peter Behrens as an arbitrator, and these two arbitrators appointed Professor Sir Elihu Lauterpacht CBE QC as Chairman. On June 20, 2002, Saluka appointed Maître Yves Fortier CC QC as an arbitrator following the resignation of Mr. Price. On March 25, 2003, the Tribunal notified the Parties of the appointment of Sir Arthur Watts KCMG QC as Chairman of the Tribunal to replace Professor Lauterpacht, who had resigned on February 24, 2003.

On August 13, 2002, the Respondent filed a Notice to Dismiss, by which it requested that the Tribunal dismiss the Claimant's claims. On September 10, 2002, the Tribunal ruled that the dismissal issue should be joined to the merits and ruled upon in the Tribunal's final award. On December 2, 2002, the Respondent submitted a Notice of Counterclaim, setting forth a counterclaim against the Claimant, which it elaborated in its Counter-Memorial ("Counterclaim").

Summary of Matters Submitted to Arbitration

A. Saluka's claim that the Czech Republic had breached Article 5 of the Treaty by depriving Saluka of its investment unlawfully and without just compensation equal to the genuine value of the investment;
B. Saluka's claim that the Czech Republic had breached Article 3 of the Treaty by failing to accord Saluka's investment fair and equitable treatment;
C. Saluka's request for an order that the Czech Republic pay Saluka compensation for the damages that it had suffered as a result of the breaches of the Treaty, with interest, and the costs of the arbitration proceedings; and
D. The Czech Republic's Counterclaim based on alleged misconduct of Nomura Europe.

Decision on Jurisdiction

On May 7, 2004, the Tribunal handed down its Decision on Jurisdiction over the Czech Republic's Counterclaim, in which it decided, *inter alia*, that it had no jurisdiction over the Counterclaim, on the grounds that the disputes underlying the Counterclaim fell to be decided under Czech law and not through the particular investment protection measures of the Treaty. Following the exchange of further written pleadings, hearings on the merits and jurisdiction were held in London from April 8 to 20, 2005. The Tribunal issued its Partial Award on March 17, 2006.

Partial Award

Jurisdiction

The Czech Republic argued in its Notice to Dismiss that Nomura had not disclosed to the Czech authorities, at the time of its purchase of the shares, the true purpose of that purchase, which was to facilitate the acquisition of Czech breweries in which IPB had a controlling interest; that Nomura was therefore not a *bona fide* investor; and that therefore Saluka, to whom Nomura had transferred its shareholding, was precluded from having recourse to arbitration under the Treaty.[1] The Czech Republic argued, further, that Saluka did not have any real and continuous *bona fide* social or economic factual links to the Netherlands, and

---

[1] Partial Award, para. 174.

should therefore be disqualified from being an investor, and that the real party in interest was Nomura, which was not an eligible claimant under the Treaty.[2]

The Tribunal noted that Article 8 of the Treaty conferred competence to make use of the arbitral process on "investors" in respect of their "investments." Under Article 1(b)(ii) of the Treaty, the term "investor" included "legal persons constituted under the laws of [the Netherlands]." The term "investments" was defined in Article 1(a), which provided:

> The term "investments" shall comprise every kind of asset invested either directly or through an investor of a third State and more particularly, though not exclusively:
>
> (i) movable and immovable property and all related property rights;
> (ii) shares, bonds and other kinds of interests in companies and joint ventures, as well as rights derived therefrom;
> (iii) title to money and other assets and to any performance having an economic value;
> (iv) rights in the field of intellectual property, also including technical processes, goodwill and know-how;
> (v) concessions conferred by law or under contract, including concessions to prospect, explore, extract and win natural resources.

The Tribunal did not interpret Article 1 of the Treaty as excluding from the definition of investor those who purchase shares as part of bare profit-making or profit-taking transactions. Even if it were possible to know an investor's true motivation in making its investment, nothing in Article 1 made the investor's motivation part of the definition of an investment.[3]

Having concluded that there were no good reasons for declining to consider the Claimant's holding of IPB shares to be an "investment" as defined in Article 1 of the Treaty,[4] the Tribunal considered the question whether Saluka was a qualified "investor" for purposes of the Treaty.

The Tribunal noted that Saluka met all requirements expressly stipulated in Article 1 of the Treaty for qualification as an investor, namely, that it be a "legal person" and be "constituted under the laws of [the Netherlands]." It rejected the argument of the Czech Republic that the relationship between Nomura and Saluka was so close that they were in effect interchangeable as parties in the proceedings.[5] The Tribunal noted that the terms of the Treaty expressly give a legal person constituted under the laws of the Netherlands the right to invoke the protection of the Treaty. The parties to the Treaty having agreed that any legal person constituted under their laws is entitled to invoke the protection of the Treaty, it was beyond the powers of the Tribunal to import into the definition of "investor" some requirement relating to such a relationship having the effect of excluding from the Treaty's protection a company which the language agreed by the parties included within it.[6]

The Tribunal also rejected the contention that Nomura Europe, by the non-disclosure of its alleged purpose in purchasing the IPB shares relating to the acquisition of Pilsner Urquell,

[2] Partial Award, para. 183.
[3] Partial Award, para. 209.
[4] Partial Award, para. 221.
[5] Partial Award, para. 227.
[6] Partial Award, para. 229.

had not acted in good faith.[7] In the Tribunal's view, it was both unreasonable and unrealistic to posit an obligation upon an investor to disclose its ultimate objectives in making a particular investment, whether through the purchase of shares or otherwise.[8]

The Czech Republic also alleged that Saluka did not have genuine, real, and continuous links to the Netherlands, and for that reason did not satisfy the requirements which are necessary to qualify as an "investor" able to benefit from the provisions of the Treaty.[9] The Tribunal, although it expressed some sympathy for the argument that a company which has no real connection with a State party to a bilateral investment treaty ("BIT") should not be entitled to invoke the provisions of that Treaty,[10] held that it was not open to the Tribunal to add requirements to the definition of the claimant-investor agreed by the parties to the Treaty.[11] The Tribunal noted that it had always been apparent to the Czech authorities that it was Nomura's intention to transfer the IPB shares it was holding to another company within the Nomura Group, and that that other company would be a special-purpose vehicle set up for the specific and sole purpose of holding those shares.[12]

Saluka's Claims under Article 5 of the Treaty

Saluka asserted that the Czech Republic, through its intervention in IPB, had deprived Saluka of the value of its shares in IPB contrary to Article 5 of the Treaty, which provides:[13]

> Neither Contracting Party shall take any measures depriving, directly or indirectly, investors of the other Contracting Party of their investments unless the following conditions are complied with:
>
> a. the measures are taken in the public interest and under due process of law;
> b. the measures are not discriminatory;
> c. the measures are accompanied by provision for the payment of just compensation. Such compensation shall represent the genuine value of the investments affected and shall, in order to be effective for the claimants, be paid and made transferable, without undue delay, to the country designated by the claimants concerned and in any freely convertible currency accepted by the claimants.

Saluka contended that the forced administration was not in the public interest; that it was not taken under due process of law; that the Czech Government granted discriminatory State aid to IPB's competitors; that the Czech Government resorted to its regulatory power unlawfully in order to transfer IPB's business to CSOB; and that the Czech Government never paid any compensation to Saluka after having deprived Saluka of its investment.[14]

The Tribunal held that Article 5 of the Treaty imported into the Treaty the customary international law notion that a deprivation can be justified if it results from the exercise of

[7] Partial Award, para. 231.
[8] Partial Award, para. 232.
[9] Partial Award, para. 239.
[10] Partial Award, para. 240.
[11] Partial Award, para. 241.
[12] Partial Award, para. 242.
[13] Partial Award, para. 245.
[14] Partial Award, para. 249.

regulatory actions aimed at the maintenance of public order.[15] In the Tribunal's opinion, "[i]t is now established in international law that States are not liable to pay compensation to a foreign investor when, in the normal exercise of their regulatory powers, they adopt in a non-discriminatory manner *bona fide* regulations that are aimed at the general welfare."[16] It further held that the principle that a State does not commit an expropriation and is thus not liable to pay compensation to a dispossessed alien investor when it adopts general regulations that are "commonly accepted as within the police power of States" forms part of customary international law today.[17] It fell to the Tribunal to determine whether particular conduct by a State "crosses the line" separating valid regulatory activity from expropriation.[18]

The Tribunal reviewed the facts which led the CNB, on June 16, 2000, to "introduce forced administration" of IPB pursuant to Section 26(1)(d) of the Czech Banking Act.[19] It reproduced *in extenso* the translation of the CNB decision of June 16, 2000, supplied by the Czech Republic.[20] Having reviewed the totality of the evidence which the CNB invoked in support of its decision, the Tribunal concluded that the CNB had been justified, under Czech law, in imposing the forced administration of IPB and appointing an administrator to exercise the forced administration.[21] The Tribunal was of the view that, in imposing the forced administration of IPB on June 16, 2000, the Czech Republic had adopted a measure which was valid and permissible as within its regulatory powers.[22]

Saluka's Claims under Article 3 of the Treaty

Saluka also contended that the way in which events unfolded with respect to its shareholding in IPB amounted to a breach by the Czech Republic of its obligation under Article 3(1) of the Treaty, which provides:

> Each Contracting Party shall ensure fair and equitable treatment to the investments of investors of the other Contracting Party and shall not impair, by unreasonable or discriminatory measures, the operation, management, maintenance, use, enjoyment or disposal thereof by those investors.

Applying Article 31(1) of the 1969 Vienna Convention on the Law of Treaties, the Tribunal held that the protection of foreign investments was not the sole aim of the Treaty, but rather a necessary element alongside the overall aim of encouraging foreign investment as well as extending and intensifying the Parties' economic relations. It noted that "an interpretation which exaggerates the protection to be accorded to foreign investments may serve to dissuade host States from admitting foreign investments and so undermine the overall aim of extending and intensifying the parties' mutual economic relations."[23] The "dominant element" of the fair and equitable treatment standard was the notion of legitimate expecta-

---

[15] Partial Award, para. 254.
[16] Partial Award, para. 255.
[17] Partial Award, para. 262.
[18] Partial Award, para. 264.
[19] Partial Award, para. 268.
[20] Partial Award, para. 270.
[21] Partial Award, para. 271.
[22] Partial Award, para. 276.
[23] Partial Award, para. 300.

tions.[24] The Tribunal held that the expectations of foreign investors included the observation by the host State of "such well-established fundamental standards as good faith, due process, and non-discrimination."[25] According to the Tribunal, the host State's legitimate right subsequently to regulate domestic matters in the public interest had to be taken into consideration as well.[26] The determination of a breach of Article 3(1) of the Treaty therefore required a weighing of the Claimant's legitimate and reasonable expectations on the one hand and the Respondent's legitimate regulatory interests on the other.[27] The Tribunal concluded that "a foreign investor whose interests are protected under the Treaty is entitled to expect that the Czech Republic will not act in a way that is manifestly inconsistent, non-transparent, unreasonable (i.e. unrelated to some rational policy), or discriminatory (i.e. based on unjustifiable distinctions)."[28]

Saluka contended that the Czech Republic gave a discriminatory response to the systemic bad debt problem in the Czech banking sector, especially by providing State financial assistance to the other Big Four banks to the exclusion of IPB, and thereby created an environment impossible for the survival of IPB.[29] The Tribunal found that, after its privatization, IPB was excluded as a beneficiary from the Czech Government's strategy to solve the bad debt problem of IPB's competitors by the provision of direct financial assistance to the banks. This exclusion continued until after the forced administration of IPB.[30] It found, further, that the Czech Republic did eventually provide assistance to all of the Big Four banks, including IPB after it had been acquired by CSOB.[31]

The Tribunal rejected the contention of the Czech Republic that the differential treatment of IPB was justified, which was based, *inter alia*, on the argument that Saluka had no reason to expect that the Czech Government would be willing to alleviate IPB's future problems by providing State financial assistance; and on the argument that the financial assistance granted to IPB's competitors was in the discretion of the Czech State as part of its privatization strategy.[32]

The Tribunal reviewed in detail the unfolding of CSOB's acquisition of IPB, which it contrasted with the unfolding of the negotiations between IPB, Saluka/Nomura, and the Czech Government.[33] It found that the Ministry of Finance and the CNB had unreasonably frustrated IPB's and its shareholders' good faith efforts to resolve IPB's crisis. The Tribunal held that the Czech Government had failed to deal with IPB's as well as Saluka's and Nomura's proposals in an unbiased, even-handed, transparent, and consistent way, and it unreasonably refused to communicate with IPB and Saluka and Nomura in an adequate manner.[34]

Saluka also alleged that the provision by the Czech Republic of significant financial assistance to IPB's business, once the beneficiary of such assistance had become CSOB, was

[24] Partial Award, para. 302.
[25] Partial Award, para. 303.
[26] Partial Award, para. 305.
[27] Partial Award, para. 306.
[28] Partial Award, para. 308.
[29] Partial Award, paras. 312–314.
[30] Partial Award, para. 326.
[31] Partial Award, para. 322.
[32] Partial Award, paras. 328–347.
[33] Partial Award, paras. 366–406.
[34] Partial Award, paras. 407–432.

unfair and inequitable contrary to Article 3(1) of the Treaty.[35] The Tribunal found that, at the time the financial assistance to CSOB was implemented, IPB had already lost its banking business to CSOB. It was therefore not conceivable that, due to the State aid provided to CSOB, IPB and its shareholders could have suffered harm in addition to the harm that had already been caused by the forced administration and the subsequent loss of the banking business.[36]

According to Saluka, the Czech Republic had failed to prevent the unjust enrichment of CSOB at the expense of the IPB shareholders, including Saluka, upon the transfer of IPB's business to CSOB.[37] The Tribunal noted that the concept of unjust enrichment is recognized as a general principle of international law, but found that the Czech Republic had not, by means of the transfer of IPB's business to CSOB and the provision of State aid following the forced administration, taken or received anything of value at the expense of Saluka. It was not the Czech Republic which received the banking business from IPB, but CSOB;[38] and it was IPB's and not Saluka's banking business that was transferred to CSOB.[39]

Non-Impairment

Saluka also presented a claim based on the non-impairment obligation contained in Article 3(1) of the Treaty, which provides that:

> [W]ith reference to the investments of investors of the other Contracting Party, each Contracting Party ... shall not impair, by unreasonable or discriminatory measures, the operation, management, maintenance, use, enjoyment or disposal thereof by those investors.

The Tribunal found that the Czech Republic, by violating the "fair and equitable treatment" standard, at the same time impaired the enjoyment of Saluka's investment – namely, the shareholding in IPB – by giving a discriminatory response to the bad debt problem in the Czech banking sector; and by refusing to negotiate in good faith on the proposals made by IPB and its shareholders, in violation of its non-impairment obligation.[40]

The Tribunal found, based on several press reports containing information said to have been received from Government sources, that the Czech Government did in fact unreasonably spread negative information on IPB to the public, and that this contributed to the aggravation of IPB's financial distress and to its subsequent failure.[41] It found that, once forced administration was publicly stated to be unavoidable, that statement became a self-fulfilling prophecy, because the bank run was certain to set in the next working day. The Tribunal held that this conduct of the Government was unjustifiable and unreasonable and "contributed in all probability to the unsustainability of IPB's situation."[42]

---

[35] Partial Award, para. 433.
[36] Partial Award, para. 447.
[37] Partial Award, para. 448.
[38] Partial Award, para. 452.
[39] Partial Award, para. 453.
[40] Partial Award, paras. 465–466.
[41] Partial Award, paras. 472–478.
[42] Partial Award, para. 481.

Full Security and Protection

Saluka further argued that the Czech Republic had violated its obligation under Article 3(2) of the Treaty, which provides:

> More particularly, each Contracting Party shall accord to such investments full security and protection which in any case shall not be less than that accorded either to investments of its own investors or to investments of investors of any third States, whichever is more favourable to the investor concerned.

Saluka contended that the Czech Republic had "failed to accord Saluka's investment full protection and security by its oppressive use of public powers, post-forced administration, with a view to depriving Saluka of any residual economic benefit of its investment," including by police searches of premises owned by Nomura.[43] The Tribunal noted that the "full protection and security" standard applies essentially when the foreign investment has been affected by civil strife and physical violence, and obliges the host State to adopt all reasonable measures to protect assets and property from threats or attacks which may target particularly foreigners or certain groups of foreigners.[44] In the Tribunal's view, nothing had emerged from the facts before it that would amount to a manifest lack of due process leading to a breach of international justice and to a failure of the Czech Republic to provide "full protection and security" to Saluka's investment.[45]

Other Matters

After setting out its conclusions,[46] the Tribunal noted that it retained its jurisdiction in order to decide the outstanding question of redress, including questions of quantum, in a second phase of the arbitration.[47]

The case was settled and resolved following issuance of the Partial Award.

---

[43] Partial Award, para. 485.
[44] Partial Award, paras. 483–484.
[45] Partial Award, para. 493.
[46] Partial Award, paras. 496–505.
[47] Partial Award, para. 508.

The MOX Plant Case

Parties:	Ireland/United Kingdom
Arbitration Agreement:	1982 United Nations Convention on the Law of the Sea
Arbitrators:	Judge Thomas A. Mensah (President), Prof. James Crawford SC, Me L. Yves Fortier CC QC, Prof. Gerhard Hafner, Sir Arthur Watts KCMG QC,[†] The Rt. Hon. Lord Mustill
Dates of Procedural Orders:	July 2, 2002; December 10, 2002; June 24, 2003; November 14, 2003; January 22, 2007; June 6, 2008.

Summary

United Kingdom operating mixed oxide ("MOX") plant on coast of Irish Sea – Ireland claimed that United Kingdom breached its obligations under 1982 United Nations Convention on the Law of the Sea ("UNCLOS") by operating MOX plant – Ireland initiated arbitral proceedings under Annex VII of UNCLOS – United Kingdom objected to jurisdiction of arbitral tribunal based on certain European Community ("EC") law issues – proceedings suspended pending decision of the European Court of Justice ("ECJ") on EC law issues – ECJ found Ireland to be in breach of EC law by bringing action before the UNCLOS arbitral tribunal – continuation of suspension of proceedings – termination of proceedings following withdrawal of claim by Ireland.

Legal Subject Matters

European Communities:
- European Court of Justice
  - Exclusive jurisdiction

Oceans:
- Law of the sea
  - Prevention, reduction and control of pollution of the marine environment

Settlement of disputes:
- Arbitration
  - Jurisdiction of the arbitral tribunal
    - Provisional measures
    - Suspension of proceedings

[†] Deceased November 16, 2007.

Bibliography

Order No. 3 published in:
- 42 I.L.M. p. 1187 (2003).

Commentary:

- Oliver Dörr, *The European Court of Justice Getting in the Way: The Abortive MOX Plant Arbitration, in* A WISER CENTURY? JUDICIAL DISPUTE SETTLEMENT, DISARMAMENT AND THE LAWS OF WAR 100 YEARS AFTER THE SECOND HAGUE PEACE CONFERENCE (Thomas Giegerich ed., 2009);
- Freya Baetens, *Muddling the Waters of Treaty Interpretation? Relevant Rules of International Law in the MOX Plant OSPAR Arbitration and EC Biotech Case*, 77 NORDIC J. INT'L L. p. 197 (2008);
- Patrick Eicher, *International Forum Shopping: The MOX Plant Case and the ECJ*, 30 DUBLIN U. L.J. p. 367 (2008);
- Normand Halde, *La Cour de Babel : entre l'incertitude scientifique et l'instabilité juridique : un cas d'analyse : l'affaire MOX*, 19 RQDI p. 199 (2007);
- Adam Stanislas, *Het Europees Hof van Justitie en andere internationale rechtsprekende organen: enkele opmerkingen naar aanleiding van het Mox-fabriek arrest*, 40 RBDI p. 113 (2007);
- Karen N. Scott, *European Court of Justice: The MOX Case Before the European Court: C-459/03 Commission v. Ireland*, 22 INT'L J. MARINE & COASTAL L. p. 303 (2007);
- Jasper Finke, *Competing Jurisdiction of International Courts and Tribunals in Light of the MOX Plant Dispute*, 49 GERMAN Y.B. INT'L L. p. 307 (2007);
- Sandrine Maljean-Dubois, *L'affaire de l'Usine MOX devant les tribunaux internationaux*, 134 JDI p. 437 (2007);
- Raphael Oen, *Streitschlichtung zwischen EG-Mitgliedstaaten im Rahmen gemischter Verträge: der MOX Plant-Fall und seine Folgen*, 45 Archiv des Völkerrechts p. 136 (2007);
- Paul James Cardwell & Duncan French, *Who Decides? The ECJ's Judgment on Jurisdiction in the* MOX Plant *Dispute*, 19 J. ENV'L L. p. 121 (2007);
- Nikolaos Lavranos, *The MOX Plant and IJzeren Rijn Disputes: Which Court is the Supreme Arbiter?*, 19 LEIDEN J. INT'L L. p. 223 (2006);
- Nikolaos Lavranos, *The "MOX Plant" Judgment of the ECJ: How Exclusive is the Jurisdiction of the ECJ?*, 15(10) EUR. ENV'L L. REV. p. 291 (2006);
- M. Bruce Volbeda, *The MOX Plant Case: The Question of "Supplemental Jurisdiction" for International Environmental Claims Under UNCLOS*, 42 TEXAS INT'L L.J. p. 211 (2006);
- Robin Churchill & Joanna Scott, *The MOX Plant Litigation: The First Half-Life*, 53 INT'L & COMP. L.Q. p. 643 (2004);
- Volker Röben, *The Order of the UNCLOS Annex VII Arbitral Tribunal to Suspend Proceedings in the Case of the MOX Plant at Sellafield: How Much Jurisdictional Subsidiarity?*, 73 NORDIC J. INT'L L. p. 223 (2004);
- Yuval Shany, *The First MOX Plant Award: The Need to Harmonize Competing Environmental Regimes and Dispute Settlement Procedures*, 17 LEIDEN J. INT'L L. p. 815 (2004);
- Maki Tanaka, *Lessons from the Protracted MOX Plant Dispute: A Proposed Protocol on Marine Environmental Impact Assessment to the United Nations Convention on the Law of the Sea*, 25 MICHIGAN J. INT'L L. p. 337 (2004);
- D.J. Devine, *Provisional Measures Ordered by the International Tribunal for the Law of the Sea in the Area of Pollution: The MOX Plant Case (Ireland v. United Kingdom) ITLOS Case No 10, 3 December 2001*, 28 SOUTH AFRICAN Y.B. INT'L L. p. 263 (2003);
- Malcolm J.C. Forster, *The MOX Plant Case: Provisional Measures in the International Tribunal for the Law of the Sea*, 16 LEIDEN J. INT'L L. p. 611 (2003);
- Barbara Kwiatkowska, *The Ireland v United Kingdom (MOX Plant) Case: Applying the Doctrine of Treaty Parallelism*, 18 INT'L J. MARINE & COASTAL L. p. 1 (2003).

Facts

A dispute arose between the Republic of Ireland ("Ireland") and the United Kingdom of Great Britain and Northern Ireland ("United Kingdom") concerning discharges into the Irish Sea of certain radioactive wastes produced by or as a result of the operation of the mixed oxide fuel reprocessing plant at Sellafield in the United Kingdom ("MOX Plant"). The MOX Plant is operated with the authorization of the United Kingdom Government by British Nuclear Fuels plc, a corporation wholly owned by the United Kingdom Government. The spent nuclear fuel reprocessed at the MOX Plant comes principally from another plant at Sellafield, the Thermal Oxide Reprocessing Plant ("THORP").

On October 25, 2001, Ireland, pursuant to Part XV of the 1982 United Nations Convention on the Law of the Sea ("UNCLOS"), submitted to the United Kingdom a Notification and Statement of Claim instituting arbitral proceedings as provided for in Annex VII to UNCLOS "in the dispute concerning the MOX plant, international movements of radioactive materials, and the protection of the marine environment of the Irish Sea."

On November 9, 2001, Ireland submitted a Request for Provisional Measures to the International Tribunal for the Law of the Sea ("ITLOS"). On December 3, 2001, ITLOS issued a Provisional Order ("ITLOS Order"), in which it found, pursuant to Article 290(5) of UNCLOS, "that the Annex VII arbitral tribunal would *prima facie* have jurisdiction over the dispute."[1]

On January 21, 2002, Ireland filed a "Notification and Amended Statement of Claim and Grounds on which it is Based" ("Amended Statement of Claim"). The Annex VII arbitral tribunal ("Tribunal") was duly constituted in February 2002. The Tribunal designated the International Bureau of the Permanent Court of Arbitration ("PCA") to serve as Registry for the proceedings. On July 2, 2002, the Tribunal approved Ireland's Amended Statement of Claim.[2] The Tribunal established the timetable for the submission of written proceedings in its Rules of Procedure, as modified by the Tribunal.[3]

The Tribunal held hearings in The Hague from June 10 to 21, 2003. On June 13, 2003, the President of the Tribunal issued a Statement announcing that, in light of certain jurisdictional issues that had been raised before the Tribunal, the Tribunal had decided to suspend further proceedings in the case.[4] The President declared that the Tribunal remained seized of the dispute in the meantime,[5] and would hear arguments from Ireland "on the content of any provisional measures that it seeks."[6]

On June 16, 2003, Ireland submitted to the Tribunal a "Request for Further Provisional Measures" pursuant to Article 290 of UNCLOS "to preserve Ireland's rights under UNCLOS and to prevent harm to the marine environment."[7]

---

[1] ITLOS Order, para. 62.

[2] Order No. 1, "Ireland's Amended Statement of Claim," July 2, 2002.

[3] Order No. 2, "Time-Limits for Submission of Pleadings," Dec. 10, 2002.

[4] President's Statement of June 13, 2003, para. 12.

[5] *Id.* para. 13.

[6] *Id.* para. 15.

[7] Order No. 3, "Suspension of Proceedings on Jurisdiction and Merits, and Request for Further Provisional Measures," June 24, 2003 [hereinafter "Order No. 3"], para. 32.

Summary of Matters Submitted to Arbitration

A. Whether the United Kingdom had breached its obligations under Articles 192, 193, 194, 207, 211, or 213 of UNCLOS, by failing to take the measures necessary to prevent, reduce, and control pollution and by failing properly to assess the risk of terrorist attack on the MOX Plant;
B. Whether the United Kingdom had breached its obligations under Articles 123 and 197 of UNCLOS by refusing to share information with Ireland or to carry out a proper environmental assessment;
C. Whether the United Kingdom had breached its obligations under Article 206 of UNCLOS by failing properly to assess the effects of the operation of the MOX Plant on the Irish Sea; and
D. Whether the Tribunal had jurisdiction to hear and decide the case on the merits.

Decisions of the Tribunal

On June 24, 2003, the Tribunal issued its Order No. 3 on "Suspension of Proceedings on Jurisdiction and Merits and Request for Further Provisional Measures." Order No. 3 dealt with the following matters.

Suspension of Proceedings on Jurisdiction and Merits

The United Kingdom had raised various objections to the jurisdiction of the Tribunal.[8] The Tribunal held that it did have *prima facie* jurisdiction, and that there was "nothing which manifestly and in terms exclude[d] the Tribunal's jurisdiction."[9] However, the Tribunal still had to establish that it had "jurisdiction in a definitive sense," and it considered that, "even to proceed to hear argument on the merits of the dispute brought before it,"[10] it needed to be satisfied that there were no substantial doubts as to its jurisdiction.

According to the Tribunal, the objections to jurisdiction raised by the United Kingdom fell into two categories, namely, (i) questions of jurisdiction and admissibility in respect of UNCLOS itself and other international agreements and instruments invoked by Ireland ("international law issues"), and (ii) questions relating to the positions of the Parties under the law of the European Communities ("EC law issues").[11] The Tribunal considered that none of the issues raised cast doubt on its *prima facie* jurisdiction.[12]

With regard to the international law issues, the Tribunal noted the relevance of the 1992 Convention for the Protection of the Marine Environment of the North-East Atlantic ("OSPAR Convention") to some of the issues in dispute, but did not consider that this altered the character of the present dispute, nor did it trigger the application of Articles 281 or 282 of UNCLOS.[13]

---

[8] President's Statement of June 13, 2003, para. 3; Order No. 3, para. 13.
[9] Order No. 3, para. 14.
[10] Order No. 3, para. 15.
[11] Order No. 3, para. 16.
[12] Order No. 3, para. 17.
[13] Order No. 3, para. 18.

With respect to the EC law issues, "certain problems" had become apparent to the Tribunal in respect of some important and interrelated areas of EC law as they applied to the dispute between the Parties before the Tribunal.[14] Those problems concerned, *inter alia*, the division of competences between the European Community and its Member States in respect of UNCLOS, particularly in the light of the declarations made by the Parties and the European Community pursuant to Article 5 of Annex IX to UNCLOS, as well as the matters which, by agreement of the Parties, were subject to the exclusive jurisdiction of the European Court of Justice ("ECJ") under European Community law.

The Tribunal noted that the Commission of the European Communities ("Commission") had indicated that it was examining the question whether to institute proceedings under Article 226 of the EC Treaty.[15] There was thus a real possibility that the ECJ might be seized of the questions (i) whether the provisions of UNCLOS on which Ireland relied were matters in relation to which competence had been transferred to the EC and (ii) whether the exclusive jurisdiction of the ECJ, with regard to Ireland and the United Kingdom as Member States of the EC, extended to the interpretation and application of UNCLOS "as such and in its entirety."[16]

The Parties agreed that, if the ECJ were to hold that the interpretation of UNCLOS in its entirety fell within the exclusive competence of the ECJ as between Member States of the EU, "it would preclude the jurisdiction of the present Tribunal entirely," by virtue of Article 282 of UNCLOS.[17]

The Tribunal recognized that the problems referred to above related to matters that essentially concerned the internal operation of a separate legal order, namely, the legal order of the European Communities, to which both of the Parties in the present proceedings were subject, and which, in the circumstances referred to above,[18] were to be determined within the institutional framework of the European Communities.[19]

The Tribunal considered that, until the EC law issues were definitively resolved, there remained substantial doubts about whether the jurisdiction of the Tribunal could be firmly established in respect of all or any of the claims in dispute.[20]

In the circumstances, and "bearing in mind considerations of mutual respect and comity which should prevail between judicial institutions both of which may be called upon to determine rights and obligations as between two States," the Tribunal decided, in the absence of a resolution of the EC law issues,[21] to suspend further proceedings on jurisdiction and the merits.[22] It decided that it remained seized of the dispute and would resume its proceedings not later than December 1, 2003, in the hope that it would at that time have a clearer picture of the position regarding EC law.[23]

---

[14] Order No. 3, para. 20.

[15] Written Answer given by the Commission in the European Parliament on May 15, 2003.

[16] Order No. 3, para. 21.

[17] *Id.* para. 22.

[18] *See* text accompanying note 16, *supra*.

[19] Order No. 3, para. 24.

[20] Order No. 3, para. 25.

[21] Order No. 3, para. 28.

[22] Order No. 3, paras. 29–30.

[23] *Id.*

Ireland's Request for Further Provisional Measures

In its "Request for Further Provisional Measures," Ireland requested that the Tribunal order, *inter alia*, that "[t]he United Kingdom shall ensure that there are no liquid waste discharges from the MOX Plant at Sellafield into the Irish Sea."[24] It further requested that the Tribunal order certain measures of cooperation between the Parties in the event "of any proposal for additional reprocessing at THORP or manufacturing at MOX."[25] Ireland had stated that "the circumstances justifying this request include the likely duration of the suspension of the hearing and the real possibility of proceedings before the [ECJ], and the conduct of the United Kingdom as outlined in the pleadings."[26]

The Tribunal did not consider that Ireland had established that any harm that might be caused to the marine environment by virtue of the operation of the MOX Plant, pending the determination of the case on the merits, would meet the threshold test prescribed by Article 290(1) of UNCLOS, which prescribes that such harm must be "serious."[27]

Ireland also argued that provisional measures were necessary to protect its rights under UNCLOS. The Tribunal was not satisfied that in the present circumstances there was an urgent and serious risk of irreparable harm to Ireland's claimed rights, which would justify it in prescribing provisional measures relating to discharges from the MOX Plant.[28] The Tribunal was satisfied that, since December 2001, there had been an increased measure of cooperation and consultation, as required by the ITLOS Order. However, the Tribunal recommended that the Parties seek to establish secure arrangements, at a suitable inter-governmental level, for coordination of all of the various agencies and bodies involved.[29]

Other Matters

The Tribunal urged the Parties, jointly and separately, to take appropriate steps to expedite the resolution of the outstanding questions of EC law.[30] The Tribunal affirmed the ITLOS Order[31] and directed, *inter alia*, that the Parties should each submit to the Tribunal and to the other Party

(i) no later than September 12, 2003, an initial report and information on compliance with the ITLOS Order and with the recommendations made by the Tribunal in Order No. 3;[32] and
(ii) no later than November 17, 2003, a further report and information on compliance.[33]

---

[24] Order No. 3, para. 33.
[25] *Id.*
[26] Order No. 3, para. 34.
[27] Order No. 3, para. 55.
[28] Order No. 3, para. 62.
[29] Order No. 3, paras. 66–67.
[30] Order No. 3, para. 69, *Dispositif*, para. 6.
[31] Order No. 3, *Dispositif*, para. 2.
[32] Order No. 3, *Dispositif*, para. 7(a).
[33] Order No. 3, *Dispositif*, para. 7(b).

Further Proceedings

By letter dated October 21, 2003, Ireland informed the Tribunal that, on October 15, 2003, the Commission had decided to authorize the institution of proceedings against Ireland before the ECJ in respect of the EC law issues.[34] On November 14, 2003, the Tribunal issued Order No. 4, in which it suspended further proceedings in the case until the ECJ had given judgment or the Tribunal otherwise determined.[35] The suspension of the proceedings was without prejudice to the continuation of the matters ordered in the Tribunal's Order No. 3 of June 24, 2003.[36] The Tribunal also ordered, *inter alia*, that:

(i) subject to any further order by the Tribunal, the Parties submit, not later than May 31, 2004 and every six months thereafter, a report and information on compliance with the provisional measure affirmed and recommendations made by the Tribunal in Order No. 3;[37] and
(ii) subject to any further order by the Tribunal, Ireland submit, not later than June 30, 2004, and every six months thereafter, reports on developments in the proceedings before the ECJ.[38]

The ECJ delivered its Judgment on May 30, 2006.[39] By letter dated June 16, 2006, the Registrar of the Tribunal requested the Parties' reactions and their intentions regarding the MOX Plant case in light of the Judgment of the ECJ. Ireland replied by letter dated June 30, 2006. The United Kingdom replied by letter dated November 30, 2006.

On January 22, 2007, the Tribunal suspended until further notice:

(a) the obligation on the Parties to submit periodic reports and information on compliance with the provisional measure affirmed and recommendations made by the Tribunal in Order No. 3 of June 24, 2003;[40] and
(b) Ireland's obligation to submit periodic reports on developments in the proceedings before the ECJ.[41]

The Tribunal decided to remain seized of the dispute[42] and reserved the subsequent procedure for further decision.[43]

---

[34] Order No. 4, "Further Suspension of Proceedings on Jurisdiction and Merits," Nov. 14, 2003 [hereinafter "Order No. 4"], preamble.

[35] Order No. 4, para. 1(a).

[36] Order No. 4, *Dispositif*, para. 1(b).

[37] Order No. 4, *Dispositif*, para. 1(d).

[38] Order No. 4, *Dispositif*, para. 1(e).

[39] *See* Case C-459/03, Comm'n v. Ireland, 2006 E.C.R. I-4635.

[40] Order No. 5, "Suspension of Periodic Reports by the Parties," Jan. 22, 2007 [hereinafter "Order No. 5"], *Dispositif*, Para. 1(a).

[41] Order No. 5, *Dispositif*, para. 1(b).

[42] Order No. 5, *Dispositif*, para. 1(c).

[43] Order No. 5, *Dispositif*, para. 2.

On January 31, 2008, the United Kingdom, pursuant to Article 7(1)(a) of the Tribunal's Rules of Procedure, appointed The Rt. Hon. The Lord Mustill as a member of the Tribunal in replacement of Sir Arthur Watts KCMG QC who had passed away on November 16, 2007.

Termination

By Order No. 6 of June 6, 2008, in which it placed on record Ireland's withdrawal of the claim made by it against the United Kingdom, the Tribunal declared the proceedings formally terminated.

Eritrea-Ethiopia Boundary Commission

Parties: Eritrea/Ethiopia

Date of Arbitration Agreement: December 12, 2000

Commissioners: Prof. Sir Elihu Lauterpacht CBE QC (President), Judge Stephen M. Schwebel, Prince Bola Ajibola, Sir Arthur Watts KCMG QC,[†] Prof. W. Michael Reisman

Date of Decision: April 13, 2002

Summary

Delimitation of boundary based on colonial treaties and applicable principles of international law – colonial treaties of 1900, 1902 and 1908 not fully delimiting boundaries – interpretation of treaties as modified by subsequent conduct of parties (*effectivités*) – principle of *uti possidetis*, or respect for colonial boundaries existing at independence – limits of the *uti possidetis* principle – boundary line delimited according to treaties as modified by subsequent conduct of parties – Commission also mandated to demarcate the boundary – parties hampered Commission's ability to proceed with emplacement of pillars on the ground – location by satellite imagery and aerial photography of sites for pillar emplacement.

Legal Subject Matters

Customary international law:
- Prescription and acquiescence
- Principle of respect for boundaries existing at independence (*uti possidetis*)

Sources of international norms:
- Treaties
  - Interpretation
    - Modification by conduct

State:
- Jurisdiction
  - Evidence of display of State authority (*effectivités*)
- Territory and boundaries
  - Delimitation
  - Demarcation

[†] Deceased November 16, 2007.

Bibliography

Decision published in:
- 41 I.L.M. p. 1057 (2002);
- XXV R.I.A.A. p. 83 (2004).

Commentary:
- *The 1998-2000 War between Eritrea and Ethiopia: An International Legal Perspective* (Andrea de Guttry, Harry H.G. Post & Gabriella Venturini eds., TMC Asser Press 2009);
- Marcel Kohen, *The Decision on the Delimitation of the Eritrea/Ethiopia Boundary of 13 April 2002: A Singular Approach to International Law Applicable to Territorial Disputes*, *in* LIBER AMICORUM LUCIUS CAFLISCH p. 767 (2007);
- Abebe Zegeye and Melakou Tegegn, *The Ethiopia-Eritrea Conflict: A Critical Observation*, Institute for Global Dialogue Occasional Paper No. 5 (April 2007);
- Malcolm Shaw, *Title, Control, and Closure? The Experience of the Eritrea-Ethiopia Boundary Commission*, 56 INT'L & COMP. L.Q. p. 755 (2007);
- Philippe Weckel, *Commission des frontières (Erythrée/Ethiopie), Communication du 27/12/06*, 1 RGDIP p. 189 (2007);
- Bruno Simma & Daniel-Erasmus Khan, *Peaceful Settlement of Boundary Disputes under the Auspices of the Organisation of African Unity and the United Nations: the Case of the Frontier Dispute between Eritrea and Ethiopia*, *in* LIBER AMICORUM JUDGE SHIGERU ODA p. 1179 (2002).

Facts

In May 1998 armed hostilities broke out between Eritrea and Ethiopia (the "Parties"). After a number of attempts to re-establish peace by the United Nations ("UN") and the Organization of African Unity ("OAU") culminating in the June 18, 2000 Agreement on Cessation of Hostilities, on December 12, 2000, the two Parties signed the "Agreement between the Government of the State of Eritrea and the Government of the Federal Democratic Republic of Ethiopia" ("Algiers Agreement"),[1] providing for the permanent termination of military hostilities between them. Article 4 of the Algiers Agreement established the Eritrea-Ethiopia Boundary Commission ("Commission"). Pursuant to the Algiers Agreement, Eritrea appointed as Commissioners Mr. Jan Paulsson and Judge Stephen M. Schwebel, and Ethiopia appointed as Commissioners His Excellency Prince Bola Adesumbo Ajibola and Sir Arthur Watts KCMG QC. The party-appointed arbitrators selected as President of the Commission Professor Sir Elihu Lauterpacht CBE QC, who accepted his appointment on February 20, 2001. On June 12, 2001, following a challenge to Mr. Paulsson by Ethiopia and his subsequent resignation, Professor W. Michael Reisman was appointed by Eritrea to fill the vacancy thus created. Mr. Paulsson's resignation "did not imply any acceptance of the validity of the alleged grounds of the challenge."[2] According to Article 4(7) of the Algiers Agreement, the Chief of the UN Cartographic Section was appointed as the Commission's Secretary to provide technical and cartographic assistance. At its first meeting in March

---

[1] Alternate title: "Agreement between the Government of the Federal Democratic Republic of Ethiopia and the Government of the State of Eritrea."

[2] Decision Regarding Delimitation of the Border between the State of Eritrea and the Federal Republic of Ethiopia [hereinafter "Decision"], para. 1.14.

2001 the Commission appointed the Permanent Court of Arbitration ("PCA") as Registry for the proceedings.

Pursuant to Article 4(8) of the Algiers Agreement, the Parties submitted their claims and evidence relevant to the mandate of the Commission to the Secretary, who, pursuant to Article 4(9), identified those portions of the border as to which there appeared to be no dispute between the Parties, although Ethiopia reserved its position with regard to those findings.

On June 20, 2001, the Commission adopted its Rules of Procedure, based, as required by Article 4(11) of the Algiers Agreement, on the 1992 Permanent Court of Arbitration Optional Rules for Arbitrating Disputes between Two States. Pursuant to those Rules, the Parties filed Memorials within the time limits provided, with the written phase of the pleadings closing upon the filing of Replies on October 29, 2001. The Commission held hearings at the Peace Palace in The Hague from December 10 to 21, 2001. Following deliberations, the Commission delivered its unanimous Decision Regarding Delimitation of the Border on April 13, 2002.

Summary of Matters Submitted to Arbitration

The Parties provided in Article 4(2) of the Algiers Agreement that the mandate of the Commission was "to delimit and demarcate the colonial treaty border based on pertinent colonial treaties (1900, 1902 and 1908) and applicable international law," and that "[t]he Commission shall not have the power to make decisions *ex aequo et bono*." In Article 4(1) of the Algiers Agreement, the Parties "reaffirm the principle of respect for the borders existing at independence as stated in resolution AHG/Res. 16(1) adopted by the OAU Summit in Cairo in 1964, and, in this regard, that they shall be determined on the basis of pertinent colonial treaties and applicable international law."

Decision of the Boundary Commission

Mandate and Applicable Law

After summarizing the procedural and relevant substantive history, the Commission examined the three elements of its mandate, namely: (i) the interpretation of the colonial treaties; (ii) applicable international law; and (iii) the significance of the reference to the OAU Summit Resolution. The Commission stated expressly that its task in the delimitation decision was not concerned with the demarcation of the boundary, namely, the physical marking out of the boundary through the emplacement of boundary pillars on the ground, which would constitute the next phase of its activities.[3]

With regard to the interpretation of the specified colonial treaties, the Commission took guidance from the international judicial precedent and general principles of international law.[4]

---

[3] Decision, para. 3.37.

[4] Decision, paras. 3.6–3.11, 3.13. Authorities cited: Serbian Loans, 1929 P.C.I.J. (ser. A) Nos. 20/21, at p. 38 (Jul. 12); Legal Consequences for States of the Continued Presence of South Africa in Namibia (South West Africa) Notwithstanding Security Council Resolution p. 276 (1970), Advisory Opinion, 1971 I.C.J. REP. p. 22 (June 21); Temple of Preah Vihear (Cambodia v. Thail.), 1962 I.C.J. REP. p. 6 (June 15); Nuclear Tests

In setting out the applicable principles of treaty interpretation, the Commission took into account the meaning of the treaty and the "common will" of the Parties,[5] the doctrine of contemporaneity,[6] the role of preparatory documents,[7] and the role of subsequent conduct of the Parties, which "may be so clear in relation to matters that appear to be the subject of a given treaty that the application of an otherwise pertinent treaty provision may be varied, or may even cease to control the situation, regardless of its original meaning."[8]

The Commission held that "[t]he nature and extent of the conduct effective to produce a variation of the treaty" was "a matter of appreciation by the tribunal in each case."[9] In this connection, it described the process known variously as "estoppel, acquiescence, preclusion, or implied or tacit agreement," as:

> an act, course of conduct or omission by or under the authority of one party indicative of its view of the content of the applicable legal rule – whether of treaty or customary origin; the knowledge, actual or reasonably to be inferred, of the other party, of such conduct or omission; and a failure by the latter party within a reasonable time to reject, or dissociate itself from, the position taken by the first.[10]

In the Commission's view, "these concepts apply to the attitude of a party to its own conduct: it cannot subsequently act in a manner inconsistent with the legal position reflected in such conduct."[11]

The Commission held, further, following the reasoning of the International Court of Justice ("ICJ") in the *Case Concerning Kasikili/Sedudu Island*, that "applicable international law" was not confined to the law governing treaty interpretation and included rules of customary international law, "even if such rules might involve a departure from the position prescribed by the relevant treaty provisions."[12]

The Commission then set out considerations relating to the three broad categories of conduct on which the Parties had pleaded: maps,[13] activities on the ground tending to show the exercise of sovereign authority by the Party engaging in that activity (*effectivités*),[14] and diplomatic and other similar exchanges tending to evidence admissions or assertions of sovereignty.[15] The Commission further examined the differing weight to be accorded to maps

---

(Austl. v. Fr.), 1974 I.C.J. REP. p. 253, at pp. 267–268 (Dec. 20); Arbitral Award in the Dispute Concerning Certain Boundary Pillars Between the Arab Republic of Egypt and the State of Israel, (1988) 80 I.L.R. p. 226, (1988) 27 I.L.M. p. 1421; Case Concerning Kasikili/Sedudu Island (Bots./Namib.), 1999 I.C.J. REP. p. 1060; Award of Her Majesty Queen Elizabeth II, Pursuant to the Agreement for Arbitration of a Controversy between the Argentine Republic and the Republic of Chile concerning certain parts of the Boundary between their Territories (Arg. v. Chile), (1969) 38 I.L.R. p. 10, at p. 89 (Dec. 9, 1966) (*Palena* Award).

[5] Decision, para. 3.4.

[6] Decision, para. 3.5.

[7] Decision, para. 3.13.

[8] Decision, para. 3.8.

[9] Decision, para. 3.9.

[10] *Id.*

[11] *Id.*

[12] Decision, paras. 3.14–3.15, citing The *Kasikili/Sedudu* Case, *supra* note 4, at paras. 91–93.

[13] Decision, paras. 3.17–3.28.

[14] Decision, para. 3.29.

[15] Decision, para. 3.30.

presented by the Parties as evidence supporting their claims. Only one of the numerous maps under consideration was annexed to a treaty, namely, the map annexed to the Treaty of 1900. The Commission held that the reference to the 1964 OAU Summit declaration in Article 4(1) of the Algiers Agreement had the particular effect of manifesting the Parties' acceptance of the date of the independence of Eritrea – April 27, 1993 – as the date at which the borders between them were to be determined, noting that developments subsequent to that date would not be taken into account, "save in so far as they can be seen as a continuance or confirmation of a line of conduct already clearly established."[16]

The Central Sector

The 1900 Treaty, a bilateral agreement between Eritrea's former colonial power, Italy, and Ethiopia, provided that it is written "in the Italian and Amharic languages, both to be considered official save that in case of error in writing the Emperor Menelik will rely on the Amharic version."[17] No difference between the texts was alleged to be material in this part of the boundary, and the Commission used an agreed English translation.

The line described in Article I of the 1900 Treaty as "Tomac-Todluc-Mareb-Belesa-Muna" was held to delimit the boundary from the frontier with Sudan in the west to a point in the east where the river Muna "in its Treaty sense" was determined to end.[18] By the adoption of the 1902 Treaty, the Parties altered the western part of the boundary, after which the 1900 Treaty "[e]ffectively ... dealt only with the central sector."[19] The Commission observed that, in adopting the line in the 1900 Treaty, the Parties were legally confirming a line that had been accepted in practice for several years on a *de facto* or provisional basis.[20] As a delimitation which could form the basis for a demarcation of the boundary on the ground, the 1900 Treaty was insufficiently detailed in its description, and therefore the annexed map was of critical importance. Because the map was considered an integral part of the Treaty, as the Parties had "clarified their agreement by adding to the brief verbal description of the boundary the words 'as traced on the map annexed,'" it was analyzed under the same rules of interpretation as those applied to the Treaty text.[21]

The Commission considered that despite the Treaty map's inadequacies as a "delimitation which could form the basis for a demarcation of the boundary on the ground,"[22] the Treaty map was, on the whole, "an acceptable indicator of key features, including the location of Barachit, Senafe, Debra Damo and Adigrat, and the flow of rivers in the area between them."[23] The Commission proceeded to determine the boundary identified by the 1900 Treaty, as amended by the 1902 Treaty, in a line from west to east starting from the confluence of the Mareb and Mai Ambessa rivers.[24] It then examined the subsequent conduct of the Parties by

---

[16] Decision, paras. 3.31–3.36.
[17] Decision, note 19.
[18] Decision, para. 4.3.
[19] Decision, para. 4.4.
[20] Decision, para. 4.5.
[21] Decision, para. 4.8.
[22] *Id.*
[23] Decision, para. 4. 36.
[24] Decision, paras. 4.11–4.54.

reference to the four regions which were the subject of dispute.[25] The first was the western part of the Belesa projection, where the Commission found evidence to justify departures from the Treaty line in two areas: (i) at Tserona and Fort Cadorna, which as a result of an admission made by Ethiopia during the course of the proceedings were placed in Eritrean territory;[26] and (ii) in the Acran region, where evidence of Eritrean activity was found to be sufficient in administrative range, quantity, area, and period to justify treating that region as part of Eritrea.[27] The second region was the eastern part of the Belesa projection, where the Commission found that the evidence of the subsequent conduct of the Parties in relation to the town of Zalambessa supported the conclusion that this was Ethiopian.[28] In the third region, the Endeli projection (Irob), the Commission found evidence that Ethiopia had established its effective sovereignty to the required degree in the more southerly and easterly parts of the Endeli projection.[29] In the fourth region, Bada, the Commission found that the evidence presented was not sufficient to justify departing from the boundary line the Commission determined as that of the 1900 Treaty.[30]

The Western Sector

The 1902 Treaty, concluded between Italy, Ethiopia, and the United Kingdom of Great Britain and Ireland, was described as an Annex not only to the 1900 Treaty but also to a separate Treaty of May 15, 1902, regarding the frontier between Sudan and Ethiopia.[31] The 1902 Treaty modified the 1900 Treaty by providing that the frontier should begin at the junction of the Khor Um Hagar with the Setit and extend to the junction of the Mareb and the Mai Ambessa.[32] The 1902 Treaty provided in its final paragraph that it had been "signed in triplicate, written in the Italian, English and Amharic languages identically, all texts being official."[33]

The location of the western terminus of the boundary as expressed in Article I, paragraph (ii) of the 1902 Treaty, although not the subject of any dispute between the Parties, differed from the terminus shown by a number of maps, namely, the Khor Royan, which was the basis of an agreed tripoint between Eritrea, Ethiopia and the Sudan, a separate agreement which the Commission was not at liberty to change.[34] The Commission found that the boundary started at the agreed tripoint, ran to the center of the Setit immediately opposite that point, and turned eastwards up the Setit until it turned to the northeast to run towards the confluence of Mareb and Mai Ambessa.[35]

The most contentious part of the boundary covered by the 1902 Treaty was the point in the Setit where the boundary turns away to follow another named river, to which different

[25] Decision, paras. 4.63–4.91.
[26] Decision, paras. 4.69–4.70.
[27] Decision, para. 4.71.
[28] Decision, paras. 4.73–4.78.
[29] Decision, paras. 4.79–4.86.
[30] Decision, paras. 4.87–4.91.
[31] Decision, paras. 5.1, 5.9.
[32] Decision, para. 5.1.
[33] Decision, para. 5.5.
[34] Decision, paras. 5.6–5.12.
[35] Decision, para. 5.12.

names had been given in the English and Amharic versions of the Treaty, namely “Maiteb” and “Maiten,” respectively.[36] The Commission thus had to determine, first, to which river the Treaty referred, and second, the course of the link between that river and the Mareb.[37] Ethiopia contended that the reference in the 1902 Treaty was to the river presently known as the Maiteb, which the Commission called the western Maiteb.[38] Eritrea contended, initially, that the original Treaty reference to the “Maiteb” referred to a river called the Mai Tenné, and later suggested that it referred to the river Sittona.[39]

After seeking to establish the proper interpretation of the 1902 Treaty through the evidence adduced as to its terms[40] in light of its object and purpose,[41] its context and negotiating history,[42] and the subsequent course of conduct of the Parties in its application,[43] the Commission assessed the legal position as it stood on the eve of the Italian invasion of Ethiopia in 1935. In the Commission’s view, this approach was proper in light of the history of the relations between Italy and Ethiopia in and after 1935 and the nature of the evidence available before and after that date.[44] The Commission found that, although Article I of the 1902 Treaty referred to a river called the Maiteb, the explicit object and purpose of the Treaty, namely, the assignment to Eritrea of the Cunama tribe, indicated that the intention of the Parties was that the boundary river should not be the western Maiteb. The Commission was satisfied on the evidence, including several key geographic features of the river marked by the negotiators of the 1902 Treaty on the sole available map, as well as the location of the territory of the Cunama, that the river marked as “Maiteb” was really the Sittona, and it therefore interpreted the name “Maiteb” in the 1902 Treaty as being the present-day Sittona.[45]

The 1902 Treaty indicated that the line from the Setit to the Mareb was yet to be delimited. The Commission therefore went on to delimit the whole border according to the colonial treaties and factors relevant according to applicable principles of international law.[46] Giving weight in this sector only to those maps produced by the Parties themselves prior to 1935, the Commission found that these maps amounted to subsequent conduct or practice of the Parties evidencing their mutual acceptance of a boundary corresponding to the Eritrea claim line,[47] with which the eastern border of Cunama territory between the Setit and the Mareb coincided.[48] Thus, as at 1935, the boundary between the Setit and the Mareb had crystallized and was binding on the Parties, and nothing in developments after 1935 was found to have had the effect of altering that boundary.[49]

---

[36] Decision, para. 5.13.
[37] *Id.*
[38] Decision, para. 5.14.
[39] Decision, para. 5.15.
[40] Decision, paras. 5.17–5.27.
[41] Decision, paras. 5.28–5.36.
[42] Decision, paras. 5.37–5.43.
[43] Decision, paras. 5.44–5.81.
[44] Decision, para. 5.82.
[45] Decision, para. 5.85.
[46] Decision, paras. 5.86–5.87.
[47] Decision, para. 5.88.
[48] Decision, para. 5.89.
[49] Decision, paras. 5.90–5.96.

The Eastern Sector

The 1908 Treaty was "done in duplicate and in identic terms" [*sic*] in Italian and Amharic, but each Party being satisfied that the English translation accurately stated its contents, the Commission used the English translation.[50] Article I of the 1908 Treaty states: "From the most easterly point of the frontier established between the Colony of Eritrea and the Tigre by the Treaty of the 10th July, 1900, the boundary continues south-east, parallel to and at a distance of 60 kilometers from the coast, until it joins the frontier of the French possessions of Somalia."[51] After setting out the relevant provisions of the Treaty and its geographic and historical context, the Commission specified the nature of the exercise under the 1908 Treaty;[52] the point from which the boundary was to commence;[53] the point where the boundary was to terminate;[54] and the geometric method by which the boundary was to be drawn.[55] The Commission determined that the optimum means of implementing Article I of the 1908 Treaty was to take a satellite image of the coastline of Eritrea and to project this line inland for a distance of 60 kilometers, so as to produce a line every point of which is exactly 60 kilometers inland from the nearest point on the coast.[56]

Turning to the question whether any subsequent conduct adduced by the Parties required the Commission to vary the boundary thus determined, the Commission found that the *effectivités*[57] adduced for the period since 1908 did not require any adjustment,[58] with the exception of the town of Bure, at which the Commission found that the historic boundary checkpoints reflected a common agreement of the Parties that the boundary passes equidistantly between the checkpoints at that town.[59] None of the maps presented led the Commission to change its conclusion regarding Article I of the 1908 Treaty as varied in relation to Bure.[60]

The Boundary Line within Rivers

With regard to the 1900 and 1902 Treaties, which designated rivers as key components of the boundaries they established, without specifying where in each river the boundary should be placed, the Commission held that, as favored by both Parties, the determination of the boundary within rivers must be deferred to the demarcation stage. In the meantime, there should be no change in the *status quo* and regard should be paid to the customary rights of the local people to have access to the river.[61]

---

[50] Decision, para. 6.1.
[51] Decision, para. 6.2.
[52] Decision, paras. 6.13–6.14.
[53] Decision, para. 6.15.
[54] Decision, para. 6.16.
[55] Decision, paras. 6.17–6.22.
[56] Decision, para. 6.21.
[57] *See* text accompanying note 14 *supra*.
[58] Decision, paras. 6.25–6.29.
[59] Decision, paras. 6.30–6.32.
[60] Decision, para. 6.33.
[61] Decision, paras. 7.1–7.3.

Conclusions

In the *dispositif*, the Commission set out its description of the boundary line, as unanimously determined by it,[62] and listed the maps illustrating the boundary, specifying that "a *definitive* map of the whole boundary on a scale of 1:25,000" would be produced "on a sector-by-sector basis as each sector is finally demarcated and the exact coordinates of the locations of the boundary markers have been determined."[63] It also included a table setting out the coordinates of all reference points mentioned in the Decision, including those not used in its description of the boundary, accurate to the equivalent of 0.18 kilometers. The Commission specified that these coordinates would be made more precise during the demarcation.[64] Appended to the Decision were the Commission's findings as to "The Subsequent Conduct of the Parties in the Sector Covered by the 1900 Treaty" (Appendix A) and as to the "Location of the Cunama" (Appendix B); and a "Technical Note Relating to Maps" (Appendix C).

The Demarcation Phase

The Parties called upon the Commission in Article 4(13) of the Algiers Agreement to arrange for "expeditious demarcation." In Article 4(15) they agreed that "the delimitation and demarcation determinations of the Commission shall be final and binding" and that "[e]ach party shall respect the border so determined, as well as the territorial integrity and sovereignty of the other party."

Both Parties immediately announced their full acceptance of the Commission's Delimitation Decision when it was delivered on April 13, 2002. The Commission promulgated the Demarcation Directions on July 8, 2002,[65] and established field offices in Asmara, Addis Ababa and Adigrat. Demarcation began in the eastern sector in March 2003 and the location of pillars was established through field assessment with the cooperation of both Parties by August 2003.[66] An impasse arose when the Commission attempted to commence demarcation in the central and western sectors. Ethiopia agreed that the Commission could continue with pillar emplacement in the eastern sector, but was not prepared to allow demarcation to begin in the central and western sectors.[67] Ethiopia raised various obstacles, such as prohibiting field-work within the territory under its control and contesting parts of the Commission's decision before the UN Security Council.[68] From October 2003, Eritrea began to take various measures impeding the Commission's field work and the ability of the United Nations Mission in Ethiopia and Eritrea to provide necessary assistance to the Commission's staff.[69]

---

[62] Decision, para. 8.1.

[63] Decision, para. 8.2.

[64] Decision, para. 8.3.

[65] *See* Commission's Statement of November 27, 2006, *annexed to* The Secretary-General, Special Report of the Secretary-General on Ethiopia and Eritrea, UN Doc. S/2006/992 (Dec. 15, 2006) [hereinafter "Statement"], para. 5.

[66] Statement, para. 8.

[67] Statement, para. 9.

[68] Statement, para. 10.

[69] Statement, para. 11.

The Commission held a meeting with the Parties on March 10, 2006, with a view to enabling the resumption of demarcation activities, but without success. A further meeting, which the Parties refused invitations to attend, was held on May 17, 2006. Meetings scheduled for June 15, 2006, and August 24, 2006, were cancelled due to refusal of one or both Parties to attend.[70]

On October 6, 2006, the Commission wrote to the Parties asking them what steps they intended to take to implement repeated requests by the Security Council to comply with their obligations under the Algiers Agreement. Ethiopia did not respond. Eritrea replied indicating that no progress could be made until Ethiopia stated without qualification that it accepted the boundary as determined by the Commission in its Decision of April 13, 2002.[71] The Commission met in private session at The Hague on November 20, 2006.[72] Both Parties declined the Commission's invitation to attend the meeting. Part of the meeting was attended by representatives of the Secretary-General of the United Nations, the European Union, the United States of America and the People's Democratic Republic of Algeria.

On November 27, 2006, the Commission issued a "Statement" announcing its decision to adopt an alternative approach of identifying the location of points for the emplacement of pillars by the use of image processing and terrain modeling techniques. The Commission provided the Parties with the list of boundary points that it had identified by those techniques along the whole length of the boundary. The Statement was annexed to the Special Report of the Secretary-General of the United Nations of December 15, 2006.[73]

Paragraph 22 of the Commission's Statement provided:

> As the Commission evidently cannot remain in existence indefinitely, it proposes that the Parties should, over the next twelve months, terminating at the end of November 2007, consider their positions and seek to reach agreement on the emplacement of pillars. If, by the end of that period, the Parties have not by themselves reached the necessary agreement and proceeded significantly to implement it, or have not requested and enabled the Commission to resume its activity, the Commission hereby determines that the boundary will automatically stand as demarcated by the boundary points listed in the Annex hereto and that the mandate of the Commission can then be regarded as fulfilled. Until that time, however, it must be emphasised that the Commission remains in existence and its mandate to demarcate has not been discharged. Until such time as the boundary is finally demarcated, the Delimitation Decision of 13 April 2002 continues as the only valid legal description of the boundary.

In June 2007, given that the Parties had not yet reached the necessary agreement to implement the demarcation process nor requested or enabled the Commission to resume its activity, the Commission invited the Parties to a meeting with the objective of recommencing the demarcation process. Both Parties having indicated that they would be willing to attend, the Commission held the meeting at The Hague on September 6 and 7, 2007. As the meeting with the Parties did not yield the necessary agreement to recommence demarcation activities, the Commission determined that its pillar locations identified in the Statement became

---

[70] Statement, para. 12.
[71] Statement, para. 14.
[72] Statement, para. 1.
[73] *Supra* note 65.

binding on the Parties at the end of November 2007, and the Commission at that point considered its mandate under the Algiers Agreement as having been fulfilled.[74]

[74] *See* Press Release, Nov. 30, 2007.

Eritrea-Ethiopia Claims Commission – General Introduction

Parties: Eritrea/Ethiopia

Date of Arbitration Agreement: December 12, 2000

Commissioners: Prof. Hans van Houtte (President), Judge George H. Aldrich, Mr. John R. Crook, Dean James Paul, Ms. Lucy Reed

Date of Awards:

***Partial Awards*:**
- Prisoners of War – Eritrea's Claim 17 (July 1, 2003)
- Prisoners of War – Ethiopia's Claim 4 (July 1, (2003)
- Central Front – Eritrea's Claims 2, 4, 6, 7, 8 & 22 (April 28, 2004)
- Central Front – Ethiopia's Claim 2 (April 28, 2004)
- Civilians Claims – Eritrea's Claims 15, 16, 23 & 27–32 (Dec. 17, 2004)
- Civilians Claims – Ethiopia's Claim 5 (Dec. 17, 2004)
- Western Front, Aerial Bombardment and Related Claims – Eritrea's Claims 1, 3, 5, 9–13, 14, 21, 25 & 26 (Dec. 19, 2005)
- Western and Eastern Fronts – Ethiopia's Claims 1 & 3 (Dec. 19, 2005)
- Diplomatic Claim – Eritrea's Claim 20 (Dec. 19, 2005)
- Diplomatic Claim – Ethiopia's Claim 8 (Dec. 19, 2005)
- Loss of Property in Ethiopia Owned by Non-Residents – Eritrea's Claim 24 (Dec. 19, 2005)
- Economic Loss Throughout Ethiopia – Ethiopia's Claim 7 (Dec. 19, 2005)
- Jus Ad Bellum – Ethiopia's Claims 1–8 (Dec. 19, 2005)

***Final Awards*:**
- Pensions – Eritrea's Claims 15, 19 & 23 (Dec. 19, 2005)
- Ports – Ethiopia's Claim 6 (Dec. 19, 2005)
- Eritrea's Damages Claims (Aug. 17, 2009)
- Ethiopia's Damages Claims (Aug. 17, 2009)

***Decisions*:**[1]
- Decision No. 1 "The Commission's Mandate/ Temporal Scope of Jurisdiction" (Aug. 2001)
- Decision No. 2 "Claims Categories, Forms and Procedures" (Aug. 2001)

---

[1] The Commission's Awards and Decisions are available at the PCA's website, www.pca-cpa.org.

- Decision No. 3 "Remedies" (Aug. 2001)
- Decision No. 4 "Evidence" (Aug. 2001)
- Decision No. 5 "Multiple Claims in the Mass Claims Process, Fixed-Sum Compensation at the $500 and $1500 Levels, Multiplier for Household Claims" (Aug. 2001)
- Decision No. 6 "Eritrea's Claim 18" (Dec. 19, 2005)
- Decision No. 7 "Guidance Regarding *Jus ad Bellum* Liability" (July 27, 2007)
- Decision No. 8 "Relief to War Victims" (July 27, 2007)

Facts

In May 1998, an armed conflict broke out between the State of Eritrea ("Eritrea") and the Federal Democratic Republic of Ethiopia ("Ethiopia") (collectively, the "Parties"). The Eritrea-Ethiopia Claims Commission ("Commission") was created pursuant to Article 5 of the Agreement between the Government of the Federal Democratic Republic of Ethiopia and the Government of the State of Eritrea of December 12, 2000 ("Agreement"). Article 1 of the Agreement provides that "[t]he parties shall permanently terminate military hostilities between themselves." Under Article 5(1) of the Agreement, the Commission has jurisdiction over "all claims for loss, damage or injury by one Government against the other, and by nationals (including both natural and juridical persons) of one party against the Government of the other party … that are (a) related to the conflict that was the subject of the Framework Agreement, the Modalities for its Implementation and the Cessation of Hostilities Agreement, and (b) result from violations of international humanitarian law, including the 1949 Geneva Conventions, or other violations of international law."

The Commission informed the Parties on August 29, 2001, that it intended to conduct proceedings in Government-to-Government claims in two stages: first, concerning liability and second, if liability was found, concerning damages. Following the exchange of written pleadings, hearings on the issue of liability were held at the Peace Palace in four rounds between November 2002 and April 2005. On April 13, 2006, the Commission issued an Order directing the Parties to proceed with a simplified damages phase. Hearings proceeded in two groups: the first, "Group Number One Claims," from April 17 to 27, 2007, and the second, "Group Number Two Claims," from May 19 to 28, 2008.

Eritrea-Ethiopia Claims Commission

Partial Award
Eritrea's Claim 17: Prisoners of War

Parties:	Eritrea/Ethiopia
Date of Arbitration Agreement:	December 12, 2000
Commissioners:	Prof. Hans van Houtte (President), Judge George H. Aldrich, Mr. John R. Crook, Dean James Paul, Ms. Lucy Reed
Date of Partial Award:	July 1, 2003

Summary

International armed conflict waged between Eritrea and Ethiopia between 1998 and 2000 – approximately 2,600 Eritrean prisoners of war ("POWs") interned by Ethiopia during that conflict – liability of Ethiopia for violations of international humanitarian law committed in treatment of POWs – Ethiopia liable for failing to prevent beating or other unlawful abuse of Eritrean POWs at capture – Ethiopia liable for frequently depriving Eritrean POWs of footwear – Ethiopia liable for failing to protect personal property of Eritrean POWs – Ethiopia liable for subjecting Eritrean POWs to enforced indoctrination at certain camps – Ethiopia liable for permitting health conditions at Mai Kenetal endangering the health of Eritrean POWs confined there – Ethiopia liable for providing all Eritrean POWs prior to December 2000 a diet seriously deficient in nutrition – Ethiopia liable for failing to provide required standard of medical care – Ethiopia liable for delaying repatriation of 1,287 Eritrean POWs for 77 days longer than reasonably required.

Legal Subject Matters

Settlement of disputes:
- Arbitration
  - Jurisdiction of the arbitral tribunal
  - Standard of proof

International humanitarian law:
- International Committee of the Red Cross
  - Confidentiality
- Sources
  - Customary international humanitarian law

  - Geneva Conventions 1949
  - Hague Regulations 1907
- Violations
  - Unlawful treatment of prisoners of war
    - Deprivation of footwear
    - Enforced indoctrination
    - Failure to protect personal property
    - Inadequate health conditions in camps
    - Inadequate medical care
    - Physical abuse

Bibliography

Award published in:
- XXVI R.I.A.A. (forthcoming 2010);
- 42 I.L.M. p. 1083 (2003).

Commentary:
- *The 1998-2000 War between Eritrea and Ethiopia: An International Legal Perspective* (Andrea de Guttry, Harry H.G. Post & Gabriella Venturini eds., TMC Asser Press 2009);
- Hans van Houtte, *The Eritrea-Ethiopia Claims Commission and International Humanitarian Law*, *in* JUDICIAL RIGHTS AND INTERNATIONAL JUSTICE, LIBER FAUSTO POCAR p. 383 (Guiffre 2009);
- Pierre d'Argent & Jean d'Aspremont, *La Commission des réclamations Érythrée-Éthiopie : un premier bilan*, 53 AFDI p. 347 (2007);
- Won Kidane, *Civil Liability for Violations of International Law: The Jurisprudence of the Eritrea-Ethiopia Claims Commission in The Hague*, 25 WIS. INT'L L.J. p. 23 (2007);
- George H. Aldrich, *The Work of the Eritrea-Ethiopia Claims Commission*, 6 Y.B. INT'L HUMAN. L. p. 435 (2006);
- Natalie Klein, *State Responsibility for International Humanitarian Law Violations and the Work of the Eritrea Ethiopia Claims Commission So Far*, 47 GERM. Y.B. INT'L L. p. 214 (2005);
- Judith I.A. Lichtenberg, *Eritrea Ethiopia Claims Commission*, 12 TILBURG FOREIGN L. REV. p. 266 (2004);
- J. Romesh Weeramantry, *Prisoners of War (Eritrea v. Ethiopia), Eritrea's Claim 17/Ethiopia's Claim 4, Partial Awards*, 99 AM. J. INT'L .L. p. 465 (2005);
- Caroline E. Foster, *The Partial Awards of the Eritrea-Ethiopia Claims Commission on the Treatment of Prisoners of War*, 1 N.Z. Y.B. INT'L L. p. 139 (2004).

Facts

The Parties waged a costly, large-scale international armed conflict along several areas of their common frontier between 1998 and 2000. Ethiopia interned a total of approximately 2,600 Eritrean POWs between the start of the conflict and November 29, 2002, when all remaining Eritrean POWs registered by the International Committee of the Red Cross were released.[1] Ethiopia utilized six permanent camps: Fiche, Bilate, Feres Mai, Mai Chew, Mai Kenetal, and Dedessa. Ethiopia also operated several transit camps.

[1] Partial Award, Eritrea's POW Claim [hereinafter "Partial Award"], para. 3.

Eritrea's Claim 17 was filed on December 12, 2001. Following the exchange of written pleadings, a hearing on the issue of liability was held at the Peace Palace in December 2002 in conjunction with a hearing in the related Claim 4 of Ethiopia.

Summary of Matters Submitted to Arbitration

A. Eritrea's claims for loss, damage, and injury suffered by it as a result of Ethiopia's alleged unlawful treatment of its Prisoners of War ("POWs"), who were nationals of Eritrea;
B. Eritrea's request for additional relief in the form of orders that Ethiopia:
   (i) cooperate with the ICRC in effecting an immediate release of all remaining POWs it held;
   (ii) return personal property of POWs confiscated by it; and
   (iii) desist from displaying information and photographs of POWs to public view.

Partial Award

Jurisdiction

The Commission determined that it had jurisdiction over Eritrea's claims concerning the treatment of its POWs by Ethiopia during the period December 12, 2000, until their final release or repatriation, including a claim for unjustified delay in the release and repatriation of some of those POWs. The Commission lacked jurisdiction over claims that were not filed by the December 12, 2001, filing deadline established by Article 5(8) of the Agreement. All other claims asserted in the proceeding were within the jurisdiction of the Commission.

Applicable Law

With respect to matters prior to Eritrea's accession to the Geneva Conventions of 1949 on August 14, 2000, the Commission held that the international law applicable to the Parties' claims was customary international law, including customary international humanitarian law as exemplified by relevant parts of the four Geneva Conventions of 1949.[2] Whenever either Party asserted that a particular relevant provision of the Geneva Conventions was not part of customary international law at the relevant time, the burden of proof would be on the asserting Party.[3] With respect to matters subsequent to August 14, 2000, the international humanitarian law applicable to the present claim was the relevant parts of the four Geneva Conventions of 1949, as well as customary international law.

Evidentiary Issues

The Commission's Rules of Procedure did not "articulate the quantum or degree of proof that a party must present" to meet the burden of proof.[4] The Commission held that it would require clear and convincing evidence to establish the liability of a Party for a violation of

---

[2] Partial Award, para. 41.
[3] Partial Award, para. 41.
[4] Partial Award, para. 44.

applicable international law.[5] It rejected any suggestion that, because some claims involved allegations of potentially criminal individual conduct, it should apply an even higher standard of proof corresponding to that in individual criminal proceedings.[6]

The Commission noted that it had "hoped to benefit" from the "experienced and objective assessment of conditions in both Parties' camps"[7] of the International Committee of the Red Cross ("ICRC"). It asked the Parties to include the ICRC reports on camp visits in their written submissions or to explain their inability to do so.[8] Both Parties responded that they wished to do so; however, the ICRC refused to permit access to information other than public documents on the grounds of its "deeply held belief that its ability to perform its mission requires strong assurances of confidentiality."[9] The Commission recorded its disappointment, in the unique situation that both Parties to the armed conflict agreed that the requested documents should be provided to it, that the ICRC was not prepared to allow it access to the requested materials.[10]

Findings of Liability for Violations of International Law

The Commission made several organizational comments before setting out its findings on liability.[11] It noted that "[u]nder customary international law, as reflected in the Geneva Convention Relative to the Treatment of Prisoners of War ("Geneva Convention III"), the requirement of treatment of POWs as human beings is the bedrock on which all other obligations of the Detaining Power rest."[12] It also stated that its task was not to determine the liability of a Party for each individual incident of illegality suggested by the evidence, but "to determine liability for serious violations of the law by the Parties, which are usually illegal acts or omissions that were frequent or pervasive and consequently affected significant numbers of victims."[13]

Mistreatment of POWs at Capture and Its Immediate Aftermath

Eritrea alleged that its POWs were mistreated at capture and its immediate aftermath. The Commission noted that many of the Eritrean POW declarants were already wounded at capture and nearly all testified to treatment of the sick or wounded by Ethiopian forces upon capture and during evacuation. Consequently, in addition to the customary standards reflected in Geneva Convention III, the Commission also applied the standards reflected in the Geneva Convention for the Amelioration of the Condition of the Wounded and Sick in Armed Forces in the Field of August 12, 1949 ("Geneva Convention I").[14]

---

[5] Partial Award, para. 46.
[6] Partial Award, para. 47.
[7] Partial Award, para. 51.
[8] Partial Award, para. 51.
[9] Partial Award, para. 53.
[10] Partial Award, para. 53.
[11] Partial Award, paras. 54–56.
[12] Partial Award, para. 55.
[13] Partial Award, para. 56.
[14] Partial Award, para. 57.

Ethiopia presented substantial evidence regarding the international humanitarian law training given to its troops. The Commission found that the evidence suggested that this training generally was effective in preventing unlawful killing.[15] It found that on balance there was insufficient corroborated evidence to find Ethiopia liable for frequent or recurring killing of Eritrean POWs at capture or its aftermath. In contrast, Eritrea did present clear and convincing evidence of frequent physical abuse of Eritrean POWs by their captors both at the front and during evacuation.[16] The evidence of frequent beatings and other unlawful physical abuse of Eritrean POWs at capture or shortly after capture was "clear, convincing and essentially unrebutted."[17] The Commission held that Ethiopia was liable for failing to take effective measures, as required by international law, to prevent such abuse.[18]

Eritrea alleged that Ethiopia failed to ensure humane evacuation conditions in accordance with the obligations of the Detaining Power as reflected by Articles 19 and 20 of Geneva Convention III. On balance, and with one exception, the Commission found that Ethiopian troops satisfied the legal requirements for evacuations from the battlefield under the harsh geographic, military and logistical circumstances. The exception was the frequent, but not invariable, practice of seizing footwear and requiring them to walk barefoot during evacuations from the battlefield, as a result of which the Commission found Ethiopia liable for inhumane treatment.[19]

Eritrea alleged widespread confiscation by Ethiopian soldiers of POWs' money and other valuables, either at or after capture, and asked the Commission to "order the return of all irreplaceable personal property to Eritrean POWs that was confiscated by Ethiopia ... and in particular that Ethiopia return identity documents and personal photographs displayed on the Internet."[20] The Commission found that personal property frequently was taken from Eritrean prisoners by Ethiopian military personnel, without receipts or any hope of return, contrary to Articles 17 and 18 of Geneva Convention III, and that Ethiopia was liable to Eritrea for the resulting losses suffered by Eritrean POWs.[21] It held that an order requiring the return of property unlawfully seized and held was not appropriate or likely to be effective.[22]

Physical and Mental Abuse of POWs in Camps

Both Parties submitted substantial amounts of evidence concerning the physical and mental abuse of POWs in the camps.[23] The Commission held that it lacked sufficient evidence to determine whether the physical punishments actually imposed on Eritrean POWs violated the standard in Article 89 of Geneva Convention III.[24] In contrast, regarding mental abuse, Ethiopia admitted that its camps were organized in a manner that resulted in the segregation

---

[15] Partial Award, para. 60.
[16] Partial Award, para. 62.
[17] Partial Award, para. 63.
[18] Partial Award, para. 63.
[19] Partial Award, para. 68.
[20] Partial Award, para. 72.
[21] Partial Award, para. 76.
[22] Partial Award, para. 78.
[23] Partial Award, para. 80.
[24] Partial Award, para. 81.

of various groups of POWs from each other according to the length of their military service.[25] Such segregation was contrary to Article 22 of Geneva Convention III. The Commission rejected Ethiopia's argument that this segregation was done to reduce hostility between the groups.[26] It noted, further, that Ethiopia conducted extensive indoctrination programs of the various groups of POWs in Bilate, Mai Chew, Mai Kenetal and Dedessa, with attendance effectively made compulsory, contrary to Article 38 of Geneva Convention III.[27]

Unhealthy Conditions in Camps

The Commission noted the fundamental principle of Geneva Convention III that detention of POWs must not seriously endanger the health of those POWs.[28] In the Commission's view, its task was to determine whether there were violations which warranted the imposition of damages because they clearly endangered the lives or health of POWs in contravention of the basic policy of the Convention and customary international law.[29] It held that, to sustain the burden of proof in the context of camp conditions, each Party had to produce credible evidence that:

(a) portrayed a serious violation;
(b) was cumulative and was reinforced by the similarity of the critical allegations;
(c) was detailed enough to portray the specific nature of the violation; and
(d) showed that the violation existed over a period of time long enough to justify the conclusion that it seriously endangered the health of at least some of the POWs in the camp.[30]

The Commission determined that a camp-by-camp analysis of the relevant evidence was appropriate in order to determine which, if any, of Eritrea's claims met the standard of endangerment of health. It then examined what it understood to be a general claim by Eritrea that the food conditions at all of Eritrea's internment camps combined over a period of time to produce serious malnutrition among a number of POWs that led to various illnesses.[31]

The Commission found the evidence relating to the short term camps at Feres Mai and Mai Chew insufficient to justify a finding that conditions there seriously endangered the health of POWs.[32] Mai Kenetal presented a different picture, as it was put into operation at the onset of winter, and in May 2000, Ethiopia launched a major offensive which produced an unanticipated camp population of around 2,000 POWs.[33] The Ethiopian declarants stated that ICRC teams regularly visited the camps and made no serious complaints about its conditions.[34] The Commission noted that this was a specific instance where access to the rel-

[25] Partial Award, para. 84.
[26] Partial Award, para. 84.
[27] Partial Award, para. 85.
[28] Partial Award, para. 87.
[29] Partial Award, para. 88.
[30] Partial Award, para. 90.
[31] Partial Award, para. 91.
[32] Partial Award, para. 92.
[33] Partial Award, para. 93.
[34] Partial Award, para. 100.

evant ICRC reports would have been helpful.[35] It found that a combination of serious, substandard health conditions did exist at Mai Kenetal for some time, that these conditions seriously and adversely affected the health of some POWs there and endangered the health of others, and that this situation constituted a violation of customary international law.[36]

Eritrea appeared in its Statement of Claim and Memorial to claim that, throughout their captivity, Eritrean POWs were provided food which was insufficient in "quantity, quality, and variety to keep them in good health and prevent loss of weight."[37] The Commission held that the food provided by Ethiopia to POWs at all camps prior to December 2000 was sufficiently deficient in needed nutrition, over time, as to endanger seriously the health of Eritrean POWs in violation of applicable international humanitarian law.[38]

Inadequate Medical Care in Camps

Eritrea claimed that Ethiopia did not provide the Eritrean POWs with the medical care required under international humanitarian law.[39] Eritrea also claimed that Ethiopia did not provide adequate infirmaries, clinics, and hospitals as required under Article 30 of Geneva Convention III,[40] and complained about the lack of preventive care in the Ethiopian camps as required by Article 31 of Geneva Convention III.[41] The Commission noted that the protections relating to medical care provided by Articles 15, 20, 29, 30, 31, 109, and 110 of Geneva Convention III are unconditional.[42] Many of these rules are broadly phrased and do not characterize precisely the quality or extent of medical care necessary for POWs.[43] Nevertheless, the Commission held that certain principles can be applied in assessing the medical care given to POWs.[44]

Many of the declarants criticized the quality of medical care[45] and complained about delays in medical treatment.[46] Ethiopia submitted extensive evidence in rebuttal, including declarations from military officers in charge of prisoners and from camp administrators and doctors.[47] The Commission relied mainly on the testimony of the Eritrean doctors, who examined the Eritrean POWs repatriated after hostilities ended in December 2000, and who were of the opinion that these wounded and sick POWs could not have received required medical care.[48]

The Commission considered monthly examinations of the camp population to be a preventive measure forming part of the Detaining Power's obligations under customary inter-

---

[35] Partial Award, para. 100.
[36] Partial Award, para. 101.
[37] Partial Award, para. 106.
[38] Partial Award, para. 114
[39] Partial Award, para. 119.
[40] Partial Award, para. 124.
[41] Partial Award, para. 126.
[42] Partial Award, para. 116.
[43] Partial Award, para. 117.
[44] Partial Award, para. 118.
[45] Partial Award, para. 121.
[46] Partial Award, para. 123.
[47] Partial Award, para. 127.
[48] Partial Award, para. 131.

national law.[49] Ethiopia neither contended that it conducted medical examinations nor attempted to justify the lack of such examinations.[50] There was limited isolation of contagious POWs, beginning only at Mai Kenetal.[51] The Commission concluded that Ethiopia failed to provide Eritrean POWs with the required minimum standard of medical care prior to December 2000,[52] but found that Eritrea had failed to prove that the medical care provided to Eritrean POWs after December 2000 was less than required by applicable law.[53]

Unlawful Assault on Female POWs

Eritrea alleged in its Statement of Claim that Ethiopian soldiers raped female POWs and, in one case, raped and killed a female prisoner. The Commission, after careful review of the evidence, found that Eritrea had not presented clear and convincing evidence of rape, killing or other assault aimed at female POWs. Without in any way undermining its recognition of the vulnerability of female POWs, the Commission did not find Eritrea liable for breaching "customary international law obligations to protect the person and honor of female Eritrean POWs."[54]

Delayed Repatriation of POWs

Eritrea alleged that Ethiopia failed to release and repatriate POWs without delay after December 12, 2000. On November 29, 2002, Ethiopia released all POWs registered by the ICRC remaining in its custody, thus rendering moot Eritrea's request for an order regarding repatriation. There remained Eritrea's claim that Ethiopia failed to repatriate the POWs it held as required.[55]

The Commission recalled that Eritrea acceded to the four Geneva Conventions of 1949 effective August 14, 2000, so they were in force between the Parties after that date. Article 118 of Geneva Convention III states that "[p]risoners of war shall be released and repatriated without delay after the cessation of active hostilities."[56]

The Commission determined that hostilities ceased after December 12, 2000, on which date the Article 118 obligation to repatriate "without delay" came into operation.[57] It held that these words "indicate that repatriation should occur at an early time and without unreasonable or unjustifiable restrictions or delays."[58] It recognized at the same time that repatriation "cannot be instantaneous," and that preparations for the safe, orderly, and consensual repatriation of POWs, especially the sick and wounded, could be time-consuming.[59] The Commission also noted that it was proper to expect that each Party's conduct with respect to

[49] Partial Award, para. 132.
[50] Partial Award, para. 134.
[51] Partial Award, para. 135.
[52] Partial Award, para. 136.
[53] Partial Award, para. 137.
[54] Partial Award, para. 142.
[55] Partial Award, para. 144.
[56] Partial Award, para. 145.
[57] Partial Award, para. 146.
[58] Partial Award, para. 147.
[59] Partial Award, para. 147.

the repatriation of POWs would be reasonable and broadly commensurate with the conduct of the other.[60]

After examining the evidence submitted by the Parties concerning the repatriation process,[61] the Commission concluded that, while Eritrea promptly released and repatriated its remaining POWs in late August 2002, Ethiopia waited three months, until November 29, 2002, to release the remainder of its POWs and to repatriate those desiring repatriation. This delay was not explained.[62] Having concluded that Ethiopia did not meet its obligation promptly to repatriate the POWs it held, as required by law, the Commission addressed the question of the date on which this failure of compliance began. Following the ICRC's announcement of the release of all remaining Ethiopian POWs from Eritrea on August 23, 2002, the Commission saw no legal justification for the continued prolonged detention by Ethiopia of the remaining Eritrean POWs, and estimated that the necessary arrangements should not have taken more than three weeks at the most. It held that Ethiopia violated its obligations under Article 118 of Geneva Convention III by failing to repatriate 1,287 POWs by September 13, 2002, and that it was responsible to Eritrea for the resulting delay of 77 days.[63]

---

[60] Partial Award, para. 149.
[61] Partial Award, paras. 150–156.
[62] Partial Award, para. 157.
[63] Partial Award, para. 163.

14.3

Eritrea-Ethiopia Claims Commission

Partial Award
Ethiopia's Claim 4: Prisoners of War

Parties:	Eritrea/Ethiopia
Date of Arbitration Agreement:	December 12, 2000
Commissioners:	Prof. Hans van Houtte (President), Judge George H. Aldrich, Mr. John R. Crook, Dean James Paul, Ms. Lucy Reed
Date of Partial Award:	July 1, 2003

Summary

International armed conflict waged between Eritrea and Ethiopia between 1998 and 2000 – approximately 1,100 Ethiopian prisoners of war ("POWs") interned by Eritrea during that conflict – liability of Eritrea for violations of international humanitarian law committed in treatment of POWs – Eritrea liable for refusing permission to International Committee of the Red Cross ("ICRC") to visit, register, interview and provide relief to Ethiopian POWs – Eritrea liable for failing to protect Ethiopian POWs from being killed at capture or immediate aftermath – Eritrea liable for permitting mental and physical abuse of Ethiopian POWs – Eritrea liable for depriving Ethiopian POWs of footwear – Eritrea liable for failing to protect personal property of Ethiopian POWs – Eritrea liable for seriously endangering health of POWs at certain camps due to inadequate housing, sanitation, drinking water, bathing opportunities and food – Eritrea liable for failing to provide required standard of medical care – Eritrea liable for subjecting Ethiopian POWs to unlawful conditions of labor – Eritrea liable for permitting unnecessary suffering of POWs during transfer between camps – Eritrea liable for failing to allow POWs to complain about conditions and frequently punishing those who complained.

Legal Subject Matters

Settlement of disputes:
- Arbitration
  - Jurisdiction of the arbitral tribunal
  - Standard of proof

International humanitarian law:
- International Committee of the Red Cross:

  - Access to prisoners
  - Confidentiality
- Sources
  - Geneva Conventions 1949
  - Hague Regulations 1907
  - Customary international humanitarian law
- Violations
  - Unlawful treatment of prisoners of war
    - Confiscation of personal property
    - Deprivation of footwear
    - Enforced indoctrination
    - Failure to allow, and punishing of, complaints by POWs
    - Failure to allow permission to ICRC to visit and register POWs
    - Inadequate health and sanitation conditions
    - Inadequate medical care
    - Killing at capture or immediate aftermath
    - Mental abuse
    - Physical abuse
    - Unlawful conditions of labor
    - Unnecessary suffering

Bibliography

Award published in:
- XXVI R.I.A.A. (forthcoming 2010);
- 42 I.L.M. p. 1056 (2003).

Commentary:
- *The 1998-2000 War between Eritrea and Ethiopia: An International Legal Perspective* (Andrea de Guttry, Harry H.G. Post & Gabriella Venturini eds., TMC Asser Press 2009);
- Hans van Houtte, *The Eritrea-Ethiopia Claims Commission and International Humanitarian Law*, *in* JUDICIAL RIGHTS AND INTERNATIONAL JUSTICE, LIBER FAUSTO POCAR p. 383 (Guiffre 2009);
- Pierre d'Argent & Jean d'Aspremont, *La Commission des réclamations Érythrée-Éthiopie : un premier bilan*, 53 AFDI p. 347 (2007);
- Won Kidane, *Civil Liability for Violations of International Law: The Jurisprudence of the Eritrea-Ethiopia Claims Commission in The Hague*, 25 Wis. Int'l L.J. p. 23 (2007);
- George H. Aldrich, *The Work of the Eritrea-Ethiopia Claims Commission*, 6 Y.B. INT'L HUMAN. L. p. 435 (2006);
- Natalie Klein, *State Responsibility for International Humanitarian Law Violations and the Work of the Eritrea Ethiopia Claims Commission So Far*, 47 GERM. Y.B. INT'L L. p. 214 (2005);
- Judith I.A. Lichtenberg, *Eritrea Ethiopia Claims Commission*, 12 TILBURG FOREIGN L. REV. p. 266 (2004);
- J. Romesh Weeramantry, *Prisoners of War (Eritrea v. Ethiopia), Eritrea's Claim 17/Ethiopia's Claim 4, Partial Awards,* 99 AM. J. INT'L L. p. 465 (2005);
- Caroline E. Foster, *The Partial Awards of the Eritrea-Ethiopia Claims Commission on the Treatment of Prisoners of War,* 1 N.Z. Y.B. INT'L L. p. 139 (2004).

Facts

The Parties waged a costly, large-scale international armed conflict along several areas of their common frontier between 1998 and 2000. Eritrea interned a total of approximately 1,100 Ethiopian POWs between the start of the conflict and August 2002, when the remaining POWs registered by the International Committee of the Red Cross ("ICRC") were released.[1] Eritrea utilized five permanent camps: Barentu, Embakala, Digdigta, Afabet, and Nafka (also known as Sahel). Eritrea utilized these camps one after the other and, with the exception of Barentu, closed each camp upon transfer of the POWs to the next camp.[2] Eritrea also used various facilities as transit camps during evacuation of the Ethiopian POWs from the various fronts.[3]

Ethiopia's Claim 4 was filed on December 12, 2001. Following the exchange of written pleadings, a hearing on the issue of liability was held at the Peace Palace in December 2002 in conjunction with a hearing in the related Claim 17 of Eritrea.

Summary of Matters Submitted to Arbitration

Ethiopia's claims for loss, damage, and injury suffered by it as a result of Eritrea's unlawful treatment of its Prisoners of War ("POWs") who were nationals of Ethiopia.

Partial Award

Jurisdiction

The Commission determined that it had temporal jurisdiction over claims by either Party based upon alleged delays in repatriation of POWs. The Commission lacked jurisdiction over claims that were not filed by the December 12, 2001, filing deadline established by Article 5(8) of the Agreement, which concerned Ethiopia's claim with respect to repatriation. All other claims asserted in the proceeding were within the jurisdiction of the Commission, including the claim concerning delayed access by the ICRC to Ethiopian POWs.

Applicable Law

With respect to matters prior to Eritrea's accession to the Geneva Conventions of 1949 on August 14, 2000, the Commission held that the international law applicable to the Parties' claims was customary international law, including customary international humanitarian law as exemplified by relevant parts of the four Geneva Conventions of 1949.[4] Whenever either Party asserted that a particular relevant provision of the Geneva Conventions was not part of customary international law at the relevant time, the burden of proof would be on the asserting Party.[5] With respect to matters subsequent to August 14, 2000, the international humani-

---

[1] Partial Award, Ethiopia's POW Claim [hereinafter "Partial Award"], para. 3.

[2] Partial Award, para. 4.

[3] Partial Award, para. 5.

[4] Partial Award, para. 29.

[5] Partial Award, para. 32.

tarian law applicable to the present claim was the relevant parts of the four Geneva Conventions of 1949, as well as customary international law.

Evidentiary Issues

The Commission's Rules of Procedure did not "articulate the quantum or degree of proof that a party must present" to meet the burden of proof.[6] The Commission held that it would require clear and convincing evidence to establish the liability of a Party for a violation of applicable international law.[7] It rejected any suggestion that, because some claims involved allegations of potentially criminal individual conduct, it should apply an even higher standard of proof corresponding to that in individual criminal proceedings.[8]

The Commission noted that it had "hoped to benefit" from the "experienced and objective assessment of conditions in both Parties' camps"[9] of the ICRC. It asked the Parties to include the ICRC reports on camp visits in their written submissions or to explain their inability to do so.[10] Both Parties responded that they wished to do so; however, the ICRC refused to permit access to information other than public documents on the grounds of its "deeply held belief that its ability to perform its mission requires strong assurances of confidentiality."[11] The Commission recorded its disappointment, in the unique situation that both Parties to the armed conflict agreed that the requested documents should be provided to it, that the ICRC was not prepared to allow it access to the requested materials.[12]

Findings of Liability for Violations of International Law

The Commission made several organizational comments before setting out its findings on liability.[13] It noted that, "[u]nder customary international law, as reflected in the Geneva Convention Relative to the Treatment of Prisoners of War ("Geneva Convention III"), the requirement of treatment of POWs as human beings is the bedrock on which all other obligations of the Detaining Power rest."[14] It also stated that its task was not to determine the liability of a Party for each individual incident of illegality suggested by the evidence, but "to determine liability for serious violations of the law by the Parties, which are usually illegal acts or omissions that were frequent or pervasive and consequently affected significant numbers of victims."[15]

Eritrea's Refusal to Permit the ICRC to Visit POWs

From the outset of the armed conflict in 1998, the ICRC was permitted by Ethiopia to visit the Eritrean POWs and the camps in which they were held. In Eritrea, all efforts by the

---

[6] Partial Award, para. 35.
[7] Partial Award, para. 37.
[8] Partial Award, para. 38.
[9] Partial Award, para. 46.
[10] Partial Award, para. 46.
[11] Partial Award, para. 48.
[12] Partial Award, para. 48.
[13] Partial Award, paras. 49–54.
[14] Partial Award, para. 53.
[15] Partial Award, para. 54.

ICRC to visit the Ethiopian POWs held by Eritrea were refused by Eritrea until August 2000, just after Eritrea acceded to the 1949 Geneva Conventions. The Commission had to decide whether such refusal by Eritrea constituted a violation of its legal obligations under the applicable law.[16]

The Commission rejected the argument of Eritrea that provisions of Geneva Convention III requiring external scrutiny of the treatment of POWs and access to POWs by the ICRC had not become part of customary international law. These requirements were indeed "treaty-based" in the sense that they were articulated in Geneva Convention III, but, as such, they incorporated past practices that had standing of their own in customary law, and they were "of such importance for the prospects of compliance with the law that it would be irresponsible for the Commission to consider them as inapplicable as customary international law."[17] It therefore held that Eritrea violated customary international law from May 1998 until August 2000 by refusing to permit the ICRC to send its delegates to all places where POWs were detained, to register those POWs, to interview them without witnesses, and to provide them with the customary relief and services.[18]

Mistreatment of POWs at Capture and Its Immediate Aftermath

Ethiopia alleged that POWs were mistreated at capture and its immediate aftermath. The Commission noted that many of the Ethiopian POW declarants were already wounded at capture and nearly all testified to treatment of the sick or wounded by Eritrean forces upon capture and evacuation. Consequently, in addition to the customary international law standards reflected in Geneva Convention III, the Commission also applied the standards reflected in the Geneva Convention for the Amelioration of the Condition of the Wounded and Sick in Armed Forces in the Field of August 12, 1949 ("Geneva Convention I").[19]

The Commission found that Ethiopia had presented a *prima facie* case that Eritrean troops regularly beat and frequently killed Ethiopians upon capture and its immediate aftermath. Eritrea offered detailed and persuasive evidence that Eritrean troops had received training on the basic requirements of the Geneva Conventions on the taking of POWs, but did not submit evidence of what steps it took, if any, to ensure that its forces actually put this extensive training to use in the field.[20] The Commission concluded that Eritrea had failed to rebut the *prima facie* case presented by Ethiopia and consequently held that Eritrea failed to comply with the fundamental obligation of customary international law that POWs, even when wounded, must be protected and may not, under any circumstances, be killed.[21]

Ethiopia alleged that Eritrea failed to ensure humane evacuation conditions in accordance with the obligations of the Detaining Power as reflected by Articles 19 and 20 of Geneva Convention III. Subject to the holding concerning unlawful physical abuse during evacuation and with one exception, the Commission found that Eritrean troops satisfied the legal requirements for evacuations from the battlefield under the harsh geographic, military,

---

[16] Partial Award, para. 55.
[17] Partial Award, para. 61.
[18] Partial Award, para. 62.
[19] Partial Award, para. 63.
[20] Partial Award, para. 67.
[21] Partial Award, para. 68.

and logistical circumstances.[22] The exception was the practice of seizing the footwear of all Ethiopian POWs and requiring them to walk barefoot during evacuations from the battlefield, as a result of which the Commission found Eritrea liable for inhumane treatment.[23]

Ethiopia also alleged frequent abuse in Eritrea's interrogation of POWs. The Commission recalled that international law does not prohibit the interrogation of POWs, but does restrict the information they are obliged to reveal and prohibits torture or other measures of coercion, including threats and "unpleasant or disadvantageous treatment of any kind."[24] The Commission found "clear and convincing evidence, unrebutted by Eritrea, that Eritrean interrogators frequently threatened or beat POWs during interrogation, particularly when they were dissatisfied with the prisoner's answers."[25]

The Commission found, further, that Eritrea failed to take the necessary measures to prevent the confiscation of prisoners' personal property, and held that, consequently, Eritrea failed to comply with its obligations under Articles 17 and 18 of Geneva Convention III and was liable to Ethiopia for the consequent losses suffered by Ethiopian POWs.[26]

Physical and Mental Abuse in Prisoner of War Camps

The Commission found Ethiopia's evidence consistent and persuasive that the Eritrean guards at the various POW camps often used force for the enforcement of rules and as means of punishment, and that guards who regularly beat POWs were not replaced as a result. The Commission held that the physical abuse of POWs violated customary law as exemplified by Articles 13, 42, 87, and 89 of Geneva Convention III.[27] There was also evidence of discrimination contrary to Article 16 of Geneva Convention III,[28] and that, after ICRC visits began, POWs were threatened with physical punishment if they reported abuses to the ICRC.[29]

Eritrea introduced little, if any, evidence to counter Ethiopia's evidence of physical and mental abuse of POWs. The Commission concluded that Eritrea violated international law from May 1998 until the last Ethiopian POWs were released in August 2002 by permitting the pervasive and continuous physical and mental abuse of Ethiopian POWs in Eritrean POW camps.[30]

Unhealthy Conditions in Camps

The Commission noted that a fundamental principle of Geneva Convention III is that detention of POWs must not seriously endanger the health of those POWs.[31] In the Commission's view, its task was to determine whether there were violations which warranted the imposition of damages because they clearly endangered the lives or health of

[22] Partial Award, para. 74.
[23] Partial Award, para. 74.
[24] Partial Award, para. 76.
[25] Partial Award, para. 76.
[26] Partial Award, para. 79.
[27] Partial Award, para. 82.
[28] Partial Award, para. 83.
[29] Partial Award, para. 84.
[30] Partial Award, para. 86.
[31] Partial Award, para. 87.

POWs in contravention of the basic policy of the Convention and customary international law.[32] It held that, to sustain the burden of proof in the context of camp conditions, each Party had to produce credible evidence that:

(a) portrayed a serious violation;
(b) was cumulative and was reinforced by the similarity of the critical allegations;
(c) was detailed enough to portray the specific nature of the violation; and
(d) showed that the violation existed over a period of time long enough to justify the conclusion that it seriously endangered the health of at least some of the POWs in the camp.[33]

The Commission then examined the health-related conditions at each of Eritrea's POW camps. It found sufficient evidence to constitute a *prima facie* case of serious violations at Embakala, Digdigta, Afabet, and Nafka, of required health-related conditions, which seriously endangered the health of prisoners.[34] The Commission found that the conditions of housing, sanitation, drinking water, bathing opportunities, and food at the prison camps at Embakala, Digdigta, Afabet, and Nakfa were such as to constitute a serious violation by Eritrea of its basic duties to protect the health of prisoners in its custody, and thus constituted a violation by Eritrea of applicable international humanitarian law.[35]

Inadequate Medical Care in Camps

The Commission noted that a Detaining Power has the obligation to provide its POW camps the medical assistance on which the POWs depend to heal their battle wounds and to prevent further damage to their health.[36] It found an abnormally high rate of deaths among the prisoners in Eritrean camps.[37] There were frequent complaints that treatment was inadequate and often delayed, and there was also evidence of a lack of basic preventive care.[38]

Overall, while the Commission was satisfied that Eritrea made efforts to provide medical care and that some care was available at each permanent camp, the evidence was inadequate to overcome Ethiopia's *prima facie* case.[39] It found insufficient evidence to establish that all POWs in need of medical attention were treated in a timely manner over the full course of their captivity.[40] It found, further, that Eritrea failed to take several important preventative care measures specifically mandated by international law, namely, the undertaking of regular medical examinations, the maintenance of personal POW medical data, and the segregation from the general POW population of POWs infected with contagious diseases.[41]

---

[32] Partial Award, para. 88.
[33] Partial Award, para. 90.
[34] Partial Award, paras. 93–94.
[35] Partial Award, para. 103.
[36] Partial Award, para. 104.
[37] Partial Award, para. 110.
[38] Partial Award, paras. 112–113.
[39] Partial Award, para. 116.
[40] Partial Award, para. 117.
[41] Partial Award, paras. 121–123.

Accordingly, the Commission held that Eritrea violated international law from May 1998 until the last Ethiopian POWs were released and repatriated in August 2002, by failing to provide Ethiopian POWs with the required minimum standard of medical care.[42]

Unlawful Conditions of Labor

Ethiopia alleged that Eritrea forced POWs to work in conditions that violated requirements of Articles 13, 14, 26, 27, 49–55, 62, 65, and 66 of Geneva Convention III.[43]

The Commission found that sick or wounded POWs who were not physically fit, and officers, were forced to work, in violation of Article 49 of Geneva Convention III,[44] and that Ethiopian POWs at Afabet, Digdigta, and Nafka were frequently beaten when they tried to take rests or were unable to carry heavy loads, in violation of Articles 13 and 51 of Geneva Convention III.[45] The Commission found, further, that POWs were forced to work without sufficient food or water or appropriate footwear, in violation of Articles 27 and 51 of Geneva Convention III,[46] that POWs were often required to work excessive hours, in violation of Article 53 of Geneva Convention III,[47] and that none of the POWs was paid for his work, as required by Articles 54 and 62 of Geneva Convention III.[48]

The Commission rejected claims by Ethiopia that the above conditions were "humiliating" under Article 52 of Geneva Convention III[49] or that POWs had been required to perform work of a military character in breach of Article 50 of Geneva Convention III.[50]

Conditions of Transfer Between Camps

Ethiopia alleged that Eritrea treated POWs inhumanely in the course of transfers between camps in breach of Articles 46 and 47 of Geneva Convention III.[51] On reviewing the evidence, the Commission recognized the effect of Eritrea's "drastically limited resources" and infrastructure.[52] However, it found that transfers were often accompanied by deliberate physical abuse by guards, including beating of the sick and wounded, and that Eritrea provided no effective measures to prevent such misconduct.[53] The Commission therefore held that Eritrea was liable for permitting unnecessary suffering of POWs during transfer between camps.[54]

---

[42] Partial Award, para. 124.
[43] Partial Award, para. 126.
[44] Partial Award, para. 127.
[45] Partial Award, para. 128.
[46] Partial Award, para. 129.
[47] Partial Award, para. 130.
[48] Partial Award, para. 131.
[49] Partial Award, para. 132.
[50] Partial Award, para. 133.
[51] Partial Award, para. 135.
[52] Partial Award, para. 136.
[53] Partial Award, para. 137.
[54] Partial Award, para. 138.

Treatment of the Dead

Ethiopia brought separate claims for alleged violations of customary international law following the death of a POW, citing Articles 120 and 121 of Geneva Convention III. In the absence of clear and convincing evidence, the Commission did not find Eritrea liable.[55]

Failure to Post Camp Rules and Allow Complaints

Ethiopia claimed violations of requirements to post camp regulations and to have complaints procedures. As regards the posting of camp regulations, the Commission recalled Article 41 of Geneva Convention III. It found that there is a customary obligation to post camp regulations in a clear and accessible location and otherwise to ensure that POWs are aware of their rights and obligations.[56] Given the sparse evidence supporting Ethiopia's claim, the Commission rejected it.[57]

As regards Ethiopia's claim that Eritrea did not provide effective complaint procedures, the Commission held that both customary law and the 1929 Geneva Convention guarantee POWs a right to complain about their conditions of detention free from retribution. The Commission found that Eritrea, in violation of its obligations under international law, did not allow Ethiopian POWs held at any of its camps to complain about their conditions and to seek redress. It also found Eritrea liable for subjecting prisoners who attempted to complain to heavy and unlawful sanctions, including segregation from the rest of the camp population and beatings by guards.[58]

---

[55] Partial Award, paras. 140–141.
[56] Partial Award, para. 144.
[57] Partial Award, para. 146.
[58] Partial Award, paras. 149–150.

Eritrea-Ethiopia Claims Commission

Partial Award
Eritrea's Claims 2, 4, 6, 7, 8 & 22: Central Front

Parties:	Eritrea/Ethiopia
Date of Arbitration Agreement:	December 12, 2000
Commissioners:	Prof. Hans van Houtte (President), Judge George H. Aldrich, Mr. John R. Crook, Dean James Paul, Ms. Lucy Reed
Date of Partial Award:	April 28, 2004

Summary

International armed conflict waged between Eritrea and Ethiopia between 1998 and 2000 – liability of Ethiopia for violations of international humanitarian law committed during conflict on Central Front – Ethiopia liable for unlawful looting and destruction of buildings whilst in occupation of several towns and villages – Ethiopia liable for permitting rape of women during its occupation of Senafe Town – Ethiopia liable for permitting deliberate damage by explosion to ancient monument – deadline for filing of claims of December 12, 2001 – dismissal of claims not filed before deadline.

Legal Subject Matters

International humanitarian law:
- Sources
  - Customary international humanitarian law
  - Geneva Conventions 1949
  - Hague Regulations 1907
- Violations
  - Destruction of property
  - Destruction of historic monument
  - Looting
  - Unlawful treatment of civilians
  - Rape

Bibliography

Award published in:
- XXVI R.I.A.A. (forthcoming 2010);
- 43 I.L.M. p. 1249 (2004).

Commentary:
- *The 1998-2000 War between Eritrea and Ethiopia: An International Legal Perspective* (Andrea de Guttry, Harry H.G. Post & Gabriella Venturini eds., TMC Asser Press 2009);
- Hans van Houtte, *The Eritrea-Ethiopia Claims Commission and International Humanitarian Law*, *in* JUDICIAL RIGHTS AND INTERNATIONAL JUSTICE, LIBER FAUSTO POCAR p. 383 (Guiffre 2009);
- Pierre d'Argent & Jean d'Aspremont, *La Commission des réclamations Érythrée-Éthiopie : un premier bilan*, 53 AFDI p. 347 (2007);
- Won Kidane, *Civil Liability for Violations of International Law: The Jurisprudence of the Eritrea-Ethiopia Claims Commission in The Hague*, 25 WIS. INT'L L.J. p. 23 (2007);
- George H. Aldrich, *The Work of the Eritrea-Ethiopia Claims Commission*, 6 Y.B. INT'L HUMAN. L. p. 435 (2006);
- Natalie Klein, *State Responsibility for International Humanitarian Law Violations and the Work of the Eritrea Ethiopia Claims Commission So Far*, 47 GERM. Y.B. INT'L L. p. 214 (2005);
- Judith I.A. Lichtenberg, *Eritrea Ethiopia Claims Commission*, 12 TILBURG FOREIGN L. REV. p. 266 (2004);
- J. Romesh Weeramantry, *Central Front (Eritrea v. Ethiopia), Eritrea's Claims 2, 4, 6, 7, 8 & 22/ Ethiopia's Claim 2, Partial Awards*, 99 AM. J. INT'L L. p. 465 (2005);
- Robert P. Barnidge, *The Eritrea-Ethiopia Claims Commission: Partial Awards, Central Front*, 6 GRIFFIN'S VIEW ON INT'L & COMP. L. p. 12 (2005);
- Weckel, Philippe, *Commission des réclamations Erithrée/Ethiopie, Sentences du 28 Avril 2004 (Front Central)*, 1 RGDIP p. 224 (2005).

Facts

The Parties waged a costly, large-scale international armed conflict along several areas of their common frontier between 1998 and 2000. After the armed conflict began on the Western Front in May 1998, both Eritrea and Ethiopia began to strengthen their armed forces along what would become the Central Front. From mid-May to early June 1998, Eritrean forces moved into areas administered prior to the conflict by Ethiopia, occupied territory, and established field fortifications and trench lines. When Ethiopia later moved substantial numbers of its armed forces into the area, a static front was created that remained largely the same for almost two years. In May 2000, Ethiopia launched a general offensive that drove all Eritrean armed forces out of the territory previously administered by Ethiopia and took Ethiopian forces deep into Eritrea. Ethiopian forces remained in occupation of parts of Tserona and Senafe Sub-Zobas until February and March 2001 when, pursuant to the December 12, 2000 Agreement Agreement, they withdrew to territory administered by Ethiopia prior to the conflict.

This Partial Award addressed allegations of illegal conduct related to military operations on the Central Front of that conflict. For the purposes of these claims, the Central Front encompassed the area of five Sub-Zobas in Southern Eritrea, namely, Adi Quala, Senafe, Areza, Tserona, and Mai Mene. These claims were filed on December 12, 2001. Following the exchange of written pleadings, a hearing on liability was held at the Peace Palace in November 2003, in conjunction with a hearing in Ethiopia's related Claim 2.

Summary of Matters Submitted to Arbitration

Eritrea's claims that Ethiopia was responsible for unlawful actions in the Central Front that resulted in the looting and destruction of property, destruction of infrastructure, personal injury to civilians, and desecration of places of worship, graves, and monuments.

Partial Award

Jurisdiction

Ethiopia challenged the jurisdiction of the Commission over certain claims that allegedly were not presented before December 12, 2001. The Commission upheld this challenge in relation to six of Eritrea's Claims, namely, (i) claims that violations of international law by Ethiopia occurred after March 2001; (ii) claims based on the alleged refusal or failure of Ethiopian military commanders to stop illegal conduct by Ethiopian soldiers in Senafe and Tserona Sub-Zobas; (iii) a claim of unlawful use of land mines in Areza Sub-Zoba; (iv) a claim that Ethiopia conducted unlawful re-education classes in Mai Mene Sub-Zoba; (v) a claim based on alleged violations of Protocol II of the 1980 Convention on Certain Conventional Weapons or of Articles 52, 57 or 59 of Additional Protocol I of 1977 to the Geneva Conventions ("Protocol I"); and (vi) a claim of alleged continuing unlawful occupation after March 2001 of Eritrean territory on the Central Front and unlawful conduct during such continued occupation. The Commission found these claims not to have been filed by December 12, 2001.[1] All other claims asserted in the proceedings were within the jurisdiction of the Commission.

Applicable Law

The Parties and the Commission proceeded on the premise that the 1998–2000 conflict between the Parties was an international armed conflict subject to the international law of armed conflict.[2] The Commission recalled its holding in its Partial Awards on Prisoners of War, in which it held that the law applicable to those claims was customary international humanitarian law as exemplified by the relevant parts of the Geneva Conventions. The Commission held that "these holdings apply as well to the Central Front claims addressed in the present Award and, indeed, to all the claims submitted to the Commission."[3] The Commission made the same holdings with respect to the customary status of the Hague Convention (IV) Respecting the Laws and Customs of War on Land of 1907 and its annexed Regulations ("Hague Regulations") as those it had made with respect to the Geneva Conventions of 1949.[4]

---

[1] Partial Award, Eritrea's Central Front Claims [hereinafter "Partial Award"], paras. 13–17.
[2] Partial Award, para. 20.
[3] Partial Award, para. 21.
[4] Partial Award, para. 22.

Evidentiary Issues

Eritrea's Claims were based on the actions within the five Sub-Zobas of the Central Front for which Ethiopia was responsible that were allegedly unlawful and resulted in the looting and destruction of property, destruction of infrastructure, personal injury to civilians, and desecration of places of worship, graves, and monuments. Following a general comment on the evidence of rape on the Central Front, the Commission dealt with these claims sub-zoba by sub-zoba.[5]

Noting that rape is an illegal act that need not be frequent to support State responsibility, the Commission looked for clear and convincing evidence of several rapes in specific geographic areas under specific circumstances.[6] It found such evidence in the Central Front regions where large numbers of opposing troops were in closest proximity to civilian populations for the longest periods of time, namely, Senafe Town in Eritrea and Irob Wereda in Ethiopia. The Parties were obliged to impose effective measures, as required by international humanitarian law, to prevent rape of civilian women. The clear and convincing evidence of several incidents of rape in these areas showed that, at a minimum, they failed to do so.[7]

Areza, Mai Mene and Adi Quala Sub-Zobas

This predominantly agricultural region became the area of initial fighting in Eritrea during Ethiopia's May 2000 offensive. The Commission rejected all claims relating to the Areza, Mai Mene, and Adi Quala Sub-Zobas for failure of proof.[8] The Parties disagreed as to whether the provisions of the Geneva Conventions applicable to occupied territory were applicable to these three sub-zobas, as Ethiopian armed forces were present only for a limited period of time. However, the Commission did not need to decide whether any areas within these three sub-zobas were occupied territory as it had dismissed all claims arising within them for failure of proof.[9]

Tserona Sub-Zoba

It was undisputed that Tserona Town, the principal town in the sub-zoba, was heavily damaged during the war. Eritrea contended that Tserona Town was subjected to massive looting by Ethiopian forces and that public buildings there were deliberately and unlawfully destroyed by Ethiopian demolition.[10] Ethiopia denied responsibility, submitting that some damage occurred in combat and asserting that some of the destruction and looting was carried out by Eritreans.[11] Eritrea submitted in evidence a satellite photograph of the town taken on May 31, 2000, a few days after Ethiopian forces occupied the town, which showed

---

[5] Partial Award, para. 35.
[6] Partial Award, para. 41.
[7] Partial Award, para. 42.
[8] Partial Award, paras. 44–47, 48–51, 52–56.
[9] Partial Award, para. 57.
[10] Partial Award, para. 59.
[11] Partial Award, para. 61.

that roofs remained on most of the structures in the town.[12] The Commission found the latter evidence persuasive that by June 2001, virtually all roofs, doors and windows were missing. It also found that three buildings that were evidently intact when the satellite photograph was taken were subsequently destroyed by explosives.[13] In view of the evident, substantial use of explosives to destroy those buildings, which were intact when the occupation began, the Commission concluded that Ethiopia, as the Occupying Power, must be held responsible for their destruction.

With respect to the claim for looting and stripping buildings in Tserona Town, the Commission, after reviewing the evidence, noted that Ethiopia occupied Tserona Town for nearly nine of the twelve months between May 31, 2000, and June 2001, when the damage was assessed. Whether or not Ethiopian military personnel were responsible for the looting and stripping of buildings in the town, Ethiopia, as the Occupying Power, was responsible for the maintenance of public order, for respecting private property, and for preventing pillage. Consequently, Ethiopia was liable for permitting the unlawful looting and stripping of buildings in the town during the period of its occupation.[14]

Given the difficulty of assessing relative responsibility for the looting and stripping of the town, and considering the evidence as a whole, the Commission found that Ethiopia was liable for 75% of the damage caused by looting and stripping in Tserona Town.[15] The Commission also found that Ethiopia was liable for 75% of the damage caused to the Tserona Patriots Cemetery, which was located immediately outside Tserona Town.[16]

Senafe Sub-Zoba

The Commission was unable to determine from the evidence the precise extent to which the damage to the village of Serha resulted from combat in late May 2000 or previously, but was satisfied that the bulk of that damage occurred while Ethiopia occupied the village and acted in violation of Article 53 of the Geneva Convention Relative to the Protection of Civilian Persons in Time of War ("Geneva Convention IV"), and consequently there was damage for which Ethiopia was liable. It held that Ethiopia was liable for 70% of the total damage inflicted on Serha from May 1998 through February 2001.[17]

Senafe Town was continuously occupied by Ethiopian forces from the time they entered the town on May 26, 2000, until they departed in February 2001. Numerous credible accounts indicated the presence of at least some Ethiopian soldiers there.

Eritrea presented detailed and cumulative evidence of several rapes by Ethiopian soldiers of Eritrean women in Senafe Town. Ethiopia's limited documentation that rape complaints were investigated and soldiers arrested and its emphasis on the scope of its humanitarian law compliance training were insufficient to rebut this *prima facie* case.[18] Accordingly, it

---

[12] Partial Award, para. 62.
[13] Partial Award, para. 62.
[14] Partial Award, para. 67.
[15] Partial Award, para. 69.
[16] Partial Award, paras. 70–71.
[17] Partial Award, para. 78.
[18] Partial Award, para. 81.

found Ethiopia liable for failure to take effective measures to prevent rape by its soldiers of Eritrean civilian women during Ethiopia's invasion and occupation of Senafe Town.[19]

Eritrea presented evidence that described a pattern of Ethiopian soldiers seizing property and widespread looting and destruction of property from homes, businesses, schools, clinics, and churches.[20] Ethiopia asserted that its troops were well trained in the rules of international humanitarian law and that Eritrean civilians were responsible for the looting, without providing any evidence directly supporting either contention.[21] The Commission held that Ethiopia, as the Occupying Power for approximately nine of the twelve months that Senafe town was not administered by Eritrea, was liable for 75% of the losses resulting from that looting that occurred in the town between May 26, 2000, and when the Eritrean administration returned in June 2001.[22]

The principal damage claim by Eritrea relating to Senafe Town was for the deliberate, unlawful destruction of infrastructure, in particular of a number of substantial buildings. The Commission received evidence from multiple sources showing that a significant number of important buildings had been destroyed by the time Eritrea resumed administration of the town in June 2001.[23] The task facing the Commission was to determine whether there was clear and convincing evidence that Ethiopia was responsible for the evident damage or destruction inflicted on these important buildings.[24]

The Commission considered the evidence relating to sixteen named buildings and complexes which constituted the complete list of destroyed buildings in Senafe Town for which Eritrea was claiming. It found Ethiopia to be liable for damage to the Electrical Authority buildings; the Ministry of Agriculture buildings; the New Town Administrative Headquarters; the Old Town Administrative Headquarters and Offices West; the Old Town Administrative Headquarters and Residence East; the Senafe Secondary School; the Senafe Hospital (for 90% of the value of the hospital); and for the destruction of the Sub-Zoba Administrative and Residential Buildings and the Telecommunications Building.[25] The Commission dismissed Eritrea's claims relating to the Bissrat Hotel, the Courthouse, the Momona Hotel, and the Police Station for failure of proof.[26] It dismissed all other claims relating to Senafe Town for lack of proof.[27]

The Stela of Matara

The Stela of Matara ("Stela") is an obelisk that is perhaps 2,500 years old and was an object of great historical and cultural significance to both Eritrea and Ethiopia. It stood alone on a plain 4.68 meters above ground, with another meter under ground. The Commission found evidence that the area where the Stela was located was controlled by Ethiopian forces

---

[19] Partial Award, para. 81.
[20] Partial Award, para. 82.
[21] Partial Award, para. 83.
[22] Partial Award, para. 84.
[23] Partial Award, para. 85.
[24] Partial Award, para. 89.
[25] Partial Award, paras. 95–103.
[26] Partial Award, paras. 104–105.
[27] Partial Award, para. 106.

at least from May 28, 2000. Witnesses stated that it was standing on the evening of May 30, 2000, and was lying on the ground on the morning of May 31.[28] Eritrea presented an expert witness who testified, to the satisfaction of the Commission, that the Stela was damaged and toppled by a military type of explosive.[29] Ethiopia asserted that it was unclear what caused the Stela to fall, that Eritrea had the burden of proof, and that it had not met that burden.[30]

The Commission held that Ethiopia was responsible for the felling of the Stela on the night of May 30-31, 2000, and that this was a violation of international humanitarian law. According to the Commission, the prohibition on the deliberate destruction of historic monuments in Article 56 of the Hague Regulations "is part of customary law."[31] As civilian property in occupied territory, the Stela's destruction was also prohibited by Article 53 of Geneva Convention IV and by Article 52 of Protocol I.[32] The Commission dismissed Eritrea's request that Ethiopia also be obligated to apologize for that damage, pursuant to its Decision No. 3 "Remedies."[33]

---

[28] Partial Award, para. 108.
[29] Partial Award, para. 109.
[30] Partial Award, paras. 110–111.
[31] Partial Award, para. 113.
[32] Partial Award, para. 113.
[33] Partial Award, para. 114.

14.5

Eritrea-Ethiopia Claims Commission

Partial Award
Ethiopia's Claim 2: Central Front

Parties:	Eritrea/Ethiopia
Date of Arbitration Agreement:	December 12, 2000
Commissioners:	Prof. Hans van Houtte (President), Judge George H. Aldrich, Mr. John R. Crook, Dean James Paul, Ms. Lucy Reed
Date of Partial Award:	April 28, 2004

Summary

International armed conflict waged between Eritrea and Ethiopia between 1998 and 2000 – liability of Eritrea for violations of international humanitarian law committed during conflict on Central Front – Eritrea liable for permitting physical abuse of civilians by intentional killing, beating and abduction in Mereb Lekhe, Ahferom, and Gulomakheda Weredas – Eritrea liable for permitting looting and stripping and deliberate unlawful destruction of structures in Zalambessa Town – Eritrea liable for failing to take effective measures to prevent rape of women by its soldiers in Irob Wereda – Eritrea liable for failing to release or provide information regarding civilians taken into custody – Eritrea liable for failing to prevent dropping of cluster bombs near a school and its civilian neighborhood.

Legal Subject Matters

International humanitarian law:
- Sources
  - Customary international humanitarian law
  - Geneva Conventions 1949
  - Hague Regulations 1907
- Violations
  - Cluster bombs
  - Destruction of property
  - Looting
  - Rape
  - Unlawful treatment of civilians
    - Abduction
    - Beating
    - Intentional killing

Bibliography

Award published in:
- XXVI R.I.A.A. (forthcoming 2010);
- 43 I.L.M. p. 1275 (2004).

Commentary:
- *The 1998-2000 War between Eritrea and Ethiopia: An International Legal Perspective* (Andrea de Guttry, Harry H.G. Post & Gabriella Venturini eds., TMC Asser Press 2009);
- Hans van Houtte, *The Eritrea-Ethiopia Claims Commission and International Humanitarian Law*, *in* JUDICIAL RIGHTS AND INTERNATIONAL JUSTICE, LIBER FAUSTO POCAR p. 383 (Guiffre 2009);
- Pierre d'Argent & Jean d'Aspremont, *La Commission des réclamations Érythrée-Éthiopie : un premier bilan*, 53 AFDI p. 347 (2007);
- Won Kidane, *Civil Liability for Violations of International Law: The Jurisprudence of the Eritrea-Ethiopia Claims Commission in The Hague*, 25 WIS. INT'L L.J. p. 23 (2007);
- George H. Aldrich, *The Work of the Eritrea-Ethiopia Claims Commission*, 6 Y.B. INT'L HUMAN. L. p. 435 (2006);
- Natalie Klein, *State Responsibility for International Humanitarian Law Violations and the Work of the Eritrea Ethiopia Claims Commission So Far*, 47 GERM. Y.B. INT'L L. p. 214 (2005);
- Judith I.A. Lichtenberg, *Eritrea Ethiopia Claims Commission*, 12 TILBURG FOREIGN L. REV. p. 266 (2004);
- J. Romesh Weeramantry, *Central Front (Eritrea v. Ethiopia), Eritrea's Claims 2, 4, 6, 7, 8 & 22/ Ethiopia's Claim 2, Partial Awards*, 99 AM. J. INT'L L. p. 465 (2005);
- Robert P. Barnidge, *The Eritrea-Ethiopia Claims Commission: Partial Awards, Central Front*, 6 GRIFFIN'S VIEW ON INT'L & COMP. L. p. 12 (2005);
- Weckel, Philippe, *Commission des réclamations Erithrée/Ethiopie, Sentences du 28 Avril 2004 (Front Central)*, 1 RGDIP p. 224 (2005).

Facts

Between 1998 and 2000, the Parties waged a costly, large-scale international armed conflict along several areas of their common frontier. After the armed conflict began on the Western Front in May 1998, both Eritrea and Ethiopia began to strengthen their armed forces along what would become the Central Front. From mid-May to early June 1998, Eritrean forces moved into areas administered prior to the conflict by Ethiopia, occupied territory, and established field fortifications and trench lines. When Ethiopia later moved substantial numbers of its armed forces into the area, a static front was created that remained largely the same for almost two years. In May 2000, Ethiopia launched a general offensive that drove all Eritrean armed forces out of the territory previously administered by Ethiopia and took Ethiopian forces deep into Eritrea. Ethiopian forces remained in Eritrean territory until late February 2001 when, pursuant to the December 12, 2000 Agreement, they returned to the pre-war line of administrative control.

This Partial Award addressed allegations of illegal conduct related to military operations of the Central Front of that conflict. For the purposes of these claims, the Central Front encompassed the area of military operations extending between Ethiopia's Mereb Lekhe Wereda on the west and Irob Wereda on the east and the corresponding areas to the north in Eritrea. These claims were filed on December 12, 2001. Following the exchange of written pleadings, a hearing on liability was held at the Peace Palace in November 2003, in conjunction with a hearing in Eritrea's related Claims 2, 4, 6, 7, 8 and 22.

Summary of Matters Submitted to Arbitration

Ethiopia's claims that Eritrea was responsible for unlawful actions in the Central Front that included the intentional killing, physical abuse, and abduction of civilians; rape; looting and destruction of property; destruction of infrastructure; and use of cluster bombs.

Partial Award

Jurisdiction and Applicable Law

Eritrea did not contest the Commission's jurisdiction over the types of claims presented by Ethiopia. The Commission found that it had jurisdiction over all of Ethiopia's claims. With respect to matters prior to Eritrea's accession to the Geneva Conventions of 1949, effective August 14, 2000, the international law applicable to this claim was customary international law, including customary international humanitarian law as exemplified by the relevant parts of the four Geneva Conventions of 1949. With respect to matters subsequent to August 14, 2000, the international law applicable to this claim was the relevant parts of the four Geneva Conventions of 1949, as well as customary international law. The holdings of the Commission to this effect in its Partial Awards on Prisoners of War applied "to all the claims submitted to the Commission."[1]

Evidentiary Issues

The Commission summarized the events on the Central Front relevant to Ethiopia's Claim.[2] It emphasized that its description of territories administered by one Party or the other prior to the conflict and the conclusions reached in this Partial Award were not intended to and could not have any effect on the lawful boundary between the two nations, the determination of that boundary being the task of the Boundary Commission established by Article 4 of the Peace Agreement of December 12, 2000.[3] The Commission noted, further, that in its Decision of April 13, 2002, Regarding Delimitation of the Border, the Boundary Commission "was not purporting to reach any conclusions as to the areas effectively administered by either Party in May 1998, when the armed conflict between them began."[4]

Ethiopia's Central Front claims were generally organized on the basis of the wereda in which each claim was alleged to have occurred. Following a general comment on the evidence of rape on the Central Front, the Commission addressed Ethiopia's claims wereda by wereda.[5]

Noting that rape is an illegal act that need not be frequent to support State responsibility, the Commission looked for clear and convincing evidence of several rapes in specific geographic areas under specific circumstances.[6] It found such evidence in the Central Front

[1] Partial Award, Ethiopia's Central Front Claim [hereinafter "Partial Award"], para. 15.

[2] Partial Award, paras. 24–33.

[3] Partial Award, para. 27.

[4] Partial Award, para. 30.

[5] Partial Award, para. 33.

[6] Partial Award, para. 38.

regions where large numbers of opposing troops were in closest proximity to civilian populations for the longest periods of time, namely, Senafe Town in Eritrea and Irob Wereda in Ethiopia. The Parties were obliged to impose effective measures, as required by international humanitarian law, to prevent rape of civilian women. The clear and convincing evidence of several incidents of rape in these areas showed that, at a minimum, they failed to do so.[7]

Mereb Lekhe Wereda[8]

Ethiopia's claims with respect to this wereda were based on allegations of physical and mental abuse of the civilian inhabitants of the wereda, the abduction of some civilians, indiscriminate shelling, indiscriminate placement of land mines, looting and unlawful destruction of private and public property, destruction of objects indispensable to the survival of the civilian population, and unlawful damage to environmental resources.

The Commission found that the military operations by Eritrea resulted in substantial numbers of Ethiopian civilians suffering prolonged danger, deprivation, and sometimes injury or death: first, while fleeing under fire; second, as displaced persons in caves and camps; and finally, from the presence of landmines when eventually they were able to return to their villages. The evidence was inadequate for the Commission to hold that either the shelling or the placement of land mines was unlawful on grounds that they targeted civilians or were indiscriminate, contrary to the Hague Regulations or customary international law.[9] Eritrea was liable for permitting frequent physical abuse of civilians by means of intentional killings, beatings, and abductions, as well as widespread looting and property destruction in the areas that were occupied by its armed forces from May 1998 to May 2000.

Ahferom Wereda[10]

Ethiopia claimed for the same types of alleged unlawful actions in Ahferom Wereda as it did in Mereb Lekhe Wereda. The Commission found clear and convincing evidence that those fleeing from Eritrean forces suffered from shelling and from small arms fired at them intentionally or indiscriminately,[11] and that many of the civilians who chose not to flee were physically abused by being beaten and, in some cases, being taken to Eritrea for interrogation and imprisonment.[12] The evidence was also adequate to show that Eritrean forces engaged in frequent destruction of property and looting of useful animals, materials, and other property. The evidence was inadequate for the Commission to hold that either the shelling or the placement of land mines was unlawful on grounds that they targeted civilians or were indiscriminate, contrary to the Hague Regulations or customary international law.[13] The Commission concluded that Eritrea was liable for permitting the frequent physical abuse of

---

[7] Partial Award, para. 39.
[8] Partial Award, paras. 41–53.
[9] Partial Award, paras. 47–50.
[10] Partial Award, paras. 54–59.
[11] Partial Award, para. 56.
[12] Partial Award, para. 57.
[13] Partial Award, para. 58.

civilians in Ahferom Wereda by means of intentional killings, killings and woundings caused by indiscriminate small-arms fire, beatings, abductions and widespread looting and property destruction in the wereda.

Gulomakheda Wereda[14]

The Commission then considered the Gulomakheda Wereda, which included the significant border town of Zalambessa. Eritrean armed forces had entered the wereda in early June 1998 and established trench lines a few kilometers south of Zalambessa and an area of military operations beyond them. In addition to claiming for the same types of alleged unlawful actions as it did in the Mereb Lekhe and Ahferom Weredas, Ethiopia claimed for forced labor, mental abuse, and the deportation of civilians to Eritrea.[15]

The Commission found adequate evidence to hold Eritrea liable for permitting frequent physical abuse of civilians in Gulomakheda Wereda during its invasion in June 1998, primarily in the form of aimed or indiscriminate small-arms fire, killings, beatings, and abductions, and less frequent, but recurring, physical abuse of civilians in the wereda during the next two years.[16] The Commission also found Eritrea liable for permitting frequent looting and destruction of property in the wereda during its occupation.

With respect to Ethiopia's claim of forced labor, the evidence described civilians being forced to work for the Eritrean armed forces for short periods, at tasks including burying bodies, digging trenches, and carrying ammunition to the front, without pay and under threats of beatings.[17] The Commission noted that while Article 51 of the Geneva Convention Relative to the Protection of Civilian Persons in Time of War ("Geneva Convention IV") permits Occupying Powers to requisition labor, it requires fair pay and work proportionate to individuals' capacities. However, the Commission concluded that, while the labor described was disturbing, it appeared to have taken place only during the early days of the occupation and was thus neither frequent nor pervasive, and did not therefore justify a finding of liability under the standards applied by the Commission.[18]

With respect to Ethiopia's claim for unlawful deportation, thousands of residents of Gulomakheda Wereda had been compelled to leave in early 1999 and go to displaced persons camps in Eritrea. Article 49 of Geneva Convention IV permits evacuation of a given area "if the security of the population or imperative military reasons so demand." The Commission accepted Eritrea's argument that the increased risks to inhabitants from Ethiopian artillery fire by February 1999 justified their mass relocation to camps for internally displaced persons ("IDP camps") and, for material reasons, such camps had to be in Eritrea.[19] The Commission therefore dismissed this claim.

---

14 Partial Award, paras. 60–70.
15 Partial Award, para. 61.
16 Partial Award, para. 62.
17 Partial Award, para. 65.
18 Partial Award, para. 66.
19 Partial Award, para. 68.

Zalambessa – Looting and Property Destruction[20]

The Parties disagreed as to which of them was responsible for the enormous damage inflicted on the town of Zalambessa, which, prior to the war, had approximately seven to ten thousand inhabitants and close to 1,400 buildings. When Ethiopia recaptured the town in May 2000, scarcely a single building remained intact, and virtually all residents had been compelled to leave by Eritrea in February 1999. Ethiopia claimed that the destruction was caused almost entirely by Eritrea during the Eritrean occupation of the town from June 1998 to May 2000. Eritrea alleged that the destruction was caused by the heavy and frequent shelling of Zalambessa by Ethiopia during the Eritrean occupation. Ethiopia denied shelling the town during that period except to destroy bulldozers that it alleged were being used to destroy buildings.

The Commission found that witness evidence from residents of Zalambessa asserting that Eritrean soldiers had looted virtually all moveable property, roofing materials, and other usable building materials by May 2000 was essentially unrebutted.[21] It was skeptical both of Eritrea's allegations of massive and sustained Ethiopian artillery fire into Zalambessa and of Ethiopia's assertions that its artillery fire into Zalambessa was limited to a few occasions when it tried to prevent bulldozers from destroying buildings.[22] It found that some destruction of structures within Zalambessa must be ascribed to lawful combat damage, but the majority of the destruction, based on the pattern of collapse of the building walls, was ascribable to deliberate actions by Eritrea. Having concluded that Eritrea's actions were the predominant cause of damage, the Commission assigned it responsibility for 75% of the physical damage to structures and infrastructure in the town and for 100% of the property looted in Zalambessa.

Irob Wereda[23]

The Commission turned, next, to Irob Wereda, at the eastern end of the Central Front. Eritrean forces were in regular contact with the civilian population over a long period in this wereda. Sovereignty over large portions of Irob Wereda was disputed. The Decision of the Boundary Commission placed in Eritrea substantial areas in northwest Irob that had been claimed and administered by Ethiopia when the war began.

The Commission rejected Eritrea's argument that, because the Boundary Commission determined the territory to be Eritrean, it could not be subject to belligerent occupation by Eritrea's own forces. The Commission did not agree that persons should be denied the protection of international humanitarian law because of disputes between the Parties to an international conflict regarding sovereignty over the territory concerned.[24]

The Commission found unrebutted evidence sufficient to establish a recurring pattern of excessive violence by Eritrean soldiers against civilians, including frequent beatings and

[20] Partial Award, paras. 71–73.
[21] Partial Award, para. 73.
[22] Partial Award, para. 73.
[23] Partial Award, paras. 74–100.
[24] Partial Award, para. 78.

deliberate killings.[25] It also found, on the basis of specific evidence, as well as cumulative general declarations of unreported, opportunistic rape by Eritrean soldiers, which Eritrea left unrebutted, that Eritrea was liable for failure to take effective measures to prevent rape by its soldiers of civilian women during Eritrea's invasion and occupation of Irob Wereda.[26] The Commission also found unrebutted evidence sufficient to establish a pattern of serious misconduct by Eritrean forces involving the detention and subsequent failure to release or provide information regarding the whereabouts of numerous civilians, and to establish a regular pattern of frequent severe beating and other physical abuse of civilians taken into custody.[27]

The Commission rejected, due to insufficient evidence, claims relating to forced labor, unlawful camp conditions, indiscriminate shelling, and the unlawful use of landmines. As to Ethiopia's allegations of frequent and widespread theft and looting, the Commission found Eritrea liable for the theft and looting of livestock, household goods, and public and community property involving churches, schools, and governmental offices.[28] It dismissed other claims by Ethiopia, including allegations of destruction of environmental resources, as falling below the standard required to establish liability.

Aerial Bombardment of Mekele[29]

On June 5, 1998, Ethiopia and Eritrea exchanged air strikes, in which Ethiopia attacked the Asmara airport and Eritrea attacked the Mekele airport. Ethiopia alleged that Eritrea intentionally targeted the civilian neighborhood in Mekele town using cluster bombs. The Parties were agreed on certain key facts. Eritrea sent four separate single aircraft sorties to Mekele. The first sortie had no bombs; the second dropped cluster bombs on or near the airport runway; and the third sortie, at about 5 p.m., dropped two cluster bombs over the Ayder School and neighborhood.[30]

Other important facts were not agreed. Ethiopia asserted that the fourth sortie did not drop a bomb on the airport and dropped at least one cluster bomb on the same Ayder neighborhood, which Eritrea denied. Compelling testimony by witnesses placed the strikes on Ayder one hour apart, and this testimony was consistent with video evidence, hospital records, and a press article by journalists in Mekele that day. The Commission concluded that the fourth sortie dropped at least one cluster bomb on the Ayder neighborhood and found no evidence that it had dropped any bomb on or near Mekele airport.[31]

The Commission was not convinced that Eritrea had deliberately targeted a civilian neighborhood.[32] It held that the governing legal standard was best set forth in Article 57 of Additional Protocol I of 1977 to the Geneva Conventions, "the essence of which is that all feasible precautions to prevent unintended injury to protected persons must be taken in choosing

[25] Partial Award, para. 82.
[26] Partial Award, para. 84.
[27] Partial Award, paras 85–88.
[28] Partial Award, paras. 96–99.
[29] Partial Award, paras. 101-113.
[30] Partial Award, para. 103.
[31] Partial Award, para. 107.
[32] Partial Award, para. 108.

targets, in the choice of means and methods of attack and in the actual conduct of operations."[33] The Commission did not question the choice of Mekele airport as a target, nor did it question the validity of Eritrea's argument that it had to use some inexperienced pilots and ground crew due to its lack of experienced personnel. However, the Commission had "serious concerns" about the manner in which these operations were carried out, holding that "[t]he failure of two out of three bomb runs to come close to their intended targets indicates a lack of essential care in conducting them, compounded by Eritrea's failure to take appropriate actions afterwards to prevent future recurrence."[34] The Commission could not determine from the evidence available to it why the bombs dropped from the third and fourth sorties hit the Ayder neighborhood, noting that all of the information critical to the issue was in the hands of Eritrea or could have been obtained by it, and that Eritrea did not make it available. The Commission was thus entitled to draw adverse inferences reinforcing the conclusions that not all feasible precautions were taken by Eritrea in its conduct of the airstrikes on Mekele on June 5, 1998.[35] It concluded that Eritrea was liable for the deaths, wounds, and physical damage to civilians and civilian objects caused in Mekele by the third and fourth sorties on June 5, 1998.

Aksum and Adigrat

The Commission rejected a claim by Ethiopia that Eritrea also bombed the Aksum civilian airport late on June 5, 1998. Eritrea denied any such bombing. The Commission found no liability for the alleged bombing in any event, as "an airfield is a legitimate target, even when there are no military personnel there at the time."[36] The Commission also rejected a claim by Ethiopia for several air strikes against targets in the town of Adigrat and for periodic shelling of the town. These claims failed for lack of proof, as it had not been proved that any bombing or artillery attacks against Adigrat were aimed at unlawful targets or were indiscriminate.[37]

---

[33] Partial Award, para. 110.
[34] Partial Award, para. 110.
[35] Partial Award, para. 112.
[36] Partial Award, para. 114.
[37] Partial Award, para. 115.

14.6

Eritrea-Ethiopia Claims Commission

Partial Award
Eritrea's Claims 15, 16, 23 & 27-32: Civilians Claims

Parties: Eritrea/Ethiopia

Date of Arbitration Agreement: December 12, 2000

Commissioners: Prof. Hans van Houtte (President), Judge George H. Aldrich, Mr. John R. Crook, Dean James Paul, Ms. Lucy Reed

Date of Partial Award: December 17, 2004

Summary

1993 Referendum on Eritrean self-determination limited to Eritrean citizens – Ethiopian nationals who acquired Eritrean nationality in order to participate in 1993 Referendum held to be dual nationals of Eritrea and Ethiopia – international armed conflict waged between Eritrea and Ethiopia between 1998 and 2000 – liability of Ethiopia for violations of international humanitarian law committed in treatment of Eritrean civilians – Ethiopia liable for erroneously depriving some Ethiopians who were not dual nationals of their Ethiopian nationality – Ethiopia liable for arbitrarily depriving of their Ethiopian nationality dual nationals who remained in Ethiopia during the war, dual nationals who were present in third countries during the war, and dual nationals who were expelled to Eritrea but were not screened pursuant to Ethiopia's security review procedure – Ethiopia liable for permitting local farmers, militia, or police forcibly to expel rural people from rural areas near the border – Ethiopia liable for permitting the forcible expulsion to Eritrea of some members of expellees' families who did not hold Eritrean nationality – Ethiopia liable for permitting local authorities to expel to Eritrea an unknown but considerable number of dual nationals for reasons that could not be established – Ethiopia liable for frequently failing to provide safe and humane treatment to persons being expelled from Ethiopia to Eritrea – Ethiopia liable for holding Eritrean civilians on security-related charges under harsh conditions and subjecting them to abuse – Ethiopia liable for detaining Eritrean civilians without apparent justification, holding them together with prisoners of war, and subjecting them to harsh treatment – Ethiopia liable for limiting to one month the period available for compulsory sale of expellees' real property – Ethiopia liable for discriminatory taxation of proceeds from some forced sales and for maintaining a system of collecting taxes from Eritrean expellees that did not meet the required minimum standards of fair and reasonable treatment – Ethiopia liable for creating and facilitating a cumulative network of economic measures that collectively resulted in loss of all or most of assets in Ethiopia of Eritrean expellees contrary to duty to ensure protection of aliens' assets.

Legal Subject Matters

International humanitarian law:
- Nationality
  - Acquisition
  - Unlawful deprivation
- Sources
  - Customary international humanitarian law
  - Geneva Conventions 1949
  - Hague Regulations 1907
- States
  - Creation
- Violations
  - Unlawful treatment of civilians
    - Deprivation of property
    - Detention without due process
    - Discrimination
    - Failure to ensure protection of aliens' assets
    - Forcible family separation
    - Unlawful expulsion

Bibliography

Award published in:
- XXVI R.I.A.A. (forthcoming 2010);
- 44 I.L.M. p. 601 (2005).

Commentary:
- *The 1998-2000 War between Eritrea and Ethiopia: An International Legal Perspective* (Andrea de Guttry, Harry H.G. Post & Gabriella Venturini eds., TMC Asser Press 2009);
- Hans van Houtte, *The Eritrea-Ethiopia Claims Commission and International Humanitarian Law*, *in* JUDICIAL RIGHTS AND INTERNATIONAL JUSTICE, LIBER FAUSTO POCAR p. 383 (Guiffre 2009);
- Pierre d'Argent & Jean d'Aspremont, *La Commission des réclamations Érythrée-Éthiopie : un premier bilan*, 53 AFDI p. 347 (2007);
- Won Kidane, *Civil Liability for Violations of International Law: The Jurisprudence of the Eritrea-Ethiopia Claims Commission in The Hague*, 25 WIS. INT'L L.J. p. 23 (2007);
- George H. Aldrich, *The Work of the Eritrea-Ethiopia Claims Commission*, 6 Y.B. INT'L HUMAN. L. p. 435 (2006);
- Natalie Klein, *State Responsibility for International Humanitarian Law Violations and the Work of the Eritrea Ethiopia Claims Commission So Far*, 47 GERM. Y.B. INT'L L. p. 214 (2005);
- Judith I.A. Lichtenberg, *Eritrea Ethiopia Claims Commission*, 12 TILBURG FOREIGN L. REV. p. 266 (2004);
- J. Romesh Weeramantry, *Civilians Claims (Eritrea v. Ethiopia), Eritrea's Claims 15, 16, 23 & 27-32/Ethiopia's Claim 5, Partial Awards*, 100 AM. J. INT'L L. p. 201 (2006);

– Philippe Weckel, *Commission des réparations (Erythrée/Ethiopie), Sentences du 17 Décembre 2004 (réclamations des victimes civiles),* 2 RGDIP p. 480 (2005).

Facts

In 1993, the Parties became two separate States, as a result of the secession of Eritrea from Ethiopia, pursuant to the April 1993 Referendum on Independence ("Referendum"). Following the Referendum, the Parties held negotiations concerning, *inter alia*, the status of Ethiopian nationals who had acquired Eritrean nationality. The Parties did not reach a formal agreement on that issue prior to the outbreak of war in May 1998. In May 1998, an armed conflict broke out between the Parties. The Parties waged a costly, large-scale international armed conflict along several areas of their common frontier between 1998 and 2000. Prior to the 1998-2000 conflict, approximately 550,000 Eritreans lived in Ethiopia. The Parties disputed the treatment received by Eritreans in Ethiopia during the war and the circumstances of those who departed.

This claim was filed on December 12, 2001. Following the exchange of written pleadings, a hearing was held at the Peace Palace in March 2004, in conjunction with Ethiopia's related Claim 5.

Summary of Matters Submitted to Arbitration

This Partial Award addressed Eritrea's claims that, beginning soon after the outbreak of war in May 1998, Ethiopia wrongfully denationalized, expelled, mistreated, and deprived of property tens of thousands of Ethiopian citizens of Eritrean origin in violation of its international legal obligations.

Partial Award

Jurisdiction and Applicable Law

The Commission considered, *inter alia*, the issue of its jurisdiction to hear claims of persons who were not nationals of the claiming state. Article 5(9) of the Agreement provides that "in appropriate cases, each party may file claims on behalf of persons of Eritrean or Ethiopian origin who may not be its nationals. Such claims shall be considered by the Commission on the same basis as claims submitted on behalf of that party's nationals." The Commission held that this provision created an exceptional procedure empowering the Commission to decide claims for the benefit of persons who were of Eritrean origin who were not Eritrean nationals. Eritrea's Statement of Claim in its Claims 15, 16, and 23 presented the claims for injuries and losses suffered by its nationals and by Ethiopians of Eritrean origin as its own. The Commission held that such claims based on injuries to non-nationals made for Eritrea's own account, not on behalf of the affected individuals, were outside the Commission's jurisdiction.[1]

As to the applicable law, the Commission recalled its Partial Awards on Prisoners of War and the Central Front, in which it held that the law applicable to those claims before August

[1] Partial Award, Eritrea's Civilians Claims [hereinafter "Partial Award"], para. 19.

14, 2000, when Eritrea acceded to the four Geneva Conventions of 1949, was customary international humanitarian law, as exemplified by the relevant parts of the four Geneva Conventions. It held that its holdings in those Awards applied in the present case and to all the claims before the Commission. Hence, Ethiopia's treatment of Eritrean nationals was subject to the relevant principles articulated in the Geneva Convention Relative to the Protection of Civilian Persons in Time of War ("Geneva Convention IV") in addition to other potentially relevant law.[2] The Parties also treated the provisions of Additional Protocol I of 1977 to the Geneva Conventions governing the protection of civilians as reflecting binding customary rules. The Commission agreed with this approach.[3]

Evidentiary Issues

As in the Parties' prior cases, the Commission required proof of liability by clear and convincing evidence and took its fundamental responsibility to be to concentrate on persistent and widespread patterns of misconduct, rather than individual acts.[4]

Introductory Observations

The Commission structured its analysis around the five major substantive breaches of international law alleged by Eritrea: mass expulsion, denationalization, detention without due process, deprivation of property, and forcible family separation.

The Parties differed as to the legal consequences of the April 1993 Referendum on Independence ("Referendum"). Pursuant to proclamations issued by the Provisional Government of Eritrea in April 1992, participation in the Referendum was limited to persons having Eritrean citizenship. The first step in registering for the Referendum was to obtain an "Eritrean Nationality Identity Card" issued by the "Provisional Government of Eritrea." These cards were not limited in duration or effectiveness and bearers of the cards could use them as travel documents to make border crossings between Eritrea and Ethiopia before the war.[5] Ethiopia argued that the Eritrean nationality acquired in order to participate in the Referendum was genuine and effective, and those who acquired Eritrean nationality thereby lost their Ethiopian nationality by virtue of Article 33 of the Ethiopian nationality law. Eritrea argued that acquiring an Eritrean nationality card before Eritrea's independence did not have legal significance, as Eritrea was not yet a State capable of conferring nationality. Ethiopia argued that Eritrea had *de facto* emerged as a State prior to the Referendum.

Taking into account the unusual transitional circumstances associated with the creation of the new State of Eritrea and both Parties' conduct before and after the 1993 Referendum, the Commission concluded that those who qualified to participate in the Referendum in fact acquired dual nationality.[6] It relied, in particular, on a formal Agreed Minute signed by both Parties in 1996, which the Commission found to indicate both Parties' awareness of the citizenship issues resulting from the separation of Eritrea and their determination to resolve

[2] Partial Award, para. 28.
[3] Partial Award, para. 29.
[4] Partial Award, para. 35.
[5] Partial Award, para. 43.
[6] Partial Award, para. 51.

them through an orderly, mandatory future choice of either nationality by affected individuals, which would only be required after the Parties set the ground rules governing their future economic relations.[7] The Commission held that the advent of war did not *per se* end these people's dual nationality.[8]

Eritrea's Claim for Deprivation of Nationality

Ethiopia contended that customary international law gives States discretion to deprive its nationals of its nationality if they acquire a second nationality. According to Ethiopia, those who acquired Eritrean nationality thereby lost their Ethiopian nationality by operation of Article 11 of the 1930 Ethiopian nationality law, which provides that Ethiopian nationality is lost when a person acquires another nationality. Eritrea claimed that those who allegedly lost their Ethiopian nationality had, in fact, not acquired Eritrean nationality, and so were unlawfully rendered stateless by Ethiopia's actions. The question before the Commission was whether Ethiopia's actions were unlawful in the unusual circumstances of the creation of the State of Eritrea.[9] The Commission noted that international law would have allowed Ethiopia to take appropriate measures to implement its 1930 nationality law at the time of the 1993 Referendum as to persons who acquired Eritrean nationality then, but Ethiopia did not do so.[10]

The Commission recognized that international law limits States' power to deprive persons of their nationality, with particular reference to Article 15(2) of the Universal Declaration of Human Rights that "no one shall be arbitrarily deprived of his nationality." In deciding whether deprivation of nationality was arbitrary, the Commission considered several factors, including whether the action had a basis in law, whether it resulted in persons being rendered stateless, and whether there were legitimate reasons for it to be taken away given the totality of the circumstances.[11]

The Commission examined Eritrea's claims separately regarding several groups deprived of their Ethiopian nationality. It considered, first, dual nationals deprived of their Ethiopian nationality and expelled for security reasons. Based on the screening process used by Ethiopia, and given the exceptional wartime circumstances, the Commission found that Ethiopia had devised and implemented a system applying reasonable criteria to identify individual dual nationals thought to pose a threat to its wartime security, and held that the loss of Ethiopian nationality after being identified through this process was not arbitrary and contrary to international law.[12]

The Commission turned, next, to dual nationals who chose to leave Ethiopia and go to Eritrea. The Commission recognized that, whatever the individual motives of such nationals, "it was a serious act that could not be without consequences for any dual national of two hostile belligerents to choose to leave one for the other while they were at war with each

[7] Partial Award, para. 53.
[8] Partial Award, para. 55.
[9] Partial Award, para. 58.
[10] Partial Award, para. 59.
[11] Partial Award, para. 61.
[12] Partial Award, paras. 65–72.

other."[13] The Commission decided that the termination of the Ethiopian nationality of these persons was not arbitrary and was not in violation of international law.[14] The Commission also held that the deprivation of nationality of dual nationals who were in Eritrea was not arbitrary or otherwise unlawful.[15]

In relation to dual nationals remaining in Ethiopia, it was undisputed that these persons had been deprived of their Ethiopian nationality and, in August 1999, required to present themselves and register as aliens and obtain a residence permit. Those who did not do so were considered as illegal entrants to the country; those who registered received distinctive yellow alien identity cards. There was no evidence that the dual nationals in this group threatened Ethiopian security or suggesting other reasons for taking away their nationality. The Commission held that this wide-scale deprivation was, under the circumstances, arbitrary and contrary to international law.[16] The Commission also found, in relation to dual nationals who were in third countries or who had left Ethiopia to go to third countries, and dual nationals who were expelled without having been subject to the security risk assessment process previously described, that those individuals had been arbitrarily deprived of their Ethiopian nationality in violation of international law.[17]

Eritrea's Claim for Expulsion

Eritrea claimed that Ethiopia had engaged in prohibited ethnically based mass expulsions or ethnic cleansing. Ethiopia maintained that 15,475 persons with Eritrean nationality were individually identified through its security process and then deprived of Ethiopian nationality and expelled. This was less than 25% of the more than 66,000 persons in Ethiopia who qualified to vote for the Referendum. The Commission found an expulsion process involving deliberation and selection, not indiscriminate mass expulsions based on ethnicity. It rejected Eritrea's claims that Ethiopia engaged in indiscriminate mass expulsions based on ethnicity or in ethnic cleansing for lack of proof.[18]

The Commission noted that international law allows a belligerent to expel the nationals of the enemy State during wartime. It rejected Eritrea's claim that the persons who were lawfully deprived of their Ethiopian nationality following identification through Ethiopia's security risk assessment process had been unlawfully expelled.[19] However, it found evidence that persons in rural areas, who were unlikely to have taken part in the Referendum and thus have acquired Eritrean nationality, had been required to leave even though there was no evidence that they posed a threat to Ethiopia's national security.[20] These expulsions, which were carried out by local farmers, militia, or police, appeared to have been based purely on the Eritrean ethnicity of the persons expelled, and were therefore clearly unlawful. Ethiopia was therefore liable to Eritrea under international law for any damages and losses

[13] Partial Award, para. 73.
[14] Partial Award, para. 73.
[15] Partial Award, para. 77.
[16] Partial Award, para. 75.
[17] Partial Award, paras. 76, 78.
[18] Partial Award, para. 80.
[19] Partial Award, para. 82.
[20] Partial Award, paras. 84–88.

to Eritrea caused by these actions.[21] In light of the Commission's earlier finding as to its jurisdiction, since these persons were not Eritrean nationals, Eritrea could only claim for the damage caused to it by these actions, and could not claim in respect of the individual injuries of these persons.

The second major group of deportees raised during the proceedings involved the family members of persons who were expelled after being identified through Ethiopia's security process. The Commission held that, to the extent that those expelled were Eritrean nationals, their expulsion was lawful, even if harsh for the individuals affected.[22] The evidence was unclear regarding the nationality of many family members. The circumstances of family members' departures showed that some departures resulted from choices made by the affected individuals or their families, which the Commission held were lawful.[23] However, there was evidence that some family members had been forcibly expelled. The Commission held that the expulsion of family members who did not hold Eritrean nationality was contrary to international law. As with the rural expellees, Eritrea could not claim damages with respect to their individual injuries, but could seek to prove any monetary damages it might have incurred as a result of Ethiopia's treatment of these persons.

As regards the other dual nationals expelled for reasons that could not be established,[24] the Commission held that these expulsions were unlawful under applicable international law, and Ethiopia was liable for permitting them to occur.[25]

Eritrea also claimed that the physical conditions under which persons were expelled from Ethiopia were inhumane and unsafe. International humanitarian law requires that all departures, whether lawful or not, be conducted humanely, in satisfactory conditions as regards safety, hygiene, sanitation, and food. Based on the totality of the record, the Commission concluded that, despite some efforts to provide for expellees during some transports, the physical conditions frequently failed to comply with international law requirements of humane and safe treatment.[26]

Detention Without Due Process

Eritrea claimed that Ethiopia detained large numbers of civilians under harsh conditions contrary to international law. This claim related to (i) persons held short-term pending their expulsion, (ii) persons held in jails or prisons for longer periods, and (iii) civilians who were allegedly wrongly detained and confined together with prisoners of war.

The Commission rejected the claim in respect of persons detained short-term pending their expulsion, as the evidence was insufficient to show a widespread or significant failure by Ethiopia to provide internationally required standards of treatment.[27] With regard to the persons taken into custody by the Ethiopian security forces and then held for longer periods,

[21] Partial Award, para. 89.
[22] Partial Award, para. 92.
[23] Partial Award, para. 95.
[24] Partial Award, para. 78.
[25] Partial Award, para. 98.
[26] Partial Award, para. 106.
[27] Partial Award, paras. 109–110.

the Commission concluded that the persons in this group were held in harsh and unsanitary conditions, contrary to international law.[28]

With regard to the other civilian detainees, the Commission dealt, first, with the group of about 85 Eritrean students who were allegedly unlawfully detained whilst studying in Ethiopia and confined under allegedly harsh conditions. This claim had been deferred by the Commission from Eritrea's Prisoner of War Claims (Claim 17).[29] The Commission held that Ethiopia could reasonably have feared that the students might have returned to Eritrea and joined the Eritrean forces if left at large. Their internment was therefore consistent with Article 35(1) of Geneva Convention IV. The Commission held, further, that the record did not establish a substantial or widespread failure to meet Geneva Convention requirements with respect to their treatment.[30]

The Commission also dealt with Eritrea's allegation in its Prisoner of War Claims that Eritrean civilians were wrongly classified and held as prisoners of war. Ethiopia did not rebut the evidence that Eritrean civilians were detained and then held as prisoners of war. The Commission held that, while international law allows the internment of civilian nationals of an enemy State under specified conditions and appropriate safeguards, the record did not show that these requirements were met. Accordingly, the continued detention of the Eritrean civilians was contrary to international law.[31]

Deprivation of Property

Eritrea alleged that Ethiopia implemented a widespread program aimed at unlawfully seizing Eritrean assets, including assets of expellees and of other persons outside of Ethiopia, and of transferring those assets to Ethiopian governmental or private interests. The Commission noted the protections of aliens' property in the modern *jus in bello.* It noted that the safeguards provided by Article 23(g) of the Hague Relations and Articles 33, 38, and 27 of Geneva Convention IV operated "in the context of another broad and sometimes competing body of belligerent rights to freeze or otherwise control or restrict the resources of enemy national so as to deny them to the enemy State."[32]

Eritrea claimed that Ethiopia designed and carried out a body of interconnected discriminatory measures to transfer the property of expelled Eritreans to Ethiopian hands, including by preventing expellees from taking effective steps to preserve their property, forcing sales of immovable property, and auctioning expellees' property to pay overdue taxes.[33] In particular, Eritrea claimed numerous deficiencies in the principal means by which expellees sought to safeguard their property, namely, the appointing of agents by means of powers of attorney. According to Eritrea, many persons in pre-expulsion detention could not execute powers of attorney due to the limited time between arrest and expulsion; others who were abroad could not make effective appointments, because Ethiopian consular officials would not provide consular formalities.[34]

---

28 Partial Award, paras. 111–113.
29 Partial Award, para. 115.
30 Partial Award, para. 117.
31 Partial Award, para. 121.
32 Partial Award, para. 127.
33 Partial Award, para. 129.
34 Partial Award, paras. 130–131.

The Commission held that the mere shortcomings of the system of powers of attorney did not establish liability.[35] However, it held that the prohibition on alien ownership of immovable property, whilst not contrary to international law, had been implemented in an arbitrary and discriminatory manner, in that Ethiopia had shortened the period for mandatory sale of deportees' assets from the six months available to other aliens to a single month.[36] Eritrea also claimed that Ethiopia had unlawfully appropriated a significant portion of the value of expellees' property by imposing a 100% "location value" tax based on the value of the land, which was imposed on forced sales of real estate. The Commission found that this tax was not applied generally to all sales of real property, but was instead imposed only on certain forced sales of expellees' property. It was therefore a discriminatory and confiscatory taxation measure contrary to international law.[37]

The Commission dismissed Eritrea's claim that Ethiopia wrongfully facilitated or participated in the process of collecting expellees' bank loans through enforced sales of collateral properties.[38] It upheld Eritrea's claim in respect of the method created by Ethiopia to collect taxes allegedly due from expellees. This process involved sending a tax demand based on an estimate, with a notification that the property of the expellee would be auctioned in the event of failure to pay. Compliance was often made impossible because of bank foreclosure proceedings and the "array of other economic misfortunes befalling expellees."[39] The Commission held that this method was approximate and arbitrary and failed to meet the minimum standards of fair and reasonable treatment necessary in the circumstances. The Commission dismissed claims by Eritrea with respect to restricted bank accounts and with respect to the dissolution of the Horn International Bank.[40]

In addition to its findings regarding particular economic measures, the Commission considered the cumulative impact of those measures. The Commission held that Ethiopia, through the network of measures it had created, had failed to meet these responsibilities. The Commission moreover noted that, if the private property of enemy nationals is to be frozen or otherwise impaired in wartime, it must be done by the State and under conditions providing for the property's protection and its eventual disposition by return to the owners or through post-war agreement.[41]

Family Separation

Eritrea claimed that Ethiopia's actions resulted in the separation of families and failures to assure the protection of children contrary to international law, in that the detention and expulsion process had led to forcible separation of spouses, forcible separation of children from one or both parents, and children being left without proper care. Ethiopia contended that it took feasible measures to avoid separating families by allowing detainees to bring their children with them and by allowing family members of expellees to leave Ethiopia

[35] Partial Award, para. 133.
[36] Partial Award, para. 136.
[37] Partial Award, para. 140.
[38] Partial Award, para. 142.
[39] Partial Award, para. 144.
[40] Partial Award, paras. 145–150.
[41] Partial Award, para. 152.

either simultaneously or subsequently. The Commission noted that both international humanitarian law and human rights law recognize that, regrettably, absolute protection of the family cannot be assured in wartime.[42] It held that Eritrea had failed to prove a pattern of frequent instances of forcible family separation or failures to assure the protection of children, and dismissed Eritrea's claim for failure of proof.[43]

Claims on Behalf of Specific Individuals

Eritrea's Claims 27–32 were brought on behalf of specific named individuals alleging injury resulting from the broader patterns of conduct considered in the present Partial Award, namely, Ethiopia's actions involving deprivation of citizenship and expulsion and Ethiopian measures affecting expellees' property. The Commission held that its Partial Award applied to all of the claims before it in the present proceedings, including Claims 27–32, and that the application of the Commission's findings to the facts of each of those claims would be assessed in the future damages phase of the proceedings.[44]

---

[42] Partial Award, para. 154.
[43] Partial Award, para. 157.
[44] Partial Award, para. 160.

14.7

Eritrea-Ethiopia Claims Commission

Partial Award
Ethiopia's Claim 5: Civilians Claims

Parties:	Eritrea/Ethiopia
Date of Arbitration Agreement:	December 12, 2000
Commissioners:	Prof. Hans van Houtte (President), Judge George H. Aldrich, Mr. John R. Crook, Dean James Paul, Ms. Lucy Reed
Date of Partial Award:	December 17, 2004

Summary

International armed conflict waged between Eritrea and Ethiopia between 1998 and 2000 – liability of Eritrea for violations of international humanitarian law committed in treatment of Ethiopian civilians – Eritrea liable for failing to ensure protection of Ethiopian civilians out of detention from acts or threats of violence by police and the civilian population – Eritrea liable for failing to ensure Ethiopians the right to find paid employment on same basis as nationals after June 2000 Cease-Fire Agreement – Eritrea liable for failing to ensure that Ethiopians able to receive medical treatment to same extent as Eritrean nationals – Eritrea liable for detaining Ethiopian nationals without clear legal basis and for concealing detainees from the International Committee of the Red Cross ("ICRC") – Eritrea liable for permitting Ethiopians so detained to be subject to physical and psychological abuse and substandard living, sanitary, and health conditions – Eritrea liable for detaining several thousand Ethiopian civilians during and after May 2000 without sufficient justification – Eritrea liable for failing to provide Ethiopians so detained humane treatment and minimum standards of food and accommodation, and for permitting Ethiopians so detained to be subjected to acts of violence and physical abuse, including indiscriminate and excessive use of lethal force against detainees at Wi'a detention camp in July 2000 – Eritrea liable for expelling several thousand Ethiopians under conditions that did not allow them to protect their property or interests in Eritrea – Eritrea liable for failing to ensure safe and humane repatriation of departing Ethiopians – departures not conducted or supervised by ICRC – Eritrea liable for allowing seizure of property belonging to Ethiopians.

Legal Subject Matters

International humanitarian law:
- Sources
  - Customary international humanitarian law
  - Geneva Conventions 1949
  - Hague Regulations 1907
- Violations
  - Unlawful treatment of civilians
    - Arrest, detention and internment
    - Conditions of detention
    - Conditions of expulsion
    - Discrimination
    - Economic loss

Bibliography

Award published in:
- XXVI R.I.A.A. (forthcoming 2010);
- 44 I.L.M. p. 630 (2005).

Commentary:
- *The 1998-2000 War between Eritrea and Ethiopia: An International Legal Perspective* (Andrea de Guttry, Harry H.G. Post & Gabriella Venturini eds., TMC Asser Press 2009);
- Hans van Houtte, *The Eritrea-Ethiopia Claims Commission and International Humanitarian Law*, *in* JUDICIAL RIGHTS AND INTERNATIONAL JUSTICE, LIBER FAUSTO POCAR p. 383 (Guiffre 2009);
- Pierre d'Argent & Jean d'Aspremont, *La Commission des réclamations Érythrée-Éthiopie : un premier bilan*, 53 AFDI p. 347 (2007);
- Won Kidane, *Civil Liability for Violations of International Law: The Jurisprudence of the Eritrea-Ethiopia Claims Commission in The Hague*, 25 WIS. INT'L L.J. p. 23 (2007);
- George H. Aldrich, *The Work of the Eritrea-Ethiopia Claims Commission*, 6 Y.B. INT'L HUMAN. L. p. 435 (2006);
- Natalie Klein, *State Responsibility for International Humanitarian Law Violations and the Work of the Eritrea Ethiopia Claims Commission So Far*, 47 GERM. Y.B. INT'L L. p. 214 (2005);
- Judith I.A. Lichtenberg, *Eritrea Ethiopia Claims Commission*, 12 TILBURG FOREIGN L. REV. p. 266 (2004);
- J. Romesh Weeramantry, *Civilians Claims (Eritrea v. Ethiopia), Eritrea's Claims 15, 16, 23 & 27-32/ Ethiopia's Claim 5, Partial Awards*, 100 AM. J. INT'L L. p. 201 (2006);
- Philippe Weckel, *Commission des réparations (Erythrée/Ethiopie), Sentences du 17 Décembre 2004 (réclamations des victimes civiles)*, 2 RGDIP p. 480 (2005).

Facts

Between 1998 and 2000, the Parties waged a costly, large-scale international armed conflict along several areas of their common frontier. Prior to the 1998-2000 conflict, between 110,000 and 120,000 Ethiopians lived in Eritrea. The situations of Ethiopians in Eritrea, which varied during the course of the conflict, became more difficult after Ethiopia's military successes in May and early June 2000, when Eritrea detained many thousands of Ethiopians in harsh conditions. The Parties disputed the treatment received by Ethiopians in Eritrea during the war and the circumstances of those who departed.

This claim was filed on December 12, 2001. Following the exchange of written pleadings, a hearing was held at the Peace Palace in March 2004, in conjunction with Eritrea's corresponding Claims 15, 16, 23 and 27–32.

Summary of Matters Submitted to Arbitration

This Partial Award addressed Ethiopia's claims that Eritrea violated international humanitarian law in its treatment of civilians of Ethiopian nationality through physical and mental abuse; unlawful arrest, detention, and internment; unlawful conditions of detention; expulsion under inhumane conditions; and confiscation and discriminatory levies.

Partial Award

Jurisdiction and Applicable Law

The Commission dismissed certain of Ethiopia's claims as not having been filed within the December 12, 2001, filing deadline established by Article 5(8) of the Agreement. The claims thus dismissed were claims that Eritrea (i) did not provide proper conditions of transport to detention or between supposed detention sites, (ii) exposed Ethiopian detainees/internees to public curiosity, and (iii) forced Ethiopians to donate blood.[1]

As to the applicable law, the Commission recalled its Partial Awards on Prisoners of War and the Central Front, in which it held that the law applicable to those claims before August 14, 2000, when Eritrea acceded to the four Geneva Conventions of 1949, was customary international humanitarian law, as exemplified by the relevant parts of the four Geneva Conventions. It held that its holdings in those Awards applied in the present case and to all the claims before the Commission.[2] The Parties also treated the provisions of Additional Protocol I of 1977 to the Geneva Conventions ("Protocol I") governing the protection of civilians as reflecting binding customary rules. The Commission agreed with this approach.[3] It held, further, that whilst the law primarily applicable to the present claim was customary international humanitarian law, customary law concerning the protection of human rights remained in force during armed conflicts, enjoying particular relevance in any situations involving persons who may not be protected fully by international humanitarian law.[4]

In relation to the duration of humanitarian law protections, the Commission held that it was the comprehensive settlement embodied in the Agreement that marked the legal turning point between the regime of the Geneva Convention Relative to the Protection of Civilian Persons in Time of War ("Geneva Convention IV") and peacetime rules. International humanitarian law protections continued to operate thereafter to protect persons in detention until their release, as well as others in the process of repatriation or re-establishment.[5]

---

[1] Partial Award, Ethiopia's Civilians Claims [hereinafter "Partial Award"], para. 20.
[2] Partial Award, para. 24.
[3] Partial Award, para. 25.
[4] Partial Award, para. 28.
[5] Partial Award, para. 31.

Evidentiary Issues

As in the Parties' prior cases, the Commission required proof of liability by clear and convincing evidence, and took its fundamental responsibility to be to concentrate on persistent and widespread patterns of misconduct, rather than individual acts.[6]

Ethiopia's Claims

The Commission organized the present Partial Award according to the seven broad categories of claims used by Ethiopia at the hearing, namely, (i) physical and mental abuse out of detention, (ii) other unlawful treatment out of detention, (iii) confiscation and discriminatory levies, (iv) unlawful arrest, detention, and internment, (v) physical and mental abuse in detention, (vi) unlawful conditions of detention, and (vii) expulsion under inhumane conditions. The Commission distinguished, in relation to the last four of these claims, between the periods before and after May 2000.[7]

Physical and Mental Abuse Out of Detention

Ethiopia alleged frequent beatings and verbal harassment of Ethiopian nationals in the streets and other public locations by Eritrean police and sometimes by civilians.[8] The Commission found that the evidence did not prove that violence and abuse were directed against Ethiopians as a matter of government policy, but it did show that violence and abuse frequently occurred at the hands of police or military personnel and sometimes at the hands of civilians. It held that Eritrea had failed to meet its legal obligation to ensure that Ethiopians in Eritrea who were not in detention were protected against acts or threats of violence on the streets and in other places.[9]

Other Unlawful Treatment Out of Detention

Ethiopia next alleged that Ethiopians who were not detained nevertheless suffered multiple forms of unlawful treatment, including discriminatory enforcement of identity card requirements and unlawful denial of employment, housing, and medical care.[10]

Identity Cards

Eritrea had first required Ethiopians to register and obtain identification cards in the spring of 1999. Ethiopia argued that Eritrea's system, particularly the requirement to carry distinctive identity cards, was actually a form of prohibited collective punishment, with the cards used to mark Ethiopians for beatings and persecution. The Commission found that the evidence did not demonstrate that identity card checks or any other aspects of administering

---

[6] Partial Award, para. 35.
[7] Partial Award, para. 39.
[8] Partial Award, para. 41.
[9] Partial Award, para. 43.
[10] Partial Award, para. 44.

the identity card system were specifically directed against Ethiopians in ways that violated international law. The Commission dismissed this claim for failure of proof.[11]

Employment, Housing and Business Licenses

Ethiopia contended that many Ethiopians lost their means of livelihood and housing because of Eritrean Government policies or actions contrary to international law. Ethiopia contended, *inter alia*, that Eritrea violated Article 39 of Geneva Convention IV, which provides that protected persons who lose their gainful employment as a result of the war "shall be granted the opportunity to find paid employment" on the same basis as nationals, "subject to security considerations."[12] The Commission found that the record did not show widespread deprivation or denial of housing or revocation of business licenses during the period prior to mid-2000.[13] In contrast, it found that Ethiopians in Eritrea experienced substantially different conditions after mid-2000. Following the June 2000 ceasefire agreement, a large number of Ethiopians were discharged from employment, both public and private; Ethiopians living in publicly-owned housing were given a month's notice to vacate; and the licenses of many Ethiopian-owned businesses were revoked. The Commission held, in respect of the period from June 2000 to the conclusion of the December 2000 Agreement, that Eritrea failed to meet its obligations under Article 39 of Geneva Convention IV.[14]

The Commission dismissed for lack of proof a claim by Ethiopia that Ethiopian students had been harassed and forced to withdraw from schools in Eritrea.[15] Ethiopia also asserted that Eritrean government hospitals unlawfully refused to treat Ethiopians on grounds of their nationality during the conflict.[16] The Commission found Eritrea's evidence insufficient to rebut Ethiopia's evidence and determined that Eritrea had violated its obligations under Article 38 of Geneva Convention IV.[17]

Confiscation and Discriminatory Levies

The Commission rejected Ethiopia's claims that Eritrea's alien registration and identity card requirements were an unlawful collective punishment[18] and that the process for obtaining exit visas was contrary to international law.[19]

Unlawful Arrest, Detentions and Internment Prior to May 2000

The Commission found that an unknown but appreciable number of Ethiopians had been detained in Eritrean prisons and jails in May 2000 without formal charges or trials, often on

[11] Partial Award, para. 46.
[12] Partial Award, para. 48.
[13] Partial Award, para. 50.
[14] Partial Award, para. 52.
[15] Partial Award, para. 55.
[16] Partial Award, paras. 56–57.
[17] Partial Award, para. 62.
[18] Partial Award, para. 66.
[19] Partial Award, para. 68.

the basis of suspicions related to security. Prisoners were sometimes concealed from the ICRC contrary to Article 143 of Geneva Convention IV. Detainees were not accorded the minimum procedural rights under Article 75 of Protocol I.[20] The Commission also found that a significant number of Ethiopians were forcibly detained at the Hawshaite internment camp for periods of up to six months after about February 1999, in harsh conditions.[21] It upheld Ethiopia's claim that Ethiopian civilians were detained at Hawshaite camp during and after February 1999 without legal justification and were subjected to physical and psychological abuse and substandard living, sanitary, and health conditions contrary to Articles 27 and 37 of Geneva Convention IV.[22]

Physical and Mental Abuse and Unlawful Conditions of Detention

The Commission then set out its findings relating to treatment in police stations, jails, and prisons, both before and after May 2000. The Commission found that detention of Ethiopians in Eritrean police stations, jails, and prisons throughout the period covered by the present claims was characterized by frequent physical and psychological abuse and by harsh and substandard living, sanitary, and health conditions, contrary to Articles 27 and 37 of Geneva Convention IV.

Ethiopia also alleged frequent rape of Ethiopian civilian women by soldiers throughout the conflict. The Commission found that Ethiopia had not presented sufficient evidence on which to base a finding of liability involving rape against the Government of Eritrea.[23] The Commission emphasized that it was not a criminal tribunal or otherwise charged with assessing liability in individual instances of violation of international humanitarian law.[24]

Expulsion under Inhumane Conditions

Ethiopia contended that Eritrea was internationally responsible for the damages suffered by every Ethiopian who left Eritrea during the period covered by its claims, including those not expelled by direct government action.[25] After reviewing the evidence, the Commission concluded that departures of Ethiopians before May 2000 resulted largely from economic or other causes, for which the Government of Eritrea was not legally responsible, and that Eritrea was not responsible for the conditions faced by those who elected to depart during this period.[26]

Claims after May 2000

The Commission recalled that Ethiopia carried out extensive attacks against Eritrea in May 2000, displacing more than 750,000 Eritrean civilians. There followed an increase in

---

[20] Partial Award, para. 75.
[21] Partial Award, para. 78.
[22] Partial Award, para. 79.
[23] Partial Award, para. 89.
[24] Partial Award, para. 90.
[25] Partial Award, para. 91.
[26] Partial Award, paras. 94–95.

previous levels of harassment and violence against Ethiopians and their property by Eritrean civilians.

In relation to Ethiopia's claim in respect of "Physical and Mental Abuse Out of Detention After May 2000," the question before the Commission was whether Eritrea met its obligation under Article 27 of Geneva Convention IV to ensure the humane treatment of Ethiopian civilians and their protection against insults and all acts or threats of violence. The Commission held that Eritrea failed to take sufficient measures to ensure the safety and protection of Ethiopian nationals during this period, contrary to Article 27 of Geneva Convention IV.[27]

As to unlawful arrest, detention, and internment after May 2000, the evidence showed that several thousand Ethiopians were arrested and forcibly held in internment or detention camps after May 2000. Many more were held in local detention facilities. Eritrea maintained that its actions were justified under Article 42 of Geneva Convention IV, which allows internment or assigned residence "if the security of the Detaining Power makes it absolutely necessary."[28] Ethiopia acknowledged that a belligerent may intern nationals of an enemy State under appropriate safeguards, but contended that Eritrea did not attempt to assess individuals' potential threat to security. The Commission found that there was no process by which detainees could secure review of their status.[29] It concluded that Eritrea had failed to show that its mass detentions of Ethiopians during and after May 2000 satisfied the requirements of Article 42 of Geneva Convention IV as being "absolutely necessary" for its security.[30]

Regarding the physical conditions of detention after May 2000, Eritrea acknowledged that these were harsh, and argued that the poor living conditions were the unavoidable result of the humanitarian crisis it was facing at the time, and that conditions were no worse than those endured by many internally displaced Eritreans.[31] The Commission recognized the challenges faced by Eritrea, but rejected them as a legal defense. It held that Geneva Convention IV reflects minimum standards of humanitarian treatment that apply whenever protected persons are detained, and that Eritrea had failed to meet the requirements of Articles 27, 85, 89, and 90 of Geneva Convention IV.[32]

Ethiopia also alleged that the poor physical conditions in detention camps were accompanied by wide-scale physical and psychological abuse of detainees. Eritrea acknowledged one serious shooting incident at Wi'a camp, but otherwise denied that the conditions were as claimed by Ethiopia.

The Commission found that camps were guarded by untrained and unqualified Eritrean personnel, whose lack of training contributed to widespread physical abuse, including recurring beatings.[33] The Commission concluded that Eritrea had failed to meet its obligation under humanitarian law to ensure the physical protection and well-being of the protected persons it detained in May 2000 and thereafter.[34]

---

[27] Partial Award, para. 99.
[28] Partial Award, para. 101.
[29] Partial Award, para. 102.
[30] Partial Award, para. 104.
[31] Partial Award, para. 106.
[32] Partial Award, para. 107.
[33] Partial Award, para. 109.
[34] Partial Award, para. 110.

The Commission also found clear and compelling evidence of a serious incident on July 11, 2000, at the Wi'a camp.[35] The Commission held that Eritrea was responsible for permitting conditions under which undisciplined camp guards used excessive and indiscriminate lethal force against protected persons, killing at least 15 and injuring 16 more.[36]

The Commission then turned to Ethiopia's claim in respect of expulsions under allegedly inhumane conditions after May 2000. As to the applicable legal considerations, Ethiopia acknowledged that States have broad powers to require aliens to leave their territory, but it contended that departures after May 2000 were unlawful because they did not result from a proper legal process and did not provide affected Ethiopians with proper respect and protection.[37] The Commission held that Eritrea acted consistently with its rights as a belligerent in compelling the departures of Ethiopians that it had detained.[38] The Commission rejected Ethiopia's claim that the other Ethiopians who left Eritrea between June and December 2000 were expelled pursuant to actions or policies of the Government of Eritrea.[39] It also rejected Ethiopia's claim that such persons had been victims of unlawful indirect or constructive expulsion, holding that the threshold for proof of such indirect expulsion had not been met in this case.[40]

As to the physical conditions of repatriation, Ethiopia contended that expellees were forced to leave Eritrea in harsh, unsafe conditions, contrary to Article 36 of Geneva Convention IV. The Commission noted the involvement of the ICRC, which publicly reported that it organized the safe return to Ethiopia of 12,000 Ethiopians during 2000.[41] However, the Commission also found that the ICRC was not involved in some transports that exposed departing Ethiopians to harsh and hazardous conditions, including one instance of forcible deportation of 2,700 people from a camp north of Asmara in August 2000, which was publicly criticized by the ICRC.[42] The Commission held that Eritrea failed to ensure safe and humane conditions in departures in which the ICRC did not play a role.[43]

The Commission turned, finally, to Ethiopia's claim regarding property losses. It noted the provisions of Articles 33 and 35 of Geneva Convention IV and Article 23(g) of the 1907 Hague Regulations. The Commission found that those Ethiopians expelled directly from Eritrean detention camps, jails, and prisons after May 2000 did not receive any opportunity to collect portable personal property or otherwise arrange their affairs before being expelled. The Commission held that Eritrea was liable for those economic losses suffered by Ethiopians expelled directly from detention. It rejected claims for economic losses based solely on short notice for departure,[44] but found Eritrea liable for economic losses suffered by Ethiopian departees that resulted from Eritrean officials' wrongful seizure of their property and wrongful interference with their efforts to secure or dispose of their property.[45]

---

[35] Partial Award, para. 111.
[36] Partial Award, para. 115.
[37] Partial Award, para. 120.
[38] Partial Award, para. 121.
[39] Partial Award, paras. 123–125.
[40] Partial Award, para. 127.
[41] Partial Award, para. 129.
[42] Partial Award, para. 130.
[43] Partial Award, para. 131.
[44] Partial Award, para. 134.
[45] Partial Award, para. 135.

14.8

Eritrea-Ethiopia Claims Commission

Partial Award
Eritrea's Claims 1, 3, 5, 9–13, 14, 21, 25 & 26: Western Front, Aerial Bombardment, and Related Claims

Parties:	Eritrea/Ethiopia
Date of Arbitration Agreement:	December 12, 2000
Commissioners:	Prof. Hans van Houtte (President), Judge George H. Aldrich, Mr. John R. Crook, Dean James Paul, Ms. Lucy Reed
Date of Partial Award:	December 19, 2005

Summary

International armed conflict waged between Eritrea and Ethiopia between 1998 and 2000 – liability of Ethiopia for violations of international humanitarian law committed during conflict on Western Front – Ethiopia liable for unlawful looting, burning, and stripping of buildings and destruction of livestock whilst in occupation of several towns and villages during May and June 2000 – Ethiopia liable for failing to prevent the rape of women in the towns of Barentu and Teseney – liability of Ethiopia for unlawful aerial bombardment – Ethiopia liable for aerial bombing of the Harsile water reservoir in February 1999 and June 2000 – claim relating to aerial bombardment of Hirgigo Power Station dismissed on the merits – dismissal of claims relating to preventing displaced persons from returning – dismissal of claims relating to indirect displacement of civilians – Ethiopia liable for unlawful displacement of residents of the village of Awgaro.

Legal Subject Matters

Arbitration:
- Jurisdiction of the arbitral tribunal

International humanitarian law:
- Sources
  - Customary international humanitarian law
  - Geneva Conventions 1949
  - Hague Regulations 1907
- Violations
  - Destruction of property

- Looting
- Rape
- Unlawful aerial bombardment
  - Attack against drinking water installations and supplies indispensable to the survival of the civilian population for the specific purpose of denying them for their sustenance value to the adverse party
- Unlawful treatment of civilians
  - Displacement

Bibliography

Award published in:
- XXVI R.I.A.A. (forthcoming 2010);
- 45 I.L.M. p. 396 (2006).

Commentary:
- *The 1998-2000 War between Eritrea and Ethiopia: An International Legal Perspective* (Andrea de Guttry, Harry H.G. Post & Gabriella Venturini eds., TMC Asser Press 2009);
- Hans van Houtte, *The Eritrea-Ethiopia Claims Commission and International Humanitarian Law, in* JUDICIAL RIGHTS AND INTERNATIONAL JUSTICE, LIBER FAUSTO POCAR p. 383 (Guiffre 2009);
- Pierre d'Argent & Jean d'Aspremont, *La Commission des réclamations Érythrée-Éthiopie : un premier bilan*, 53 AFDI p. 347 (2007);
- Won Kidane, *Civil Liability for Violations of International Law: The Jurisprudence of the Eritrea-Ethiopia Claims Commission in The Hague*, 25 WIS. INT'L L.J. p. 23 (2007);
- George H. Aldrich, *The Work of the Eritrea-Ethiopia Claims Commission*, 6 Y.B. INT'L HUMAN. L. p. 435 (2006);
- Natalie Klein, *State Responsibility for International Humanitarian Law Violations and the Work of the Eritrea Ethiopia Claims Commission So Far*, 47 GERM. Y.B. INT'L L. p. 214 (2005);
- Judith I.A. Lichtenberg, *Eritrea Ethiopia Claims Commission*, 12 TILBURG FOREIGN L. REV. p. 266 (2004);
- Philippe Weckel, *Commission des réclamations (Erythrée/Ethiopie), Sentences du 19 Décembre 2005 (Front ouest, bombardement aérien)*, 1 RGDIP p.198 (2006).

Facts

Between 1998 and 2000, the Parties waged a costly, large-scale international armed conflict along several areas of their common frontier. In May and June of 2000, Ethiopia launched a major offensive on the Western Front. This offensive was successful in breaking through the defensive lines of Eritrea and reaching Tokombia on May 15, 2000, and Barentu on May 18, 2000, after heavy fighting. After the capture of Barentu, Ethiopia began to redeploy several of the divisions used in these attacks. Following combat between Ethiopia's 15th Division and Eritrean forces outside of Teseney on June 4, 2000, the 15th Division withdrew to the South. In the process of that withdrawal, a significant battle took place near the town of Guluj. The Ethiopian forces moved back north on June 12, 2000, capturing Guluj, Teseney, and Alighidir by June 14, 2000. On June 18, 2000, the Parties signed a cease-fire agreement.

This Partial Award addressed allegations of illegal conduct related to military operations on the Western Front of the international armed conflict between the Parties, as well as allegations of illegal conduct in the course of Ethiopia's aerial bombardment at various places in Eritrea, and allegations of internal displacement of Eritreans. For the purpose of these claims, the Western Front encompassed the area of eight sub-zobas in southern Eritrea: Teseney, Guluj, Barentu, Shambuko, Lalaigash, Haykota, Molki, and Gogne Sub-Zobas.

Eritrea filed these claims on December 12, 2001. Following the exchange of written pleadings, a hearing was held at the Peace Palace in April 2005, in conjunction with a hearing on several other claims by both Parties, including Ethiopia's related Claims 1 and 3.

Summary of Matters Submitted to Arbitration

This Partial Award addressed:

A. Eritrea's claims relating to the Western Front;
B. Eritrea's claims relating to aerial bombardment at various places in Eritrea; and
C. Eritrea's claims relating to the displacement of Eritrean civilians, including in areas to which Ethiopian armed forces withdrew following the end of the war.

Partial Award

Eritrea's Claims

Eritrea submitted eight separate claims, one for each of the affected sub-zobas on the Western Front in Eritrea. All of these Claims alleged abuse of civilians, looting, and loss of property. The Commission addressed each of these Claims in the geographical order used by Eritrea, starting with the farthest west.

Claim 3 – Teseney Sub-Zoba

Eritrea claimed that, during two brief Ethiopian occupations of the sub-zoba in late May and June 2000, Ethiopian armed forces abused civilians, looted and destroyed property, including water supply systems, and laid landmines in central areas of Teseney town, thus endangering civilians.

Ethiopia argued that it did not "occupy" this sub-zoba (or others) in May and June 2000, as its forces were fighting and moving too quickly to make Ethiopia an "Occupying Power" as that term is used in the Geneva Convention Relative to the Protection of Civilian Persons in Time of War ("Geneva Convention IV"). The Commission agreed that the Ethiopian military presence was more transitory in most towns and villages on the Western Front than it was on the Central Front, where the Commission found Ethiopia to be an Occupying Power.[1]

The Commission found that the evidence did not establish a pattern of frequent or pervasive abuse of civilians. It held that the claim for abuse of civilians failed for lack of proof.[2] With respect to property loss, the Commission found an abundance of clear and convincing evidence of violations. It found that, during the second occupation of Teseney, looting and burning of homes and shops were widespread, a commercial bank, hospital and two grain

[1] Partial Award, Eritrea's Western Front Claims [hereinafter "Partial Award"], para. 26.

[2] Partial Award, para. 28.

warehouses were looted and burned, and there was also clear and convincing evidence of wholesale theft and destruction of domestic animals.[3] Ethiopia alleged that it had taken measures to prevent Ethiopian civilians from entering Eritrea, but the evidence indicated that those measures were not always sufficient. The Commission held that Ethiopia was liable to Eritrea for permitting the widespread and severe looting and burning of buildings and destruction of livestock in Teseney town by its soldiers and civilians. The Commission also found clear and convincing evidence of the unlawful destruction of property and livestock in Alighidir village during the times when Ethiopian armed forces were present, including the destruction of a large new cotton-processing plant.[4]

Claim 13 – Guluj Sub-Zoba

Eritrea presented evidence of isolated incidents of the abuse of civilians. This claim therefore failed for lack of proof. The Commission found consistent and convincing evidence that Ethiopian military and civilian personnel looted the shops and houses of Guluj, and military personnel then destroyed animals and burned the structures until there was little left in the town. Taking into account collateral damage from combat action, the Commission assessed Ethiopia's liability at 90% of the loss and damage to property and livestock in Guluj during May and June 2000.[5] The Commission also found Ethiopia liable for permitting looting in the villages of Tabaldia and Gergef.[6] It found Ethiopia liable for 75% of the damage caused to the border town of Omhajer from May 16, 2000, until Ethiopian forces left in September 2000, during which time Ethiopia was the Occupying Power.[7]

Claim 9 – Barentu Sub-Zoba

The town of Barentu was a significant military base for Eritrea. Ethiopian forces reached it on May 18, 2000, after three days of heavy fighting. Most residents fled before the arrival of the Ethiopian forces. For eight days from May 18 until May 26, 2000, Ethiopian armed forces were in uncontested control of the town.[8] The evidence was consistent that, except for limited bomb and artillery damages, the town was intact on May 17.[9] Several Ethiopian officers asserted that Eritrean forces had destroyed and looted buildings before retreating. The Commission concluded that the weight of the conflicting evidence placed the reality closer to the circumstances described by the Eritrean declarants.[10] Aside from allegations of rape (as to which see below), the Commission found insufficient evidence to support Eritrea's allegation of the abuse of civilians and dismissed that claim.[11] It found detailed and consistent evidence that many locked buildings were forced open and looted by Ethiopian soldiers

[3] Partial Award, para. 29.
[4] Partial Award, para. 31.
[5] Partial Award, para. 36.
[6] Partial Award, paras. 37–38.
[7] Partial Award, para. 39.
[8] Partial Award, para. 44.
[9] Partial Award, para. 41.
[10] Partial Award, para. 43.
[11] Partial Award, para. 45.

and civilians. There was also credible evidence that the local hospital and warehouses belonging to the Ministry of Agriculture were looted and partially burned. The Commission found Ethiopia, as the Occupying Power, liable for unlawfully permitting these acts.[12]

Eritrea also claimed that Ethiopian forces destroyed by detonation a number of buildings in Barentu. The Commission found, based on the evidence as a whole, that four significant structures, namely, the police station, the courthouse, an hotel and a bakery, were destroyed by explosives during the occupation. In these circumstances the burden was on Ethiopia, as the Occupying Power, to prove that the damage was caused by others or was otherwise not attributable to Ethiopia. Since Ethiopia had not proved how the destruction was caused, the Commission held Ethiopia liable for the damage to these buildings.[13]

Claim 12 – Shambuko Sub-Zoba

On the basis of the limited and conflicting evidence, the Commission found that the town of Shambuko and the villages of Bishuka and Bimbina suffered significant damage from combat actions in 1999 and 2000. The Commission found that there was little evidence of civilian abuse and held that the claim for the abuse of civilians failed for lack of proof.[14] On balance, it found that the evidence was insufficient to prove that Ethiopia was liable for the damage to Shambuko, Bishuka, and Bimbina.[15]

Claim 5 – Lalaigash Sub-Zoba

Lalaigash Sub-Zoba was the site of strong Ethiopian attacks on May 12, 2000, against the Eritrean trench lines protecting the principal town in the sub-zoba Tokombia. At least from May 12 to May 15, 2000, this area was a war zone where Ethiopia carried out attacks against heavily defended Eritrean positions.[16] The Commission found the evidence insufficient to support Eritrea's claim in respect of the abuse of civilians.[17] It found consistent evidence that Ethiopian soldiers deliberately detonated a tobacco plant outside Tokombia and the police station in Tokombia. It held that Ethiopia, as the Occupying Power, was liable for unlawfully permitting the destruction of the tobacco plant and police station, and for unlawfully permitting the looting of other buildings in Tokombia.[18] Eritrea's claims for property losses in villages in this sub-zoba failed for lack of proof.[19]

Claim 10 – Haykota Sub-Zoba, Claim 1 – Molki Sub-Zoba, and Claim 11 – Gogne Sub-Zoba

Eritrea claimed for alleged abuse of civilians and for looting and property destruction by Ethiopian soldiers in Haykota Sub-Zoba. Ethiopian forces traversed this sub-zoba on their

---

[12] Partial Award, para. 46.
[13] Partial Award, para. 47.
[14] Partial Award, para. 51.
[15] Partial Award, para. 53.
[16] Partial Award, para. 55.
[17] Partial Award, para. 56.
[18] Partial Award, para. 57.
[19] Partial Award, para. 58.

advance from Barentu to Teseney, and they fought with Eritrean soldiers also passing through the sub-zoba in the same period.[20] The Commission found the evidence insufficient to prove a pattern of frequent or pervasive abuse of civilians,[21] and that Eritrea had failed to establish a pattern of misconduct by Ethiopian soldiers. Eritrea's claims in relation to this sub-zoba failed for lack of proof. Ethiopia was held liable for permitting the looting of buildings in Molki Sub-Zoba on May 15-16, 2000, which was the scene of bitter fighting on May 14 and 15, 2000.[22] Eritrea's claims in respect of the alleged abuse of civilians and destruction of property in Molki Sub-Zoba and Gogne Sub-Zoba failed for lack of proof.[23]

Allegations of Rape

In setting out its general comments concerning rape, the Commission accepted that rape is such a sensitive matter in the Parties' culture that victims are extremely unlikely to come forward, and the evidence available is likely to be far less detailed and explicit than for non-sexual offenses.[24] The Commission recalled that it had not required evidence of a pattern of frequent or pervasive rapes and that rape, which "by definition involves intentional and grievous harm to an individual civilian victim," was an illegal act which did not need to be frequent to support State responsibility.[25]

The Commission found clear and convincing evidence of several incidents of rape of Eritrean civilian women in Barentu and Teseney, unrebutted by Ethiopia, and concluded that Ethiopia failed to impose effective measures on its troops, as required by international humanitarian law, to prevent rape of civilian women in Barentu and Teseney.[26] For other areas in the Western Front, the Commission did not find sufficient evidence on which to find Ethiopia liable for failing to protect civilian women from rape by its troops.[27]

Eritrea's Claim 26 – Unlawful Aerial Bombardment

This claim was for the allegedly unlawful aerial bombardment of civilian targets in six places, namely Asmara, Assab, Adi Keih, Mendefera, Forto, and Massawa. This claim was organized not as a series of claims for separate incidents, but rather as a claim that Ethiopia carried out a pattern of indiscriminate and disproportionate aerial bombardments that caused civilian casualties and property losses at a number of different places.[28] Eritrea cited evidence that civilians were killed and injured and civilian objects destroyed or damaged in a number of towns, villages, and internally displaced persons ("IDP") camps during the armed conflict. Eritrea alleged that these losses occurred because the Ethiopian Air Force failed to distinguish between military objectives and civilians and civilian objects and failed to avoid

---

[20] Partial Award, para. 59.
[21] Partial Award, para. 61.
[22] Partial Award, paras. 64, 66.
[23] Partial Award, paras. 64–67, 68–73.
[24] Partial Award, para. 77.
[25] Partial Award, paras. 78–79.
[26] Partial Award, para. 83.
[27] Partial Award, para. 84.
[28] Partial Award, para. 91.

disproportionate civilian losses. Eritrea relied particularly on the rules of law contained in Articles 48, 51, 52, and 57 of Additional Protocol I of 1977 to the Geneva Conventions ("Protocol I").[29] Ethiopia accused Eritrea of failing to comply with its obligations, under Article 58 of Protocol I, to take appropriate measures to separate civilians and civilian objects from military objects to the maximum extent feasible.[30]

The Commission considered the provisions of Protocol I cited by the Parties to express customary international humanitarian law.[31] After careful consideration of all the evidence, including the testimony at the hearing of a military expert presented by Eritrea and by a senior Ethiopian Air Force officer, the Commission concluded that Eritrea had not proved its claim that Ethiopia's aerial bombing was indiscriminate or disproportionate within the meaning of Article 51 of Protocol I. It held that Claim 26, except for that part relating to the Harsile water reservoir, failed for lack of proof.

As to the Harsile water reservoir, Ethiopia acknowledged that it made several air strikes on this reservoir, which is located in a harsh desert region. Eritrea submitted evidence that this reservoir, which was not damaged in the attacks, served only civilians and was the sole source of drinking water for the town of Assab, located about 17 kilometers away. The Commission found that the Government of Ethiopia knew that the reservoir was a vital source of water for the city of Assab, and that Ethiopia's purpose in targeting it was to deprive Eritrea of the sustenance value of its water.[32]

The Parties agreed that Article 54 of Protocol I, if it applied between them, would have prohibited the targeting of the Harsile water reservoir. However, Ethiopia asserted that the Harsile water reservoir was a legitimate military objective under the applicable customary international law. Ethiopia maintained, further, that Article 54 of Protocol I was a new development in 1977 that had not become a part of customary international law by the 1998-2000 war.[33] In the Commission's view, a treaty provision of a compelling humanitarian nature that has not been questioned by any statements of reservation or interpretation and is not inconsistent with general State practice in the two decades since the conclusion of the treaty may reasonably be considered to have come to reflect customary international humanitarian law.[34] The Commission held that the provisions of Article 54, that prohibit attacks against drinking water installations indispensable to the survival of the civilian population for the specific purpose of denying them their sustenance value to the adverse party, had become part of customary international humanitarian law by 1999. Those aerial bombardments were therefore in violation of applicable international humanitarian law. As no damage to the reservoir had been shown, the Commission held that the finding of liability was itself satisfaction to Eritrea for that violation.[35]

---

[29] Partial Award, para. 93.
[30] Partial Award, para. 94.
[31] Partial Award, para. 95.
[32] Partial Award, para. 100.
[33] Partial Award, para. 103.
[34] Partial Award, para. 105.
[35] Partial Award, para. 105.

Eritrea's Claim 25 – Aerial Bombardment of Hirgigo Power Station

Eritrea also claimed in respect of the bombing by Ethiopia on May 28, 2000, of Hirgigo Power Station, located about ten kilometers from the port of Massawa. While not yet fully operational, the power station had supplied some power briefly to Asmara and Mendefera. Eritrea asserted that the bombing of the plant was unlawful as the plant was not a legitimate military objective, and requested the Commission to find Ethiopia liable to compensate Eritrea for that violation.[36] Eritrea relied on Article 52(2) of Protocol I. Ethiopia did not dispute that that provision reflects customary international law.[37]

Ethiopia contended that the objective assigned to the two jet aircraft that had carried out the bombing had been the port of Massawa, and that those aircraft had been responding to an anti-aircraft missile launched from an anti-aircraft installation inside the perimeter of the plant at Hirgigo.[38] The Commission rejected this explanation based on the evidence before it and went on to consider whether the power plant was a legitimate military objective. The Commission therefore addressed the question whether the power plant was an object that, by its nature, location, purpose, or use, made an effective contribution to military action at the time it was attacked.[39] The Commission considered that, while the fact that Eritrea placed anti-aircraft guns in the vicinity of the power station did not, by itself, make the power station a military objective, it indicated that Eritrean military authorities themselves viewed the station as having military significance.[40] The Commission, by a majority,[41] found that the port and naval base at Massawa were legitimate military objectives. It followed that the generating facilities providing the electric power needed to operate them were objects that made an effective contribution to military action.[42] It then addressed the question whether the Hirgigo plant's total or partial destruction, in the circumstances ruling in May 2000, offered a definite military advantage. The Commission found, by a majority, that in the circumstances prevailing on May 28, 2000, the Hirgigo power station was a military objective, as defined in Article 52(2) of Protocol I, and that Ethiopia's aerial bombardment of it was not unlawful. It therefore dismissed this claim on the merits.[43]

Eritrea's Claim 14 – Preventing Displaced Persons from Returning

The Commission rejected a claim by Eritrea in respect of Ethiopia's alleged forcible prevention of displaced Eritreans from returning to their homes in violation of Article 49 of Geneva Convention IV, inasmuch as this was directed at events after the conflict was ended definitively on December 12, 2000.[44] It found that, to the extent that any part of this claim could be based on events occurring during the conflict, it was dismissed for lack of proof.[45]

---

[36] Partial Award, para. 111.

[37] Partial Award, para. 113.

[38] Partial Award, para. 114.

[39] Partial Award, para. 117.

[40] Partial Award, para. 119.

[41] This part of the Partial Award was supported by a majority comprising Commissioners Aldrich, Crook, Paul, and Reed.

[42] Partial Award, para. 120.

[43] Partial Award, para. 121.

[44] Partial Award, paras. 128–129.

[45] Partial Award, para. 130.

Eritrea's Claim 21 – Displacement of Civilians

Eritrea claimed for (i) indirect displacement, namely, displacement of civilians caused by their fear of alleged Ethiopian violations of international law in the conduct of military operations, and (ii) direct displacement, namely, displacement resulting from orders and forceful actions by Ethiopian armed forces designed to compel such displacement.

As regards indirect displacement, the Commission found that such displacements standing alone were not evidence of violations of international law. The Commission recalled its holding in its Central Front Partial Awards that the flight of civilians from the perceived danger of hostilities does not, as such, give rise to liability under international humanitarian law.[46] The Commission considered that it had fully addressed Eritrea's claims for indirect displacement as regards the Western Front in its prior Partial Award in Eritrea's Central Front Claims.[47] Eritrea's claims for indirect displacement as regards the Eastern Front were dismissed for lack of proof.

With regard to direct displacement, Eritrea claimed that, after Ethiopian armed forces entered Eritrean villages, they frequently ordered and compelled Eritrean residents to leave. The Commission noted that direct displacement claims were inadmissible to the extent that they related to places within the area administered by Ethiopia prior to the conflict, meaning south of the United Nations Mission in Ethiopia and Eritrea ("UNMEE") line, as these had been dealt with in the Commission's decision relating to rural expellees in its Partial Award in Eritrea's Civilians Claims.[48] The Commission found the evidence insufficient regarding those claims it held to be admissible, with the exception of the village of Awgaro. The Commission found that the entire population of this undefended village, comprising about 600 families, was displaced in May 2000 as a result of the order of an Ethiopian officer. The evidence consistently indicated forced expulsion from Awgaro based on ethnicity.[49] Ethiopia did not present rebuttal evidence.[50]

Although the Awgaro incident did not establish a pattern of systematic, frequent, or pervasive direct displacements, the Commission held that it was sufficiently serious to engage State responsibility. It therefore held Ethiopia liable for the unlawful direct displacement of the Eritrean residents of Awgaro.[51]

Eritrea's Claim 25 – Aerial Bombardment of Hirgigo Power Station – Separate Opinion of President Hans van Houtte

President van Houtte attached a Separate Opinion in respect of Eritrea's Claim 25, in which he dissented from the majority as to the lawfulness of the bombing of the Hirgigo power station, firstly, as regards its characterization as a legitimate military objective, and secondly, as regards the proportionality of the bombing.

---

[46] Partial Award, para. 135, *citing* Partial Award, Ethiopia's Central Front Claims, para. 53.

[47] Partial Award, para. 136.

[48] Partial Award, para. 137.

[49] Partial Award, para. 139.

[50] Partial Award, para. 140.

[51] Partial Award, para. 142.

In President van Houtte's opinion, the Hirgigo power station unquestionably had a civilian purpose. Ethiopia had not sufficiently specified the extent to which Hirgigo power station, which was not yet operational, by its nature or purpose, made or would make an effective contribution to the military action or that its destruction offered a definite military advantage. Ethiopia therefore had not discharged the burden of proving that the power plant was a military objective.[52]

President van Houtte also took the view that Eritrea had failed, as required by Article 57 of Protocol I, to investigate beforehand whether the concrete and direct military advantage of this bombing outweighed the damage to civil society. He noted that, if different means are available to block harbor activities, the method that is most effective and causes least damage to civilians should be chosen. In President van Houtte's opinion, the potential military advantage caused by the bombing was disproportionate to the damage to civilian objects and the civilian population.[53]

[52] Partial Award, Separate Opinion of President van Houtte, paras. 6–8.
[53] *Id.*, para. 11.

14.9

Eritrea-Ethiopia Claims Commission

Partial Award
Ethiopia's Claims 1 & 3: Western and Eastern Fronts

Parties:	Eritrea/Ethiopia
Date of Arbitration Agreement:	December 12, 2000
Commissioners:	Prof. Hans van Houtte (President), Judge George H. Aldrich, Mr. John R. Crook, Dean James Paul, Ms. Lucy Reed
Date of Partial Award:	December 19, 2005

Summary

International armed conflict waged between Eritrea and Ethiopia between 1998 and 2000 – liability of Eritrea for violations of international humanitarian law committed during conflict on Western and Eastern Fronts – Western Front – Eritrea liable for permitting beating and abduction of civilians – Eritrea liable for permitting looting of property and livestock – Eastern Front – Eritrea liable for permitting intentional and indiscriminate killings of civilians – Eritrea liable for failure to prevent rape of women – Eritrea liable for permitting beatings, abduction, forced labor, and conscription of civilians – Eritrea liable for permitting looting and destruction of property.

Legal Subject Matters

International humanitarian law:
- Sources
  - Customary international humanitarian law
  - Geneva Conventions 1949
- Violations
  - Abduction
  - Destruction of property
  - Looting
  - Rape
  - Unlawful killing
  - Unlawful treatment of civilians

Bibliography

Award published in:
- XXVI R.I.A.A. (forthcoming 2010).

Commentary:
- *The 1998-2000 War between Eritrea and Ethiopia: An International Legal Perspective* (Andrea de Guttry, Harry H.G. Post & Gabriella Venturini eds., TMC Asser Press 2009);
- Hans van Houtte, *The Eritrea-Ethiopia Claims Commission and International Humanitarian Law*, *in* JUDICIAL RIGHTS AND INTERNATIONAL JUSTICE, LIBER FAUSTO POCAR p. 383 (Guiffre 2009);
- Pierre d'Argent & Jean d'Aspremont, *La Commission des réclamations Érythrée-Éthiopie : un premier bilan*, 53 AFDI p. 347 (2007);
- Won Kidane, *Civil Liability for Violations of International Law: The Jurisprudence of the Eritrea-Ethiopia Claims Commission in The Hague*, 25 WIS. INT'L L.J. p. 23 (2007);
- George H. Aldrich, *The Work of the Eritrea-Ethiopia Claims Commission*, 6 Y.B. INT'L HUMAN. L. p. 435 (2006);
- Natalie Klein, *State Responsibility for International Humanitarian Law Violations and the Work of the Eritrea Ethiopia Claims Commission So Far*, 47 GERM. Y.B. INT'L L. p. 214 (2005);
- Judith I.A. Lichtenberg, *Eritrea Ethiopia Claims Commission*, 12 TILBURG FOREIGN L. REV. p. 266 (2004);
- Philippe Weckel, *Commission des réclamations (Erythrée/Ethiopie), Sentences du 19 Décembre 2005 (Front ouest, bombardement aérien)*, 1 RGDIP pp.198–202 (2006).

Facts

Between 1998 and 2000, the Parties waged a costly, large-scale international armed conflict along several areas of their common frontier. On May 12, 1998, at least two brigades of Eritrean soldiers, supported by tanks and artillery, invaded and captured the town of Badme and several other border areas in Ethiopia's Tahtay Adiabo Wereda. Ethiopian armed resistance was offered initially only by local militia and police, who were forced to flee. Ethiopia responded quickly to Eritrea's attacks, moving elements of its army into defensive positions in Tahtay Adiabo Wereda. During the following months of 1998, the conflict spread to other areas of the border. In February 1999, Ethiopia launched a successful offensive named "Operation Sunset" on the Western Front, restoring control over virtually all of the territory that Eritrea had occupied for the preceding nine months.

This Partial Award addressed allegations of illegal conduct related to military operations on the Western Front and Eastern Front of the international armed conflict between the Parties. For the purpose of these claims, the Western Front encompassed the area of military operations in Kafta Humera Wereda, Tahtay Adiabo Wereda, and Laelay Adiabo Wereda. The Eastern Front encompassed much of the Afar region of northeastern Ethiopia, in the Elidar, Dalul, and Afdera Weredas.

Ethiopia filed these claims on December 12, 2001. Following the exchange of written pleadings, a hearing on liability was held at the Peace Palace in April 2005, in conjunction with a hearing on several other claims by both Parties, including Eritrea's related Claims 1, 3, 5, 9–13, 14, 21, 25 and 26.

Summary of Matters Submitted to Arbitration

1. Ethiopia's claims that Eritrea violated international law on the Western Front by:
   (i) physical abuse of civilians;
   (ii) property loss through looting or deliberate and unlawful destruction;
   (iii) indiscriminate aerial bombing, shelling, and use of landmines; and
   (iv) displacement of Ethiopian civilians; and
2. Ethiopia's claims that on the Eastern Front Eritrea engaged in a systematic pattern of abuse against civilians.

Partial Award

Western Front

Ethiopia claimed that Eritrea violated international law on the Western Front in four categories, namely: (i) physical abuse of civilians, (ii) property loss through looting or deliberate and unlawful destruction, (iii) indiscriminate aerial bombing, shelling, and use of landmines, and (iv) displacement of Ethiopian civilians. The bulk of Ethiopia's Western Front Claims arose during the nine-month period between May 1998 and February 1999. Some claims also involved alleged incursions and shelling after February 1999 and before the conclusion of the Agreement in December 2000.[1]

The Commission addressed the third and fourth categories for the Western Front as a whole, before evaluating the first two categories on a wereda-by-wereda basis, followed by the rape allegations.

Indiscriminate Aerial Bombing, Shelling, and Use of Landmines; Displacement of Civilians

The evidence showed that by far the largest number of civilians killed and injured during the war on the Western Front were victims either of shelling or of landmines. The Commission found that Ethiopia was unable to demonstrate that the shelling and use of landmines were indiscriminate or otherwise unlawful.[2] It held that Article 51(1) of Additional Protocol I of 1977 to the Geneva Conventions ("Protocol I"), which sets out the types of attacks which are to be considered indiscriminate, reflects a rule of customary international law. The Commission found that the towns and villages that Ethiopia claimed had been subjected to unlawful shelling had not been shelled indiscriminately, as the military objectives of those towns were not sufficiently distinct so as to permit their being targeted separately. The relevant towns and villages were all close to the front, sometimes squarely between the opposing armies, and many were located on the communication and supply lines on which soldiers in combat depend.[3] All of Ethiopia's claims for unlawful shelling on the Western Front failed for lack of proof.

---

[1] Partial Award, Ethiopia's Western and Eastern Front Claims [hereinafter "Partial Award"], para. 27.
[2] Partial Award, para. 29.
[3] Partial Award, para. 32.

The Commission found abundant evidence that both Parties used landmines widely, and that they killed and wounded many civilians, as well as domestic animals. However, there was little or no evidence as to the circumstances in which the mines were laid. Given that both Parties dug trenches and placed landmines to defend those positions, and that forces in retreat often lack the time and incentive to remove such mines, the Commission held that Ethiopia's claims based on Eritrea's use of landmines on the Western Front failed for lack of proof.[4]

The evidence regarding aerial bombing was insufficient to enable the Commission to evaluate any particular bombing. Ethiopia's claims based on aerial bombing on the Western Front therefore failed for lack of proof.[5] The Commission also dismissed Ethiopia's claims for the displacement of civilians on the Western Front due to a failure to establish a violation of international law.[6]

Physical Abuse and Property Loss

Tahtay Adiabo Wereda

The Commission rejected Ethiopia's claims for injury to civilians who were shot while fleeing Eritrean attacks in Tahtay Adiabo Wereda, because there was evidence that the armed Ethiopian militia members who were defending the area were frequently dressed in civilian clothes. Militia members who ceased firing on the enemy and turned to flee remained enemy combatants and therefore legitimate targets; if civilians who were non-combatants were fleeing at the same time, the Commission held that "one cannot assume that any who were hit by enemy bullets had been recognized as non-combatants or that the Eritrean fire was indiscriminate."[7]

There was no evidence that Eritrea permitted frequent or pervasive shootings of civilians; however, the Commission drew attention to "one shooting of an Ethiopian civilian in Badme that can only be described as murder," namely, the execution on May 12, 1998, of a one-armed man who was not trying to flee, which was "so flagrant a violation of international humanitarian law that the Commission expresses its sincere hope that those responsible either have been or will be punished."[8]

The Commission found Eritrea liable for permitting frequent beating of civilians in Tahtay Adiabo Wereda[9] and for the frequent abduction of Ethiopian civilians from Tahtay Adiabo Wereda to Eritrea and for unexplained disappearances. There was unrebutted evidence showing that half of the individuals abducted had not been accounted for by the time the witness declarations were collected.[10] The Commission found sufficient evidence to hold Eritrea liable for permitting looting by Eritrean soldiers to occur in areas occupied by its armed

---

[4] Partial Award, para. 35.
[5] Partial Award, para. 36.
[6] Partial Award, para. 37.
[7] Partial Award, para. 38.
[8] Partial Award, para. 39.
[9] Partial Award, para. 40.
[10] Partial Award, para. 41.

forces.[11] Ethiopia's claims for deliberate and unlawful property destruction in Tahtay Adiabo Wereda failed for lack of proof.

Laelay Adiabo Wereda

As in Tahtay Adiabo Wereda, there was some evidence of shooting of civilians, but virtually all related to civilians who were fleeing along with militia members. On balance, the Commission could not find that Eritrea permitted frequent or pervasive shootings of civilians in Laelay Adiabo Wereda.[12] It did find sufficient evidence to hold Eritrea liable for permitting the frequent abduction of Ethiopian civilians from Laelay Adiabo Wereda to Eritrea and for unexplained disappearances,[13] and for permitting looting by Eritrean soldiers, particularly of livestock.[14] Ethiopia's claims for deliberate and unlawful property destruction in Laelay Adiabo Wereda failed for lack of proof.

Kafta Humera Wereda

In the absence of sufficient eyewitness evidence of physical abuse, Ethiopia's claims for frequent or pervasive shooting, beating, or other types of physical abuse in this wereda failed for lack of proof. However, the Commission found sufficient evidence to hold Eritrea liable for permitting the frequent abduction of Ethiopian civilians and for unexplained disappearances. It also found sufficient evidence to hold Eritrea liable for permitting looting of property and livestock by Eritrean soldiers.[15] Ethiopia's claims for deliberate and unlawful property destruction in Kafta Humera Wereda failed for lack of proof.

Allegations of Rape

The Commission recalled its previous holdings as to the standard which it applied in the case of allegations of rape, namely, clear and convincing evidence of several rapes in specific geographic areas.[16] In setting out its general comments concerning rape, the Commission accepted that rape is such a sensitive matter in the Parties' culture that victims are extremely unlikely to come forward, and the evidence available is likely to be far less detailed and explicit than for non-sexual offenses. Considering the very small number of witness declarations and the very limited detail in them, the Commission dismissed Ethiopia's claim for lack of proof.[17]

Eastern Front

For the purpose of these Claims, the Eastern Front encompassed much of the Afar region of northeastern Ethiopia, an extremely harsh and dry environment populated by the nomadic

---

[11] Partial Award, para. 42.
[12] Partial Award, para. 44.
[13] Partial Award, para. 45.
[14] Partial Award, para. 46.
[15] Partial Award, para. 48.
[16] Partial Award, paras. 49–54.
[17] Partial Award, para. 56.

Afar people, who have a distinctive language and culture and a largely oral tradition. The Commission noted the resulting difficulties for its assessment of the evidence in these circumstances.[18]

Ethiopia's Eastern Front claims were based on allegations that Eritrean forces engaged in a systematic pattern of abuse against civilians in Elidar, Dalul, and Afdera Weredas, including intentional killings and a massacre in Dabu and Wahan, beatings and rapes, rampant looting, forcible conscription and forced labor, indiscriminate shelling, and indiscriminate planting of land mines. Ethiopia submitted sufficient evidence for Elidar and Dalul Weredas to establish a *prima facie* case of frequent or systematic violations of international humanitarian law by Eritrean armed forces, but there was too little evidence relating to Afdera Wereda to constitute even a *prima facie* case for liability for actions there.[19] Eritrea argued in rebuttal that its troops could not have breached Ethiopian trench lines and consequently could not have physically reached the alleged victims. The Commission was not convinced by this argument and held that Eritrea had failed to produce sufficient factual evidence to overcome Ethiopia's evidence showing certain frequent or systematic violations of international humanitarian law by Eritrean armed forces.[20]

The most serious of Ethiopia's claims for physical abuse on the Eastern Front was an alleged massacre or massacres of civilians at or near a place called Dabu in Elidar Wereda. From the contradictory and confusing evidence, two main accounts emerged, one dated 1998 or 1999, according to which between 20 and 40 Ethiopian civilians were shot, and a second dated 1999 or 2000, involving some 18 or 19 victims. Neither version included a clear geographic reference. Having weighed all the evidence before it, the Commission was of the view that a serious and deadly incident did occur somewhere in the region but that Ethiopia had failed to present clear and convincing evidence of a massacre on which the Commission could found liability.[21]

Elsewhere in the Eastern Front, the Commission found sufficiently detailed and consistent evidence to support a *prima facie* case of a pattern of intentional and indiscriminate killings, which was effectively unrebutted by Eritrea.[22] The Commission found clear and convincing evidence of several incidents of rape of Ethiopian women by Eritrean soldiers in Elidar and Dalul Weredas. It held that Eritrea was liable for failing to impose effective measures on its troops, as required by international humanitarian law, to prevent rape of women in Elidar and Dalul Weredas.[23] The Commission also found sufficient evidence to hold Eritrea liable for permitting beatings by Eritrean forces in Elidar and Dalul Weredas,[24] and for permitting widespread looting and willful property destruction, including the violent and deliberate destruction of camels and other livestock, which formed the primary livelihood for many in the region.[25]

---

[18] Partial Award, para. 57.
[19] Partial Award, para. 61.
[20] Partial Award, para. 63.
[21] Partial Award, para. 66.
[22] Partial Award, para. 67.
[23] Partial Award, para. 69.
[24] Partial Award, para. 70.
[25] Partial Award, para. 71.

On the basis of unrebutted evidence that civilians were taken prisoner and forced to dig trenches and clear roads for the Eritrean army, the Commission held Eritrea liable for abduction, forced labor, and conscription in Dalul Wereda in violation of international law.[26]

As to Ethiopia's claim for indiscriminate or otherwise unlawful shelling and planting of landmines in this area, particularly in Bure town, the Commission found the limited evidence before it insufficient to prove that the civilian losses incurred due to landmines and shelling resulted from violations of international humanitarian law.[27]

---

[26] Partial Award, paras. 72–73.
[27] Partial Award, para. 74.

Eritrea-Ethiopia Claims Commission

Partial Award
Ethiopia's Claims 1-8: *Jus Ad Bellum*

Parties: Eritrea/Ethiopia

Date of Arbitration Agreement: December 12, 2000

Commissioners: Prof. Hans van Houtte (President), Judge George H. Aldrich, Mr. John R. Crook, Dean James Paul, Ms. Lucy Reed

Date of Partial Award: December 19, 2005

Summary

International armed conflict waged between Eritrea and Ethiopia between 1998 and 2000 – liability of Eritrea for violation of prohibition on resort to armed force – Eritrea found to have resorted to armed force on May 12, 1998, to attack and occupy the town of Badme and other territory then peacefully administered by Ethiopia – Eritrea liable for violation of Article 2(4) of United Nations Charter – scope of damages for which Eritrea liable to be determined in damages phase of the proceedings.

Legal Subject Matters

Arbitration:
- Jurisdiction of the arbitral tribunal

International law:
- Prohibition on resort to armed force
  - Application where title to territory in dispute
  - Self-defense

Bibliography

Award published in:
- XXVI R.I.A.A. (forthcoming 2010);
- 45 I.L.M. p. 430 (2006).

Decision No. 7 "Guidance Regarding *Jus Ad Bellum* Liability" published in:
- 46 I.L.M. p. 1121

Commentary:

- *The 1998-2000 War between Eritrea and Ethiopia: An International Legal Perspective* (Andrea de Guttry, Harry H.G. Post & Gabriella Venturini eds., TMC Asser Press 2009);
- Hans van Houtte, *The Eritrea-Ethiopia Claims Commission and International Humanitarian Law*, *in* Judicial Rights and International Justice, Liber Fausto Pocar p. 383 (Guiffre 2009);
- Susan A. Notar, *Eritrea Ethiopia Claims Commission Decision No. 7 Guidance Regarding* Jus Ad Bellum *Liability: Introductory Note*, 46 I.L.M. p. 1119;
- Pierre d'Argent & Jean d'Aspremont, *La Commission des réclamations Érythrée-Éthiopie : un premier bilan*, 53 AFDI p. 347 (2007);
- Won Kidane, *Civil Liability for Violations of International Law: The Jurisprudence of the Eritrea-Ethiopia Claims Commission in The Hague*, 25 Wis. Int'l L.J. p. 23 (2007);
- George H. Aldrich, *The Work of the Eritrea-Ethiopia Claims Commission*, 6 Y.B. Int'l Human. L. p. 435 (2006);
- Natalie Klein, *State Responsibility for International Humanitarian Law Violations and the Work of the Eritrea Ethiopia Claims Commission So Far*, 47 Germ. Y.B. Int'l L. p. 214 (2005);
- Judith I.A. Lichtenberg, *Eritrea Ethiopia Claims Commission*, 12 Tilburg Foreign L. Rev. p. 266 (2004).
- Luisa Castagnetti, *Il problema del diritto all'uso della forza nelle relazioni internazionali di fronte alla Eritrea-Ethiopia Claims Commission*, 90 Rivista di diritto internazionale p. 738 (2007);
- Christine Gray, *The Eritrea/Ethiopia Claims Commission Oversteps Its Boundaries: A Partial Award?*, 17 Eur. J. Int'l L. p. 699 (2006);
- Philippe Weckel, *Commission des réclamations (Erythrée/Ethiopie), Sentences du 19 Décembre 2005 (*jus ad bellum*)*, 1 RGDIP p. 195 (2006).

Facts

In May 1998, an armed conflict broke out between the Parties. The Parties disagreed as to the cause of this armed conflict. Ethiopia alleged that, between May 12 and June 11, 1998, Eritrea launched a "full scale" invasion of Ethiopia at many points along the Parties' mutual border from Badme in the West to Bure in the East. Eritrea contended *inter alia* that Ethiopia was unlawfully occupying Eritrean territory in the area around Badme, which was the area of much of the initial hostilities in May 1998, citing the Decision of the Eritrea-Ethiopia Boundary Commission of April 13, 2002.[1] Eritrea argued that its actions in taking Badme and adjacent areas on May 12, 1998, were lawful measures of self-defense, consistent with Article 51 of the UN Charter, taken in response to fighting near Badme that began on May 6 and 7, 1998.[2]

This Partial Award addressed a claim that was included as a component of all of Ethiopia's Claims 1–8. Ethiopia asked the Commission to find Eritrea responsible for loss, damage, and injury suffered by Ethiopia's nationals as a result of the alleged use of force against Ethiopia in violation of the rules of international law regulating the use of force, the *jus ad bellum*, in May and June 1998. Ethiopia filed these claims on December 12, 2001. Following the exchange of written pleadings, a hearing on liability was held at the Peace Palace in April 2005, in conjunction with a hearing on several other claims by both Parties.

---

[1] Partial Award, Ethiopia's *Jus Ad Bellum* Claim [hereinafter "Partial Award"], para. 9. *See also* Summary, Eritrea-Ethiopia Boundary Commission, p. 144.

[2] Partial Award, para. 9.

Summary of Matters Submitted to Arbitration

Ethiopia's Claim that Eritrea carried out a series of unlawful armed attacks against it, beginning on May 12, 1998, in violation of the *jus ad bellum.*

Partial Award

Jurisdiction

Eritrea contested the jurisdiction of the Commission on the grounds that Article 3 of the Agreement assigned the responsibility to address this issue to another body. Article 3 of the Agreement provides for the creation of an "independent and impartial body," whose task is defined in the following terms:

> In order to determine the origins of the conflict, an investigation will be carried out on the incidents of 6 May 1998 and on any other incident prior to that date which could have contributed to a misunderstanding between the parties regarding their common border, including the incidents of July and August 1997.

According to the Commission, the determination of the origins of the conflict and the nature of any misunderstandings about the border, had they been made by the impartial body anticipated by Article 3 of the Agreement, which had not been constituted, would not have answered the question of the legality of Eritrea's resort to force. The body anticipated by Article 3 was directed to inquire into matters of fact; the Commission was the only body assigned by the Agreement with the duty of deciding claims of liability for violations of international law.[3]

The Parties had agreed that the last sentence of Article 5 of the Agreement, which provides that "[t]he Commission shall not hear claims arising from the cost of military operations, preparing for military operations, or the use of force, except to the extent that such claims involve violations of international humanitarian law," was limited to claims solely for the costs of the enumerated activities. The Commission concluded that it had jurisdiction pursuant to Article 5 of the Agreement over Ethiopia's *Jus Ad Bellum* Claim.[4]

Merits

Ethiopia contended that Eritrea planned and carried out attacks against Ethiopia in violation of its obligations under international law, including the requirement of Article 2(4) of the Charter of the United Nations ("UN Charter") that all Members refrain from the threat or use of force against the territorial integrity or political independence of any State. The Commission rejected the first defensive argument by Eritrea that recourse to force by Eritrea would have been lawful because some of the territory concerned was territory to which Eritrea had a valid claim. In the Commission's view, "the practice of States and the writings of eminent publicists show that self-defense cannot be invoked to settle territorial disputes."[5]

---

[3] Partial Award, para. 4.
[4] Partial Award, para. 5.
[5] Partial Award, para. 10.

Eritrea also contended that Ethiopian armed militia near Badme carried out forcible incursions into Eritrea in early May 1998 and fired on Eritrean forces on May 6 and 7, killing eight Eritrean soldiers and setting off fighting in the area between small units during the next several days.[6] The Commission rejected this second defensive argument, holding that localized border encounters between small infantry units, even those involving the loss of life, do not constitute an armed attack for purposes of Article 51 of the UN Charter.[7] The Commission was satisfied that the events that occurred in the vicinity of Badme during the period from May 6 to 12, 1998, were not of a magnitude to constitute an armed attack by either State against the other within the meaning of Article 51 of the UN Charter.[8]

The Commission noted that a joint body of the Parties met in Addis Ababa on May 8, 1998, to discuss border problems. It was undisputed that the head of the Eritrean delegation to that meeting was its Minister of Defense and that following the meeting on May 8, its delegation left Addis Ababa during the night.[9] Ethiopia asserted that agreement had been reached at the meeting that both sides should avoid border crossings by armed personnel and that the two sides would meet again in two months in Asmara to seek agreement on border issues.[10] The Commission found that on May 12, 1998, at about 5:30 a.m., Eritrean armed forces attacked the town of Badme and several other border areas that were all either within undisputed Ethiopian territory or within territory that was peacefully administered by Ethiopia and that later would be on the Ethiopian side of the line to which Ethiopian armed forces were obligated to withdraw in 2000 under the Cease-Fire Agreement of June 18, 2000.[11] The Commission, recalling its Partial Award in Ethiopia's Central Front Claims, held that that line was the best available evidence of the areas effectively administered by Ethiopia in early May 1998. The Commission held, further, that its holdings concerning conduct during the war had no effect on the international boundary as subsequently determined by the Eritrea-Ethiopia Boundary Commission.[12]

The Commission concluded that Eritrea had violated Article 2(4) of the UN Charter by resorting to armed force to attack and occupy Badme as well as other territory in the Tahtay Adiabo and Laelay Adiabo Weredas of Ethiopia, in an attack that began on May 12, 1998, and was liable to compensate Ethiopia for the damages caused by that violation of international law.[13]

The Commission rejected the third defensive argument put forward by Eritrea that Ethiopia had declared war on Eritrea.[14]

The Commission found, further, that Ethiopia had failed to prove that the unlawful armed attack that began on May 12, 1998, in what became known as the Western Front, should be considered to include all of Eritrea's subsequent attacks in May and June 1998 as one continuous second phase.[15] Ethiopia's contention that subsequent attacks by Eritrea along other

---

[6] Partial Award, para. 9.
[7] Partial Award, para. 11.
[8] Partial Award, para. 12.
[9] Partial Award, para. 13.
[10] Partial Award, para. 13.
[11] Partial Award, paras. 14–15.
[12] Partial Award, para. 15.
[13] Partial Award, para. 16.
[14] Partial Award, para. 17.
[15] Partial Award, para. 18.

parts of their common border were pre-planned and coordinated unlawful uses of force failed for lack of proof.

The Commission could not resolve whether the Eritrean military operations from mid-May to mid-June 1998, in what became the Central and Eastern Fronts, were pre-planned attacks or were determined by developing military demands after it became clear that Ethiopia would not acquiesce in Eritrea's captures of territory on the Western Front.[16] It therefore decided to request further briefing in the damages phase concerning the scope of the damages for which Eritrea was liable by reason of that attack.[17]

Decision No. 7 "Guidance Regarding *Jus Ad Bellum* Liability"

The Commission held its first round of hearings in the damages phase of the proceedings in April 2007. At the hearing, Ethiopia contended that Eritrea bore very extensive liability on account of its violation of the *jus ad bellum*. Eritrea contended that, because the manner in which Ethiopia presented its claim did not conform to the Commission's procedural instructions prior to the hearing, the Claim should be dismissed in its entirety. On July 27, 2007, the Commission issued its Decision Number 7 "Guidance Regarding *Jus Ad Bellum* Liability" ("Decision No. 7"), in which it set out to provide guidance for the Parties' pleadings and arguments in the final round of hearings of the damages phase of the proceedings, regarding the extent of Eritrea's liability to pay damages for its breach of the *jus ad bellum*.

As to the applicable standard of legal causation, the Commission reviewed the findings of various international bodies on the determination of damages having a sufficient causal connection with conduct violating international law to be compensable. It concluded that the necessary connection is best characterized through the term "proximate cause."[18] The Commission noted that, in assessing whether this test had been met, and whether the chain of causation was sufficiently close in a particular situation, it would give weight to whether particular damage reasonably should have been foreseeable to an actor committing the international delict in question.[19]

The Commission also addressed the contention by Ethiopia that the *jus ad bellum* violation identified by the Commission "inescapably resulted in [the] wider condition [of wide-scale hostilities]" and that any "loss, damage or injury associated with it … is compensable." Having rejected the arguments of the Parties as an appropriate basis for determining this issue, the Commission reserved its decision on Ethiopia's *jus ad bellum* claims.[20]

As regards the considerations relevant to assessing *jus ad bellum* responsibility, the Commission noted that the few twentieth-century cases in which States had been held to be internationally responsible for extensive war damages counseled caution rather than providing clear guidance.[21] The Commission noted, in particular, that the resolutions adopted by the UN Security Council in relation to the war between Eritrea and Ethiopia were markedly different in substance and tone from those adopted regarding the 1990–1991 invasion and

[16] Partial Award, para. 19.
[17] Partial Award, para. 20.
[18] Decision No. 7, para. 13.
[19] *Id.*
[20] Decision No. 7, para. 20.
[21] Decision No. 7, para. 22.

occupation of Kuwait by Iraq. In relation to the war between Eritrea and Ethiopia, none of the Security Council's resolutions assigned responsibility for the conflict to either Party, and all of the resolutions spoke to both Parties, not to Eritrea alone.[22] When hostilities intensified in early 1999 during Ethiopia's Operation Sunset, and at the time of Ethiopia's May 2000 incursion into Eritrea, the Security Council again addressed both Parties in equal terms.

The Commission invited the Parties, at the next stage of the proceedings, to address in a more considered and precise manner the scope of damages flowing from the Commission's Partial Award in relation to the specific elements claimed by Ethiopia on the basis of *jus ad bellum*, taking full account of Decision No. 7.[23]

[22] Decision No. 7, para. 31.
[23] Decision No. 7, para. 33.

Eritrea-Ethiopia Claims Commission

Partial Award
Eritrea's Claim 20: Diplomatic Claim

Parties:	Eritrea/Ethiopia
Date of Arbitration Agreement:	December 12, 2000
Commissioners:	Prof. Hans van Houtte (President), Judge George H. Aldrich, Mr. John R. Crook, Dean James Paul, Ms. Lucy Reed
Date of Partial Award:	December 19, 2005

Summary

International armed conflict waged between Eritrea and Ethiopia between 1998 and 2000 – Parties maintained diplomatic ties during armed conflict between them – liability of Ethiopia for violations of international law committed in relation to Eritrean diplomatic personnel and property – departure of Eritrean diplomatic personnel from Addis Ababa airport in May 1998 – Ethiopian officials searched and interfered with luggage or person or both of Ambassador and other departing diplomats – Ethiopia liable for violating Articles 36 and 29 of the Vienna Convention on Diplomatic Relations – entering, ransacking, searching, and seizure of the Eritrean Embassy Residence and other property without Eritrea's consent by Ethiopia – Ethiopia liable for violating Article 22 of the Vienna Convention on Diplomatic Relations.

Legal Subject Matters

Diplomatic relations:
- Vienna Convention on Diplomatic Relations
  - Application during international armed conflict
    - Exemption from search of personal baggage of diplomatic agents
    - Inviolability of diplomatic agents
    - Principle of reciprocity

Bibliography

Award published in:
- XXVI R.I.A.A. (forthcoming 2010).

Commentary:
- *The 1998-2000 War between Eritrea and Ethiopia: An International Legal Perspective* (Andrea de Guttry, Harry H.G. Post & Gabriella Venturini eds., TMC Asser Press 2009);
- Hans van Houtte, *The Eritrea-Ethiopia Claims Commission and International Humanitarian Law*, *in* JUDICIAL RIGHTS AND INTERNATIONAL JUSTICE, LIBER FAUSTO POCAR p. 383 (Guiffre 2009);
- Pierre d'Argent & Jean d'Aspremont, *La Commission des réclamations Érythrée-Éthiopie : un premier bilan*, 53 AFDI p. 347 (2007);
- Won Kidane, *Civil Liability for Violations of International Law: The Jurisprudence of the Eritrea-Ethiopia Claims Commission in The Hague*, 25 WIS. INT'L L.J. p. 23 (2007);
- George H. Aldrich, *The Work of the Eritrea-Ethiopia Claims Commission*, 6 Y.B. INT'L HUMAN. L. p. 435 (2006);
- Natalie Klein, *State Responsibility for International Humanitarian Law Violations and the Work of the Eritrea Ethiopia Claims Commission So Far*, 47 GERM. Y.B. INT'L L. p. 214 (2005);
- Judith I.A. Lichtenberg, *Eritrea Ethiopia Claims Commission*, 12 TILBURG FOREIGN L. REV. p. 266 (2004);
- J. Romesh Weeramantry, *Diplomatic Claims (Eritrea v. Ethiopia), Eritrea's Claim 20/Ethiopia's Claim 8, Partial Awards*, 101 AM. J. INT'L L. p. 616 (2007).

Facts

Between 1998 and 2000, the Parties waged a costly, large-scale international armed conflict along several areas of their common frontier. Throughout the armed conflict, the Parties maintained their diplomatic ties with each other. In 1998, Eritrea was represented in Ethiopia by Ambassador Ghirma Asmeron ("Ambassador Ghirma"), who was also the accredited representative of Eritrea to the Organization of African Unity ("OAU") and the United Nations Economic Commission for Africa ("UNECA"). Shortly after the armed conflict began in May 1998, Ethiopia ordered Ambassador Ghirma to reduce the diplomatic staff to three, including himself. Ethiopia declared all but those three *persona non grata* and ordered them to leave the country within 48 hours. In February 1999, after Ethiopia initiated a counteroffensive in the Badme region, Ethiopia declared the Ambassador himself *persona non grata* and gave him 25 hours to depart, which he did by plane.

This Partial Award addressed claims arising out of injuries alleged to have been suffered by the Eritrean diplomatic mission and consular posts and personnel in Ethiopia, including Ambassador Ghirma, as a result of Ethiopia's alleged violations of the international law of diplomatic and consular relations. Eritrea requested monetary compensation and additional remedies, including orders that Ethiopia desist from interference with Eritrean diplomatic personnel and that it restore the Embassy Residence to Eritrea. Eritrea filed these claims on December 12, 2001. Following the exchange of written pleadings, a hearing on liability was held at the Peace Palace in April 2005, in conjunction with a hearing on several other claims by both Parties, including Ethiopia's related Claim 8.

Summary of Matters Submitted to Arbitration

This Partial Award addressed Eritrea's claims in relation to:

A. Alleged illegal expulsion of diplomatic and consular agents and staff, including alleged interference with Eritrea's participation in meetings of the OAU and UNECA;

B. Alleged seizure of the Embassy Residence and detention of personnel; and
C. Alleged interference with Embassy and Consulate Operations.

Partial Award

Introductory Comment

The Commission stressed the Parties' commendable decisions not to sever their diplomatic links despite the armed conflict.[1] It noted that this unusual situation presented unusual challenges for the application of diplomatic law, as certain of the premises of diplomatic relations "cannot be presumed to continue without strain during hostilities."[2]

Jurisdiction

The Commission upheld a jurisdictional challenge by Ethiopia in relation to two of Eritrea's claims which it found had not been identified in its Statement of Claim and therefore had not been filed within the time limit imposed by Article 5(8) of the Agreement.[3] Ethiopia also challenged Eritrea's pursuit of a claim based on Ethiopia's alleged interference with Eritrea's effective participation in the OAU and UNECA in Addis Ababa. The Commission rejected this challenge on the basis that Eritrea's claim, although not explicitly alleged in its Statement of Claim, was sufficiently clear in the context of its objections to the expulsion of Ambassador Ghirma, who was ambassador to Ethiopia and the accredited representative of Eritrea to the OAU and UNECA.[4]

The Commission also dismissed for lack of jurisdiction two other claims of alleged mistreatment involving the Chargé. Given that these claims on their face dated from after December 2000 and did not arise as a result of the armed conflict, they were extinguished pursuant to Article 5(8) of the Agreement.[5]

Applicable Law

Both Parties relied on the Vienna Convention on Diplomatic Relations of 1961 ("VCDR") and the Vienna Convention on Consular Relations of 1963, which "largely codify customary international diplomatic and consular law," as the sources of applicable law for the Diplomatic Claims.[6] Ethiopia took the position that a state of war must modify the application of international diplomatic law; Eritrea argued for strict application of the standards in the VCDR despite a state of war.[7] The Commission faced the task of considering the largely unprecedented question of how the principles in the VCDR should be construed and applied in the course of the Parties' armed conflict. However, the Commission did not accept that the

---

[1] Partial Award, Eritrea's Diplomatic Claim [hereinafter "Partial Award"], para. 4.
[2] Partial Award, para. 6.
[3] Partial Award, para. 11.
[4] Partial Award, para. 12.
[5] Partial Award, para. 51.
[6] Partial Award, para. 15.
[7] Partial Award, para. 17.

Parties could derogate from their fundamental obligations under the VCDR, notably, those relating to the inviolability of diplomatic agents and premises, because of the exigencies of war.[8] In light of the limited time and resources allocated to the Commission, and paying particular attention to the principle of reciprocity, the Commission held that it was constrained to look for serious violations impeding the effective functioning of the diplomatic mission.[9]

Categories of Claims

Eritrea organized its claim into three categories, namely, (i) alleged expulsion of diplomatic and consular agents and staff, (ii) alleged seizure of the Embassy Residence and detention of personnel, and (iii) alleged interference with Embassy and Consulate operations.

Expulsion of Diplomats and Staff

As regards the expulsion of diplomats and staff, Eritrea claimed in respect of (a) the short length of time allowed by Ethiopia for the departure of Eritrean diplomats and staff, (b) Ethiopian treatment of such personnel during departure, and (c) the size and make-up of the Eritrean mission following the departures.

Eritrea alleged that the 25-hour and 48-hour departure periods for the Ambassador and diplomatic staff, respectively, were unreasonably short under Article 9(2) of the VCDR. The Commission, particularly given the circumstances of the armed conflict, did not find a violation of international law based on the time periods allowed for Ambassador Ghirma and other diplomats to depart Eritrea.[10] The Commission did find violations of Articles 29 and 36 of the VCDR with respect to Ethiopia's treatment of the Eritrean diplomats during their departures.[11] The Commission noted that the treatment allegedly accorded by Ethiopia to the departing Eritrean diplomats in this regard approximated that allegedly accorded by Eritrea to Ethiopian diplomats departing Asmara.[12]

The Commission found no violation of the VCDR in Ethiopia's setting limits on the size and make-up of Eritrea's mission staff. It found that Eritrea had presented insufficient evidence to prove that the small size of the Embassy staff allowed by Ethiopia, which was no smaller than Eritrea allowed the Ethiopian Embassy in Asmara, left it unable to perform its diplomatic functions.[13]

Seizure of the Embassy Residence and Detention of Personnel

Eritrea alleged that Ethiopia entered and seized the Embassy Residence and took diplomatic property shortly after Ambassador Ghirma's departure in February 1999, in violation of Article 22 of the VCDR.[14] The Commission found that Eritrea had presented clear and

[8] Partial Award, paras. 19–20.
[9] Partial Award, para. 22.
[10] Partial Award, para. 33.
[11] Partial Award, para. 36.
[12] Partial Award, para. 37.
[13] Partial Award, para. 41.
[14] Partial Award, para. 43.

convincing evidence that Ethiopian security agents entered, ransacked, searched, and seized the Eritrean Embassy Residence, as well as vehicles and other property, without Eritrea's consent. Ethiopia admitted "sealing off" the Residence from Eritrean use on the basis of "credible internal intelligence and national security reports" that Eritrea was using the Residence for illegal purposes. The Commission held that this was not a legal defense and that the Residence, as part of the diplomatic premises, is absolutely inviolable under Article 22 of the VCDR.[15]

In relation to Eritrea's claim for detention of Embassy personnel, the Commission, whilst it found the evidence clear and convincing, found that there was no evidence that these detentions had compromised the essential functioning of the Eritrean mission.[16] It therefore rejected this claim for lack of proof.

Interference with Embassy Operations

Eritrea complained of several types of official action allegedly interfering with the functioning of its mission in violation of international diplomatic law.

Eritrea claimed that Ethiopian security agents increasingly monitored, harassed, and intimidated visitors to the Embassy as well as Embassy staff. The Commission noted that each Party increased its monitoring of the other's Embassy and its scrutiny of staff and visitors to the Embassy, and that each mission sometimes requested and at other times objected to an increased security presence, as the need for extra protection in wartime competed with the problems inherent in the enemy's serving as security provider. On balance, the Commission did not find that Ethiopia's security measures involving the Eritrean Embassy, while sometimes intrusive and even perhaps abusive, compromised the basic functioning of the Eritrean mission in violation of the applicable international diplomatic law.[17] The Commission also dismissed, for failure of proof, Eritrea's claims of unlawful interference with free Embassy communications through disconnection and tapping of telephone lines and opening Embassy mail.[18]

Interference with OAU and UNECA Participation

Eritrea claimed that Ethiopia had interfered with Eritrea's' full participation in the OAU and UNECA, at a critical time in the peacemaking process, by peremptorily rejecting Ambassador Ghirma and then his nominated replacement as Eritrea's accredited representative to those international organizations.[19]

The Commission recognized that this claim implicated a complex area of international organization law.[20] It considered the question whether Ethiopia, as the host State, had a legal obligation to allow Eritrea absolute discretion to designate particular individuals to serve as its representatives to the OAU and the UNECA. Having found nothing to this effect in the OAU Privileges and Immunities Convention, the OAU Headquarters Agreement, or the

---

[15] Partial Award, para. 46.
[16] Partial Award, para. 49.
[17] Partial Award, para. 55.
[18] Partial Award, para. 58.
[19] Partial Award, para. 59.
[20] Partial Award, para. 60.

UNECA Headquarters Agreement, it therefore dismissed the claim. The Commission found, further, that Eritrea had failed to prove that Ethiopia had interfered with its full participation in the OAU and UNECA.[21] The record showed that Eritrea had waited nine months to make its first and only proposal for a new permanent representative to the OAU to replace Ambassador Ghirma, that Ethiopia rejected the candidate on the reasonable ground that he had been declared *persona non grata* in 1997, and that Eritrea's Chargé was promptly accredited to the OAU after Ambassador Ghirma's departure and was able to attend OAU sessions.[22]

Eritrea's Request for Additional Remedies

The Commission found that Eritrea had not shown, as required pursuant to the Commission's Decision No. 3 "Remedies" of July 24, 2001, that the non-monetary remedies it had requested were "in accordance with international practice."[23]

The Commission asserted throughout the Award that, to the extent that Embassy staff and family members or visitors who were mistreated, denationalized, and/or expelled or lost property in the course of denationalization and expulsion fell within the categories for which the Commission assessed liability in the Partial Award in Eritrea's Civilians Claims, Eritrea could assert damages claims with respect to them in the damages phase in that case.[24]

---

[21] Partial Award, para. 62.
[22] *Id.*
[23] Partial Award, para. 65.
[24] Partial Award, paras. 42, 50, 56, 65.

Eritrea-Ethiopia Claims Commission

Partial Award
Ethiopia's Claim 8: Diplomatic Claim

Parties: Eritrea/Ethiopia

Date of Arbitration Agreement: December 12, 2000

Commissioners: Prof. Hans van Houtte (President), Judge George H. Aldrich, Mr. John R. Crook, Dean James Paul, Ms. Lucy Reed

Date of Partial Award: December 19, 2005

Summary

International armed conflict waged between Eritrea and Ethiopia between 1998 and 2000 – Parties maintained diplomatic ties during armed conflict between them – liability of Eritrea for violations of international law committed in relation to Ethiopian diplomatic personnel and property – arrest and detention of Ethiopian Chargé d'Affaires in September 1998 and October 1999 – Eritrea liable for violating Article 29 of Vienna Convention on Diplomatic Relations – retention by Eritrea for 5 years of a box containing Ethiopian Embassy correspondence including blank passports – Eritrea liable for violating official Ethiopian diplomatic correspondence and interfering with functioning of mission in breach of Articles 24 and 29 of Vienna Convention on Diplomatic Relations.

Legal Subject Matters

Diplomatic relations:
- Vienna Convention on Diplomatic Relations
  - Application during international armed conflict
    - Inviolability of diplomatic agents
    - Inviolability of diplomatic correspondence
  - Principle of reciprocity

Bibliography

Award published in:
- XXVI R.I.A.A. (forthcoming 2010);
- 45 I.L.M. p. 621 (2006).

Commentary:

- *The 1998-2000 War between Eritrea and Ethiopia: An International Legal Perspective* (Andrea de Guttry, Harry H.G. Post & Gabriella Venturini eds., TMC Asser Press 2009);
- Hans van Houtte, *The Eritrea-Ethiopia Claims Commission and International Humanitarian Law*, *in* Judicial Rights and International Justice, Liber Fausto Pocar p. 383 (Guiffre 2009);
- Pierre d'Argent & Jean d'Aspremont, *La Commission des réclamations Érythrée-Éthiopie : un premier bilan*, 53 AFDI p. 347 (2007);
- Won Kidane, *Civil Liability for Violations of International Law: The Jurisprudence of the Eritrea-Ethiopia Claims Commission in The Hague*, 25 Wis. Int'l L.J. p. 23 (2007);
- George H. Aldrich, *The Work of the Eritrea-Ethiopia Claims Commission*, 6 Y.B. Int'l Human. L. p. 435 (2006);
- Natalie Klein, *State Responsibility for International Humanitarian Law Violations and the Work of the Eritrea Ethiopia Claims Commission So Far*, 47 Germ. Y.B. Int'l L. p. 214 (2005);
- Judith I.A. Lichtenberg, *Eritrea Ethiopia Claims Commission*, 12 Tilburg Foreign L. Rev. p. 266 (2004);
- J. Romesh Weeramantry, *Diplomatic Claims (Eritrea v. Ethiopia), Eritrea's Claim 20/Ethiopia's Claim 8, Partial Awards*, 101 Am. J. Int'l L. p. 616 (2007).

Facts

Between 1998 and 2000, the Parties waged a costly, large-scale international armed conflict along several areas of their common frontier. During the armed conflict, the Parties maintained their diplomatic ties with each other. On April 29, 1999, Eritrean Customs officials intercepted and retained a diplomatic bag sent from the Ethiopian Consulate in Jeddah to the Embassy. Eritrea did not release this diplomatic bag to Ethiopia despite formal demands. The Parties disagreed as to other matters concerning the treatment of Ethiopian diplomatic personnel and property throughout the armed conflict. Ethiopia alleged that in September 1998 and in October 1999, Eritrea twice arrested and then briefly detained and interrogated the Ethiopian Chargé d'Affaires. Eritrea denied this claim. Ethiopia also alleged that Eritrean security agents harassed Embassy personnel.

This Partial Award addressed claims arising out of the injuries alleged to have been suffered by the Ethiopian diplomatic mission and consular posts and personnel in Eritrea as a result of Eritrea's alleged violations of the international law of diplomatic and consular relations. Ethiopia filed these claims on December 12, 2001. Following the exchange of written pleadings, a hearing on liability was held at the Peace Palace in April 2005, in conjunction with a hearing on several other claims by both Parties, including Eritrea's related Claim 20.

Summary of Matters Submitted to Arbitration

This Partial Award addressed Ethiopia's claims relating to:

A. Alleged arrest, detention, and interrogation of the Ethiopian Chargé d'Affaires;
B. Alleged harassment of Embassy personnel;
C. Alleged seizure of Embassy documents;
D. Alleged interference with Embassy access; and
E. Alleged failure to protect the security of the Embassy and its personnel.

Partial Award

Introductory Comment

The Commission stressed the Parties' commendable decisions not to sever their diplomatic links despite the armed conflict.[1] It noted that this unusual situation presented unusual challenges for the application of diplomatic law, as certain of the premises of diplomatic relations "cannot be presumed to continue without strain during hostilities."[2]

Jurisdiction

The Commission upheld Eritrea's jurisdictional objection to Ethiopia's claims concerning the status and treatment of the Assab Consulate under international diplomatic and consular law as these had not been filed within the time limit imposed by Article 5(8) of the Agreement.[3] The Commission rejected a number of claims concerning alleged arrests of Embassy staff because they concerned events allegedly occurring after December 2000 that do not fall within the extended parameters of Commission Decision No. 1 "The Commission's Mandate/Temporal Scope of Jurisdiction."[4]

Applicable Law

Both Parties relied on the Vienna Convention on Diplomatic Relations of 1961 ("VCDR") and the Vienna Convention on Consular Relations of 1963, which "largely codify customary international diplomatic and consular law," as the sources of applicable law for the Diplomatic Claims.[5] Ethiopia took the position that a state of war must modify the application of international diplomatic law; Eritrea argued for strict application of the standards in the VCDR despite a state of war.[6] The Commission faced the task of considering the largely unprecedented question of how the principles in the VCDR should be construed and applied in the course of the Parties' armed conflict. However, the Commission did not accept that the Parties could derogate from their fundamental obligations under the VCDR, notably, those relating to the inviolability of diplomatic agents and premises, because of the exigencies of war.[7] In light of the limited time and resources allocated to the Commission, and paying particular attention to the principle of reciprocity, the Commission held that it was constrained to look for serious violations impeding the effective functioning of the diplomatic mission.[8]

---

[1] Partial Award, Ethiopia's Diplomatic Claim [hereinafter "Partial Award"], para. 4.
[2] Partial Award, para. 6.
[3] Partial Award, para. 12.
[4] Partial Award, para. 15.
[5] Partial Award, para. 19.
[6] Partial Award, para. 22.
[7] Partial Award, para. 24.
[8] Partial Award, para. 26.

Categories of Claims

Ethiopia presented six categories of claims, namely, (i) alleged arrest, detention, and interrogation of the Chargé d'Affaires, (ii) alleged harassment of Embassy personnel, (iii) alleged seizure of Embassy documents, (iv) alleged interference with Embassy access, (v) alleged failure to protect the security of the Embassy and its personnel, and (vi) alleged failure to facilitate the repatriation of staff of the Consulate in Assab and their families, and restriction of their freedom of movement and communication.

Treatment of the Chargé d'Affaires

Ethiopia claimed that Eritrea violated Articles 26, 29, and 31 of the VCDR by mistreating the Ethiopian Chargé d'Affaires. The Commission held Eritrea liable for violating Article 29 of the VCDR by arresting and briefly detaining the Chargé in September 1998 and October 1999 without regard to his diplomatic immunity.[9] It did not consider that these circumstances also gave rise to breaches of Article 26 of the VCDR, which protects free travel in the territory of the receiving State, or Article 31, which guarantees immunity from criminal prosecution and compulsion to give evidence.[10]

Ethiopia also claimed for two instances in which Eritrea summoned the Chargé to the Ministry of Foreign Affairs to question him about a letter he had written and circulated to foreign governments. The Commission noted that the VCDR does not prohibit the receiving State from calling for meetings with accredited diplomats and that such meetings are an integral part of effective diplomacy and, absent clear and convincing proof that the Chargé was coerced, the Commission dismissed the claim.[11]

Harassment of Embassy Personnel

Ethiopia presented broad claims that Eritrean security agents "consistently engaged in harassment, intimidation, abusive search, interrogation, arrest, and detention" of non-diplomatic Embassy staff who were Ethiopian nationals. The Commission was unable to find clear and convincing evidence that the treatment of permanent resident service staff compromised the essential functioning of the Ethiopian mission.[12] Ethiopia made a separate claim that Eritrean officials mistreated a group of Ethiopian diplomats in the course of their departure from Asmara in June 1998, in violation of Articles 29 and 44 of the VCDR. Ethiopia alleged that Eritrean security officers obstructed the departing diplomats at the airport and put them at risk of missing the 48-hour departure deadline imposed by Eritrea. The Commission dismissed this claim for lack of proof.[13]

The Commission noted that, to the extent that individual Embassy staff members fell within the categories for which the Commission assessed liability in the Partial Award in

---

[9] Partial Award, para. 33.
[10] Partial Award, para. 34.
[11] Partial Award, para. 36.
[12] Partial Award, para. 39.
[13] Partial Award, para. 41.

Ethiopia's Civilians Claims, including liability for wrongful and abusive detention, Ethiopia could assert damages claims with respect to them in the damages phase in that case.[14]

Seizure of Embassy Documents

Ethiopia claimed that on April 29, 1999, Eritrean Customs officials at the Asmara airport intercepted and retained a diplomatic bag sent from the Ethiopian consulate in Jeddah to the Embassy, which contained 100 blank passports, invoices, and receipts, in violation of Articles 24, 27, and 29 of the VCDR.[15] The Commission found that the package at issue was not labeled in any fashion to indicate its character as a diplomatic bag and hence Ethiopia could not prove a violation of Article 27 of the VCDR. However, it was not disputed that Eritrea had refused to release the box, which constituted official Ethiopian correspondence, to Ethiopia for more than five years. The Commission held Eritrea liable for violating official Ethiopian diplomatic correspondence and interfering with the functioning of the mission in breach of Articles 24 and 29 of the VCDR.[16]

Interference with Embassy Access

Ethiopia complained of increased monitoring of its Embassy by security agents after the outbreak of the war, alleging that Eritrean security personnel outside the Ethiopian Embassy searched, questioned, and sometimes assaulted visitors and staff members.[17] The Commission noted that each Party increased its monitoring of the other's Embassy and its scrutiny of staff and visitors to the Embassy, and that each mission sometimes requested and at other times objected to an increased security presence, as the need for extra protection in wartime competed with the problems inherent in the enemy's serving as security provider. On balance, the Commission did not find that Eritrea's security measures involving the Ethiopian Embassy, while sometimes intrusive and even perhaps abusive, compromised the basic functioning of the Eritrean mission in violation of the applicable international diplomatic law.[18]

The Commission then examined Ethiopia's contentions that Eritrea unlawfully interfered with Ethiopian Embassy communications by disconnecting some telephone lines and tapping others, locking the Embassy mail box, routinely opening and seizing official correspondence, and denying the Embassy's request, which was made on an unspecified date, for Internet service. The Commission dismissed these claims for failure of proof.[19] It held, further, that Ethiopia's claim concerning denial of Internet service fell outside the Commission's temporal jurisdiction, on the basis of evidence that Internet service was not available in Eritrea until after December 2000.

---

[14] Partial Award, para. 40.
[15] Partial Award, para. 42.
[16] Partial Award, para. 44.
[17] Partial Award, para. 45.
[18] Partial Award, para. 50.
[19] Partial Award, para. 52.

Failure to Protect the Security of the Embassy and Its Personnel

Ethiopia charged Eritrea with violating Article 22 of the VCDR by failing to protect the Embassy and its personnel from intrusion by two individuals, one on August 10, 1999, and the second on June 23, 2000. In the second case the intruder tried to burn the Embassy flag. Eritrean police arrested both intruders. The Commission found that Eritrea had taken action consistent with its obligations under the VCDR in both instances, and found no violation of the applicable law in connection with these claims.[20]

[20] Partial Award, para. 54.

Eritrea-Ethiopia Claims Commission

Partial Award
Eritrea's Claim 24: Loss of Property in Ethiopia Owned by Non-Residents

Parties:	Eritrea/Ethiopia
Date of Arbitration Agreement:	December 12, 2000
Commissioners:	Prof. Hans van Houtte (President), Judge George H. Aldrich, Mr. John R. Crook, Dean James Paul, Ms. Lucy Reed
Date of Partial Award:	December 19, 2005

Summary

International armed conflict waged between Eritrea and Ethiopia between 1998 and 2000 – liability of Ethiopia for violations of international humanitarian law committed in its treatment of property belonging to Eritrean nationals – requisitioning by Ethiopia during conflict of trucks and buses owned by Eritreans – Ethiopia liable for failing to provide full compensation to owners of vehicles so requisitioned – economic measures taken by Ethiopia resulting collectively in loss of businesses and immovable property in Ethiopia of non-resident Eritreans – Ethiopia liable for creating and facilitating cumulative network of economic measures resulting in property losses contrary to duty to ensure protection of aliens' assets.

Legal Subject Matters

Arbitration:
- Jurisdiction of the arbitral tribunal

Diplomatic protection:
- Nationality of claims

International armed conflict:
- Duty to protect from despoliation
- Expropriation
  - Duty to pay full compensation
- Treatment of alien property

Bibliography

Award published in:
- XXVI R.I.A.A. (forthcoming 2010).

Commentary:
- *The 1998-2000 War between Eritrea and Ethiopia: An International Legal Perspective* (Andrea de Guttry, Harry H.G. Post & Gabriella Venturini eds., TMC Asser Press 2009);
- Hans van Houtte, *The Eritrea-Ethiopia Claims Commission and International Humanitarian Law*, *in* Judicial Rights and International Justice, Liber Fausto Pocar p. 383 (Guiffre 2009);
- Pierre d'Argent & Jean d'Aspremont, *La Commission des réclamations Érythrée-Éthiopie : un premier bilan*, 53 AFDI p. 347 (2007);
- Won Kidane, *Civil Liability for Violations of International Law: The Jurisprudence of the Eritrea-Ethiopia Claims Commission in The Hague*, 25 Wis. Int'l L.J. p. 23 (2007);
- George H. Aldrich, *The Work of the Eritrea-Ethiopia Claims Commission*, 6 Y.B. Int'l Human. L. p. 435 (2006);
- Natalie Klein, *State Responsibility for International Humanitarian Law Violations and the Work of the Eritrea Ethiopia Claims Commission So Far*, 47 Germ. Y.B. Int'l L. p. 214 (2005);
- Judith I.A. Lichtenberg, *Eritrea Ethiopia Claims Commission*, 12 Tilburg Foreign L. Rev. p. 266 (2004).

Facts

Between 1998 and 2000, the Parties waged a costly, large-scale international armed conflict along several areas of their common frontier. Before the outbreak of the conflict in May 1998, persons with Eritrean nationality or antecedents owned real property and conducted businesses in Ethiopia. In particular, Eritrean nationals owned and operated many of the heavy trucks that carried fuel and freight from Eritrean ports to Ethiopia. When hostilities began in 1998, Ethiopian officials took possession of many of these trucks, and enacted certain other measures limiting the property and economic rights of Eritrean nationals.

This Partial Award addressed Eritrea's claims regarding losses caused to the businesses and real property of Eritreans who were not resident in Ethiopia, in particular, non-resident Eritrean truck owners. Ethiopia filed these claims on December 12, 2001. Following the exchange of written pleadings, a hearing on liability was held at the Peace Palace in April 2005, in conjunction with a hearing on several other claims by both Parties.

Summary of Matters Submitted to Arbitration

This Partial Award addressed Eritrea's Claims relating to:

A. Alleged seizure of movable property;
B. Alleged interference with Eritrean-owned businesses; and
C. Alleged violations of Eritreans' real property rights.

Partial Award

Jurisdiction

Article 5(9) of the Agreement provides that, "in appropriate cases, each party may file claims on behalf of persons of Eritrean or Ethiopian origin who may not be its nationals." The Agreement thus gave the Commission jurisdiction to consider claims presented by the Parties on behalf of certain non-nationals. The Commission recalled its holding in the Partial Award in Eritrea's Civilians Claims as to its jurisdiction regarding claims based on injuries to non-nationals, and noted that it would apply it in this case, so that "claims based on injuries to non-nationals made for Eritrea's own account, and not on behalf of the affected individuals, are outside the Commission's jurisdiction."[1]

Ethiopia contended that certain of Eritrea's claims based upon injuries to nationals possessing both the nationality of Eritrea and that of a third State were within the Commission's jurisdiction only if Eritrea showed that the Eritrean nationality was the dominant and effective one. Eritrea contended that the dominant and effective nationality test should be limited to instances where the claimant has the nationality of the two States involved in a dispute-settlement procedure. The Commission, noting that doctrine was divided on this question, held that "a dominant and effective nationality test must be restrictively applied, and limited to cases where a claimant holds the nationality of the two disputing States," as the purpose of this test is to determine whether the international dispute has the required "international element that is absent if the claim involves a person with the nationality of the defendant State."[2]

Eritrea presented claims for illegal detention and conscription into Ethiopian military service of numerous drivers and their assistants. Ethiopia responded that this issue should have been pleaded and raised in the context of the Civilians Claims proceedings. The Commission noted that its Partial Award in Eritrea's Civilians Claims covered the illegal detention and conscription of the drivers and their assistants. The Commission held that Eritrea's request for a further, separate finding of liability with respect to these persons therefore was not admissible, but the evidence presented in connection with this claim would be considered during the damages phase.[3]

The Commission upheld an objection by Ethiopia to Eritrea's claims, raised in its Memorial, based on losses associated with diversion of vessels, as it held that these claims had not been identified with sufficient particularity in Eritrea's Statement of Claim and therefore had not been filed within the one-year filing deadline established by the Agreement.[4]

---

[1] Partial Award, Eritrea's Claim 24 [hereinafter "Partial Award"], para. 7, *citing* Partial Award, Eritrea's Civilians Claims, para. 19.

[2] Partial Award, para. 11.

[3] Partial Award, para. 13.

[4] Partial Award, para. 14.

Merits

Seizures and Other Losses Involving Movable Property

Eritrea contended that, shortly after hostilities began, the Ethiopian authorities systematically confiscated trucks with Eritrean registrations and trucks with Ethiopian registrations owned by Eritreans, without providing any compensation.[5] The Commission found ample evidence regarding the widespread confiscation of trucks with no compensation,[6] and limited evidence regarding the confiscation of buses.[7] In rebuttal, Ethiopia presented a statement by an Ethiopian official who acknowledged that some 4,000 trucks had been requisitioned, and maintained that compensation had been paid.[8] Considering all the evidence, the Commission found a systematic confiscation of trucks, for which no compensation had been provided, including trucks with Eritrean plates as well as those with Ethiopian plates owned by Eritreans. The Commission held that the evidence supported a similar conclusion with regard to buses.[9]

The Commission rejected Eritrea's contention that this widespread confiscation was discriminatory and in itself contrary to international law. It held that, given the circumstances facing Ethiopia, its acts of confiscation appeared to have been for legitimate public purposes and consistent with international law applicable during an international armed conflict.[10] However, the Commission recalled that the Parties had agreed that, notwithstanding the latitude afforded to belligerents to place discriminatory controls on enemy property during an international armed conflict, the basic international legal rules regulating expropriation continue to apply. Where aliens' property is taken for State purposes in wartime, the obligation to provide full compensation continues to operate, even if the payment of that compensation may be delayed by the interruption of economic relations between belligerents. The Commission therefore held that Ethiopia was liable for failing to pay full compensation for those Eritrean-owned trucks and buses requisitioned by Ethiopia during the conflict and not returned to their owners.[11]

The Commission also noted that, had Eritrea's claim regarding the diversion of ships containing Eritrea-bound cargo fallen within its jurisdiction, this claim would have been rejected on the merits, as Eritrea had failed to prove any violation of international law or humanitarian law with regard to the diversion of Eritrea-bound cargo.[12]

Interference with Businesses and Immovable Property in Ethiopia Owned by Non-Resident Eritreans

Eritrea claimed that Ethiopia interfered with the rights of Eritreans living outside of Ethiopia who owned businesses or real property in Ethiopia through (i) detention and intimidation

[5] Partial Award, para. 16.
[6] Partial Award, para. 17.
[7] Partial Award, para. 19.
[8] Partial Award, para. 20.
[9] Partial Award, para. 22.
[10] Partial Award, para. 23.
[11] Partial Award, para. 24.
[12] Partial Award, para. 26.

of Eritrean property owners temporarily present in Ethiopia, (ii) expulsion of agents, and (iii) refusal to issue visas or otherwise facilitate the appointment of new agents.

The Commission held that, even though the operation of businesses owned by nationals of an opposing belligerent may be lawfully suspended during hostilities, confiscation of assets or other measures making a business property *res derelicta* without compensation are unacceptable. It found that Eritrea had presented convincing if limited evidence of Ethiopian harassment of Eritrean nationals or of third State nationals of Eritrean origin attempting to protect their property.[13]

The Commission dismissed Eritrea's claim regarding the expulsion of Eritrean-origin agents and employees of non-residents and regarding Ethiopia's restrictive policies on visas and the appointment of new agents, in application of the relevant conclusions in its Partial Award in Eritrea's Civilians Claims.

The Commission then considered the collective impact of Ethiopia's measures on non-resident businesses and real property owners. It recalled that a belligerent is bound to ensure insofar as possible that the property of protected persons and of other enemy nationals are not despoiled and wasted.[14] The Commission found that, as a result of the cumulative effects of the measures applied by Ethiopia, many non-resident business and real property owners lost everything they had in Ethiopia. The Commission held that the lawfulness of some of those measures did not preclude that their cumulative effect resulted in the despoliation of non-residents' properties. It concluded that Ethiopia had failed in its duty to protect aliens' assets.[15]

---

[13] Partial Award, para. 29.

[14] Partial Award, para. 31, *citing* Partial Award, Eritrea's Civilians Claims, para. 151.

[15] Partial Award, para. 32.

14.14

Eritrea-Ethiopia Claims Commission

Partial Award
Ethiopia's Claim 7: Economic Loss Throughout Ethiopia

Parties: Eritrea/Ethiopia

Date of Arbitration Agreement: December 12, 2000

Commissioners: Prof. Hans van Houtte (President), Judge George H. Aldrich, Mr. John R. Crook, Dean James Paul, Ms. Lucy Reed

Date of Partial Award: December 19, 2005

Summary

International armed conflict waged between Eritrea and Ethiopia between 1998 and 2000 – liability of Eritrea for economic damages allegedly resulting from Eritrea's breach of *jus ad bellum* in May 1998 – first stage of proceedings concerning liability – second stage concerning quantum of damages to be conducted at a later date – Ethiopia's claims for economic damages not admissible in first stage of the proceedings – deferral of consideration of Ethiopia's claims for economic damages until second stage of the proceedings.

Legal Subject Matters

Arbitration:
- Jurisdiction of the arbitral tribunal

Diplomatic protection:
- Nationality of claims

International armed conflict:
- Duty to protect from despoliation
- Expropriation
  - Duty to pay full compensation
- Treatment of alien property

Bibliography

Award published in:
- XXVI R.I.A.A. (forthcoming 2010).

Commentary:
- *The 1998-2000 War between Eritrea and Ethiopia: An International Legal Perspective* (Andrea de Guttry, Harry H.G. Post & Gabriella Venturini eds., TMC Asser Press 2009);
- Hans van Houtte, *The Eritrea-Ethiopia Claims Commission and International Humanitarian Law*, *in* JUDICIAL RIGHTS AND INTERNATIONAL JUSTICE, LIBER FAUSTO POCAR p. 383 (Guiffre 2009);
- Pierre d'Argent & Jean d'Aspremont, *La Commission des réclamations Érythrée-Éthiopie : un premier bilan*, 53 AFDI p. 347 (2007);
- Won Kidane, *Civil Liability for Violations of International Law: The Jurisprudence of the Eritrea-Ethiopia Claims Commission in The Hague*, 25 WIS. INT'L L.J. p. 23 (2007);
- George H. Aldrich, *The Work of the Eritrea-Ethiopia Claims Commission*, 6 Y.B. INT'L HUMAN. L. p. 435 (2006);
- Natalie Klein, *State Responsibility for International Humanitarian Law Violations and the Work of the Eritrea Ethiopia Claims Commission So Far*, 47 GERM. Y.B. INT'L L. p. 214 (2005);
- Judith I.A. Lichtenberg, *Eritrea Ethiopia Claims Commission*, 12 TILBURG FOREIGN L. REV. p. 266 (2004).

Facts

Between 1998 and 2000, the Parties waged a costly, large-scale international armed conflict along several areas of their common frontier. This Partial Award addressed Ethiopia's claims in respect of a wide range of economic damage allegedly suffered by Ethiopia between 1998 and 2000 as the result of unlawful conduct by Eritrea. Ethiopia relied on two legal bases in support of Claim 7, namely, (i) the *jus ad bellum*, that is, Eritrea's allegedly unlawful use of force against Ethiopia, and (ii) five bilateral agreements regulating trade and commercial relationships between the Parties.

Ethiopia claimed in respect of:

(a) Loss, damage, and injury to Ethiopia's national airline, Ethiopian Airlines;
(b) Disruption of Ethiopia's international trade;
(c) Substantial losses to Ethiopian tourism;
(d) Losses to Ethiopia's international development assistance;
(e) Damage, loss, or injury to projects run by Ethiopia's Road Authority;
(f) Losses of tax revenue;
(g) Declines in Ethiopia's foreign and domestic investment; and
(h) Costs incurred for the reconstruction and rehabilitation of areas damaged or destroyed as a result of Eritrea's violations of international law.

Eritrea denied liability.

Ethiopia filed these claims on December 12, 2001. Following the exchange of written pleadings, a hearing on liability was held at the Peace Palace in April 2005, in conjunction with a hearing on several other claims by both Parties.

Summary of Matters Submitted to Arbitration

This Partial Award addressed:

A. Ethiopia's claim for loss, damage, and injury suffered by Ethiopia as a result of the alleged use of force by Eritrea in violation of the *jus ad bellum*;

B. Ethiopia's claim for loss, damage, and injury to Ethiopia's National Airline and other claims for large-scale economic damage stemming from the 1998-2000 conflict between the Parties; and
C. Ethiopia's claim that five bilateral agreements regulating trade and commercial relationships between the Parties were violated by Eritrea.

Partial Award

Jurisdiction and Admissibility

The Commission confirmed, with reference to its Partial Award on the portions of Ethiopia's Claims 1–8 alleging violation of the *jus ad bellum*, that it had jurisdiction to decide alleged violations of international law relating to a breach of the *jus ad bellum*.[1] Recalling its findings in that Partial Award, the Commission held that Ethiopia's claims for economic damages allegedly suffered as the legal consequence of Eritrea's violation of the *jus ad bellum* in May 1998 were not admissible at the first stage of the proceedings, which concerned liability.[2]

The Merits

Loss, Damage, and Injury to Ethiopia's National Airline

Ethiopia claimed compensation for several different types of losses allegedly suffered by Ethiopian Airlines ("EAL"), Ethiopia's national airline, including, *inter alia*, costs incurred due to the relocation of EAL activities in Addis Ababa to Nairobi during the conflict and losses of revenue resulting from disruption of EAL's Asmara operations. The Commission found that these claims appeared to rest on the general contention that Eritrea was legally obliged to provide compensation for wartime injury to Ethiopia's economy resulting from Eritrea's violation of the *jus ad bellum*. The Commission had held that it would address questions regarding the scope of Eritrea's potential liability for breach of the *jus ad bellum* at the next (damages) stage of the proceedings. The Commission therefore held that the claims were not admissible at this stage.[3] The Commission dismissed for failure of proof a claim by Ethiopia for the taking of office furniture and equipment contained in Ethiopian Airlines' offices in Asmara and Assab.[4]

Other Claims for Economic Damage

As regards Ethiopia's allegations of other forms of large-scale economic damage stemming from the 1998–2000 conflict, the Commission also held that those claims were not admissible at this stage of the proceedings.[5]

---

[1] Partial Award, Ethiopia's Claim 7 [hereinafter "Partial Award"], para. 6.
[2] Partial Award, para. 9.
[3] Partial Award, para. 11.
[4] Partial Award, para. 12.
[5] Partial Award, paras. 13–14.

Violation of Bilateral Agreements

Ethiopia alleged that five bilateral agreements regulating trade and commercial relationships between the Parties were violated by Eritrea. These were: (i) the Transit and Port Services Agreement of September 27, 1993; (ii) the Protocol Agreement on traffic between Eritrea and Ethiopia of September 27, 1993; (iii) the Air Services Agreement of September 27, 1993; (iv) the Trade Agreement of September 27, 1993, and its Protocol (on trade in goods and services) of September 27, 1993; and (v) the Commercial Road Agreement of September 27, 1993.

Ethiopia contended that the eruption of the war did not *ipso facto* terminate these agreements, and that "Eritrea was responsible for the violations of agreements it had entered into with Ethiopia when it unlashed [*sic*] its unlawful aggression against Ethiopia."[6] The Commission took note of the "broad consensus" in the literature that bilateral treaties, especially those of a political or economic nature, are at the very least suspended by the outbreak of a war.[7] The Commission, taking into account the nature and objectives of the five agreements cited by Ethiopia to support its economic claims, considered that they fell within the category of treaties which become ineffective in time of war (either through termination or suspension). It therefore dismissed on the merits Ethiopia's claim for compensation for economic losses because of violation of those treaties.[8]

---

[6] Partial Award, para. 16.
[7] Partial Award, para. 18.
[8] Partial Award, para. 18.

14.15

Eritrea-Ethiopia Claims Commission

Final Award
Eritrea's Claims 15, 19 & 23: Pensions

Parties: Eritrea/Ethiopia

Date of Arbitration Agreement: December 12, 2000

Commissioners: Prof. Hans van Houtte (President), Judge George H. Aldrich, Mr. John R. Crook, Dean James Paul, Ms. Lucy Reed

Date of Award: December 19, 2005

Summary

International armed conflict waged between Eritrea and Ethiopia between 1998 and 2000 – Ethiopia responsible prior to conflict for paying pensions of former Ethiopian state employees resident in Eritrea – cessation of cooperation in pension arrangements following outbreak of armed hostilities between the Parties – liability of Ethiopia for ceasing to perform the Parties' pre-war pension arrangements – claims dismissed.

Legal Subject Matters

International humanitarian law:
- Sources
  - Additional Protocol I
  - Customary international humanitarian law
  - Geneva Conventions of 1949

Sources of international norms:
- Treaties
  - Vienna Convention on the Law of Treaties
    - Treaties between belligerents
      - Performance
      - Suspension
      - Termination

Bibliography

Award published in:
- XXVI R.I.A.A. (forthcoming 2010);
- 45 I.L.M. p. 633 (2006).

Commentary:
- *The 1998-2000 War between Eritrea and Ethiopia: An International Legal Perspective* (Andrea de Guttry, Harry H.G. Post & Gabriella Venturini eds., TMC Asser Press 2009);
- Hans van Houtte, *The Eritrea-Ethiopia Claims Commission and International Humanitarian Law*, *in* JUDICIAL RIGHTS AND INTERNATIONAL JUSTICE, LIBER FAUSTO POCAR p. 383 (Guiffre 2009);
- Pierre d'Argent & Jean d'Aspremont, *La Commission des réclamations Érythrée-Éthiopie : un premier bilan*, 53 AFDI p. 347 (2007);
- Won Kidane, *Civil Liability for Violations of International Law: The Jurisprudence of the Eritrea-Ethiopia Claims Commission in The Hague*, 25 WIS. INT'L L.J. p. 23 (2007);
- George H. Aldrich, *The Work of the Eritrea-Ethiopia Claims Commission*, 6 Y.B. INT'L HUMAN. L. p. 435 (2006);
- Natalie Klein, *State Responsibility for International Humanitarian Law Violations and the Work of the Eritrea Ethiopia Claims Commission So Far*, 47 GERM. Y.B. INT'L L. p. 214 (2005);
- Judith I.A. Lichtenberg, *Eritrea Ethiopia Claims Commission*, 12 TILBURG FOREIGN L. REV. p. 266 (2004);
- Philippe Weckel, *Commission des réparations (Erythrée/Ethiopie), Sentence du 19 Décembre 2005 (pensions)*, 1 RGDIP p. 192 (2007).

Facts

In 1993, the Parties entered into discussions and arrangements regarding the rights and obligations of the previously unitary State of Ethiopia, following the independence of Eritrea. These arrangements concerned, *inter alia*, the pensions of former Ethiopian state employees, military personnel, and employees of nationalized state enterprises who now resided in Eritrea. The Parties cooperated for several years in developing and implementing the arrangements to pay pensions to certain persons in Eritrea under three pension programs that the Parties had created. By 1998, systems were operating under which Eritrean agencies administered payment of pensions to former Ethiopian civil servants, military personnel, and state enterprise employees in Eritrea, utilizing funds that were periodically transferred by Ethiopia, with the last transfer occurring on April 30, 1998. These arrangements were based on the Parties' September 1993 Protocol Agreement on Labour, Social Affairs and Pensions ("1993 Protocol").

After armed hostilities between the Parties began in May 1998, the Parties' cooperation with respect to these pension arrangements ended. Between 1998 and 2000, the Parties waged a costly, large-scale international armed conflict along several areas of their common frontier.

Eritrea filed these claims on December 12, 2001. Following the exchange of written pleadings, a hearing on liability was held at the Peace Palace in April 2005, in conjunction with a hearing on several other claims by both Parties.

Summary of Matters Submitted to Arbitration

This Final Award addressed:

A. Eritrea's claim that Ethiopia ceased to perform the Parties' pre-war pension arrangements in violation of its legal obligations;
B. Eritrea's claim that Ethiopia's actions resulted in an uncompensated taking of property contrary to international law;

C. Eritrea's claim that Ethiopia's actions resulted in an unjust enrichment; and
D. Eritrea's claim that Ethiopia's obligations to pay pensions arose pursuant to customary international law regulating the succession of States.

Final Award

Jurisdiction

The Commission determined that Eritrea's claims were within its jurisdiction under Article 5 of the Agreement,[1] and that the legal theories invoked by Eritrea were consistent with the Commission's mandate to apply international law.[2]

Merits

Eritrea claimed that Ethiopia, in violation of international law, had repudiated its obligations under the governing bilateral agreements by ceasing to transfer funds to Eritrea after the outbreak of hostilities.[3] Ethiopia contended that the Parties' agreements regarding pensions were not intended to survive a war between them, and viewed the 1998-2000 war as involving a fundamental transformation of circumstances that terminated agreements bearing on pensions.[4]

The Commission held that Article 3.4 of the 1993 Protocol created an obligation under treaty law for Ethiopia "to pay eligible pensioners effectively and efficiently in Eritrea" while the Parties worked to develop permanent pension arrangements.[5] The Parties' practice subsequent to the 1993 Protocol confirmed that the Parties viewed the 1993 Protocol as giving rise to legal obligations.[6]

In the Commission's view, the impact of the 1998-2000 war on obligations under the Protocol and its associated documents concerned two strands of customary international law. The first of these strands was the nature and extent of belligerents' rights under customary international law to regulate or prohibit financial transactions with an opposing power during an international armed conflict. The Commission, in reliance on "the widespread and generally accepted modern practice of extensive … prohibitions on financial transactions between belligerents, regardless of the transaction's purpose," rejected the argument by Eritrea that customary international law prevents belligerents from barring pensions-related payments to an opposing belligerent.[7]

The second strand of customary international law addressed by the Commission was the effect of the 1998-2000 war on Ethiopia's treaty obligations under the 1993 Protocol and related documents. The Commission noted the absence of any provision in the Vienna Conven-

[1] Final Award, Eritrea's Pensions Claim [hereinafter "Final Award"], paras. 6–9.
[2] Final Award, para. 10.
[3] Final Award, para. 17.
[4] Final Award, para. 24.
[5] Final Award, para. 25.
[6] Final Award, para. 26.
[7] Final Award, para. 27.

tion on the Law of Treaties on the impact of hostilities on treaties between belligerents, and noted that modern doctrine "does not provide settled guidance on significant points."[8]

The Commission held that, in cases where the intention to maintain a treaty in operation during hostilities is not plainly apparent from the text or the surrounding circumstances, the parties should be presumed to intend that such treaties be at least suspended during the hostilities; and thus that the 1993 Protocol and its associated agreements were, at the least, suspended during the hostilities between the Parties and their immediate aftermath.[9] The Commission stated that it did not need to decide whether, as argued by Ethiopia, the treaty obligations were suspended or terminated in order to decide the issues falling within the limited temporal scope of its jurisdiction under the Agreement.[10] It dismissed on the merits Eritrea's claims based on Ethiopia's alleged non-performance of the 1993 Protocol and associated documents during that period.

Eritrea's Taking Claims

Eritrea contended that Ethiopia took individuals' property rights to receive pensions, and that Ethiopia took from Eritrea its rights to monies set aside and held in Ethiopia for future pension payments.[11] Ethiopia denied any taking of property.[12] The Commission found that the record did not establish that public pension entitlements under Ethiopian law were sufficiently concrete to constitute property protected by international law. It held, further, that there was no proof of an unlawful taking during the jurisdictional period as it had determined that it was lawful for Ethiopia to cease performing the bilateral agreements relating to pensions during the hostilities between the Parties.[13]

The Commission also dismissed Eritrea's contention that Ethiopia took a property interest belonging to the State of Eritrea in some part of a pool of pension assets held by Ethiopia. It found that the record did not establish the existence of any such asset pool.[14] It held, further, that Eritrea had not established a legal right to receive any specific amount from Ethiopia, and that even if Eritrea had claims to money or other property interests in Ethiopia, those interests would have been subject to Ethiopia's wartime rights in relation to the State property of an opposing belligerent under customary international law.[15]

Eritrea's State Succession and Unjust Enrichment Claims

The Commission also considered two theories advanced by Eritrea at the hearing. Those were, first, that customary international law relating to State succession required Ethiopia to fund pensions for former Ethiopian civil servants, and, second, that Ethiopia was unjustly enriched by its actions. Eritrea claimed that, once the Parties agreed on the 1993 Protocol

---

[8] Final Award, para. 28.
[9] Final Award, para. 30.
[10] Final Award, para. 32.
[11] Final Award, para. 33.
[12] Final Award, para. 34.
[13] Final Award, para. 36.
[14] Final Award, para. 37.
[15] Final Award, para. 38.

and its associated documents, the customary law of State succession constituted an additional source of obligation reinforcing Ethiopia's obligations under those arrangements.[16] The Commission, noting that State practice on this issue varied, found that there was no established customary rule allocating to the predecessor State primary responsibility for official pensions when unitary States divide.[17] As regards Eritrea's invocation of the customary international law doctrine of unjust enrichment, the Commission noted that this doctrine must be applied cautiously given its imprecise and subjective character. The Commission concluded that the record did not demonstrate unjust enrichment by Ethiopia during the Commission's jurisdictional period.[18]

Concluding Observations

Ethiopia had emphasized, at the hearing and in its written pleadings, its willingness to resume negotiations on pension matters interrupted by the 1998-2000 conflict. The Commission viewed Ethiopia's statements as serious and important undertakings, and encouraged the Parties to act upon them and to renew good-faith negotiations on reaching a permanent arrangement regarding pensions for those who had served Ethiopia prior to 1993.[19]

---

[16] Final Award, para. 40.
[17] Final Award, para. 41.
[18] Final Award, para. 43.
[19] Final Award, para. 44.

Eritrea-Ethiopia Claims Commission

Final Award
Ethiopia's Claim 6: Ports

Parties:	Eritrea/Ethiopia
Date of Arbitration Agreement:	December 12, 2000
Commissioners:	Prof. Hans van Houtte (President), Judge George H. Aldrich, Mr. John R. Crook, Dean James Paul, Ms. Lucy Reed
Date of Award:	December 19, 2005

Summary

International armed conflict waged between Eritrea and Ethiopia between 1998 and 2000 – most of Ethiopia's export and import cargo prior to conflict shipped from Eritrean ports of Assab and Massawa – closing of ports due to armed conflict – some property stranded at Eritrean ports – liability of Eritrea for closing of ports to Ethiopian trade and for taking of property of Ethiopia and of Ethiopian nationals – lack of evidence that Eritrea acted unreasonably or unlawfully in relation to property – claims dismissed.

Legal Subject Matters

International humanitarian law:
- Rights and duties of belligerents
  - Property of enemy State
  - Property of nationals of enemy State
- Sources
  - Additional Protocol I
  - Customary international humanitarian law
  - Geneva Conventions of 1949

Bibliography

Award published in:
- XXVI R.I.A.A. (forthcoming 2010).

Commentary:
- *The 1998-2000 War between Eritrea and Ethiopia: An International Legal Perspective* (Andrea de Guttry, Harry H.G. Post & Gabriella Venturini eds., TMC Asser Press 2009);

- Hans van Houtte, *The Eritrea-Ethiopia Claims Commission and International Humanitarian Law*, *in* Judicial Rights and International Justice, Liber Fausto Pocar p. 383 (Guiffre 2009);
- Pierre d'Argent & Jean d'Aspremont, *La Commission des réclamations Érythrée-Éthiopie : un premier bilan*, 53 AFDI p. 347 (2007);
- Won Kidane, *Civil Liability for Violations of International Law: The Jurisprudence of the Eritrea-Ethiopia Claims Commission in The Hague*, 25 Wis. Int'l L.J. p. 23 (2007);
- George H. Aldrich, *The Work of the Eritrea-Ethiopia Claims Commission*, 6 Y.B. Int'l Human. L. p. 435 (2006);
- Natalie Klein, *State Responsibility for International Humanitarian Law Violations and the Work of the Eritrea Ethiopia Claims Commission So Far*, 47 Germ. Y.B. Int'l L. p. 214 (2005);
- Judith I.A. Lichtenberg, *Eritrea Ethiopia Claims Commission*, 12 Tilburg Foreign L. Rev. p. 266 (2004);
- Philippe Weckel, *Commission des réparations (Erythrée/Ethiopie), Sentence du 19 Décembre 2005 (ports)*, 1 RGDIP pp. 198–202 (2007).

Facts

In 1993, the Parties became two separate States upon Eritrea's gaining independence from Ethiopia, leaving Ethiopia without a direct outlet to the sea. Most of Ethiopia's export and import cargo thereafter continued to be shipped via the Eritrean ports of Assab and Massawa. In May 1998, an armed conflict broke out between the Parties. Between 1998 and 2000, the Parties waged a costly, large-scale international armed conflict along several areas of their common frontier. When hostilities began in May 1998, cargo bound to or from Ethiopia, primarily import cargo located at the port of Assab, was stranded in Eritrea.

Eritrea filed these claims on December 12, 2001. Following the exchange of written pleadings, a hearing on liability was held at the Peace Palace in April 2005, in conjunction with a hearing on several other claims by both Parties.

Summary of Matters Submitted to Arbitration

This Final Award addressed Ethiopia's claim regarding cargo bound to or from Ethiopia that was stranded in Eritrea when hostilities began in 1998.

Final Award

Jurisdiction

Ethiopia's claim represented a Government-to-Government claim predicated on injuries allegedly suffered by Ethiopia due to the closings of Eritrean ports to Ethiopian trade and due to takings of the property of Ethiopia and Ethiopian nationals by Eritrea, in violation of international law and in circumstances related to the 1998-2000 conflict between the Parties. In addressing Eritrea's contention that a significant proportion of the property held at Assab was owned by foreign donors of bulk food aid and other material for drought relief or development assistance, the Commission noted that it did not have jurisdiction over Ethiopia's claim for the loss of property in Eritrea's ports to the extent that it was based on property not owned by Ethiopia or Ethiopian nationals.[1]

---

[1] Final Award, Ethiopia's Ports Claim [hereinafter "Final Award"], para. 6.

Merits

Ethiopia claimed that Eritrean actions on three key dates in May 1998 gave rise to takings of Ethiopian property located at Assab when hostilities began. Ethiopia alleged that (i) on May 8, Eritrean officials directed Ethiopia's Maritime and Transit Service Enterprise ("MTSE") to close its office in Assab; (ii) on May 14, Eritrea blocked access by trucks seeking to pick up bulk fuel from fuel depots; and (iii) on May 22, Eritrea finally closed the border to freight traffic. Eritrea disputed this claim and insisted that the port of Assab remained available to handle cargo to and from Ethiopia in the days after hostilities began and that it did not prevent Ethiopian cargo from being loaded for import or export.

Taking into account the totality of the record, the Commission was not persuaded that the events of May 8, 14, and 22, 1998, cited by Ethiopia in fact resulted in takings of Ethiopian property. It found that the port of Assab remained open to movements of Ethiopian cargo for a number of days after hostilities began and that, during this period, Ethiopian cargo at Assab continued to be loaded either onto ships for export or onto trucks for transit to Ethiopia. It also found that a significant volume of Ethiopian property stranded by the events of May 1998 remained available for delivery to Ethiopia, if the Parties could agree on terms to bring this about.[2]

The Commission held that the record did not establish any other violations of international law regarding the stranded property. By the time movements of cargo to Ethiopia ended in May 1998, leaving Ethiopian property stranded at Assab, the Parties were engaged in an international armed conflict. In the Commission's view, in the course of the conflict, it was lawful for Eritrea to terminate Ethiopia's access to the port of Assab and the movement of Ethiopian cargo from Assab to Ethiopia.[3]

Ethiopia also contended that Eritrea violated international humanitarian law in blocking shipments of humanitarian food cargoes present at Assab, contrary to Article 23 of the Geneva Convention Relative to the Protection of Civilian Persons in Time of War ("Geneva Convention IV").[4] The Commission rejected this claim on the grounds that while some medical supplies may have been included in the mass of property remaining at Assab in May 1998, the record did not show that any meaningful portion was potentially subject to Article 23 of Geneva Convention IV, that Ethiopia requested the passage of any such goods, or that Ethiopia had any control measures in place to prevent their diversion.[5]

The Commission distinguished between the rights of a belligerent to prevent commerce from its territory with another belligerent and the question of belligerent rights to appropriate the property of an enemy State or of its nationals. The Commission set out the rules of law applicable to the confiscation of public property of the opposing belligerent and those applicable to private property of the other belligerent's nationals, which are limited to controls of a custodial character.[6] Eritrea contended that it sought to act in a fair and reasonable manner in relation to the stranded property, and that Eritrean domestic legislation provided

---

[2] Final Award, para. 19.
[3] Final Award, para. 20.
[4] Final Award, para. 22.
[5] *Id.*
[6] Final Award, paras. 24–26.

an appropriate benchmark for assessing this action.[7] The Commission rejected this argument on the grounds that the law applicable to this claim was international law, not Eritrean warehouseman's law, and that national warehouseman's law, which often imposes rigid deadlines for removing cargo and gives warehousemen broad rights to dispose of cargo not removed within those deadlines, is not appropriate in a wartime situation where foreign cargo owners may be unable to protect their property.[8]

The Commission concluded that the record did not establish that Eritrea had acted in an unreasonable or unlawful fashion in relation to the property covered by this claim during the Commission's jurisdictional period, and accordingly dismissed Ethiopia's claim.

The Commission noted that Eritrea was prepared to transfer to Ethiopia the stranded property remaining in Eritrea, to provide an accounting for funds received for property it had disposed of, and to transfer the balance to Ethiopia.[9] The Commission observed that this offer appeared to be broadly in line with Eritrea's belligerent obligations in relation to the property, but was able to make no findings in this respect as no claims relating to the implementation of the post-war return of the stranded property were filed by December 12, 2001.[10] The Commission encouraged the Parties to consider some arrangement regarding the return or other appropriate disposition of the remaining stranded property and noted that it remained ready to assist if jointly requested by the Parties in connection with this matter.[11]

---

[7] Final Award, para. 27.
[8] Final Award, para. 29.
[9] Final Award, para. 31.
[10] Final Award, para. 32.
[11] Final Award, paras. 33–34.

Eritrea-Ethiopia Claims Commission

Final Award
Eritrea's Damages Claims

Parties: Eritrea/Ethiopia

Date of Arbitration Agreement: December 12, 2000

Commissioners: Prof. Hans van Houtte (President), Judge George H. Aldrich, Mr. John R. Crook, Dean James Paul, Ms. Lucy Reed

Date of Final Award: August 17, 2009

Summary

International armed conflict waged between Eritrea and Ethiopia between 1998 and 2000 – liability of Ethiopia for violations of international humanitarian law – damages for Eritrea's claims on its own behalf – US$13,500,000 for losses of residential and business property on the Central and Western Fronts – US$35,965,000 for damage to and destruction of buildings on the Central and Western Fronts – US$1,500,000 in respect of injuries to civilians due to loss of access to health care – US$100,000 for damage to cultural property – US$4,000,000 for mistreatment of prisoners of war – US$2,000,000 for failing to prevent the rape of known and unknown victims in the towns of Senafe, Barentu and Teseney – US$1,550,000 for forcible expulsion of the population of Awgaro – US$50,000 in respect of dual Eritrean-Ethiopian nationals arbitrarily deprived of their Ethiopian nationality while present in third countries – US$15,000,000 in respect of wrongful expulsion of dual nationals by local Ethiopian authorities – US$11,000,000 for receiving, caring for and resettling rural Ethiopian nationals wrongfully expelled from Ethiopia – US$2,000,000 for failure to provide humane and safe treatment for persons being expelled from Ethiopia – US$46,000,000 for expellees' losses of property on account of Ethiopia's wrongful actions – US$24,525,000 for Ethiopia's failure to return or provide compensation after the war for vehicles it requisitioned from non-resident Eritreans – US$1,500,000 for other property losses of non-resident Eritreans – US$2,600,000 for imprisoning or detaining Eritrean civilians under harsh and unacceptable conditions – US$155,000 for violation of Eritrea's diplomatic premises and property – satisfaction – satisfaction in form of declaration of wrongfulness in respect of findings that Ethiopia unlawfully deprived dual Eritrean-Ethiopian nationals of their Ethiopian nationality and that Ethiopia unlawfully interfered with Eritrea's departing diplomats – all of Eritrea's other claims on its own behalf dismissed – total monetary compensation of US$161,455,000 awarded to Eritrea – claims by Eritrea on behalf of named individuals – damages – total award of US$2,065,865 in respect of Eritrea's claims on behalf of named individuals.

Legal Subject Matters

Arbitration:
- Admissibility of claims
- Jurisdiction of the arbitral tribunal
- Remedies

Compensation:
- Damages
  - Evidence
  - Failing to provide full compensation to owners of requisitioned property
  - Failure to ensure protection of aliens' assets
  - Procedure
    - Individual claims
    - Inter-State claims
    - Mass claims processes
  - Scope of liability findings
  - Seriousness of violation

Bibliography

Award published in:
- XXVI R.I.A.A. (forthcoming 2010)

Commentary:
- Michael J. Matheson, *Eritrea-Ethiopia Claims Commission: Damages Awards*, 13 ASIL Insight (Sept. 4, 2009).

Facts

Following the completion of hearings on the issue of liability in 2005, the Commission issued an Order on April 13, 2006, directing the Parties to proceed with a simplified damages phase. Hearings proceeded in two groups: the first, "Group Number One Claims," from April 17 to 27, 2007, and the second, "Group Number Two Claims," from May 19 to 28, 2008.

Summary of Matters Submitted to Arbitration

The damages appropriate to compensate Eritrea for the Commission's findings of liability in the following Awards:

- Prisoners of War (Eritrea's Claim 17) (Partial Award, July 1, 2003)
- Central Front (Eritrea's Claims 2, 4, 6, 7, 8 & 22) (Partial Award, April 28, 2004)
- Civilians Claims (Eritrea's Claims 15, 16, 23 & 27-32) (Partial Award, December 17, 2004)
- Western Front, Aerial Bombardment and Related Claims (Eritrea's Claims 1, 3, 5, 9-13, 14, 21, 25 & 26) (Partial Award, December 19, 2005)

- Loss of Property in Ethiopia Owned by Non-Residents (Eritrea's Claim 24) (Partial Award, December 19, 2005)
- Diplomatic Claim (Eritrea's Claim 20) (Partial Award, December 19, 2005)

Final Award

Preliminary Remarks

The Commission began with some remarks on some of the procedural challenges presented by the structure of the damages phase.[1] It also made some preliminary remarks concerning the Parties' situations as "among the poorest countries on earth,"[2] since the fact that both Parties had made claims worth billions of U.S. dollars raised potentially serious questions involving human rights norms. In particular, common Article I(2) of the International Covenant on Economic, Social and Cultural Rights ("ICESCR") and the International Covenant on Civil and Political Rights ("ICCPR") provides that "[i]n no case may be a people be deprived of its own means of subsistence."[3] The Commission also noted that in cases of diplomatic protection, compensation must be assessed in light of the actual social and economic circumstances of the injured individuals in respect of whom the State is claiming.[4] It also noted the need to avoid large diversions of national resources from the paying country, as evidenced in State practice since the Treaty of Versailles.[5]

Applicable Legal Principles[6]

Article 5(13) of the Agreement provided that the Commission should "apply relevant rules of international law" and that it "shall not have the power to make decisions *ex aequo et bono*." Compensation could only be awarded for injuries if those injuries bore a sufficiently close causal connection with conduct that the Commission had previously found to violate international law.[7]

Regarding the standard of proof, the Commission had required clear and convincing evidence in the liability phase. At the damages phase, the Commission ruled that the appropriate standard for quantification of damage was an amalgam of the standard of "clear and convincing evidence" and one based on preponderance of the evidence.[8] To require proof of quantification of damage by clear and convincing evidence would often preclude recovery, frustrating the Commission's mandate to address "the socio-economic impact of the crisis on the civilian population" under Article 5(1) of the Agreement.[9] In some cases, the Commission reduced the amount of compensation awarded to balance the uncertainties flowing

---

[1] Final Award on Eritrea's Damages Claims [hereinafter "Final Award"], paras. 8–17.
[2] Final Award, para. 18.
[3] Final Award, paras. 18–19.
[4] Final Award, para. 26.
[5] Final Award, para. 21.
[6] Final Award, paras. 28–39.
[7] Final Award, para. 29.
[8] Final Award, para. 36.
[9] *Id.*

from the lower standard of proof.[10] As determined in its Decision No. 7 of July 2007, the Commission adopted the test of "proximate cause" in assessing causation, and gave weight to "whether particular damage reasonably should have been foreseeable to an actor committing the international delict in question."[11]

Assessing Compensation and Technical Financial Issues[12]

The Parties agreed that the final awards rendered by the Commission should denominate compensation in United States dollars, but in some instances the Parties' claims and evidence reflected amounts denominated in Ethiopia birr, Eritrean nakfa and occasionally other currencies. In those circumstances, the Commission generally made conversions to U.S. dollars utilizing the exchange rate prevailing at the time of the injury underlying the compensation claim.[13] Article 5(14) of the Agreement provides that "interest ... may be awarded"; in the circumstances, the Commission decided not to award interest on the amounts awarded to either Party.[14]

Eritrea's Group Number One Damages Claims

Eritrea's claims in Group Number One related to the Central and Western Front Partial Awards. Eritrea's claim grouped together and sought compensation for all of the Commission's findings involving loss of property on the Central and Western Fronts, except for Eritrea's separate claims for destruction or damage involving 201 identified structures. Eritrea claimed for these combined losses, calculating the amounts on the basis of data from claim forms collected from over 28,000 affected households and businesses.[15] The claim forms were designed by Eritrea's Office of the Legal Advisor and were filled out by or for individual claimants through local collection programs administered by local officials working in cooperation with Eritrea's lawyers.[16] Eritrea used data from what it determined to be representative sample sizes of 548 business and 540 residential claims forms to determine fixed amounts reflecting average amounts of injury claimed. It then selected at random the individual claim forms to populate these samples.[17] The questions posed in the claims forms were not correlated to the Commission's specific liability findings, and there was no indication that the amounts claimed were verified through sampling of the underlying evidence (if any) or any other means.[18] Based on its analysis of the sample claims forms, Eritrea derived common average claim amounts for the Central and Western Fronts and applied the averages to the total claims form populations for those regions. It arrived at totals of 1,751,183,196 nakfa for business claims and 3,805,065,870 nakfa for residential claims.[19]

---

[10] Final Award, para. 38.
[11] Final Award, para. 39, *citing* Decision No. 7 of July 2007.
[12] Final Award, paras. 40–46.
[13] Final Award, para. 41.
[14] Final Award, paras. 43–44.
[15] Final Award, para. 52.
[16] Final Award, para. 54.
[17] Final Award, para. 57.
[18] Final Award, para. 58.
[19] Final Award, para. 59.

Ethiopia pointed out that the amounts claimed were extremely high in relation to per capita incomes in Eritrea, contending that the average residential claim was seventy-five times per capita gross national income.[20] It noted that the Commission's findings were usually stated in terms of specific towns or villages, and contended that those findings should be construed in a limited and precise way, to apply only to the numbers of persons shown by Eritrea's census to live within the political boundaries of those specific towns or villages.[21]

The claims form process that Eritrea designed and implemented for its property loss claims had significant weaknesses and persons who filled out claims forms were not required to provide supporting evidence. Thus the record available to the Commission offered no means to test or verify the very large amounts claimed.[22] The evidence at the liability phase had proved that many Eritreans had suffered significant losses of property during and after Ethiopia's 2000 invasion, however neither that evidence nor the evidence presented from the claims form process quantified the extent of injury or proved entitlement to the large amounts Eritrea claimed.[23] Rather than dismiss the claim outright, the Commission sought to develop a reasonable estimate of the losses resulting from the injuries it found, taking account of the likely population of the affected areas and estimates of the frequency and extent of loss.[24] The Commission assessed the losses by household rather than by individual and took account of, *inter alia*, the amounts claimed for similar losses from looting of households in Ethiopia's claims, the amounts established in 2001 as appropriate levels of fixed-sum compensation, and the seriousness of the losses to those who suffered them.[25] It awarded Eritrea US$13,500,000 as compensation for losses of residential and business property attributable to looting or other damage for which Ethiopia was found liable in Molki Sub-Zoba and the eleven towns and villages listed in the Commission's Partial Award on liability.[26]

Damage to or Destruction of Buildings

Eritrea claimed compensation exceeding two billion nakfa plus US$38 million in connection with its claim for damaged and destroyed structures on the Central and Western Fronts ("Building Claims").[27] Its claims related to 54 structures on the Central Front and 147 structures on the Western Front.[28] The evidence it presented varied widely from building to building and included witness statements, property inventories, and repair and reconstruction estimates.[29] Ethiopia challenged Eritrea's reliance on property inventories and reconstruction estimates prepared post-war with an eye toward litigation and presented without supporting evidence.[30] It presented specific defences in relation to the 15 highest-value struc-

[20] Final Award, para. 62.
[21] Final Award, para. 64.
[22] Final Award, paras. 66–67.
[23] Final Award, para. 70.
[24] Final Award, para. 72.
[25] Final Award, paras. 73–75.
[26] Final Award, para. 76.
[27] Final Award, para. 78.
[28] Final Award, para. 79.
[29] Final Award, para. 80.
[30] Final Award, para. 84.

tures claimed by Eritrea, to illustrate its objections to the scope and magnitude of Eritea's claims.[31]

Regarding the 23 structures that were specifically identified and included in the Central and Western Front Partial Awards, the Commission considered the claims on a building-by-building basis. For the more than 175 additional buildings for which Eritrea claimed compensation, the Commission required reasonable and credible evidence that: (a) the relevant building existed before the war, in the relevant location; (b) the building was damaged or destroyed during the war, in the time period designated in the relevant provision of the award; (c) the damage or destruction was unlawful, within the four corners of the relevant liability finding; and (d) the amount would approximately compensate for actual damages at the relevant time,[32] i.e. applying the principle set out by the Permanent Court of International Justice in the *Chorzow Factory* case.[33] Where the Commission had limited Ethiopia's liability to a percentage of the damage caused by looting and stripping of buildings, it applied the percentage factor in its award on damages.[34] With the exception of Senafe Hospital, the Commission excluded claims for the building or renting of substitute space.[35] It converted the claims from Eritrean nakfa to U.S. dollars on a building-by-building basis as of the year for which the relevant repair or replacement costs were estimated.[36] The Commission then set out its analyses of Eritrea's claims on the 23 specific structures identified in the Central and Western Front Partial Awards, as well as other building claims that served as models for broad categories of claims.[37] It assessed the other individual claims in groups, and within each group it offered examples of successful, unsuccessful and partially successful claims based on the evidence.[38] In sum, the total compensation awarded for Eritrea's building claims was US$13,140,000 for the Central Front and US$22,825,000 for the Western Front.[39]

Claim for Consequential Damages

Eritrea claimed US$400 million as consequential damages for 800,000 individuals allegedly injured by Ethiopian conduct, contending that Ethiopia carried out a concerted and deliberate program to destroy civilian infrastructure in areas occupied or transited by Ethiopian forces during and after the 2000 invasion.[40] Eritrea's claim related to consequential injury to every resident in and around the occupied territories in the form of disruption to educational and telecommunications services, unemployment and poverty, and loss of access to health care.[41] It argued that Ethiopia's conduct had caused a breakdown of systems required to sustain human life in violation of Article 54 of Additional Protocol I to the Geneva

[31] Final Award, para. 85.
[32] Final Award, para. 87.
[33] Final Award, paras. 25–26.
[34] Final Award, para. 91.
[35] Final Award, para. 94.
[36] Final Award, para. 96.
[37] Final Award, paras. 98–193.
[38] Final Award, para. 98.
[39] Final Award, paras. 139, 193.
[40] Final Award, para. 195.
[41] Final Award, para. 196.

Conventions ("Protocol I").[42] Ethiopia contended that this argument was inadmissible as it was a new claim, and that Eritrea had not presented any evidence that compensable damage had resulted from the conduct alleged.[43]

The Commission did not consider Eritrea's request for damages to be a new claim of liability and noted that "international law does not recognize a separate category of 'consequential damages' involving different standards of legal causation or other distinctive legal elements."[44] It therefore examined this claim in accordance with the principles generally applicable in determining damages in international claims.[45] The Commission rejected Eritrea's claim in respect of the disruption of its education system, the destruction of its electrical and telecommunications infrastructure, and adverse economic conditions,[46] but did consider injuries to Eritrea's nationals resulting from loss of access to medical care on account of unlawful destruction or damage to medical facilities in assessing compensation.[47] The Commission had found liability for unlawful damage or destruction of numerous medical facilities in Eritrea including all three regional hospitals in the affected areas.[48] The Commission emphasized that international humanitarian law accords special protection to medical facilities, medical personnel, and patients needing medical care, and noted that these protections "should have led commanders to recognize the likely consequences for civilians of widespread damage to medical facilities and loss of medical supplies."[49] It cited, in particular, Articles 18, 20, 23, and 55 of Geneva Convention IV, and Articles 12 and 15 of Protocol I, and held that it was not necessary to decide whether Article 54 of Protocol I provided an additional layer of protection.[50] Taking account of all the relevant circumstances, the Commission awarded Eritrea US$1,500,000 as compensation in respect of injuries to civilians due to loss of access to health care on account of damage to or destruction of Eritrean hospitals and other medical facilities and loss of medical supplies.[51]

Damage to Cultural Property[52]

At the liability phase, the Commission had found Ethiopia liable "[f]or permitting, while occupying the area, deliberate damage by explosion to the Stela of Matara, an ancient monument in the Senafe Sub-Zoba."[53] The explosion had destroyed all of the 2,500 year-old Stela below ground level and its lower portion above ground. The Stela was restored by local and international artisans who replaced the destroyed section with locally-quarried stone and attached the intact upper portion to the newly cut lower portion.[54] The repair and restoration

42 Final Award, para. 199.

43 Final Award, para. 200.

44 Final Award, paras. 202, 203.

45 Final Award, para. 203.

46 Final Award, paras. 204–207.

47 Final Award, paras. 210.

48 Final Award, para. 208.

49 Final Award, para. 210.

50 Final Award, paras. 211–213.

51 Final Award, para. 216.

52 Final Award paras. 217–226.

53 Final Award, para. 217, *citing* the Partial Award in Eritrea's Central Front Claims, *dispositif*, Section V.D.8.

54 Final Award, para. 219.

work cost 450,106 nakfa. Ethiopia accepted this as an appropriate measure of compensation. Eritrea claimed an additional US$8,000,000 as additional compensation for damage to a significant cultural monument.[55] This measure was the amount expended by Ethiopia in its efforts to recover the Obelisk of Axum from Rome. Ethiopia argued that this additional claim was in fact a claim for punitive damages.[56]

The Commission rejected Ethiopia's expenditures for the return of the Obelisk of Axum as an analogous measure of compensation but held that serious damage to a significant object of cultural patrimony warranted some award of compensation going beyond the mere costs of attempting to restore the object to its earlier appearance.[57] It awarded Eritrea the amounts expended to attempt to restore the Stela, plus an additional amount to reflect its unique cultural significance, for a total award of US$50,000.[58]

The Commission had found Ethiopia responsible for permitting the looting and stripping of the Tserona Patriots (or Martyrs) Cemetary and found it liable for 75% of the total damage caused, which included the looting of metals and of one thousand mango trees that had been planted as memorials.[59] Eritrea quantified the allowable 75% of the damage at 750,000 nakfa. The 2005 repair estimate that Eritrea presented in evidence was "skeletal."[60] Balancing the relatively weak evidentiary record against the severity of the violation of international law, the Commission awarded the full amount claimed, converted at the 2005 exchange rate to US$50,000.[61]

Prisoners of War[62]

In its Partial Award in Eritrea's Prisoners of War Claim 17, the Commission had found Ethiopia liable for eight violations of international law.[63] The Commission stressed that the claims before it were the claims of the Parties, not of individual victims. While it encouraged the Parties to compensate appropriately the individual victims of warfare, it calculated the damages owed by one Party to the other, including for mistreatment of POWs, on the basis of its evaluation of the evidence with respect to the seriousness of the unlawful acts or omissions, the total numbers of probable victims of those unlawful acts or omissions (where those numbers could be identified with reasonable certainty), and the extent of the injury or damage suffered because of those unlawful acts or omissions.[64] The Commission noted that the most serious violations were those relating to beating and unlawful abuse at or after capture, enforced indoctrination, and inadequate health conditions, nutrition, and medical care.[65] Many of the 2,600 Eritreans detained as POWs

---

[55] Final Award, paras. 220–221.

[56] Final Award, para. 221.

[57] Final Award, para. 222.

[58] Final Award, para. 223.

[59] Final Award, para. 224, *citing* the Partial Award in Eritrea's Central Front Claims, *dispositif*, Section V.D.2.

[60] Final Award, para. 225.

[61] Final Award, para. 226.

[62] Final Award paras. 227–233.

[63] Final Award, para. 227, *and see* Partial Award in Eritrea's Prisoners of War Claims, *dispositif*, Section V.D.

[64] Final Award, para. 229.

[65] Final Award, para. 230.

during the armed conflict[66] suffered long-lasting damage to their physical and mental health as a result of the violations of international law from which they suffered.[67] The Commission awarded Eritrea US$4,000,000 for the unlawful treatment of Eritrean POWs.[68]

Rape[69]

Concerning rape, the Commission acknowledged, first, the cultural sensitivities surrounding rape in both Eritrea and Ethiopia, and the unwillingness of victims to come forward, stating that "the full number of victims and the full magnitude of the harm they suffered cannot and will not ever be known."[70]

In the Eritrean Central Front and Western Front Partial Awards, respectively, the Commission found Ethiopia liable for "failure to take effective measures to prevent rape of women by its soldiers during the occupation of Senafe Town"[71] and "failure to take effective measures to prevent the rape of women in the towns of Barentu and Teseney."[72] Eritrea had originally proposed that each Party set aside US$500,000 to US$1,000,000 for self-administered programs for women's health care and support services in the areas where the Commission had found liability for rape. Ethiopia did not agree and instead claimed material and moral damages of US$6,739,641 representing loss of 50% of average lifetime earnings and moral damage in respect of 1% of the pre-war female population.[73] Eritrea subsequently requested an award of US$6,750,000, without explanation.[74]

Despite the shortcomings of both Parties' damages methodologies, the Commission considered this serious violation of international humanitarian law to demand serious relief. The Commission stated that "[n]either symbolic nor nominal damages will suffice in the face of the physical, mental and emotional harm known to be suffered by rape victims."[75] It awarded Eritrea (as it did Ethiopia in its parallel Award) US$2,000,000 in damages for failing to prevent the rape of known and unknown victims in the towns of Senafe, Barentu and Teseney, and expressed the hope that the Parties would use the funds awarded to develop and support health programs for women and girls in the affected areas.[76]

Displacement of the Population of Awgaro[77]

In the liability phase, the Commission had found Ethiopia liable for the forcible displacement of the population of Awgaro during Ethiopia's May 2000 attack on Eritrea.[78] Eritrea

---

[66] Final Award, para. 231.

[67] Final Award, para. 232.

[68] Final Award, para. 233.

[69] Final Award paras. 234–239.

[70] Final Award, para. 234.

[71] Final Award, para. 236, *citing* the Partial Award in Eritrea's Central Front Claims, *dispositif*, Section V.D.5.

[72] *Id.*, *citing* the Partial Award in Eritrea's Western Front and Related Claims, *dispositif*, Section IV.M.2.k.

[73] Final Award, para. 236.

[74] Final Award, paras. 236–237.

[75] Final Award, para. 238.

[76] Final Award, para. 239.

[77] Final Award, paras. 240–246.

[78] Final Award, para. 240, *citing* the Partial Award in Eritrea's Western Front and Related Claims, *dispositif*, Section VIII.E.2.b.

requested a fixed amount of US$500 per person for 3,100 persons allegedly expelled, amounting to US$1,550,000, plus the additional fixed-sum amount of US$500 per person for lost property.[79] Ethiopia contended that the per capita sum should be smaller and that the Commission's finding of liability applied only to persons residing within the legal boundaries of the village of Awgaro according to Eritrean census figures from 2000.[80]

The Commission, which understood the term "Awgaro" to describe the general area from which Eritreans had been forcibly and wrongfully expelled, concluded, on the basis of the declaration of the relief official who registered the expelled persons in the displaced persons camp to which most of them went, that at least 3,100 persons were wrongfully and forcibly expelled.[81] The Commission awarded the full amount sought, US$1,550,000, as compensation for this violation.[82]

Eritrea's Group Number Two Damages Claims

General Issues[83]

Ethiopia contended that many of Eritrea's Group No. 2 claims were barred by the customary international law rules precluding a State from claiming in the exercise of diplomatic protection if the injured individual has the nationality of the State against which the claim is made.[84] It also contended that claims involving persons whom the Commission found were dual nationals at relevant times were barred because those persons' dominant nationality was Ethiopian.[85] Eritrea argued, *inter alia*, that in the present context, the rule of dominant and effective nationality could only operate to bar a claim if the injured person's non-Eritrean nationality was continuous from the date of the injury to the date of the claim.[86]

The Commission ruled that the application of the rule of dominant and effective nationality must be qualified in situations, such as those in the present case, involving claims concerning expulsion or deprivation of nationality by the respondent State. "It cannot be that ... international law allows a State wrongfully to expel persons or deprive them of its own nationality, but then deny State responsibility because of the very social connections or bonds of nationality it wrongfully ended."[87]

Deprivation of Nationality[88]

The Commission had found Ethiopia liable "[f]or arbitrarily depriving dual nationals who remained in Ethiopia during the war of their Ethiopian nationality." These persons were not expelled, but they were required to register with Ethiopia's security authorities and to

[79] Final Award, para. 240.
[80] Final Award, para. 241.
[81] Final Award, paras. 243, 244.
[82] Final Award, para. 246.
[83] Final Award, paras. 248–251.
[84] Final Award, para. 248.
[85] Final Award, para. 248.
[86] Final Award, para. 250.
[87] Final Award, para. 251.
[88] Final Award, paras. 252–288.

surrender their passports, identity cards, and other official documents identifying them as Ethiopians. They were given distinctive yellow cards and were referred to by both Parties and by the Commission as the "yellow card people." The evidence at the liability phase indicated that 24,018 yellow cards were issued. Eritrea contended that the number of persons in this group should be increased to 36,000 to reflect persons who were obliged to register, but did not,[89] and claimed US$10,000 with respect to each person.[90] The Commission dismissed Eritrea's claim on the grounds that Eritrea had not produced evidence sufficient to establish that the "yellow card people" experienced any economic or social burdens or dislocations justifying an award of compensation.[91]

The Commission had found Ethiopia liable "for arbitrarily depriving dual nationals who were present in third countries during the war of their Ethiopian nationality." Eritrea claimed US$10,000 per person in respect of 66.1% of persons whom the International Organization for Migration had tallied as having voted in the referendum in third countries. The Commission, given the severe limitations in the record, awarded compensation in the amount of US$50,000 "in respect of the unknown, but apparently small, number of dual nationals who were arbitrarily deprived of their Ethiopian nationality while present in third countries."[92]

The Commission had also found Ethiopia liable for arbitrarily depriving dual nationals who were expelled to Eritrea but who were not screened pursuant to Ethiopia's security review procedure of their Ethiopian nationality.[93] Eritrea calculated its claimed number of 43,319 wrongful deprivations of nationality beginning with the 65,535 persons in the Eritrean Relief and Refugee Commission ("ERREC") database who registered as having entered Eritrea from Ethiopia between May 1998 and December 2000, reducing this number by those who identified themselves as having left Ethiopia voluntarily and by an estimate of those of Eritrean nationality only.[94] The Commission found that approximately 15,475 dual nationals were lawfully deprived of their nationality pursuant to a screening process by Ethiopia's state security agency (Security, Immigration and Refugees Authority, or "SIRAA")[95] and that many thousands of dual nationals left Ethiopia for Eritrea voluntarily, and their resulting loss of nationality was not arbitrary and unlawful.[96] The Commission concluded that approximately 15,000 dual nationals were arbitrarily deprived of their Ethiopian nationality in conjunction with their unlawful expulsion from Ethiopia and decided, taking into account the paucity of the evidence regarding the practical consequences following from loss of nationality, that satisfaction in the form of its earlier liability findings constituted sufficient reparation for Eritrea's claims for compensation for unlawful deprivation of some dual nationals' Ethiopian nationality.[97]

---

[89] Final Award, para. 256.
[90] Final Award, para. 257.
[91] Final Award, para. 260.
[92] Final Award, para. 267.
[93] Final Award, para. 268.
[94] Final Award, paras. 269–275.
[95] Final Award, para. 281.
[96] Final Award, para. 285.
[97] Final Award, paras. 287–288.

Wrongful Expulsion[98]

The Commission had found Ethiopia liable for the wrongful expulsion of three groups of people, namely (i) people from rural areas near the border; (ii) some members of expellees' families who did not hold Eritrean nationality; and (iii) an unknown but considerable number of dual nationals for reasons that could not be established.[99] With respect to the first and second of these groups, the Commission had found that Eritrea could only claim for direct costs incurred by it as a result of these expulsions, as these persons were not Eritrean nationals[100] and Eritrea had presented this claim on its own account and not on behalf of the affected individuals.[101]

Regarding the dual nationals, the Commission rejected both Parties' proposed methods for calculating the number of dual nationals who were wrongly expelled, and concluded, based on its best assessment of the evidence, that approximately 15,000 dual nationals were wrongly expelled.[102] In light of the unusual circumstances, including a highly disputed record regarding the extent of wrongful expulsion, and the serious character of the event for many of those affected, the Commission awarded compensation in the total amount of US$15,000,000 in respect of the wrongful expulsion of an unknown, but considerable, number of dual nationals by local Ethiopian authorities.[103]

Regarding Eritrea's claim of approximately 1.4 billion nakfa and 28 million birr for its alleged expenditure in resettling a large group of rural Ethiopians found to have been wrongfully expelled from Ethiopia, the Commission found it to be insufficiently supported by evidence. However, given the severity of the violation of international law, the Commission accepted Eritrea's estimate given in the liability phase of 15,000 rural expellees and that Eritrea had paid approximately 230 nakfa as a one-time cash subsidy to rural expellees, and found that two or three years was a reasonable transition period for the temporary provision of social services. The Commission awarded Eritrea compensation of US$11,000,000 for expenses it incurred in receiving, caring for and resettling rural Ethiopian nationals wrongfully expelled from Ethiopia.[104]

The Commission dismissed for lack of evidence Eritrea's claim for direct costs incurred in receiving non-Eritrean family members of SIRAA expellees who were also forcibly expelled from Ethiopia.[105]

Harsh Conditions of Departure[106]

The Commission had found Ethiopia liable for "frequently failing to provide humane and safe treatment to persons being expelled from Eritrea to Ethiopia."[107] Eritrea claimed

---

[98] Final Award, paras. 289–309.

[99] Final Award, para. 289; Partial Award in Eritrea's Civilians Claims, *dispositif*, Section XIII.E.

[100] Art. 5(9) of the Agreement provides that "in appropriate cases, each party may file claims on behalf of persons of Eritrean or Ethiopian origin who may not be its nationals. Such claims shall be considered by the Commission on the same basis as claims submitted on behalf of that party's nationals."

[101] Final Award, para. 290; Partial Award in Eritrea's Civilians Claims, para. 19.

[102] Final Award, para. 295.

[103] Final Award, para. 302.

[104] Final Award, paras. 303, 306–308.

[105] Final Award, para. 309.

[106] Final Award, paras. 310–315.

[107] Final Award, para. 310.

US$92,728,000 as compensation with respect to this liability finding, based on the contention that 46,364 persons experienced such conditions.[108] Ethiopia argued that persons "expelled" should be read restrictively to exclude persons who had left voluntarily.[109] The Commission held that its reference in the liability finding to persons "expelled" was not intended to exclude other persons who were made to suffer harsh and potentially dangerous conditions of transport, since persons who left Ethiopia voluntarily did not waive their right to humane and safe treatment.[110] To reflect the seriousness of the violation, the Commission awarded US$2,000,000 as compensation for failure to provide humane and safe treatment in transport.[111]

Property Losses by Persons Previously Residing in Ethiopia[112]

Eritrea's Group Number Two damages claim did not distinguish between claims involving persons previously residing in Ethiopia and those involving non-residents' property, and did not conform to the Commission's specific liability findings. Instead, Eritrea made a single claim for property losses, which included over ten million birr, US$47 million, and additional amounts in nakfa and Saudi rials, for departees' and non-residents property losses combined.[113] Concerning Eritrea's claims in respect of property losses by persons who resided in Ethiopia prior to their departure during the war, the Commission considered Eritrea's argument that expellees' overall social and economic circumstances provided substance and credibility to the very large amounts claimed based on the claims forms. The Commission found that this group was more economically diverse and less affluent overall than Eritrea contended.[114] Due to its doubts concerning the claims form process used by Eritrea to quantify individuals' losses, the Commission did not regard these as a credible measure of damages and instead made its best approximation of the expellees' aggregate property losses.[115] Based on the available evidence, the Commission awarded Eritrea US$46,000,000 as compensation in respect of expellees' losses of property on account of Ethiopia's unlawful actions.[116]

Property Losses by Non-Residents[117]

The Commission had found Ethiopia liable (1) for failing to provide full compensation for trucks and buses owned by Eritreans that were requisitioned by Ethiopia during the conflict and were not returned to their owners, and (2) for creating and facilitating a cumulative network of economic measures, some lawful and others not, that collectively resulted in the loss of all or most of the business and immovable property in Ethiopia of non-resident

[108] Final Award, para. 311.
[109] Final Award, para. 312.
[110] Final Award, para. 313.
[111] Final Award, para. 315.
[112] Final Award, paras. 316–340.
[113] Final Award, para. 319.
[114] Final Award, paras. 331, 332.
[115] Final Award, paras. 333–337.
[116] Final Award, para. 340.
[117] Final Award, paras. 341–363.

Eritreans, contrary to Ethiopia's duty to ensure the protection of aliens' assets.[118] As noted above, Eritrea's Group Number Two damages claim did not distinguish between claims for residents' or non-residents' property and did not conform to the Commission's specific liability findings.[119]

The Commission found credible evidence showing that Ethiopian authorities had systematically seized many Eritrean-owned trucks and buses in Addis Ababa, in other cities, and on the roads to border crossings, and that these trucks were not returned to their owners, nor was compensation offered after the war.[120] Taking into account all the evidence from the liability phase, including official Ethiopian records and press reports, the Commission concluded that Ethiopia seized at least six hundred trucks and buses that were in Ethiopia and were owned by Eritreans.[121] It accepted 327,000 birr as reflecting the average value of the vehicles Ethiopia seized.[122] Accordingly, the Commission awarded Eritrea compensation of US$24,525,000 for the unlawful failure by Ethiopia to return or compensate Eritrea after the war for the vehicles it requisitioned from non-resident Eritreans.

Eritrea claimed approximately 625 million birr for other losses by non-residents on the basis of its claims forms. Although this claim suffered from significant uncertainties, the Commission, based on its best estimate of the number of non-residents who lost property covered by its liability findings, awarded Eritrea US$1,500,000 as compensation for this group.[123]

Unlawful Detention of Eritrean Civilians[124]

Eritrea claimed US$40 million as compensation in respect of the wrongful detention by Ethiopia of 2,000 Eritrean civilians.[125] Its claim at the damages phase included several groups of civilians allegedly wrongfully detained, including those wrongfully detained as prisoners of war.[126] The evidence presented in support during the damages phase "did not greatly increase the available information on the number of civilians Ethiopia imprisoned or detained" but the Commission found the total of 1,200 civilians reported by Amnesty International and the U.S. State Department to be credible evidence of the total number affected.[127] It awarded Eritrea compensation of US$2,600,000 in respect of Eritrean civilians who were held on security charges, or for unknown reasons, under harsh and unacceptable conditions.[128]

---

[118] Final Award, para. 342; Partial Award in Eritrea's Claims for Loss of Property in Ethiopia Owned by Non-Residents, para. 14.
[119] Final Award, para. 343.
[120] Final Award, paras. 346–347.
[121] Final Award, paras. 356–361.
[122] Final Award, para. 362.
[123] Final Award, paras. 364-365.
[124] Final Award, paras. 366–376.
[125] Final Award, para. 367.
[126] Final Award, para. 368.
[127] Final Award, para. 375.
[128] Final Award, para. 376.

Diplomatic Claim[129]

The Commission had found Ethiopia liable for two serious violations of the international law of diplomatic and consular relations.[130] Eritrea claimed total monetary compensation of US$2,611,500 and 77,500 birr.[131] Ethiopia took the position, consistently with its own Diplomatic Claim, that satisfaction was a sufficient form of reparation.[132] The Commission held that satisfaction in the form of a declaration of wrongfulness was the appropriate remedy for the claims of wrongful searches of departing diplomatic personnel other than the Ambassador, where the proven damage was non-material.[133] Relief in the form of "a strong declaration of wrongfulness" was warranted in respect of the serious violation of the Ambassador's diplomatic immunity for the attempted search of the Ambassador's person and Ethiopia's actual search of and seizure of papers and personal property from his briefcase and hand luggage.[134] The Commission rejected Eritrea's claim for monetary compensation in respect of that violation as it was not supported by any independent documentation.[135]

Ethiopia conceded that Eritrea was entitled to satisfaction in the form of a declaration of the serious wrongfulness of Ethiopia's actions in entering, ransacking, searching, and seizing Eritrea's Embassy Residence and seizing both diplomatic property and the Ambassador's personal property.[136] The Commission noted that the question of monetary compensation was difficult to assess since the evidence on quantum was sparse, but appreciated that documentation could have been lost with the seizure of the Embassy Residence.[137] Weighing the extreme seriousness of the violation against the paucity of the valuation evidence for such large claims, the Commission awarded Eritrea US$155,000, representing approximately half of the total amount claimed for the contents of the three buildings in the Embassy Residence compound and three vehicles.[138]

Individual Claims[139]

Six of Eritrea's claims, numbered 27-32, were filed on behalf of named individuals. The Commission, in its Partial Award in Eritrea's Civilians Claims, held: "The Commission's findings of liability apply fully to [Claims 27-32] to the extent indicated by the particular facts. The application of the Commission's findings to the facts of each of these claims will be assessed in the future damages phase of these proceedings." The Commission proceeded to make that assessment in its Final Award.

The Commission dismissed Claims 27 and 28 (Hiwot Nemariam and Belay Redda) for unlawful deprivation of nationality and unlawful expulsion since the Claimants were dual

---

[129] Final Award, paras. 377–392.
[130] Final Award, para. 379; Partial Award in Eritrea's Diplomatic Claim, *dispositif*, Section IV.D.1 & 2.
[131] Final Award, para. 381.
[132] Final Award, para. 382.
[133] Final Award, paras. 385–386.
[134] Final Award, para. 387.
[135] Final Award, para. 388.
[136] Final Award, para. 389.
[137] Final Award, para. 390.
[138] Final Award, para. 391.
[139] Final Award, paras. 393–436.

nationals who were interrogated and deported for security reasons.[140] The Commission also dismissed their claims for allegedly unlawful conditions of detention pending expulsion, and Claimant 28's claims for family separation, loss of certain investments, and loss of his pension. However, the Commission awarded US$100 to each Claimant in recognition that the physical conditions of their transport failed to comply with the international law requirements of humane and safe treatment.[141] It also awarded US$56,915 to the Claimants jointly for lack of access to their bank accounts after the end of the war; US$125,000 for deprivation of business property; and US$137,500 for loss of other property, including a residence and personal property.[142]

The Commission dismissed the claims by Claimant 29 (Serztu Gebre Meskel), a dual national expelled for security reasons, for damages for unlawful deprivation of nationality and expulsion, unlawful conditions of detention, and loss of certain investments for the same reasons as those claims by Claimants 27 and 28, and also dismissed his claim for unlawful conditions of departure and other claims for property loss.[143] It awarded him US$1,500,000 for loss of his 50% interest in the Nile Construction Co., which was taken over by an Ethiopian bank after his expulsion.[144]

The Commission dismissed claims by Claimant 30 (Fekadu Andemeskal), a dual national expelled for security reasons, for unlawful deprivation of Ethiopian nationality, expulsion, and unlawful conditions of detention for the same reasons as those claims by Claimants 27 and 28, and dismissed his claims for unlawful conditions of transport and for compensation for property loss for failure of proof. His claim for lack of access to his bank accounts was dismissed because the evidence indicated that access was permitted to a former employee of the Claimant, which access was accepted by the bank.[145]

The Commission dismissed claims by Claimant 31 (Mebrahtu Gebremedhin), a dual national and U.S. permanent resident who had been detained and interrogated whilst leaving Ethiopia voluntarily, for deprivation of nationality and expulsion, for the same reasons as for Claimants 27 and 28.[146] It awarded him US$2,500 for loss of property in a bank account and US$18,750 for loss of a house, car, and personal effects.[147]

The Commission dismissed the claims by Claimant 32 (Mebrat Gebreamlak) for damages for deprivation of Ethiopian nationality and expulsion because she had left Ethiopia voluntarily, albeit after threats of expulsion.[148] It awarded her US$100,000 for inaccessible bank accounts and US$125,000 damages for loss of the assets of the Feruth International Trading Company, which Claimant 32 had owned jointly with her late husband.[149]

---

[140] Final Award, para. 397.
[141] Final Award, para. 400.
[142] Final Award, paras. 401–406.
[143] Final Award, paras. 409–413.
[144] Final Award, paras. 414–417.
[145] Final Award, paras. 419–425.
[146] Final Award, para. 427.
[147] Final Award, para. 429.
[148] Final Award, para. 432.
[149] Final Award, para. 435.

Award

The Commission set out all of its awards of compensation to Eritrea in the *dispositif* of the Final Award, and reiterated its confidence that the Parties would ensure that the compensation awarded would be paid promptly, and that funds received in respect of their claims would be used to provide relief to their civilian populations injured in the war.[150]

---

[150] Final Award, section IX.

Eritrea-Ethiopia Claims Commission

Final Award
Ethiopia's Damages Claims

Parties: Eritrea/Ethiopia

Date of Arbitration Agreement: December 12, 2000

Commissioners: Prof. Hans van Houtte (President), Judge George H. Aldrich, Mr. John R. Crook, Dean James Paul, Ms. Lucy Reed

Date of Final Award: August 17, 2009

Summary

International armed conflict waged between Eritrea and Ethiopia between 1998 and 2000 – liability of Ethiopia for violations of international humanitarian law – damages – US$11,000,000 for death, physical injury, disappearance, forced labor and conscription of Ethiopian civilians – US$2,000,000 for failing to prevent rape – US$13,900,000 for looting, and destruction of and damage to houses – US$20,195,000 for damage, destruction and looting in Zalambessa – US$2,500,000 for death, injury and property damage in Mekele – US$315,000 for looting of and damage to government buildings and infrastructure – US$4,500,000 for looting, destruction and damage to religious institutions – US$3,216,000 for seizure and looting of the Saba Dimensional Stones Share Company – US$7,500,000 for mistreatment of Ethiopian prisoners of war – US$2,000,000 for failure to protect Ethiopian civilians in Eritrea from threats and violence – US$1,500,000 for failure to ensure Ethiopian civilians in Eritrea access to employment – US$50,000 for failure to ensure that Ethiopian civilians in Eritrea were able to receive medical care to the same extent as Eritrean nationals – US$2,000,000 for wrongful detention and abusive treatment of Ethiopian civilians in Eritrean custody – US$1,500,000 for harsh treatment of Ethiopian civilians at the Hawshaite detention camp – US$10,000,000 for detaining significant numbers of Ethiopian civilians under harsh conditions during and after May 2000 – US$500,000 for deaths and injuries suffered by detainees at Wi'a Camp – US$2,000,000 for failure to protect the property of Ethiopian detainees expelled from Eritrea – US$1,000,000 for failure to protect the property of other departing Ethiopians – US$1,100,000 for failing to ensure the safe and humane repatriation of departing Ethiopians – liability for Eritrea's violations of the *jus ad bellum* – scope of liability – damages – US$45,000,000 for human suffering and lost income associated with internal displacement of persons – US$8,500,000 for Ethiopian civilian deaths and injuries – US$6,000,000 for damage to civilian property, primarily from shelling – US$3,500,000 for damage to public buildings and infrastructure – US$2,500,000 for looting, destruction and damage to religious institutions – US$5,605,000 for destruction in Zalambessa –

US$1,500,000 for deaths and injuries caused by landmines – US$250,000 for destruction of Disaster Prevention and Preparedness Bureau facilities in Adigrat – US$162,500 for damage to other government facilities on the Central Front – US$75,000 for other government losses on the Central Front – US$125,000 for looting of property from the Relief Society of Tigray – US$150,000 for damage in Adi Goshu – US$625,000 for shelling damage in Sheraro – US$65,000 for damage caused by the attack on the Mekele airport – US$4,000,000 for profits lost by Ethiopian Airlines ("EAL") – US$1,703,020 for failing to provide EAL access to its bank accounts at the Bank of Eritrea – US$7,500,000 for reconstruction and assistance to internally displaced persons – satisfaction – satisfaction in form of declaration of wrongfulness in respect of finding that Eritrea violated the Vienna Convention on Diplomatic Relations by arresting and detaining the Ethiopian Chargé d'Affaires and by violating official Ethiopian diplomatic correspondence and interfering with the functioning of the Ethiopian diplomatic mission – all of Ethiopia's other claims dismissed – total monetary compensation of US$174,036,520 awarded to Ethiopia.

Legal Subject Matters

Arbitration:
- Admissibility of claims
- Jurisdiction of the arbitral tribunal
- Remedies

Compensation:
- Damages
  - Evidence
  - Procedure
    - Individual claims
    - Inter-State claims
    - Mass claims processes
  - Scope of liability findings
  - Seriousness of violation

International law:
- Prohibition on resort to armed force
  - Evidence
    - Standard of proof
  - Violation
    - Damages
    - Foreseeability of harm
    - Scope of liability findings

Bibliography

Award published in:
- XXVI R.I.A.A. (forthcoming 2010).

Commentary:
- Michael J. Matheson, *Eritrea-Ethiopia Claims Commission: Damages Awards*, 13 ASIL Insight (Sept. 4, 2009).

Facts

Following the completion of hearings on the issue of liability in 2005, the Commission issued an Order on April 13, 2006, directing the Parties to proceed with a simplified damages phase. Hearings proceeded in two groups: the first, "Group Number One Claims," from April 17 to 27, 2007, and the second, "Group Number Two Claims," from May 19 to 28, 2008.

Summary of Matters Submitted to Arbitration

(1) The damages appropriate to compensate Ethiopia for each of the Commission's findings of liability in the following Awards:
   - Prisoners of War (Ethiopia's Claim 4) (Partial Award, July 1, 2003)
   - Central Front (Ethiopia's Claim 2) (Partial Award, April 28, 2004)
   - Civilians Claims (Ethiopia's Claim 5) (Partial Award, December 17, 2004)
   - *Jus Ad Bellum* (Ethiopia's Claims 1-8) (Partial Award, December 19, 2005)
   - Western and Eastern Fronts (Ethiopia's Claims 1 & 3) (Partial Award, December 19, 2005)
   - Ports (Ethiopia's Claim 6) (Final Award, December 19, 2005)
   - Economic Loss Throughout Ethiopia (Ethiopia's Claim 7) (Partial Award, December 19, 2005)
   - Diplomatic Claim (Ethiopia's Claim 8) (Partial Award, December 19, 2005)

(2) The extent of liability for Eritrea's violation of the *jus ad bellum*, which was not fully resolved by the Commission's Partial Award on Ethiopia's Claims 1–8.

Final Award

Preliminary Remarks

The Commission began with some remarks on some of the procedural challenges presented by the structure of the damages phase.[1] It also made some preliminary remarks concerning the Parties' situations as "among the poorest countries on earth,"[2] since the fact that both Parties had made claims worth billions of U.S. dollars raised potentially serious questions involving human rights norms. In particular, common Article I(2) of the International Covenant on Economic, Social and Cultural Rights ("ICESCR") and the International Covenant on Civil and Political Rights ("ICCPR") provides that "[i]n no case may be a people be deprived of its own means of subsistence."[3] The Commission also noted that in cases of

[1] Final Award on Ethiopia's Damages Claims [hereinafter "Final Award"], paras. 8–17.

[2] Final Award, para. 18.

[3] Final Award, paras. 18–19.

diplomatic protection, compensation must be assessed in light of the actual social and economic circumstances of the injured individuals in respect of whom the State is claiming.[4] It also noted the need to avoid large diversions of national resources from the paying country, as evidenced in State practice since the Treaty of Versailles.[5]

Applicable Legal Principles[6]

Article 5(13) of the Agreement provides that the Commission should "apply relevant rules of international law" and that it "shall not have the power to make decisions *ex aequo et bono*." The Commission therefore considered certain elements of international law affecting the proceedings. Compensation could only be awarded for injuries if those injuries bore a sufficiently close causal connection with conduct that the Commission had previously found to violate international law.[7]

Regarding the standard of proof, the Commission had required clear and convincing evidence in the liability phase. At the damages phase, the Commission ruled that the appropriate standard for quantification of damage was an amalgam of the standard of "clear and convincing evidence" and one based on preponderance of the evidence.[8] To require proof of quantification of damage by clear and convincing evidence would often preclude recovery, frustrating the Commission's mandate to address "the socio-economic impact of the crisis on the civilian population" under Article 5(1) of the Agreement.[9] In some cases, the Commission reduced the amount of compensation awarded to balance the uncertainties flowing from the lower standard of proof.[10] As determined in its Decision No. 7 of July 27, 2007, the Commission adopted the test of "proximate cause" in assessing causation, and gave weight to "whether particular damage reasonably should have been foreseeable to an actor committing the international delict in question."[11]

Assessing Compensation and Technical Financial Issues[12]

The Parties agreed that the final awards rendered by the Commission should denominate compensation in United States dollars. The Commission generally made conversions to U.S. dollars utilizing the official exchange rate prevailing at the time of the injury underlying the compensation claim.[13] Article 5(14) of the Agreement provides that "interest … may be awarded"; in the circumstances, the Commission decided not to award interest on the amounts awarded to either Party.[14]

---

[4] Final Award, para. 26.
[5] Final Award, para. 21.
[6] Final Award, paras. 28–39.
[7] Final Award, para. 29.
[8] Final Award, para. 36.
[9] *Id.*
[10] Final Award, para. 38.
[11] Final Award, para. 39, citing Decision No. 7 of July 27, 2007.
[12] Final Award, paras. 40–46.
[13] Final Award, para. 41.
[14] Final Award, para. 43.

The Commission's Liability Findings and the Structure of Ethiopia's Damages Claims[15]

Ethiopia assembled its claims regarding the Commission's liability findings into six large groups, claiming fixed-sum damages in some groups and actual amount damages in others, namely:

(i) fixed-sum damages for injuries and deaths inflicted upon Ethiopian nationals;
(ii) fixed-sum damages for loss of Ethiopian nationals' property;
(iii) actual amount damages for damage to the town of Zalambessa, damage to hundreds of churches and government facilities in Ethiopia, and damages allegedly suffered by numerous Ethiopian entities and government agencies;
(iv) material damages resulting from Eritrea's aerial operations in Mekele, use of landmines, and harm to natural resources and the environment;
(v) damages in respect of prisoners of war; and
(vi) moral damages.[16]

The Commission addressed each of these groups of claims in its Final Award.

Moral Damages Claims[17]

Ethiopia claimed, in addition to damages determined in accordance with general principles of international law, an "enormous separate increment" of damages to reflect moral injury, both to its nationals and to the State of Ethiopia itself,[18] which it calculated using an elaborate matrix of base impact values, family multipliers, and severity factors.[19] The Commission rejected this claim, holding that large per capita awards of moral damages might be appropriate in some contexts involving an individual, or identifiable members of small groups, but could not be reasonably expanded to situations involving claimed moral injury to whole populations of large areas.[20] Where appropriate, the Commission weighed considerations such as the gravity of a particular type of violation or the extent and consequences of the resulting human injury, as an integral part of its damages awards.[21]

Fixed-Sum *jus in bello* Damages Claims[22]

Deaths and Injuries[23]

The Commission turned next to Ethiopia's first and second groups of claims, beginning with Ethiopia's claims in respect of deaths and injuries. Ethiopia claimed US$434,726,251

[15] Final Award, paras. 47–53.
[16] Final Award, para. 52.
[17] Final Award, paras. 54–65.
[18] Final Award, paras. 54–55.
[19] Final Award, paras. 56–57, 158.
[20] Final Award, paras. 61–65.
[21] Final Award, para. 65.
[22] Final Award, paras. 66–135.
[23] Final Award, paras. 66–103.

for injuries and deaths suffered by Ethiopian nationals in violation of the *jus in bello*.[24] Ethiopia divided its claims into groups by offence according to gravity, namely, (a) intentional killings, (b) rape, (c) beatings and wounds caused by small arms fire, (d) abductions, and (e) forced labor and conscription.[25] Its claims for each group were based on percentages of undiscounted projected lifetime earnings of rural people in Tigray or Afar, which it calculated at US$5,060 in Tigray and US$5,588 in Afar.[26] It estimated fixed compensation for a killing to equal a lifetime's earnings; a rape to cause injury equal to 50% of lifetime earnings; beatings and wounds to cause injury equal to 50% of lifetime earnings; abductions to cause injury equal to 75% of lifetime earnings; and forced labor and conscription to cause injury equal to 85% of lifetime earnings.[27] Ethiopia then estimated the populations of areas affected by the war and the percentage of each such population that suffered specific types of violations.[28]

The Commission expressed its doubts regarding Ethiopia's approach in its calculation of amounts which were said to reflect the full extent of injuries suffered by its nationals,[29] as well as specific elements of its analysis, including the use of undiscounted unadjusted projections of lifetime earnings and its estimation of the affected population, which had to be reduced to take into account 15,000 rural expellees of Eritrean origin.[30] The available evidence suggested that the population potentially exposed to violations of the *jus in bello* was much smaller than the 242,000 claimed by Ethiopia.[31] The Commission made its own appraisal of the evidence previously adduced in respect of Ethiopia's claims of damages for each of the groups of violations identified.

Ethiopia claimed that, in the relevant areas under the Commission's liability findings, 13,935 civilians were killed intentionally or otherwise in violation of the *jus in bello* on all three fronts of the war;[32] 82,223 people suffered from beating, wounding or other physical abuse at the hands of Eritrean forces;[33] 20,354 people were abducted;[34] and 9,443 persons were made to perform forced labour or were forcibly conscripted.[35] The evidence previously submitted, which included reports from Ethiopian and government officials and witness testimony in some cases, suggested that the numbers of victims were much smaller than those claimed.[36] Based on its best estimates of the gravity and extent of Eritrea's *jus in bello* violations, and giving weight to the seriousness of the offenses against life and human dignity proved at the liability phase, the Commission awarded Ethiopia US$11,000,000 in respect of those claims.[37]

---

[24] Final Award, para. 66.
[25] Final Award, para. 71.
[26] Final Award, para. 72.
[27] Final Award, para. 73.
[28] Final Award, paras. 74–76.
[29] Final Award, para. 84.
[30] Final Award, para. 87.
[31] Final Award, para. 90.
[32] Final Award, para. 95.
[33] Final Award, para. 98.
[34] Final Award, para. 99.
[35] Final Award, para. 101.
[36] Final Award, paras. 95–102.
[37] Final Award, para. 103.

Rape[38]

Concerning rape, the Commission acknowledged, first, the cultural sensitivities surrounding rape in both countries and the unwillingness of victims to come forward, stating that "the full number of victims and the full magnitude of the harm they suffered cannot and will not ever be known."[39]

Ethiopia, in a three-step process using its general methodology, (a) estimated that 1% of the pre-war female population suffered rape in the relevant areas, totaling 236 women, (b) estimated the resultant injury at 50% of the total average lifetime lost earnings in Tigray and Afar, and (c) added large moral damages intended to reflect the gravity of the injury. On this basis, Ethiopia claimed material and moral damages of US$6,739,641.[40] The Commission found the estimated percentage of the population to be "unduly low in light of the social stigma of reporting rape and the comparatively large number of women and girls in the vulnerable population"; it also refused to accept the equation of the financial impact of a rape with that of a beating.[41]

Despite the shortcomings of both Parties' damages methodologies, the Commission considered this serious violation of international humanitarian law to demand serious relief. The Commission stated that "[n]either symbolic nor nominal damages will suffice in the face of the physical, mental and emotional harm known to be suffered by rape victims."[42] It awarded Ethiopia (as it did Eritrea in its parallel Award) US$2,000,000 in damages for failing to prevent the rape of known and unknown victims in Irob, Dalul and Elidar Weredas, and expressed the hope that the Parties would use the funds awarded to develop and support health programs for women and girls in the affected areas.[43]

Loss of Ethiopian Nationals' Property

In the liability phase, the Commission found Eritrea liable for frequent destruction of property in six weredas, and for looting in nine.[44] Ethiopia, based on a method similar to that used in its corresponding claims for injury to persons, claimed US$30,073,424 for looting and US$24,879,342 for destruction of real property in the areas covered by the Commission's *jus in bello* liability findings.[45]

Looting

Concerning looting, whilst the available evidence was fragmentary and imprecise, useful reference points were provided by the number of internally displaced persons ("IDPs") and the pre-war population of areas exposed to looting.[46] Ethiopia's estimation of the population

---

38 Final Award, paras. 104–110.
39 Final Award, para. 104.
40 Final Award, para. 106.
41 Final Award, para. 107.
42 Final Award, para. 109.
43 Final Award, para. 110.
44 Final Award, para. 112.
45 Final Award, paras. 113–114.
46 Final Award, paras. 120–123.

had to be reduced to take account of approximately 15,000 rural expellees of Eritrean origin.[47] Based on the available evidence of these numbers and of the value of looted property, and taking into account the devastating effect of loss of subsistence property on the rural poor, the Commission concluded that US$12,000,000 fairly reflected the value of property lost to looting by Eritrean soldiers.[48]

Destruction of and Damage to Houses and Real Property

Ethiopia claimed US$24,879,342 for destruction of property; its claim related to a total of 77,000 houses in the affected areas, of which Ethiopia claimed 35% had been destroyed by conduct found to violate the *jus in bello*.[49] Ethiopia did not allocate the assumed damage among houses that were wholly or partially destroyed, nor did it allocate particular housing damage to either its *jus in bello* or *jus ad bellum* claims.[50] Ethiopia's earlier evidence, including reports from Ethiopian government sources and assessments by international relief agencies, indicated that wartime damage to houses was far less extensive than Ethiopia claimed, and not all damage to housing resulted from actions for which Ethiopia was liable.[51] The Commission also found that the majority of damage that had been caused in towns had been due to shelling, which it had previously determined was not compensable under the *jus in bello*.[52] Giving weight to estimates by international agencies, and to evidence indicating that shelling was a major cause of damage to housing,[53] it awarded US$1,900,000 for the *jus in bello* component of its claims for damage to housing.[54]

Actual Amount *jus in bello* Damages Claims[55]

Destruction in Zalambessa

Ethiopia claimed an amount it converted to about US$120 million for damage to the town of Zalambessa, to churches and government facilities, and to numerous Ethiopian enterprises and government facilities. It also claimed actual amounts of damages said to result from Eritrea's bombing at the Ayder School in Mekele.[56]

At the liability phase, the Commission had found Eritrea liable for 75% of the physical damage and 100% of the looting in the town of Zalambessa. Ethiopia claimed an amount it converted to equal US$29,489,000 as material damages for destruction and looting, reflecting the full amount of damage allegedly inflicted.[57] The primary evidence for this claim was a detailed engineering survey prepared for Tigray local authorities by a team of engineers,

---

[47] Final Award, para. 123. *See also* text accompanying notes 25–27 *supra*.
[48] Final Award, para. 126.
[49] Final Award, para. 131.
[50] Final Award, paras. 131, 133.
[51] Final Award, paras. 132, 134.
[52] Final Award, paras. 129, 133.
[53] Final Award, para. 135.
[54] Final Award, para. 135.
[55] Final Award, paras. 136–206.
[56] Final Award, para. 136.
[57] Final Award, para. 137.

surveyors, local elders and others and completed in December 2000, before the creation of the Commission.[58] The Commission found the engineering study to be thorough, reasonable, and credible.[59] It took account of the total repair costs estimated in the engineering study, which it increased by 20% due to documented post-war shifts in exchange rates and construction costs, giving a sum of 179,329,400 birr. The Commission awarded Ethiopia 75% of this amount, or US$16,815,000, as compensation for damage to and destruction of buildings in Zalambessa in violation of the *jus in bello*.[60] It treated Ethiopia's claim for the remaining 25% in its consideration of Ethiopia's *jus ad bellum* claims.[61]

Looting in Zalambessa

Ethiopia also claimed US$3,056,771 for property looted from private homes in Zalambessa, basing its quantification on a governmental survey carried out for reconstruction purposes in October to December 2001.[62] It claimed smaller amounts in respect of property allegedly looted from businesses, government agencies, and other entities, including two churches and a mosque.[63] The Commission, after reviewing the evidence presented for each claim, awarded Ethiopia US$2,500,000 in respect of losses of personal property due to looting, and US$3,380,000 in respect of losses from looting of the businesses premises and other buildings.[64]

Deaths, Injuries and Property Damage in Mekele

The Commission had previously found Eritrea had violated the *jus in bello* in the conduct of its air operations in May 1998, in connection with two attacks that dropped cluster bombs near the Ayder School in Mekele. Ethiopia claimed an amount it converted to equal US$882,539 for deaths, injuries, and damage from the bombings, including the deaths of sixty persons and injuries to 168 others.[65] The Commission accepted the claimed numbers of deaths and injuries, which were based on substantial and uncontested evidence, but rejected Ethiopia's use of undiscounted projected future earnings and its mechanistic calculation of additional moral damages.[66] Ethiopia's evidence included reasonable and adequately documented costs of medical treatment and damage to the school and its contents.[67] Taking into account the consequences of this serious violation of international law, the Commission awarded Ethiopia US$2,500,000 in respect of deaths and injuries, medical expenses and property damage resulting from the dropping of cluster bombs in the vicinity of the Ayder School in Mekele.[68]

---

[58] Final Award, para. 139.
[59] Final Award, para. 140.
[60] Final Award, para. 144.
[61] Final Award, para. 145.
[62] Final Award, para. 146.
[63] Final Award, paras. 148–152.
[64] Final Award, paras. 147, 153.
[65] Final Award, paras. 154–155.
[66] Final Award, paras. 156, 158.
[67] Final Award, paras. 159–160.
[68] Final Award, para. 161.

Other Looting and Damage to Property

Ethiopia also claimed US$13,963,982 in damages for the destruction and looting of other buildings on the Central and Western Fronts, and US$2,566,002 for destruction and looting of buildings on the Eastern Front.[69] Due to lack of specificity in the evidence and the absence of liability for property damage on the Western Front, the Commission rejected Ethiopia's claims for property damage on all three fronts.[70] Based on evidence submitted in the liability phase, it awarded Ethiopia US$315,000 for damage caused by looting on all three fronts.[71]

Religious Institutions

Ethiopia's other actual amount damages claims included a claim of US$9,238,669 in compensation for material damages resulting from looting, destruction, and damage to "at least" 164 churches, monasteries, mosques, church-run clinics and parochial schools in the regions of Tigray and Afar.[72] Based on the evidence of religious officials as to the value of the items looted or destroyed, and on evidence from the liability phase regarding the Central Front which conveyed "serious disregard for the sanctity of religious institutions," the Commission awarded Ethiopia US$5,229,389 in compensation for looting, destruction and damage to religious institutions.[73]

Saba Marbles Quarry

Ethiopia claimed US$3,252,961 for looted equipment and lost profits on account of Saba Dimensional Stones Share Company ("Saba Marbles") which had a large marble quarry and associated camp in Tahtay Adiabo Wereda.[74] Eritrea's defence included the assertion that the quarry was located in Eritrea, not Ethiopia. The Commission rejected this defence on the grounds that, in any event, it was not lawful for Eritrean troops to seize the company's property and remove it by force in the manner described by the witnesses.[75] The Commission awarded Ethiopia a total of US$3,216,000 in respect of looted machinery and for loss of profits from May 1998 until some point in 2000.[76]

Ethiopia's Other *jus in bello* Claims[77]

Ethiopia's other *jus in bello* claims related to prisoners of war (POWs),[78] treatment of Ethiopian civilians in Eritrea,[79] and treatment of diplomatic property and personnel.[80]

---

[69] Final Award, para. 162.
[70] Final Award, para. 172.
[71] Final Award, paras. 173–179.
[72] Final Award, para. 180.
[73] Final Award, para. 189.
[74] Final Award, para. 199.
[75] Final Award, para. 202.
[76] Final Award, paras. 203–206.
[77] Final Award, paras. 207–270.
[78] Final Award, paras. 207–213.
[79] Final Award, paras. 214–262.
[80] Final Award, paras. 263–270.

Prisoners of War

In its Partial Award in Ethiopia's Prisoners of War Claim 4, the Commission had found Eritrea liable for twelve violations of international law.[81] The Commission stressed that the claims before it were the claims of the Parties, not of individual victims. While it encouraged the Parties to compensate appropriately the individual victims of warfare, it calculated the damages owed by one Party to the other, including for mistreatment of POWs, on the basis of its evaluation of the evidence with respect to the seriousness of the unlawful acts or omissions, the total numbers of probable victims of those unlawful acts or omissions (where those numbers could be identified with reasonable certainty), and the extent of the injury or damage suffered because of those unlawful acts or omissions.[82] The Commission identified those violations which it found to be particularly serious, including the refusal of proper access to POW camps by ICRC officials, which it noted is the most effective means of restraining abuses of POWs, as well as killings, beatings, mental and physical abuse in camps, and endangering health by failing to provide adequate standards of living including drinking water and food.[83] The total number of victims approached 1,100 and the Commission ruled that all were adversely affected by the serious violations of international law, which often resulted in lingering mental and physical injuries.[84] The Commission awarded Ethiopia US$7,500,000 for the unlawful treatment of Ethiopian POWs.[85]

Treatment of Ethiopian Civilians in Eritrea

Ethiopia claimed US$2,055,188,660 in respect of injuries allegedly inflicted on more than 120,000 Ethiopian civilians present in Eritrea at some time during the war.[86] Ethiopia divided its claim into the following categories: (i) 35,000 persons who left Eritrea before May 2000, some of whom were detained under harsh conditions at the Hawshaite camp beginning in February 1999; (ii) 69,700 persons who remained in Eritrea as of May 2000 but were not detained; and (iii) 15,300 persons who remained in Eritrea as of May 2000 who were detained in Eritrean detention camps.[87] Ethiopia claimed totals of US$509,932,000 with respect to the first category, US$1,213,362,700 with respect to the second, and US$331,893,960 with respect to the third.[88]

Ethiopia's claims were not directly related to the Commission's *jus in bello* liability findings, and its techniques of calculating damages, which were based on percentages of projected lifetime earnings, did not appear to the Commission to be appropriate in the circumstances.[89] The Commission sought to assess damages due within the framework of its actual liability findings and, due to the lack of persuasive evidence presented at the damages

---

[81] Final Award, para. 207; and *see* Partial Award, Prisoners of War, Ethiopia's Claim 4 Between the Federal Democratic Republic of Ethiopia and the State of Eritrea (July 1, 2003), *dispositif*, Section V.D.

[82] Final Award, para. 209.

[83] Final Award, para. 210.

[84] Final Award, paras. 210–212.

[85] Final Award, para. 213.

[86] Final Award, para. 214.

[87] Final Award, para. 218.

[88] Final Award, paras. 221–226.

[89] Final Award, paras. 231–232.

phase, on the basis of the evidence previously in the record.[90] Based on the available evidence, and taking into account the varying gravity of the violations concerned, the Commission awarded Ethiopia US$2,000,000 for failure to protect Ethiopian civilians in Eritrea from threats and violence;[91] US$1,500,000 for failure to ensure Ethiopian civilians in Eritrea access to employment;[92] and US$50,000 for failure to ensure that Ethiopian civilians in Eritrea had equal access to medical care.[93] In respect of Ethiopian civilians detained in Eritrea, the Commission awarded US$2,000,000 for wrongful detention and abusive treatment of Ethiopians in Eritrean custody;[94] US$1,500,000 in respect of the harsh treatment of civilian detainees at Hawshaite Camp;[95] US$10,000,000 for detention of Ethiopian civilians under harsh conditions during and after May 2000;[96] and US$500,000 in respect of the serious shooting incident that took place at Wi'a Camp on July 11, 2000, in which at least fifteen detainees were killed.[97] The Commission awarded US$2,000,000 for Eritrea's failure to protect the property of detainees who were expelled;[98] US$1,000,000 for not protecting the property of other departing Ethiopians;[99] and US$1,100,000 for Eritrea's failure to ensure the safe and humane repatriation of departing Ethiopians.[100]

Treatment of Diplomatic Property and Personnel

At the liability phase, the Commission had found Eritrea liable for (a) violating Article 29 of the Vienna Convention on Diplomatic Relations by arresting and briefly detaining the Ethiopian Chargé d'Affaires in September 1998 and October 1999 without regard to his diplomatic immunity; and (b) having retained a box containing Ethiopian Embassy correspondence including blank passports and interfering with the functioning of the mission in breach of Articles 24 and 29 of the Vienna Convention on Diplomatic Relations.[101] The Commission determined that, since the interference with Ethiopia's Chargé and official correspondence had been "serious but non-material," the appropriate relief was satisfaction in the form of a declaration of wrongfulness, and made a declaration accordingly.[102]

Ethiopia's Claims for Compensation for Eritrea's Violation of the *Jus Ad Bellum*[103]

The final section of the Award concerned the scope of damages for which Eritrea was liable because of its violation of Article 2(4) of the Charter of the United Nations by its resort

[90] Final Award, para. 233.
[91] Final Award, paras. 237–238.
[92] Final Award, paras. 239–241.
[93] Final Award, paras. 242–243.
[94] Final Award, paras. 244–247.
[95] Final Award, paras. 248–249.
[96] Final Award, paras. 250–254.
[97] Final Award, para. 255.
[98] Final Award, paras. 256–258.
[99] Final Award, paras. 259–260.
[100] Final Award, paras. 261–262.
[101] Final Award, para. 265.
[102] Final Award, paras. 269–270.
[103] Final Award, paras. 271–479.

to force against Ethiopia on May 12, 1998, and the immediately following days.[104] The question of the scope or extent of Eritrea's breach of the *jus ad bellum* pervaded Ethiopia's Group Number One and Group Number Two damages claims.[105] Ethiopia advanced claims for *jus ad bellum* damages for 19 separate types of damage.[106] The Commission addressed, first, two preliminary issues: (a) the geographical and temporal scope of liability following from the violation of the *jus ad bellum* claim; and (b) the principles applicable to determining compensation for such a violation.[107]

The Scope of Liability

The Parties' portrayal of the extent of *jus ad bellum* liability differed dramatically. Ethiopia had maintained that Eritrea should bear the full costs for all loss, damage or injury associated with the armed conflict, whereas Eritrea contended that relief should be limited to satisfaction in the form of a declaration that Eritrea had violated international law.[108] In its Decision No. 7 of July 27, 2007, the Commission had reviewed the question of the legal connection between an international delict and the scope of compensable injury in international law, concluding that this connection was best understood through the concept of proximate cause, "informed by judgments on whether particular types of damage were foreseeable consequences of a delict."[109] The Commission further examined the views of international tribunals on this question in its Final Award, noting that "[s]ince at least the *Alabama* arbitration, panels have rejected claims for damages to generalized economic interests of the victorious State or its nationals, or to its expenses in waging war."[110] In assessing causation, the Commission tried, *inter alia*, to weigh whether particular consequences were or should have been foreseen by Eritrea's leaders in the exercise of reasonable judgment at the time of Eritrea's delict in May 1998.[111]

Concerning the temporal and territorial scope of liability, the Commission concluded that injuries involving Ethiopians and Ethiopian civilian property connected with the conflict were proximately caused by Eritrea's May 1998 delict in the following areas and periods: (i) on the Western Front, in the area including Badme and its environs, and throughout all other areas on the Western Front where Ethiopian forces faced Eritrean forces occupying, or engaging in hostilities within, territory in Ethiopia or peacefully under Ethiopian administration prior to May 1998, during the period from May 1998 until the end of Ethiopia's Operation Sunset offensive in March 1999;[112] (ii) on the Central Front, at Zalambessa and other areas where serious fighting occurred, throughout the period of Eritrean forces' presence or operations, which in some cases extended until June 2000;[113] and (iii) on the Eastern Front, in Elidar and Dalul Weredas, throughout the period of Eritrean forces' presence or

[104] Final Award, para. 271.
[105] Final Award, para. 272.
[106] Final Award, paras. 273–274.
[107] Final Award, para. 275.
[108] Final Award, paras. 276–277.
[109] Final Award, para. 279.
[110] Final Award, para. 286.
[111] Final Award, para. 290.
[112] Final Award, paras. 292–297.
[113] Final Award, paras. 298–300.

operations, which sometimes extended until June 2000.[114] On all three fronts, Eritrea was liable for certain types of damage not subject to temporal limitation, notably injuries caused by landmines, and documented costs of care for internally displaced persons unable to return to their homes.[115]

Determining the Amount of Compensation

In assessing compensation for violation of the *jus ad bellum*, the Commission rejected the idea that damages should have a deterrent effect; it sought to link the amount of compensation to the gravity of each type of violation, and ruled that the level of compensation should not be the same as for violations of the *jus in bello*.[116]

Ethiopia brought fixed amount claims for internally displaced persons; civilian deaths and injuries on the war fronts; civilian property damage; deaths and injuries attributed to landmines; deaths of Ethiopian prisoners of war in Eritrean camps; and departures of Ethiopians from Eritrea.[117] The Commission addressed these claims in respect of each category.

Internally Displaced Persons

Large-scale internal displacement in the areas and times indicated above, including the evacuation of civilians from areas potentially affected by conflict, was the direct and foreseeable result of Eritrea's breach of the *jus ad bellum*.[118] The displacement of many thousands of persons on account of Eritrea's violation of the *jus ad bellum* was a most serious consequence of the conflict,[119] and most of those displaced were women and children.[120] The total number of persons whose displacement was proximately caused by Eritrea's May 1998 delict was substantially less than the total of 349,837 claimed by Ethiopia – perhaps two thirds of that number, perhaps somewhat less – and the periods of displacement varied.[121] The Commission awarded US$45,000,000 to Ethiopia on account of this claim.[122]

Civilian Deaths and Injuries

Ethiopia claimed US$205,167,028 on account of 39,881 civilians whose deaths were said to result from the war on all three fronts but who were not covered by Ethiopia's other claims, and US$102,583,514 on account of an equivalent number of injuries.[123] The Commission ruled that Eritrea was liable for deaths and injuries caused by shelling and gunfire in the regions for which there was *jus ad bellum* liability.[124] Ethiopia's claim in respect of

---

[114] Final Award, paras. 301–304.
[115] Final Award, paras. 296, 300, 304.
[116] Final Award, paras. 306–317.
[117] Final Award, para. 318.
[118] Final Award, paras. 321, 323.
[119] Final Award, para. 322.
[120] Final Award, para. 323.
[121] Final Award, paras. 324, 331.
[122] Final Award, para. 332.
[123] Final Award, para. 333.
[124] Final Award, para. 334.

deaths of militia members was excluded by the last sentence of Article 5(1) of the December 2000 Agreement.[125] The available evidence identified injuries numbering at most in the hundreds, and in some cases deaths and injuries were covered by Ethiopia's other claims.[126] The Commission awarded Ethiopia US$8,500,000 in respect of civilian deaths and injuries related to Eritrea's breach of the *jus ad bellum*.[127]

Damage to Property

Ethiopia's *jus ad bellum* claim for property damage included an additional US$77 million as *jus ad bellum* damages for damage to housing and real property.[128] Taking account of uncertainties and ambiguities in the evidence,[129] the Commission awarded US$6,000,000 for damage to housing and real property.[130]

Ethiopia's claim for damage to public buildings was not separated according to liability *jus ad bellum* and *jus in bello*. The Commission, after deconstructing this claim, awarded Ethiopia US$3,500,000 for Eritrea's violation of the *jus ad bellum* with respect to public buildings and infrastructure.[131] Regarding religious institutions, the Commission emphasized that "[d]amage to religious institutions is a particularly severe consequence of armed conflict that tears at the fabric of the affected communities and deprives them of safe places of worship."[132] It awarded Ethiopia an additional US$2,500,000 for damage to religious institutions on all three fronts.[133] It also awarded US$5,605,000 in *jus ad bellum* compensation for the remaining 25% of the damage to the town of Zalambessa.[134]

Deaths and Injuries Caused by Landmines

Ethiopia claimed US$1,635,622 in respect of deaths and injuries caused by landmines, which it calculated in the same manner as its other fixed amount claims for deaths and injuries.[135] The Commission ruled that deaths and injuries caused by landmines justified compensation if they resulted from mines that were laid in the areas and during the periods for which Eritrea bore *jus ad bellum* liability, including those resulting from detonations occurring after the liability periods, and to casualties resulting from mines laid by either Party.[136] The Commission awarded Ethiopia US$1,500,000 for deaths and injuries caused by landmines.[137]

---

[125] Final Award, para. 338.
[126] Final Award, para. 349.
[127] *Id.*
[128] Final Award, para. 350.
[129] Final Award, paras. 351–356.
[130] Final Award, para. 356.
[131] Final Award, paras. 357–379.
[132] Final Award, para. 381.
[133] Final Award, para. 386.
[134] Final Award, para. 387.
[135] Final Award, para. 389.
[136] Final Award, para. 391.
[137] Final Award, para. 393.

Business Losses and Other Actual Amount Damages

Ethiopia claimed substantial damages in respect of injuries said to have been suffered by many businesses, government agencies, and organizations, including some claims for damages resulting from the general disruption of the civilian economy in wartime.[138] The Commission rejected several of these claims for failure of proof.[139] It awarded US$250,000 for the destruction of facilities owned by the Tigray Disaster Prevention and Preparedness Bureau in Adigrat[140] and US$162,500 for its other claims relating to government losses on the Central Front.[141]

Ethiopia sought an amount said to equal US$388,212 for certain categories of government loss on the Western Front not covered by its other claims.[142] The Commission awarded US$75,000 for those claims.[143] It awarded Ethiopia compensation of US$125,000 for losses suffered by the Relief Society of Tigray; US$150,000 for damage to the town of Adi Goshu; and US$625,000 for shelling damage to the town of Sheraro, both on the Western Front.[144] It dismissed Ethiopia's claim equivalent to over one billion U.S. dollars for environmental damage in Tigray on account of the huge amount claimed and the lack of supporting evidence.[145]

The Mekele Bombings

At the liability phase, the Commission had ruled that Eritrea had not violated the *jus in bello* by its attack on Mekele airport on June 5, 1998.[146] The Commission accepted Ethiopia's contention that this attack was sufficiently linked to Eritrea's initial *jus ad bellum* violation to warrant compensation, and awarded US$65,000 in compensation for this violation.[147]

Prisoners of War, Departures from Eritrea and Ports Claim

The Commission dismissed Ethiopia's *jus ad bellum* claims in respect of prisoners of war and departures of Ethiopians from Eritrea for lack of a sufficiently clear and direct causal connection between Eritrea's violation of the *jus ad bellum* and the injuries claimed.[148] It found that Ethiopia had failed to prove a compensable loss of property in respect of its claim for property lost at Eritrean ports following the outbreak of the war.[149]

---

138 Final Award, paras. 394–395.
139 Final Award, paras. 396–409.
140 Final Award, paras. 410–412.
141 Final Award, para. 416.
142 Final Award, para. 417.
143 *Id.*
144 Final Award, paras. 418–420.
145 Final Award, paras. 421–425.
146 Final Award, para. 426.
147 Final Award, para. 427.
148 Final Award, paras. 428–435.
149 Final Award, paras. 436–444.

Ethiopian Airlines

Ethiopia claimed an amount it converted to equal US$14,464,729 for losses allegedly incurred by Ethiopian Airlines ("EAL") on account of Eritrea's violation of the *jus ad bellum*, most of which represented lost profits "for one year following the conclusion of service to and from Asmara."[150] Given the exceptional circumstance that airline service between the Parties' capitals was not a commercial endeavour but was closely linked to their overall political and economic relationship, the Commission concluded that documented lost profits from termination of the Addis Ababa service were the proximate result of Eritrea's *jus ad bellum* breach[151] and awarded US$4,000,000 with respect to this claim.[152] It awarded Ethiopia US$1,703,020 for EAL's bank accounts at the Bank of Eritrea in respect of funds that EAL had not been able to access after the war,[153] and dismissed Ethiopia's other *jus ad bellum* claims with respect to EAL.[154]

Loss of Tourism, Declines in International Development Assistance and Lost Foreign and Domestic Investment

Ethiopia made claims of (i) slightly over US$104 million for lost revenue from tourism; (ii) US$1.694 billion for foreign assistance from third parties allegedly frozen, suspended or terminated on account of the war, and (iii) US$2 billion for foreign and domestic investment in the Ethiopian economy that allegedly was not made during the war years because of Eritrea's *jus ad bellum* violation. These claims were dismissed for insufficient evidence.[155]

Reconstruction and Assistance

Ethiopia clamed a total amount it converted to equal US$99,957,819 for expenses related to the Disaster Prevention and Preparedness Commission ("DPPC") (totaling US$32,563,967) and the Relief Society of Tigray ("REST") for assisting persons displaced on account of the war and returnees from Ethiopia.[156] The Commission ruled that Ethiopia was entitled to damages reflecting demonstrated expenses reasonably incurred by Ethiopia, or by Ethiopian public or private entities, to assist and support IDPs displaced on account of Ethiopia's *jus ad bellum* violation.[157] The Commission awarded Ethiopia US$6,000,000 for Ethiopia's claim in respect of the DPPC claim and, after making the necessary deductions to take into account the value of commodities donated by foreign aid donors, it awarded US$1,500,000 for Ethiopia's claim in respect of REST.[158] Accordingly, it awarded a total of US$7,500,000 for Ethiopia's *jus ad bellum* claim for reconstruction and assistance.[159]

---

150 Final Award, paras. 446–447.
151 Final Award, para. 449.
152 Final Award, paras. 450–451.
153 Final Award, paras. 454–455.
154 Final Award, paras. 452–453, 456–457.
155 Final Award, paras. 458–469.
156 Final Award, para. 470.
157 Final Award, para. 471.
158 Final Award, paras. 473–478.
159 Final Award, para. 479.

Award

The Commission set out all of its awards of compensation to Ethiopia in the *dispositif* of the Final Award, and reiterated its confidence that the Parties would ensure that the compensation awarded would be paid promptly, and that funds received in respect of their claims would be used to provide relief to their civilian populations injured in the war.[160]

---

160 Final Award, section XII.

Government of Sudan / Sudan People's Liberation Movement/Army ('Abyei')

Parties: Government of Sudan/Sudan People's Liberation Movement/Army

Date of Arbitration Agreement: July 8, 2008

Tribunal: Prof. Pierre-Marie Dupuy (President), H.E. Judge Awn S. Al-Khasawneh, Prof. Dr. Gerhard Hafner, Prof. W. Michael Reisman, Judge Stephen M. Schwebel

Date of Award: July 22, 2009

Summary

Government of Sudan (GoS) and Sudan People's Liberation Movement/Army (SPLM/A) unable to agree on boundaries of the Abyei region – Abyei Boundaries Commission (ABC) established in 2004 to delimit the territory of Abyei – Parties agreed to define territory as "the area of the nine Ngok Dinka chiefdoms transferred to Kordofan in 1905" – ABC included five independent and impartial Experts tasked with delimiting boundaries according to agreed definition – dispute between GoS and SPLM/A over whether ABC Experts exceeded their mandate – present Tribunal established to determine whether ABC Experts exceeded their mandate – in the event of finding of excess of mandate, Tribunal mandated to carry out delimitation – Tribunal required to annul only those portions of ABC Experts' decision that exceeded mandate – ABC Experts' *interpretation* of mandate reasonable – partial annulment of ABC Experts' decision relating to *implementation* of mandate for failure to state reasons – no excess of mandate in respect of ABC Experts' decision on northern extent of Ngok "legitimate dominant claim" to 10°10'N – excess of mandate in respect of fixing of northern boundary as line bisecting the "shared secondary rights" area at 10°22'30"N – excess of mandate in respect of eastern and western boundaries – eastern and western boundaries fixed at longitudes 27°50'E and 29°E respectively – no excess of mandate with respect to ABC Experts' decision on "established secondary rights."

Legal Subject Matters

Settlement of disputes:
- Arbitration
  - Applicable Law
    - Application of international law in intra-State proceedings
  - Evidence
    - Oral evidence
    - Standard of proof

- Jurisdiction of the arbitral tribunal
- Procedure
  - Fast-track arbitral proceedings
  - Permanent Court of Arbitration Optional Rules for Arbitrating Disputes between Two Parties of Which Only One is a State, to the extent not modified by the Arbitration Agreement
  - Transparency; public nature of proceedings
  - Use of PCA Financial Assistance Fund
- Review of decisions of bodies imbued with adjudicatory powers
  - Excess of mandate
    - Error in implementation of mandate
    - Failure to state reasons
    - Procedural excess of mandate
  - Reasonableness
  - Standard of review

Fact-finding Commissions of Inquiry:
- Nature of boundary commissions
- Powers
- Standard of review

State:
- Territory and boundaries
  - Delimitation
  - Respect for traditional rights
  - Secession
  - Self-determination

Sources of international norms:
- Customary international law
- General principles of international law
- Treaties
  - Interpretation
    - Context
    - Object and purpose
    - Terms

Bibliography

Commentary:

- Gary Born & Wendy Miles, *The Sudan Case and the Inclusion of Arbitration Clauses in Peace Treaties*, 1 J. INT'L. DISPUTE SETTLEMENT (forthcoming 2010);
- Coalter Lathrop, *Abyei Arbitration (Sudan/Sudan People's Liberation Movement/Army)*, 103 AM. J. INT'L L. (forthcoming 2009);
- Jennifer McKay, *Case Note*, AUST. J. INT'L. L. (forthcoming);
- John Crook, *Abyei Arbitration – Final Award*, 13 ASIL Insight (Sept 16, 2009).

Facts

In 1983, a second civil war broke out between Northern Sudan and Southern Sudan, with its geographic center said to be in the region of Abyei, located in the province of Kordofan between Northern and Southern Sudan. In July 2002, the Government of Sudan ("GoS") and the Sudan People's Liberation Movement/Army ("SPLM/A") (hereinafter, collectively, the "Parties") signed the Machakos Protocol, which provided for the implementation of a peace agreement between the Parties, including, amongst other things, an internationally monitored referendum entitling the people from Southern Sudan to vote on whether to secede from Sudan ("Southern Referendum").[1] On May 26, 2004, the Parties signed the Protocol on Resolution of Abyei Conflict ("Abyei Protocol"), which provided that, simultaneously with the Southern Referendum, the residents of Abyei would cast a separate ballot to determine, irrespective of the results of the Southern Referendum, whether (1) Abyei would retain its special administrative status in the north, or (2) Abyei would be part of Bahr el Ghazal.[2] The Parties established the Abyei Boundaries Commission ("ABC"), which was given the task of defining and demarcating the Abyei Area.[3] The Parties defined the territory of the "Abyei Area" as "the area of the nine Ngok Dinka chiefdoms transferred to Kordofan in 1905"[4] (also referred to as the "Formula").

On December 17, 2004, the Parties signed an "Understanding on Abyei Boundaries Commission" ("Abyei Appendix") which determined the composition of the ABC. The ABC was to include, in addition to one representative and four nominees of each of the Parties, "five impartial experts knowledgeable in history, geography and any other relevant expertise" nominated by the United States of America, the United Kingdom and the Inter-Governmental Authority on Development (a seven-State regional development organization in East Africa). On January 9, 2005, the Parties signed the Comprehensive Peace Agreement ("CPA") in which they reaffirmed their commitment to, *inter alia*, the Machakos Protocol, the Abyei Protocol, and the Abyei Appendix.

With the approval of the Parties, the ABC Experts drew up their rules of procedure on April 11, 2005 and proceeded to hear testimony, conduct site visits, and obtain archival evidence. The ABC Experts presented their report ("ABC Experts' Report," "Report") to the Sudanese Presidency on July 14, 2005. The Report consisted of over 250 pages, and its "Final and Binding Decision" was as follows:

> 1) The Ngok have a legitimate dominant claim to the territory from the Kordofan-Bahr el-Ghazal boundary north to latitude 10°10' N, stretching from the boundary with Darfur to the boundary with Upper Nile, as they were in 1956;
>
> 2) North of latitude 10°10' N, through the Goz up to and including Tebeldia (north of latitude 10°35'N) the Ngok and Misseriya share isolated occupation and use rights, dating from at least the Condominium period. This gave rise to the shared secondary rights for both the Ngok and Misseriya;

[1] Award, para. 110.
[2] Abyei Protocol, section 1.3.
[3] Abyei Protocol, section 5.1.
[4] Abyei Protocol, section 1.1.2.

3) The two Parties lay equal claim to the shared area and accordingly it is reasonable and equitable to divide the Goz between them and locate the northern boundary in a straight line at approximately latitude 10°22'30" N. The western boundary shall be the Kordofan-Darfur boundary as it was defined on 1 January 1956. The southern boundary shall be the Kordofan- Bahr el-Ghazal-Upper Nile boundary as it was defined on 1 January 1956. The eastern boundary shall extend the line of the Kordofan-Upper Nile boundary at approximately longitude 29°32'15" E northwards until it meets latitude 10°22'30" N;

4) The northern and eastern boundaries will be identified and demarcated by a survey team comprising three professional surveyors: one nominated by the National Government of the Sudan, one nominated by the Government of the Southern Sudan, and one international surveyor nominated by IGAD. The survey team will be assisted by one representative each from the Ngok and Misseriya, and two representatives of the Presidency. The Presidency shall send the nominations for this team to IGAD for final approval by the international ABC Experts;

5) The Ngok and Misseriya shall retain their established secondary rights to the use of land north and south of this boundary.

Following the delivery of the ABC Experts' Report, a dispute arose between the Parties as to whether the ABC Experts had committed an excess of mandate in their delimitation of the Abyei area. On June 8, 2008, the Parties agreed, as part of the "Road Map for Return of IDPs and Implementation of Abyei Protocol" ("Abyei Road Map"), to refer this dispute to arbitration.[5] On July 7, 2008, the Parties signed the Arbitration Agreement, in which they agreed to refer their dispute to final and binding arbitration under the Arbitration Agreement and the PCA Optional Rules for Arbitrating Disputes between Two Parties of Which Only One is a State. The Parties provided that the PCA was to act as registry and designated the Secretary-General of the PCA as the appointing authority for the proceedings. Within the time limits provided under the Arbitration Agreement, the GoS appointed as arbitrators H.E. Judge Awn Shawkat Al-Khasawneh and Professor Dr. Gerhard Hafner, and the SPLM/A appointed as arbitrators Professor W. Michael Reisman and Judge Stephen M. Schwebel. In accordance with Articles 5.8 and 5.12 of the Arbitration Agreement, the Secretary-General of the PCA, in consultation with the four party-appointed arbitrators, appointed Professor Pierre-Marie Dupuy as the fifth and presiding arbitrator.

On the funding of the arbitration, on July 11, 2008, the Presidency of the Republic of Sudan submitted a request to the PCA Secretary-General for financial assistance from the PCA Financial Assistance Fund ("FAF"). With the aid of substantial contributions from Norway, the Netherlands, and France, the FAF contributed EUR500,000 towards financing part of the costs of the proceedings.[6]

The Tribunal held a preliminary procedural meeting with the Parties on November 24, 2008, at the Peace Palace, The Hague, at which the Parties and Members of the Tribunal signed the Terms of Appointment. The Parties filed written pleadings in three rounds in accordance with Article 8.3 of the Arbitration Agreement and the schedule set by the Tribunal.

On March 30, 2009, following correspondence between the Tribunal and the Parties concerning the disclosure of certain sketch maps and records and possible adverse inferences to

[5] Award, para. 134.

[6] Award, paras. 39–35.

be derived in the event of non-disclosure, the GoS provided copies of certain sketch maps and records, and explained that certain other sketch maps and records could not be provided.[7] On April 11, 2009, following further communications with the Parties, the Tribunal observed that the SPLM/A had merely "put the GoS on notice about the adverse inferences that the former will seek from the Tribunal … during the oral pleadings," declined to derive any such inferences at that stage in the proceedings, and decided to remain seized of the issue.

On March 30, 2009, the GoS, by letter addressed to the PCA, referring to certain allegations made in the Sudanese press, claimed that the four Ngok Dinka witnesses for the GoS had been harassed by members of the SPLM/A to deter them from testifying at the hearings or to convince them to change their testimony. On April 14, 2009, the SPLM/A stated in a letter to the PCA that it had investigated the allegations reported by the Sudanese press and found these to be without basis.

On April 7, 2009, the SPLM/A informed the Tribunal that the Presidency of the Republic of Sudan had allegedly not provided any portion of a US$1,000,000 sum previously requested as funding for the SPLM/A's costs. In response, the GoS explained that the Parties had previously agreed on the procedure to be used for the allocation of funds, which should be followed. On April 11, 2009, the Tribunal stated that it "expects that the GoS will facilitate and ensure the immediate release by the Presidency of the Republic of Sudan of the US$1,000,000 in funding …" On April 15, 2009, the GoS confirmed to the Tribunal that the entire amount sought by SPLM/A had been paid.[8]

On April 16, 2009, the Tribunal appointed Mr. Bill Robertson and Mr. Vincent Belgrave as Experts. Public hearings were held at the Peace Palace from April 18 to 23, 2009. Pursuant to the Parties' intention that the proceedings be conducted in a public and transparent manner, a live webcast of the hearings was made available to the public. The Parties presented two rounds of evidence and submissions, first on the Excess of Mandate issue and second on the Delimitation issue. The Tribunal declared the closure of submissions at the conclusion of the hearings on April 23, 2009.

Under Article 9(1) of the Arbitration Agreement, the Tribunal was given a maximum of 90 days from the closure of submissions to render its final award. Overall, Article 4(3) of the Arbitration Agreement required the Tribunal to complete the arbitration proceedings within nine months (six months plus a three month extension) from the date of commencement of the proceedings. The Tribunal rendered its Final Award on July 22, 2009, within both prescribed time limits, through a formal ceremony at the Peace Palace in the presence of the Parties and representatives of the States and institutions who witnessed the signing of the Comprehensive Peace Agreement.[9]

Summary of Matters Submitted to Arbitration

Article 2 of the Arbitration Agreement provided that the issues to be determined by the Tribunal were the following:

---

[7] Award, paras. 46–55.

[8] Award, paras. 67–73.

[9] The award-rendering ceremony was webcast live and remains available (as are all written pleadings and a webcast of the hearings) at the PCA website, www.pca-cpa.org.

(a) Whether or not the ABC Experts had, on the basis of the agreement of the Parties as per the CPA, exceeded their mandate which is "to define (i.e. delimit) and demarcate the area of the nine Ngok Dinka chiefdoms transferred to Kordofan in 1905" as stated in the Abyei Protocol, and reiterated in the Abyei Appendix and the ABC Terms of Reference and Rules of Procedure.

(b) If the Tribunal determines, pursuant to Sub-article (a) herein, that the ABC Experts did not exceed their mandate, it shall make a declaration to that effect and issue an award for the full and immediate implementation of the ABC Report.

(c) If the Tribunal determines, pursuant to Sub-article (a) herein, that the ABC Experts exceeded their mandate, it shall make a declaration to that effect, and shall proceed to define (i.e. delimit) on map the boundaries of the area of the nine Ngok Dinka chiefdoms transferred to Kordofan in 1905, based on the submissions of the Parties.

Award

The Tribunal's Task pursuant to the Arbitration Agreement

After setting out the arguments of the Parties,[10] the Tribunal[11] set out its task pursuant to the Arbitration Agreement. Recalling the terms of Article 2 of the Arbitration Agreement, it determined that it was to proceed in two distinct and contingent stages under Article 2(a) and Article 2(c).[12] The Tribunal emphasized the sequence of Article 2 of the Arbitration Agreement, which prohibited a *de novo* review of the ABC's findings under the initial stage (Article 2(a))[13] and the legal principles of institutional review suggesting that the "correctness" of a decision is beyond review.[14]

The Tribunal then considered whether Article 2 permitted a finding of partial nullity over certain portions of the ABC Experts' Report, "while retaining those parts found to be within the ABC Experts' mandate."[15] The Tribunal held that the power to make a finding of partial nullity, if appropriate, was required by Article 2, was permitted by general principles of law and practices[16] and was to be imputed to the Tribunal in the absence of a clear, express and unequivocal agreement to the contrary.[17]

Article 3 of the Arbitration Agreement provided that, in addition to the provisions of the CPA and the Interim National Constitution, the Tribunal was to apply "general principles of law and practices" which it determined to be relevant. A number of factors indicated that the Parties intended that international law would apply in this intra-State arbitration.[18] In particular, the essential purpose of the delimitation exercise was to determine a boundary that could potentially become an international boundary.[19] The Tribunal therefore ruled that the applicable law was international law.

---

[10] Award, paras. 136–394.

[11] Judge Al-Khasawneh attached a dissenting opinion to the Award in which he disagreed with the reasoning and conclusions of the majority. References to the Tribunal hereinafter refer to the majority.

[12] Award, para. 397.

[13] Award, paras. 398–400.

[14] Award, paras. 401–409.

[15] Award, paras. 414–415.

[16] Award, paras. 416–421.

[17] Award, para. 423.

[18] Award, para. 427.

[19] Award, para. 428.

Alleged Procedural Violations; Waiver, Estoppel, **res judicata** *Issues*[20]

The GoS argued that certain acts and omissions of the ABC Experts violated the procedures specified by the Parties in the Abyei Appendix, Terms of Reference, and Rules of Procedure, and asserted that the Tribunal should interpret a violation of the procedures specified in those instruments as an excess of mandate.[21] The SPLM/A contended that a dispute regarding excess of mandate did not extend to procedural complaints and that, alternatively, a party seeking to invalidate an arbitral award on procedural grounds must demonstrate serious prejudice.[22] The Tribunal, based on its interpretation of Article 2(a) of the Arbitration Agreement, held that the words "exceeded their mandate" referred to situations where the ABC Experts might have gone beyond the scope of the substantive issues submitted to them, and that Article 2(a) did not recognize putative violations of procedural rights within the concept of "excess of mandate."[23] As the alleged acts and omissions fell outside the category of permissible review under Article 2(a) of the Arbitration Agreement, the Tribunal rejected the arguments of the GoS.[24] Even assuming *arguendo* that procedural irregularities did occur, a significant injustice must also have occurred as a result of the irregularity. For the Tribunal, the GoS did not demonstrate that the decision outcome would have been affected by the alleged procedural violations.[25]

The Tribunal rejected the argument that the GoS had effectively waived its objections to the ABC Experts' Report through its prior agreement (in the ABC's constitutive instruments) that the Report would be "final and binding."[26] The Tribunal pointed to the GoS' expression of disagreement with the Report from its initial presentation, and of the GoS' recourse to this arbitration (to which the SPLM/A consented) precisely to seek a review of the Report.[27] On the question whether the ABC Experts' Report enjoyed *res judicata* status, the Tribunal determined that "whatever the status of the ABC Experts' Report, the Arbitration Agreement concluded by the Parties in 2008 had the effect of reopening questions that had been accepted as 'final and binding,' thus novating the issues for decision in accordance with the contingencies in Article 2."[28]

Characterization of the ABC

Three members of the Tribunal were of the view that that the ABC Experts' essential function was to reach a final decision with regard to the boundaries of the Abyei Area, even in the face of scarce factual evidence.[29] In the Tribunal's view, the ABC's role was best assessed in relation to its two essential features: its fact-finding powers and its powers to

---

[20] Award, paras. 436–451.
[21] Award, para. 437.
[22] Award, para. 438.
[23] Award, paras. 440–441.
[24] Award, para. 442.
[25] Award, para. 443.
[26] Award, paras. 445–448.
[27] Award, para. 446.
[28] Award, paras 449–450.
[29] Award, para. 455.

reach a final and binding decision.[30] First, the ABC Experts were not tasked merely to ascertain the facts surrounding a particular incident, but "to scientifically research, select and weigh such facts on the basis of a Formula that was susceptible to several, contradictory interpretations, with a view to arriving at a 'final and binding' decision that 'defined (i.e. delimited) and demarcated' the Abyei Area."[31] The Tribunal also found that the ABC Experts' role in the larger Sudan peace process, particularly the political objective of delimiting the Abyei Area, implied that they were "precluded from returning a factual *non-liquet* based on the paucity of evidence."[32] The Tribunal noted that the composition of the ABC did not preclude the attribution to it of a conclusive decision-making role and drew parallels between this case and the *Treaty of Lausanne Advisory Opinion*.[33]

Professor Hafner differed from the majority regarding the characterization of the ABC. According to Professor Hafner, the fact that the ABC Experts' decision was binding was not sufficient evidence that they possessed any powers beyond those vested in a fact-finding body.[34] Thus the ABC Experts were not empowered to make any decision having an *ex nunc*, constitutive effect; moreover, they would not have acted *infra petita* had they chosen to find a factual *non liquet*. Nevertheless, he agreed that these observations did not affect the substance of the conclusions drawn by the Tribunal.[35]

Reasonableness was the Applicable Standard for Reviewing the Interpretation and Implementation of the ABC Experts' Mandate[36]

The Parties agreed in principle that a misinterpretation by the ABC Experts of their mandate could amount to an excess of mandate, but put forward different conceptions of the standard of review applicable to determine whether the ABC Experts in fact "misinterpreted" their mandate.[37] In the Tribunal's view, the structure of Article 2 of the Arbitration Agreement and the object and purpose of the Tribunal's review of the ABC Experts' findings required it to confine itself to determining whether the ABC Experts' interpretation of their mandate was *reasonable*; the question of which interpretation the Tribunal deemed *correct* was not a question of "excess of mandate" but rather a component of the Tribunal's contingent delimitation inquiry under Article 2(c).[38]

The Tribunal found broad support in the practice of courts and tribunals for the proposition that "an instance of review must defer, and give special weight, to the interpretation of a jurisdictional instrument by the decision-making body designated under that instrument."[39] The Tribunal's own mandate pursuant to Article 2(a) of the Arbitration Agreement was to determine whether the ABC Experts' conduct and decision were within the range of what the

[30] Award, para. 475.
[31] Award, para. 477.
[32] Award, para. 479.
[33] Award, para. 481–482.
[34] Award, para. 484.
[35] Award, para. 485.
[36] Award, paras. 486–536.
[37] Award, paras. 488–492.
[38] Award, para. 496.
[39] Award, paras. 505-507, *citing*, in particular, the decision of the International Court of Justice ("ICJ") in the *Case concerning the Arbitral Award of 31 July 1989*.

Parties could have expected when consenting to the delimitation and demarcation of the Abyei Area by the ABC. To the extent that the ABC Experts' findings could still be squared with the Parties' consent, the ABC should remain the preferred forum for the delimitation of the Abyei Area.[40] In its analysis, the Tribunal distinguished between the question of the ABC Experts' *interpretation* of their mandate and the question of *implementation* or execution of that mandate.[41]

The Tribunal then turned to the next ground of review, namely, failure to state reasons. The GoS averred a requirement incumbent upon arbitrators to explain the basis for their decision, and the SPLM/A claimed that there was no such requirement, both Parties relying on arbitral precedent.[42] The Tribunal held that this issue could not be conclusively resolved by "general principles of law and practices," but was a question of proper interpretation of the ABC's constitutive instruments in light of their ordinary meaning and object and purpose.[43] It determined that the words "based on scientific analysis and research" in Section 4 of the Abyei Appendix clearly imported an exposition of the key evidence in support of the ABC Experts' findings.[44] Moreover, the object and purpose of the ABC's constitutive instruments revealed its important role in the Sudanese peace process. Because uncertainty as to the boundaries of the Abyei Area contibuted to the civil war, the Report would obviously have a major political impact on the country and the Misseriya and Ngok Dinka in and around the area; knowledge of the grounds on which the ABC Experts' Report was made "could be critical to the legitimacy and acceptability of the decision."[45]

Concerning the minimum standard of reasoning required of the ABC Experts, the Tribunal concluded that "[t]o meet the minimum requirement, an award should contain sufficient ratiocination to allow the reader to understand how the tribunal reached its binding conclusions (regardless of whether the ratiocination might persuade a disengaged third party that the award is substantively correct)."[46] In light of the object and purpose of the ABC's constitutive instruments, including the allotted time frame of three months from the beginning of the ABC Experts' fact-finding procedure until the rendering of their Report, the Parties reasonably expected and were entitled, as a matter of fairness, that each of the Report's essential rulings be supported by sufficient reasons, and the degree of reasoning provided in the Report for each of its conclusions had to be commensurate with the importance of those conclusions.[47]

Assessing the Reasonableness of the ABC Experts' Interpretation of the Formula

The Tribunal then proceeded to assess the reasonableness of the ABC Experts' interpretation of their mandate, which was "to define (i.e. delimit) and demarcate the area of the nine Ngok Dinka chiefdoms transferred to Kordofan in 1905," as stated in the Abyei Protocol and

---

[40] Award, para. 508.
[41] Award, para. 511.
[42] Award, para. 519.
[43] Award, para. 520.
[44] Award, para. 521.
[45] Award, para. 522.
[46] Award, para. 531.
[47] Award, para. 534.

reiterated in the Abyei Appendix and the ABC Terms of Reference and Rules of Procedure.

The Tribunal first discussed whether the ABC Experts could reasonably interpret the "Formula" as relating to the transfer in 1905 of the nine Ngok Dinka chiefdoms "as opposed to a defined area of land."[48] The Tribunal examined this issue in light of the textual interpretation of the Formula, its object and purpose within the meaning of Article 31(1) of the Vienna Convention, the context of the Formula, and the drafting history of the Abyei Protocol. In the Tribunal's opinion, both Parties' divergent interpretations of the Formula were tenable. It concluded that the ABC Experts' own construction was not unreasonable and that it accordingly did not constitute an excess of mandate.[49] The Tribunal noted the context of the ABC proceedings within the peace process in Sudan and that a predominantly territorial approach, whereby the 1905 provincial boundary would be the determining criterion, could lead to a definition of the Abyei Area that "potentially risks defeating the main purpose of the referendum, to empower '[t]he Members of the Ngok Dinka community and other Sudanese residing in the area' to choose whether the Abyei Area should retain its special administrative status in the north or be part of Bahr el Ghazal in the south."[50]

The Tribunal held that the predominantly tribal interpretation of the Formula was reasonable in the light of the historic facts of 1905. It recalled the "key passage" describing the transfer of the official document from the Condominium administration, the Sudan Intelligence Report of March 1905 (relied upon by the ABC Experts and the Parties),[51] and found that it was reasonable for the ABC Experts to interpret that text as referring to a transfer of administrative control over a people from one province to the other. This interpretation was confirmed by several factors including the historic confusion surrounding the location and course of the Bahr el Arab and the uncertainty of the provincial boundary and the lack of effective administration and governmental knowledge regarding the extent of the territory occupied and used by the nine Ngok Dinka chiefdoms.[52]

In light of the objectives of the 2008 Agreements, the adoption by the ABC Experts of a "predominantly tribal" approach could plausibly be regarded as furthering the stated goals of peace and reconciliation, as it would result in "incorporating into the Abyei Area the entirety of the community that was expressly mentioned in the definition of the Abyei Area as found in Section 1.1.2 of the Abyei Protocol and specifically referred to in Section 8 of the Abyei Protocol describing the process of the Abyei Referendum."[53]

The Tribunal considered, finally, whether the ABC Experts took sufficient account of the date of 1905.[54] The ABC Experts "consistently repeated that their analysis of the evidence was solely based on the attempt to determine the area predominantly occupied by the nine Ngok Dinka chiefdoms transferred in 1905."[55] The ABC Experts' reasons for examining post-1905 evidence to determine the continuity of the Ngok Dinka historical title, namely, that there was no 1905 map showing the location of the Ngok Dinka in 1905 and no suffi-

---

[48] Award, paras. 574–615.

[49] Award, para. 582.

[50] Award, para. 595, *citing* the Abyei Protocol, Section 6.1(a).

[51] Award, para. 616.

[52] Award, para. 617.

[53] Award, para. 659.

[54] Award, paras. 660–664.

[55] Award, para. 660.

cient official documentation, were clearly stated at the beginning of the Report.[56] The ABC Experts had rejected the post-1905 southern expansion of the Ngok Dinka and Misseriya as evidence of occupation by either tribe in 1905,[57] and had clearly explained to speakers and attendees at the ABC interviews with residents of the Abyei and surrounding areas that their purpose was to ascertain the location of the Ngok Dinka in 1905.[58]

Having determined that the ABC Experts' recourse to a predominantly "tribal" interpretation of the Formula was reasonable, the Tribunal considered itself bound not to go any further, "as its Article 2(a) mandate does not authorize a review beyond the threshold of 'reasonableness.'"[59] However, the Tribunal set out its reasons for considering that the ABC Experts could also have reasonably understood the Formula as expressing a predominantly "territorial" meaning, namely, evidence that there was a "working boundary" situated along the Bahr el Arab, despite the uncertainty surrounding the exact location of that river.[60] The Tribunal noted that one member of the Tribunal, Professor Hafner, believed that the "territorial" interpretation was more correct, but considered the Tribunal bound strictly by the limits of its Article 2(a) mandate, which in his opinion required that the Tribunal not review the ABC Experts' findings to the extent that they were not unreasonable, and go no further in matters of substance.[61]

Failure to State Reasons in the Implementation of the Mandate

The Tribunal noted that "[o]ne of the limited criteria of permissible review for the Tribunal was whether each of the binding decisions by the ABC Experts was supported by sufficient reasoning to allow the reader of the ABC Experts' Report to appreciate the key elements of the ABC Experts' justification."[62] Thus, the Tribunal next turned to examining whether the ABC Experts, when implementing their mandate on the basis of a tribal interpretation, stated reasons in support of their definition of each of the boundaries of the Abyei Area and remained within their mandate.[63]

The Northern Boundary of the Abyei Area

As regards the northern boundary of the Abyei Area, the Tribunal found that whilst the ABC Experts had provided sufficient reasons for their decision to adopt latitude 10°10'N as the northern limit of the Area of permanent Ngok Dinka habitation, they provided insufficient motivation for drawing the northernmost limit of a "'shared rights' area" at latitude 10°35'N, and by implication, the northern limit of the Abyei Area at 10°22'30"N, was deficient.[64] On the 10°10'N line, the Tribunal rejected the argument of the GoS that the ABC

[56] Award, para. 661.
[57] Award, para. 662.
[58] Award, para. 663.
[59] Award, para. 665.
[60] Award, paras. 667–671.
[61] Award, para. 666.
[62] Award, para. 673.
[63] *Id.*
[64] Award, para. 674.

Experts' reasoning was internally contradictory because they established that the Ragaba ez Zarga (which was historically often confused with the Bahr el Arab) had been treated as the provincial boundary but abandoned that conclusion by drawing the boundary further north.[65] In the Tribunal's view, a disagreement with the ABC Experts as to whether geographical evidence such as patterns of population settlements should prevail over historical evidence of the Condominium officials' conception of the Kordofan boundary would be a disagreement of substance and not a failure to state reasons.[66]

The Tribunal also rejected the argument of the GoS that there was no justification for latitude 10°10'N in the ABC Experts' Report since, in the Tribunal's view, the ABC Experts' reasoning for adopting that line constituted their assessment of the factual question of "where the line between Ngok Dinka 'dominant rights' and Misseriya and Ngok Dinka 'shared rights' runs" based on "permanent settlements and land use, as it appeared from administrative records and clues from human geography."[67] The Tribunal found that the arguments presented by the GoS related in reality to the substance of the dispute, namely, the evidence and the ABC Experts' appreciation of it, rather than to a failure to state reasons.[68]

Concerning the line along latitude 10°35'N, the Tribunal noted that the ABC Experts, although they noted the existence of Dinka names at that latitude on certain maps, had expressly stated that they did *not* consider that fact to constitute sufficient evidence for any boundary line.[69] The only remaining justification found in the Report was the observation that this latitude was the northern limit of the SPLM/A's claim, which coincided roughly with the northernmost extension of the goz, a desert area which the ABC Experts had found was "settled by nobody" and was regularly used on a seasonal basis both by Misseriya and Ngok Dinka.[70] In the Tribunal's view, "if a decision-maker wishes to base its decision on geographical features, some additional explanation is in order as to why that geographical feature should be determinative for the location of the boundary, thereby overriding other evidence that may have been presented by the parties."[71] A mere observation of coincidence between the limit of one Party's claim and a geographic feature could not replace "a searching inquiry and principled decision as to the northernmost area of the nine Ngok Dinka chiefdoms transferred in 1905, as was the ABC Experts' task."[72]

The Tribunal concluded that the ABC Experts' principal finding that "[t]he Ngok have a legitimate dominant claim to the territory from the Kordofan-Bahr el Ghazal boundary north to latitude 10°10'N" was supported by sufficient reasons. It recalled however that for one member of the Tribunal, Professor Hafner, "the applicability of latitude 10°10'N as the northern boundary of the transferred territory follows exclusively from the fact that the Tribunal is precluded by its mandate from reviewing it."[73]

---

[65] Award, para. 675.
[66] Award, para. 677.
[67] Award, paras. 680–681.
[68] Award, paras. 681–682.
[69] Award, para. 687 (emphasis in the original).
[70] Award, paras. 689–691.
[71] Award, para. 692.
[72] Award, para. 695.
[73] Award, para. 696.

The Southern Boundary of the Abyei Area

The southern boundary of the Abyei Area was not the focus of dispute between the Parties over the course of the ABC proceedings. The ABC Experts, having reviewed the evidence, adopted "the Kordofan – Bahr el Ghazal – Upper Nile boundary as it was defined on 1 January 1956" ("1956 Kordofan southern boundary") as the southern limit of the area of the nine Ngok Dinka chiefdoms transferred in 1905. There was no submission that this conclusion exceeded the ABC Experts' mandate, and the Tribunal found that it did not.[74] The Tribunal concluded that, to the extent that the 1956 Kordofan southern boundary met the eastern and western boundaries delimited by the Tribunal,[75] the southern boundary of the Abyei Area had been defined in compliance with the ABC Experts' mandate.[76]

The Eastern and Western Boundaries of the Abyei Area

The Tribunal found that the ABC Experts' decision regarding the eastern and western boundary lines was insufficiently motivated, and that this absence of sufficient reasoning constituted an excess of mandate concerning those parts of the ABC Experts' findings.[77]

The ABC Experts had adopted longitude 29°32'E as the eastern boundary line, on the grounds that neither the Ngok nor the SPLM/A had presented claims east of longitude 29°32'15"E.[78] According to the Tribunal, this was not a sufficiently reasoned justification of the eastern boundary but a mere summary of one of the Parties' positions.[79] The only other possible justification which the ABC Experts had identified for adopting longitude 29°32'E as the eastern boundary was a sketch map produced by the SPLM/A, which the ABC Experts had qualified as "inconclusive."[80] The Tribunal held that it was contradictory for the ABC Experts to base their decision exclusively on evidence which they themselves had qualified as inconclusive.[81]

The Tribunal noted that the ABC Experts' selection of the 1956 Kordofan-Darfur boundary as the western boundary line was "entirely unreasoned." Rather than making any specific pronouncement as to the location of that line, the ABC Experts had stated that "[a]ll other boundaries of the area that coincide with the provincial boundaries as they were at independence on 1 January 1956 shall remain as they are,"[82] without presenting any supporting evidence or analysis. The Experts' reliance on the Darfur-Kordofan boundary, without any supporting analysis, did not allow the Tribunal or readers of the ABC Experts' Report to understand how the ABC Experts arrived at this conclusion.[83]

---

[74] Award, paras. 698–701.

[75] *See infra,* text accompanying notes 86–99.

[76] Award, para. 701.

[77] Award, para. 702.

[78] Award, para. 704.

[79] *Id.*

[80] Award, para. 705.

[81] *Id.*

[82] Award, para. 706, *citing* the ABC Experts' Report, Part I, p. 45.

[83] Award, para. 706.

The Tribunal determined that a failure to state reasons constitutes an excess of mandate when it relates to a point "necessary to the tribunal's decision."[84] It held that the requirement to provide sufficient reasoning with respect to the delimitation of the eastern and western components of the Abyei Area was an integral part of the delimitation task of the ABC.[85] The Tribunal concluded that the ABC Experts had exceeded their mandate by failure to state sufficient reasons in respect of the eastern boundary and failure to state any reasons at all in respect of the western boundary.

The Tribunal's Determination of the Abyei Area's Eastern and Western Boundaries pursuant to Article 2(c) of the Arbitration Agreement

Having upheld the reasonableness of the ABC Experts' predominantly tribal interpretation of the Formula, the Tribunal considered itself "obliged to proceed with the delimitation phase of the mandate without departing from the same predominantly tribal approach."[86] It determined, further, that by "invalidating the 10°35'N and 10°22'30"N lines while upholding the 10°10'N line," it had fulfilled its mandate with respect to the northern limit of the Abyei Area, which it accordingly did not address any further.[87] It therefore proceeded to "define (i.e. delimit) on map" the eastern and western boundaries pursuant to Article 2(c) of the Arbitration Agreement.[88]

The Parties had contested the ABC's reliance both on contemporaneous Condominium records and on contemporary witness statements. Regarding contemporary witness evidence, the Tribunal, citing the decision of the Supreme Court of Canada concerning the evidentiary value of oral tradition, stated that oral evidence would be "duly taken into account, in particular, in so far as it corroborates other sources of evidence."[89]

The evidence provided by anthropological experts, in particular, District Commissioner Paul P. Howell and Professor Ian Cunnison, had not been questioned by either Party and was central to the Tribunal's decision.[90] The Tribunal relied in particular on a statement by Howell, in a document that had been submitted to the ABC and included in the ABC Experts' Report as well as relied on by both Parties before the Tribunal, that the Ngok Dinka occupied "the area between approximately Long. 27°50'E and 29°E on the Bahr el Arab, extending northwards along the main watercourses of which the largest is the Ragaba Um Biero."[91] According to the Tribunal, Howell provided "specific indications of where the Ngok Dinka's western and eastern limits lie,"[92] and these, although not contemporaneous to the 1905 transfer, provided "the best and most specific available data, especially in light of the continuity, within a largely unchanged ecology, of the Ngok Dinka's historic settlements and Humr's

---

[84] Award, para. 708, *citing Vivendi Universal* v. *Republic of Argentina*, Decision on Annulment, July 3, 2002, 6 ICSID Rep. (2002) 358.

[85] Award, para. 708.

[86] Award, para. 710.

[87] Award, para. 711.

[88] Award, para. 712.

[89] Award, paras. 717–718, *citing Delgamuukw* v. *British Columbia* (1997) S.C.R. 1010, para. 87.

[90] Award, para. 719.

[91] Award, para. 721, *citing* P.P. Howell, "Notes on the Ngork Dinka of Western Kordofan" (1951) 32 Sudan Notes and Records 329, p. 242.

[92] Award, para. 722.

migrating patterns."[93] The Tribunal found support for this position in the evidence of Professor Cunnison, who had lived for more than two years in a Humr camp between 1952 and 1955, and whose analysis had not been challenged by the Parties.[94]

The Tribunal reviewed other sources and found that all authors defining the location of the Ngok Dinka did so "by reference to the Bahr region, which they describe in a similar fashion."[95] The Tribunal emphasized the fact that the Humr had no permanent settlements on the Bahr whilst recalling Article 1.1.3 of the Abyei Protocol, which provides that "[t]he Misseriya and other nomadic peoples retain their traditional rights to graze cattle and move across the territory of Abyei."[96] The Tribunal also relied on earlier sources, published in the period 1912-1916, to confirm the presence of Ngok Dinka in the area "between the longitudes provided by Howell, up to latitude 10°10'N."[97] The Tribunal then set out additional evidence which corroborated the western and eastern longitudes indicated by Howell as the limits of the Ngok Dinka location in 1905, including, given the paucity of the contemporaneous evidence, the oral testimony of the Ngok Dinka presented by the SPLM/A.[98] The Tribunal deemed it proper to delimit the eastern and western boundaries based on lines of longitude, as the ABC had done, because there were few "non-topographic circa-1905 features that survive intact today to aid in delimitation."[99]

The Boundary delimited by the Tribunal was without Prejudice to Traditional Grazing Rights

The GoS alleged that the ABC Experts' pronouncement in their Report's "Final and Binding Decision" that "[t]he Ngok and Misseriya shall retain their established secondary rights to the use of land north and south of this boundary" was rendered in excess of the ABC Experts' mandate.[100] The Tribunal rejected this argument on the basis that, according to general principles of law, as expressed in the jurisprudence of international courts and tribunals as well as in international treaty practice, traditional rights are not extinguished by boundary delimitations. In the absence of an explicit agreement to the contrary,[101] Section 1.1.3 of the Abyei Protocol confirmed the continued application of that principle with respect to traditional rights to graze cattle and move across the Abyei Area.[102]

Final Observations

The Tribunal concluded by taking note of its role within the greater Sudanese peace process, recalling that it was for the Parties to take the next steps pursuant to the Arbitration Agreement, which provides that "the Presidency of the Republic of Sudan shall ensure the

[93] Award, para. 723.
[94] Award, para. 724.
[95] Award, paras. 726–730.
[96] Award, para. 732.
[97] Award, paras. 733–735.
[98] Award, paras. 738–744.
[99] Award, para. 747.
[100] Award, para. 749.
[101] Award, paras. 753–765.
[102] Award, para. 766.

immediate execution of the final arbitration award,"[103] and expressing the hope that the spirit of reconciliation and cooperation visible throughout the proceedings would continue to animate the Parties on this matter.[104]

The Tribunal set out its conclusions regarding the northern, southern, eastern, and western boundaries and regarding grazing and other traditional rights in the *dispositif* of the Award, and provided the coordinates of selected reference points in terms of WGS84 datum.[105] A map illustrating the boundary as defined by the Tribunal on a scale of 1:750,000 was appended to the Award.

Pursuant to the Arbitration Agreement, Arabic translations of the Final Award and Dissenting Opinion, together with their map annexes, were produced and are available for download at the PCA website.[106]

Dissenting Opinion of Judge Al-Khasawneh

Judge Al-Khasawneh appended a dissenting opinion to the Award, in which he set out his disagreement with the conclusions and reasoning of the majority.

According to Judge Al-Khasawneh, the ABC Experts had a relatively clear mandate, namely to delimit the area of the nine Ngok Dinka Chiefdoms transferred to Kordofan in 1905. It was not to locate where the Ngok Dinka were in 1905 or at any other date, which was a totally different question. In case of doubt, the ABC Experts should have sought clarification of their mandate from the Parties. Instead, they had gone on "a frolic of their own."[107] Judge Al-Khasawneh disagreed strongly with the reasoning of the majority regarding the western and eastern lines of longitude adopted by the Tribunal, and consequently with the basis for drawing the northern boundary line at latitude 10°10'N.[108] For him, the Tribunal had adopted these lines without adequate reasoning. Judge Al-Khasawneh also dissented on the issue of severability, since – the western, eastern and northern boundaries adopted by the Experts having been impugned by the Tribunal – what remained of the Experts' decision was so thin and truncated that it could not stand on its own.[109]

For Judge Al-Khasawneh, the first pillar of the Experts' misinterpretation of their mandate was based on the paradigm of "dominant" (Ngok) rights versus "secondary" (Humr) rights over certain portions of the Abyei area.[110] This was for him a discriminatory concept which had no basis in the law and custom of Kordofan.[111] The second pillar of the Experts' reasoning was their assumption, without convincing evidence, of continuity of Ngok Dinka occupation from 1905 to 1965, the year of their maximum expansion to the North. In this way, the ABC Experts, without supporting evidence, had ascribed vast tracts of land to the Ngok in areas where they never had any collective presence in 1905 or indeed in 1965.[112]

---

[103] Award, paras. 767–769.
[104] Award, para. 769.
[105] Award, para. 770.
[106] *Supra* note 9.
[107] Dissenting Opinion, para. 1.
[108] Dissenting Opinion, paras. 6–33, 34–39.
[109] Dissenting Opinion, paras. 40–51.
[110] Dissenting Opinion, paras. 52–66.
[111] Dissenting Opinion, para. 66.
[112] Dissenting Opinion, paras. 68–98.

Judge Al-Khasawneh viewed this not as a difference as to appreciation of the evidence, but an instance of misuse of the evidence to support a certain result.[113] Judge Al-Khasawneh undertook a review, illustrated on a map, of the contemporaneous and near-contemporaneous sources in the record before the ABC and the Tribunal of the locations of the Ngok and the Humr around 1905, including permanent settlements of the Humr on, and south of, the Ragaba ez Zarga, and evidence of continuity in the seasonal use by the Humr of the Bahr region.[114] Judge Al-Khasawneh concluded that even on a predominantly tribal interpretation of the ABC Experts' mandate, the extent of the location of the Ngok Dinka was nowhere near that of the area ascribed to them by the Experts or the Tribunal.

Judge Al-Khasawneh would have upheld the claims of procedural excess of mandate made by the GoS,[115] and disagreed with the Tribunal's findings that the Experts' characteristics went beyond fact-finding; that the Experts were the preferred arbiters of fact, and that the standard of review should be reasonableness, rather than correctness.[116] In conclusion, Judge Al-Khasawneh stated that the Tribunal itself was in excess of mandate, (i) by effecting a partial annulment of the Experts' delimitation without authority from its own mandate; and (ii) by replacing the Experts' unreasoned delimitation lines by equally unreasoned lines of its own.[117]

---

[113] Dissenting Opinion, para. 69.
[114] Dissenting Opinion, paras. 100–164.
[115] Dissenting Opinion, paras. 165–169.
[116] Dissenting Opinion, paras. 172–191.
[117] Dissenting Opinion, paras. 192–203.

APPENDICES

TABLE OF AUTHORITIES AND INSTRUMENTS

Treaty	Provision	Summary	Page
Aarhus Convention on Access to Information, Public Participation in Decision-Making and Access to Justice in Environmental Matters, June 25, 1998	Art. 2(3)	OSPAR Arbitration	52
Agreement between the Government of the Federal Democratic Republic of Ethiopia and the State of Eritrea, signed at Algiers, Dec. 12, 2000	Art. 4	Eritrea-Ethiopia Boundary Commission	144
	Art. 5	Eritrea-Ethiopia Claims Commission (EECC)	155
Agreement between France (Guadeloupe and Martinique) and Dominica, Sept. 7, 1987		Barbados/Trinidad & Tobago	97
Agreement on Encouragement and Reciprocal Protection of Investments Between the Kingdom of the Netherlands and the Czech and Slovak Federal Republic, April 29, 1991	Arts. 1, 1(a), 1(b)(ii), 3, 3(1), 3(2), 5, 8, 8(5)	Saluka v. Czech Republic	126
American Convention on Human Rights, Nov. 22, 1969	Art. 21(2)	Bank for International Settlements	62
Arbitration Agreement between Belgium and The Netherlands, July 22 and 23, 2003		Iron Rhine Arbitration	81
Arbitration Agreement between the Government of the State of Eritrea and the Government of the Republic of Yemen, Oct. 3, 1996	Arts. 2(3), 7(2), 7(4)	Eritrea/Yemen	39
Agreement regarding the Complete and Final Settlement of the Question of Reparations ("1930 Hague Agreement"), Jan. 20, 1930	Art. XV; Annex XII	Bank for International Settlements	62
Charter of the United Nations, June 26, 1945		Guyana/Suriname	117
	Arts. 2(4), 51	EECC Ethiopia's *Jus Ad Bellum* Claim	225
	Art. 2(4)	EECC Ethiopia's Damages Claims	278
Statute of the International Court of Justice, annexed to the Charter of the United Nations, June 26, 1945	Art. 38	Guyana/Suriname	117
"Colonial Treaty of 1900" (Treaty between Italy and Ethiopia for the Delimitation of the Frontier between Eritrea and Ethiopia), July 10, 1900		Eritrea-Ethiopia Boundary Commission	144

"Colonial Treaty of 1902" (Annex to the Treaty of 10th July, 1900, regarding the frontier between Ethiopia and Eritrea, and the Treaty of 15th May, 1902, regarding the frontier between the Soudan and Ethiopia), May 15, 1902		Eritrea-Ethiopia Boundary Commission	144
"Colonial Treaty of 1908" (Convention between Ethiopia and Italy settling the Frontier between the Italian Possessions of Somalia and the Ethiopian Empire), May 16, 1908		Eritrea-Ethiopia Boundary Commission	144
Convention between Belgium and the Netherlands relative to the Payment of the Belgian Debt, the Abolition of the Surtax on Netherlands Spirits, and the Passing of a Railway Line from Antwerp to Germany across Limburg of 1873 ("Iron Rhine Treaty")	Art. IV(4)	Iron Rhine Arbitration	81
Convention for the Protection of the Marine Environment of the North-East Atlantic ("OSPAR Convention"), Sept. 22, 1992	Arts. 1(a), 1(b), 2(2)(a), 9(1), 9(2), 9(3), 9(3)(d), 32	OSPAR Arbitration	52
		MOX Plant Arbitration	136
Convention on the Protection of the Rhine against Pollution by Chlorides, Dec. 3, 1976	Art. 13	Netherlands/France	73
Additional Protocol to the Convention on the Protection of the Rhine against Pollution by Chlorides, Sept. 25, 1991	Arts. 4, 7; Annex III, Point 1.2.3, 1.2.4, 1.2.6, 2.1.1, 3.2.3, 4.2.1	Netherlands/France	73
Convention Respecting the Bank for International Settlements, Jan. 20, 1930		Bank for International Settlements	62
Statutes of the Bank for International Settlements, annexed to the Convention Respecting the Bank for International Settlements, Jan. 20, 1930	Arts. 1, 2, 3, 13, 16, 18A, 54, 54(1), 57, 58	Bank for International Settlements	62
Geneva Convention for the Amelioration of the Wounded and Sick in Armed Forces in the Field ("Geneva Convention I"), Aug. 12, 1949		EECC Prisoners of War Claims	157, 166
Geneva Convention Relative to the Treatment of Prisoners of War ("Geneva Convention III"), Aug. 12, 1949	Arts. 15, 17, 18, 19, 20, 22, 29, 30, 31, 38, 89, 109, 110, 118	EECC Eritrea's Prisoners of War Claims	157
	Arts. 13, 14, 16-20, 26, 27, 41, 42, 49-55, 62, 65, 66, 87, 89, 120, 121	EECC Ethiopia's Prisoners of War Claims	166

Geneva Convention Relative to the Protection of Civilian Persons in Time of War ("Geneva Convention IV"), Aug. 12, 1949	Art. 53	EECC Eritrea's Central Front Claims	175
	Arts. 49, 51	EECC Ethiopia's Central Front Claims	182
	Arts. 27, 33, 35(1), 38	EECC Eritrea's Civilians Claims	190
	Arts. 27, 33, 35, 36, 37, 38, 39, 42, 85, 89, 90, 143	EECC Ethiopia's Civilians Claims	200
	Art. 49	EECC Eritrea's Western Front etc. Claims	208
	Art. 23	EECC Ethiopia's Ports Claims	257
	Arts. 18, 20, 23, 55	EECC Eritrea's Damages Claims	261
Protocol Additional to the Geneva Conventions of 12 August 1949, and Relating to the Protection of Victims of International Armed Conflicts ("Additional Protocol I"), June 8, 1977	Art. 52	EECC Eritrea's Central Front Claims	175
	Art. 57	EECC Ethiopia's Central Front Claims	182
	Art. 75	EECC Ethiopia's Civilians Claims	200
	Arts. 48, 51, 52, 52(2), 54, 57	EECC Eritrea's Western Front etc. Claims	208
	Arts. 12, 15, 54	EECC Eritrea's Damages Claims	261
Hague Convention for the Pacific Settlement of International Disputes, Oct. 18, 1907	Art. 85; Ch. III	Bank for International Settlements	62
International Covenant on Civil and Political Rights, Dec. 16, 1962	Art. I(2)	EECC Damages Claims	261, 278
International Covenant on Economic, Social and Cultural Rights, Dec. 16, 1962	Art. I(2)	EECC Damages Claims	261, 278
Memorandum of Understanding between Belgium and the Netherlands, March 28, 2000		Iron Rhine Arbitration	81

Memorandum of Understanding between Eritrea and Yemen for Cooperation in the Area of Maritime Fishing, Trade, Investment and Transportation, 1994		Eritrea/Yemen	39
Hague Regulations of 1907, annexed to the Hague Convention (IV) Respecting the Laws and Customs of War on Land, Oct. 18, 1907	Art. 56 Art. 23(g)	EECC Eritrea's Central Front Claims EECC Ethiopia's Civilians Claims	175 200
Treaty between Belgium and the Netherlands relative to the Separation of their Respective Territories, 1839		Iron Rhine Arbitration	81
Treaty between the French Republic and the United Kingdom of Great Britain and Northern Ireland Concerning the Construction and Operation by Private Concessionaires of a Channel Fixed Link signed at Canterbury on 12 Feb. 1986	Arts. 3(1), 10, 19, 19 (2)(f)	Eurotunnel Arbitration	106
Treaty of Friendship, Commerce and Navigation between the Hawaiian Kingdom and the United States of America, 1849		Larsen/Hawaiian Kingdom	46
Treaty between the Republic of Trinidad and Tobago and the Republic of Venezuela on the Delimitation of Marine and Submarine Areas, April 18, 1990		Barbados/Trinidad and Tobago	97
Treaty Establishing the European Community as Amended by Subsequent Instruments, May 25, 1957	Art. 249 Arts. 154-156, 226, 227, 234, 239, 292 Art. 226	OSPAR Arbitration Iron Rhine Arbitration MOX Plant Arbitration	52 81 136
Treaty Establishing the Joint Yemeni-Eritrean Committee for Bilateral Cooperation Between the Government of the Republic of Yemen and the Government of the State of Eritrea, Oct. 16, 1998		Eritrea/Yemen	39

United Nations Convention on the Law of the Sea, Dec. 10, 1982	Arts. 3, 5, 6, 7, 7(4), 15, 121(1)	Eritrea/Yemen	39
	Arts. 287, 290	Malaysia/Singapore	93
	Arts. 63(1), 74, 83, 283, 283(1), 286, 287(1), 287(3), 287(3(a), 298; Part XV	Barbados/Trinidad and Tobago	97
	Arts. 15, 74, 74(3), 83, 83(3), 286, 287, Part XV section 3	Guyana/Suriname	117
	Arts. 123, 192, 193, 194, 197, 206, 207, 211, 213, 281, 282, 290(1), 290(5)	MOX Plant Arbitration	136
Annex VII to the United Nations Convention on the Law of the Sea	Art. 1	Malaysia/Singapore	93
	Art. 3	Barbados/Trinidad and Tobago	97
	Art. 3	Guyana/Suriname	117
		MOX Plant Arbitration	136
Annex IX to the United Nations Convention on the Law of the Sea	Art. 5	MOX Plant Arbitration	136
Vienna Convention on Diplomatic Relations, Apr. 18, 1961	Arts. 9(2), 22, 29, 36	EECC Eritrea's Diplomatic Claims	231
	Arts. 22, 24, 26, 27, 29, 31, 44	EECC Ethiopia's Diplomatic Claims	237
	Arts. 24, 29	EECC Ethiopia's Damages Claims	278

Vienna Convention on the Law of Treaties, May 23, 1969		Larsen/Hawaiian Kingdom	39
	Arts. 31(1), 31(3)(c), 32(2)(b)	OSPAR Arbitration	52
	Art. 31(3)(b)	Bank for International Settlements	62
	Arts. 31, 31(1), 31(2), 31(30, 31(4), 31(3)(c), 32(2)(b), 62(1)	Netherlands/France	73
	Arts. 32, 33	Eurotunnel	106
	Art. 31(1)	Saluka v. Czech Republic	126
	Art. 31(1)	Abyei Arbitration	296
Other Instruments			
Arbitration Agreement between Lance Paul Larsen and the Hawaiian Kingdom by its Council of Regency, Oct. 30, 1999		Larsen/Hawaiian Kingdom	46
Concession Agreement, March 14, 1986	Clauses 2.1, 15.3, 20, 27, 27.1, 27.5, 27.7, 34, 34.1, 34.2, 34.3, 40, 40.4	Eurotunnel Arbitration	106
EC Council Directive 92/43/EEC on the Conservation of Natural Habitats and of Wild Fauna and Flora, May 21, 1992		Iron Rhine Arbitration	81
EC Directive 90/313/EEC on the Freedom of Access to Information on the Environment, June 7, 1990	Art. 4	OSPAR Arbitration	52
International Law Commission (Draft) Articles on State Responsibility, 2001	Arts. 4, 5	OSPAR Arbitration	52
	Art. 47	Eurotunnel Arbitration	106
Resolution AHG/Res. 16 (I) adopted by the Organization for African Unity Summit, July 1964		Eritrea-Ethiopia Boundary Commission	144
Permanent Court of Arbitration Optional Rules for Arbitrating Disputes between Two Parties of which Only One is a State	Arts. 1(1), 3(1)	Larsen/Hawaiian Kingdom	46
		Abyei Arbitration	296

Permanent Court of Arbitration Optional Rules for Arbitrating Disputes between Two States		Eritrea-Ethiopia Boundary Commission	144
Protocol on Resolution of Abyei Conflict, May 26, 2004		Abyei Arbitration	296
Record of the Decisions of the 56th Plenary Meeting of the International Commission for the Protection of the Rhine held on July 2, 1991		Netherlands/France	73
Rio Declaration on Environment and Development, 1992	Principle 4	Iron Rhine Arbitration	81
Rules for Arbitration between the Bank for International Settlements and Private Parties	Art. 20	Bank for International Settlements	62
United Nations Commission on International Trade Law (UNCITRAL) Arbitration Rules		Larsen/Hawaiian Kingdom Saluka v. Czech Republic	46 126
Domestic Legislation/Instrument			
Czech Republic - Banking Act	Section 26(1)(d)	Saluka v. Czech Republic	126
Netherlands - Wet Geluidhinder (Noise Abatement Act)		Iron Rhine Arbitration	81
UK - Immigration and Asylum Act, 1999		Eurotunnel Arbitration	106
USA - Joint Resolution No. 55 of the House of Representatives and Senate, 1898		Larsen/Hawaiian Kingdom	46

CHRONOLOGY OF AWARDS AND DECISIONS

1998

October 9, 1998	Award of the Tribunal, Eritrea/Yemen – Sovereignty of Various Red Sea Islands

1999

December 17, 1999	Award of the Tribunal, Eritrea/Yemen – Maritime Delimitation

2001

February 5, 2001	Award of the Tribunal, Larsen v. Hawaiian Kingdom

2002

April 13, 2002	Decision of the Eritrea-Ethiopia Boundary Commission concerning Delimitation
November 22, 2002	Partial Award of the Tribunal, Bank for International Settlements

2003

July 1, 2003	Partial Award, Eritrea-Ethiopia Claims Commission, Eritrea's Claim 17: Prisoners of War
July 1, 2003	Partial Award, Eritrea-Ethiopia Claims Commission, Ethiopia's Claim 4: Prisoners of War
July 2, 2003	Award, Dispute Concerning Access to Information under Article 9 of the OSPAR Convention
September 19, 2003	Final Award of the Tribunal, Bank for International Settlements

2004

March 12, 2004	Award of the Tribunal, The Rhine Chlorides Arbitration concerning the Auditing of Accounts
April 28, 2004	Partial Award, Eritrea-Ethiopia Claims Commission, Eritrea's Claims 2, 4, 6, 7, 8 & 22: Central Front
April 28, 2004	Partial Award, Eritrea-Ethiopia Claims Commission, Ethiopia's Claim 2: Central Front
December 17, 2004	Partial Award, Eritrea-Ethiopia Claims Commission, Eritrea's Claims 15, 16, 23 & 27-32: Civilians Claims
December 17, 2004	Partial Award, Ethiopia's Claim 5: Civilians Claims, Eritrea-Ethiopia Claims Commission

2005

May 24, 2005	Award of the Tribunal, The Iron Rhine ("IJzeren Rijn") Arbitration
September 1, 2005	Award of the Tribunal, Case Concerning Land Reclamation by Singapore In and Around the Straits of Johor
September 20, 2005	Decision of the Tribunal concerning Interpretation of the Award, The Iron Rhine ("IJzeren Rijn") Arbitration

December 19, 2005	Partial Award, Eritrea-Ethiopia Claims Commission, Eritrea's Claims 1, 3, 5, 9-13, 14, 21, 25 & 26: Western Front, Aerial Bombardment and Related Claims
December 19, 2005	Final Award, Eritrea-Ethiopia Claims Commission, Eritrea's Claims 15, 19 & 23: Pensions
December 19, 2005	Partial Award, Eritrea-Ethiopia Claims Commission, Eritrea's Claim 24: Loss of Property in Ethiopia Owned by Non-Residents
December 19, 2005	Partial Award, Eritrea-Ethiopia Claims Commission, Diplomatic Claim (Eritrea's Claim 20)
December 19, 2005	Partial Award, Eritrea-Ethiopia Claims Commission, Ethiopia's Claims 1-8: *Jus Ad Bellum*
December 19, 2005	Partial Award, Eritrea-Ethiopia Claims Commission, Ethiopia's Claims 1& 3: Western and Eastern Fronts
December 19, 2005	Final Award, Eritrea-Ethiopia Claims Commission, Ethiopia's Claim 6: Ports
December 19, 2005	Partial Award, Eritrea-Ethiopia Claims Commission, Ethiopia's Claim 7: Economic Loss Throughout Ethiopia
December 19, 2005	Partial Award, Eritrea-Ethiopia Claims Commission, Ethiopia's Claim 8: Diplomatic Claim

2006

March 17, 2006	Partial Award of the Tribunal, Saluka Investments B.V. v. The Czech Republic
April 11, 2006	Award of the Tribunal, Barbados/Republic of Trinidad and Tobago

2007

January 20, 2007	Partial Award of the Tribunal, The Eurotunnel Arbitration
September 17, 2007	Award of the Tribunal, Guyana/Suriname
November 30, 2007	Determination of the Eritrea-Ethiopia Boundary Commission concerning Demarcation

2008

July 6, 2008	Order No. 6 of the Tribunal terminating the proceedings, The MOX Plant Case (Ireland v. United Kingdom)

2009

July 22, 2009	Award of the Tribunal, Government of Sudan / Sudan People's Liberation Movement/Army (Abyei Arbitration)
August 17, 2009	Final Award, Eritrea-Ethiopia Claims Commission, Eritrea's Damages Claims
August 17, 2009	Final Award, Eritrea-Ethiopia Claims Commission, Ethiopia's Damages Claims

INDEX OF SUBJECT MATTERS